"The greatest Christian writers are th spiritual readers the knowledge of God, of ourselves, and of the grace of our Lord Jesus Christ. Among these are Augustine, Calvin, Edwards, and the Puritan John Owen, who ought to be better known than he is. The editors of this volume have worked hard to make Owen's unrivalled insight into the Christian's inner war with sin accessible to all, and the result is truly a godsend. Filled with classic devotional theology which, like Bunyan's *Pilgrim's Progress,* needs to be read again and again to be properly grasped, we have in the three treatises presented here a companion for life."

J. I. PACKER, Professor of Theology, Regent College

"John Owen's three treatises on sin, mortification, and temptation are a priceless treasure. To read them is to mine pure spiritual gold. Unfortunately, as in mining, reading Owen is hard work. Now, through skillful editing, Kelly Kapic and Justin Taylor have made Owen's work accessible to modern readers while still retaining his unique writing style. Anyone concerned about personal holiness will profit from reading this new edition of a classic work."

JERRY BRIDGES, Navigators Community Ministries Group

"Sin is tenacious, but by God's grace we can hate it and hunt it. John Owen provides the master guide for the sin-hunter. Kapic and Taylor bring together three of Owen's classics, clarifying them in simple ways—but all the substance, the careful, hounding arguments are still there to train our spiritual sight and love our souls."

MARK DEVER, Senior Pastor, Capitol Hill Baptist Church, Washington, D.C.

"With a volume of Owen in your hands you may wonder why you have wasted so much time reading lesser things. True, as Dr. John ("Rabbi") Duncan once said, if you are going to read this you will need to 'prepare yourself for the knife.' But that knife is the scalpel of one of the finest spiritual surgeons in the history of the church. Owen understood as few have how the gospel makes us well. Three cheers for everything Kapic and Taylor are doing to introduce a new generation of Christians to Owen's peerless works."

SINCLAIR B. FERGUSON, Senior Minister, First Presbyterian Church, Columbia, S.C.

"For over three hundred years the doctrinal and devotional works of John Owen have been a classic resource for the church. Though unusually insightful, Owen may be too challenging for many to read with benefit. Now, with brilliant editorial efforts and insightful introductions by Kelly Kapic and Justin Taylor, Owen's magnificent treatises on sin and sanctification have been made available for a new generation. I am confident that this welcomed volume will provide guidance and enablement for believers in need of God's grace and blessing. The editors are to be congratulated for their fine work!"

DAVID S. DOCKERY, President, Union University,
Jackson, Tenn.

"John Owen is a spiritual surgeon with the rare skill to cut away the cancer of sin and bring gospel healing to the sinner's soul. Apart from the Bible, I have found his writings on sin and temptation to be the best books ever written for helping me to stop sinning the same old sins. Now Owen's profound thinking on spiritual change in the Christian life is available in a user-friendly format that will help a new generation gain gospel victory over the power of remaining sin."

PHILIP GRAHAM RYKEN, Senior Minister,
Tenth Presbyterian Church, Philadelphia

"No writer has taught me more about the dynamics of the heart and the deceitfulness of sin than John Owen. Reading his writing has been life-changing, although at times his seventeenth-century style can be a challenge to modern ears. How grateful I am that Kapic and Taylor have invested their time and considerable skills to bring Owen's profound and practical teaching to a modern audience. Read this book carefully; it will help you understand your heart and experience God's grace."

C. J. MAHANEY, Sovereign Grace Ministries,
Gaithersburg, Md.

OVERCOMING SIN and TEMPTATION

EDITED BY

KELLY M. KAPIC

AND

JUSTIN TAYLOR

JOHN OWEN

FOREWORD BY

JOHN PIPER

CROSSWAY

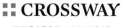

WHEATON, ILLINOIS

Overcoming Sin and Temptation

Published by Crossway
1300 Crescent Street
Wheaton, Illinois 60187

Cover design: Studio Gearbox

Reprinted with new cover 2015

First printing 2006

Printed in the United States of America

ISBN-13: 978-1-4335-5008-9
ISBN-10: 1-4335-5008-3
ePub ISBN: 978-1-4335-5011-9
PDF ISBN: 978-1-4335-5009-6
Mobipocket ISBN: 978-1-4335-5010-2

Library of Congress Cataloging-in-Publication Data

Owen, John, 1616–1683
Overcoming sin and temptation : three classic works by John Owen / edited by Kelly M. Kapic and Justin Taylor ; foreword by John Piper.
p. cm.
Includes texts of Of the Mortification of sin in believers, Of temptation, and Indwelling sin.
Includes bibliographical references and index.
ISBN 13: 978-1-58134-649-7 (tpb)
ISBN 10: 1-58134-649-2 (tpb)
1. Sin—Christianity. 2. Temptation. 3. Christian life—Puritan authors. I. Kapic, Kelly M., 1972– . II. Taylor, Justin, 1976– . III. Title.
BT715.O932 2006
241'.3—dc22 2006015124

Crossway is a publishing ministry of Good News Publishers.

VP 24 23 22 21 20 19 18 17 16 15
13 12 11 10 9 8 7 6 5 4 3 2

This volume is dedicated to our children
Jonathan Taylor Kapic and Margot Monroe Kapic

and

Claira Lucile Taylor and Malachi Xavier Taylor
Incredible gifts from God

Contents

Foreword

I REJOICE AT THIS publication of John Owen's works on the nature of our battle with sin. It is the kind of thinking we need. Therefore, I thank God for Kelly Kapic and Justin Taylor. They have done a good service for the church. I hope teachers and pastors will help their people benefit from this book.

As I look across the Christian landscape, I think it is fair to say concerning sin, "They have healed the wound of my people lightly" (Jer. 6:14; 8:11, ESV). I take this to refer to leaders who should be helping the church know and feel the seriousness of indwelling sin (Rom. 7:20), and how to fight it and kill it (Rom. 8:13). Instead the depth and complexity and ugliness and danger of sin in professing Christians is either minimized—since we are already justified—or psychologized as a symptom of woundedness rather than corruption.

This is a tragically light healing. I call it a tragedy because by making life easier for ourselves in minimizing the nature and seriousness of our sin, we become greater victims of it. We are in fact not healing ourselves. Those who say that they already feel bad enough without being told about the corruptions of indwelling sin misread the path to peace. When our people have not been taught well about the real nature of sin and how it works and how to put it to death, most of the miseries people report are not owing to the disease but its symptoms. They feel a general malaise and don't know why, their marriages are at the breaking point, they feel weak in their spiritual witness and devotion, their workplace is embattled, their church is tense with unrest, their fuse is short with the children, etc. They report these miseries as if they were the disease. And they want the symptoms removed.

We proceed to heal the wound of the people lightly. We look first and mainly for circumstantial causes for the misery—present or past. If we're good at it, we can find partial causes and give some relief. But the healing is light. We have not done the kind of soul surgery that is possible only when the soul doctor knows the kind of things Owen talks about in these books, and when the patient is willing to let the doctor's scalpel go deep.

What Owen offers is not quick relief, but long-term, deep growth in grace that can make strong, healthy trees where there was once a fragile sapling. I pray that thousands—especially teachers and pastors and other leaders—will choose the harder, long-term path of growth, not the easier, short-term path of circumstantial relief.

The two dead pastor-theologians of the English-speaking world who have nourished and taught me most are Jonathan Edwards and John Owen. Some will say Edwards is unsurpassed. Some say Owen was the greater. We don't need to decide. We have the privilege of knowing them both as our friends and teachers. What an amazing gift of God's providence that these brothers were raised up and that hundreds of years after they have died we may sit at their feet. We cannot properly estimate the blessing of soaking our minds in the Bible-saturated thinking of the likes of John Owen. What he was able to see in the Bible and preserve for us in writing is simply magnificent. It is so sad—a travesty, I want to say—how many Christian leaders of our day do not strive to penetrate the wisdom of John Owen, but instead read books and magazines that are superficial in their grasp of the Bible.

We act as though there was nothing extraordinary about John Owen's vision of biblical truth—that he was not a rare gift to the church. But he was rare. There are very few people like this whom God raises up in the history of the church. Why does God do this? Why does he give an Owen or an Edwards to the church and then ordain that what they saw of God should be preserved in books? Is it not because he loves us? Is it not because he would share Owen's vision with his church? Great trees that are covered with the richest life-giving fruit are not for museums. God preserves them and their fruit for the health of his church.

I know that all Christians cannot read all such giants. Even one mountain is too high to climb for most of us. But we can pick one or two, and then ask God to teach us what he taught them. The really great writers are not valuable for their cleverness but for their straightforward and astonishing insight into what the Bible really says about great realities. This is what we need.

The Bible is God's word. Therefore, it is profound. How could it not be? God inspired it. He understands himself and the human heart infinitely. He is not playing games with us. He really means to communicate the profoundest things about sin and hell and heaven and Christ and faith and salvation and holiness and death. Paul does not sing out in vain, "Oh, the depth of the riches and wisdom and knowledge of God! How unsearchable are his judgments and how inscrutable his ways!" (Rom. 11:33, ESV). No. He summons us to stop settling for pop culture and to learn what the Bible really has to say about the imponderable depths of sin and grace.

Owen is especially worthy of our attention because he is shocking in his insights. That is my impression again and again. He shocks me out of my platitudinous ways of thinking about God and man. Here are a few random recollections from what you are (I hope) about to read. You will find others on your own.

"There is no death of sin without the death of Christ" (*Of the Mortification of Sin in Believers,* chapter 7). Owen loves the cross and knows what happened there better than anyone I have read. The battle with sin that you are about to read about is no superficial technique of behavior modification. It is a profound dealing with what was accomplished on the cross in relation to the supernatural working of the Holy Spirit through the deep and wonderful mysteries of faith.

"To kill sin is the work of living men; where men are *dead* (as all unbelievers, the best of them, are dead), sin is *alive,* and will live" (chapter 7). Oh, the pastoral insights that emerge from Owen! As here: If you are fighting sin, you are alive. Take heart. But if sin holds sway unopposed, you are dead no matter how lively this sin makes you feel. Take heart, embattled saint!

"God says, 'Here is one, if he could be rid of this lust I should never hear of him more; let him wrestle with this, or he is lost'" (chapter 8). Astonishing! God ordains to leave a lust with me till I become the sort of warrior who will still seek his aid when this victory is won. God knows when we can bear the triumphs of his grace.

"Is there the guilt of any great sin lying upon you unrepented of? A new sin may be permitted, as well as a new affliction sent, to bring an old sin to remembrance" (chapter 9). What? God ordains that we be tested by another sin so that an old one might be better known and fought? Sin is one of God's weapons against sin?

"The difference between believers and unbelievers as to knowledge is not so much in the *matter* of their knowledge as in the *manner* of knowing. Unbelievers, some of them, may know more and be able to say more of God, his perfections, and his will, than many believers; but they know nothing as they ought, nothing in a right manner, nothing spiritually and savingly, nothing with a holy, heavenly light. The excellency of a believer is, not that he has a large apprehension of things, but that what he does apprehend, which perhaps may be very little, he sees it in the light of the Spirit of God, in a saving, soul-transforming light; and this is that which gives us communion with God, and not prying thoughts or curious-raised notions" (chapter 12). How then will we labor to help people know much and know it "in a right manner"? What is that?

"[Christ] is the head from whence the new man must have influences of life and strength, or it will decay every day" (chapter 14). Oh, that our people would feel the urgency of daily supplies of grace because "grace decays." Do they know this? Is it a category in their mind—that grace decays? How many try to live their lives on automatic pilot with no sense of urgency that means of grace are given so that the riches of Christ may daily be obtained with fresh supplies of grace.

The list could go on and on. For me, to read Owen is to wake up to ways of seeing that are so clearly biblical that I wonder how I could have been so blind. May that be your joyful experience as well.

—John Piper, Pastor for Preaching and Vision
Bethlehem Baptist Church, Minneapolis

PREFACE

READING JOHN OWEN: WHY A NEW EDITION?

JUSTIN TAYLOR

READING OWEN IS WORTH THE EFFORT

One of our goals in publishing this volume is to reintroduce John Owen to the church today. And one of the hindrances in the way of his reception is his reputation for being hard to read. There is no glossing over the fact that studying Owen's writings requires hard work. But we would also insist—alongside many of the great saints in the history of the church—that the effort required to read Owen is richly repaid. We agree with the judgment of J. I. Packer regarding Owen's works: "I did not say that it was easy to read them!—that would not be true; yet I do venture to say that the labour involved in plodding through these ill-arranged and tediously-written treatises will find them abundantly worthwhile."[1] Our goal has been to produce a faithful and accurate edition of Owen's writings on sin and temptation that begins to overcome some of these barriers to understanding his profound and practical insights and instruction.

OWEN'S WRITING STYLE

In order to understand Owen's literary style, it is worth quoting Packer at length:

> There is no denying that Owen is heavy and hard to read. This is not so much due to obscure arrangement as to two other factors. The first is his lumbering literary gait. 'Owen travels through it [his subject] with the elephant's grace and solid step, if sometimes also with his ungainly

[1] J. I. Packer, *A Quest for Godliness* (Wheaton, Ill.: Crossway Books, 1990), 84.

> motion,' says [Andrew] Thomson. That puts it kindly. Much of Owen's prose reads like a roughly-dashed-off translation of a piece of thinking done in Ciceronian Latin. It has, no doubt, a certain clumsy dignity; so has Stonehenge; but it is trying to the reader to have to go over sentences two or three times to see their meaning, and this necessity makes it much harder to follow an argument. The present writer, however, has found that the hard places in Owen usually come out as soon as one reads them aloud. The second obscuring factor is Owen's austerity as an expositor. He has a lordly disdain for broad introductions which ease the mind gently into a subject, and for comprehensive summaries which gather up scattered points into a small space. He obviously carries the whole of his design in his head, and expects his readers to do the same. Nor are his chapter divisions reliable pointers to the discourse, for though a change of subject is usually marked by a chapter division, Owen often starts a new chapter where there is no break in the thought at all. Nor is he concerned about literary proportions; the space given to a topic is determined by its intrinsic complexity rather than its relative importance, and the reader is left to work out what is basic and what is secondary by noting how things link together.[2]

At the same time, we shouldn't exaggerate the difficulties of Owen's prose when set before a certain sort of reader:

> His studied unconcern about style in presenting his views, a conscientious protest against the self-conscious literary posturing of the age, conceals their uncommon clarity and straightforwardness from superficial readers; but then, Owen did not write for superficial readers. He wrote, rather, for those who, once they take up a subject, cannot rest till they see to the bottom of it, and who find exhaustiveness not exhausting, but satisfying and refreshing. . . .
>
> Owen's style is often stigmatized as cumbersome and tortuous. Actually it is Latinised spoken style, fluent but stately and expansive, in the elaborate Ciceronian style. When Owen's prose is read aloud, as didactic rhetoric (which is, after all, what it is), the verbal inversions, displacements, archaisms and new coinages that bother modern readers cease to obscure and offend. Those who think as they read find Owen's expansiveness suggestive and his fulsomeness fertilising.[3]

---

[2] Ibid., 147.
[3] Ibid., 193, 194.

Reading Owen: A New Option

Up until now, there have been two main options for those who want to read Owen's writings on sin and temptation. One could work through volume 6 of *The Works of John Owen* as edited by William Goold in the 1850s,[4] or one could use a contemporary abridgement or paraphrase.[5] In this volume we are seeking to present something new: an unabridged but updated edition of Owen's three classic works that preserves all of Owen's original content but seeks to make it a bit more accessible. In so doing, we hope to play a small part in reintroducing Owen to both the church and the academy.[6]

Features of This New Edition

What changes have we made to the original edition of Owen's works? We have:

- provided overviews of the thesis and arguments for all three books
- footnoted difficult vocabulary words or phrases (at their first occurrence in each book) and collected them into a glossary
- Americanized the British spelling (e.g., behaviour to behavior)
- updated archaic pronouns (e.g., thou to you)
- updated other archaic spellings (e.g., hath to have; requireth to requires)
- updated some archaic word forms (e.g., concernments to concerns, surprisals to surprises)
- corrected the text in places where the nineteenth-century edition incorrectly deviated from the original
- modernized some of the punctuation

[4] There are two main collections of Owen's works: a 21-volume set edited by Thomas Russell (1826), and a 24-volume set edited by William Goold (1850–1853). The former is long out of print; the latter, save for one volume, has been reprinted in facsimile by the Banner of Truth Trust in Edinburgh (1965–1968) and has remained in print for the last 40 years. *The Works of John Owen,* with some slight updates, have also been included on a CD-Rom published by Ages Software of Rio, Wisconsin.

[5] For an edited abridgement, see John Owen, *Triumph Over Temptation: Pursuing a Life of Purity,* Victor Classics, ed. James M. Houston (Colorado Springs: Victor, 2004). (This volume was formerly titled *Sin and Temptation: The Challenge of Personal Godliness,* originally published by Multnomah in 1983, followed by Bethany in 1996.) The principle was "to seek the kernel and remove the husk," which involved cutting about half of the original work and extensive rewriting. See also Kris Lundgaard's popular work, *The Enemy Within: Straight Talk About the Power and Defeat of Sin* (Phillipsburg, N.J.: Presbyterian & Reformed, 1998), which is not an edition of Owen's writings per se, but rather an effort by Lundgaard to restate and recast Owen's arguments for today. In addition, the Banner of Truth Trust and Christian Focus Publications in the UK have each produced small paperback editions of *The Mortification of Sin,* with only slight modifications contained therein.

[6] We are also editing a new edition of Owen's *Communion with God* (Wheaton, Ill.: Crossway, forthcoming).

- placed Owen's Scripture references in parentheses[7]
- added our own Scripture references in brackets when Owen quotes or alludes to a passage but does not provide a reference
- transliterated all Hebrew and Greek words, and provided a translation if Owen didn't provide one
- translated all Latin phrases that Owen leaves untranslated
- provided sources for quotations and allusions where possible
- removed Owen's intricate numbering system, which functioned as an extensive outline
- added headings and italics throughout this volume, and extensive outlines of our own at the end, to aid the reader in following the flow of Owen's thought

As an example of the sort of limited modernizing that we have done to the text, the following is a reproduction of an original paragraph from Owen's *The Nature, Power, Deceit, and Prevalency of Indwelling Sin* (from his exposition of Revelation 2) . . .

> The fame might alfo be fhewed concerning the reft of thofe *Churches,* only one or two of them excepted. *Five* of them are charged with decays and declensions. Hence there is mention in the Scripture of the *Kindnefs of Youth,* öf the *Love of Efpoufals,* with great commendation, *Jer.* 2. 2, 3. of our *firft Faith,* I Tim. 5. 12. of the *beginning of our confidence, Heb.* 3.14.

. . . and this is our edited version as it appears in this volume:

> The same also might be showed concerning the rest of those churches, only one or two of them excepted. Five of them are charged with decays and declensions. Hence there is mention in the Scripture of the "kindness of youth," of the "love of espousals," with great commendation (Jer. 2:2-3); of our "first faith" (1 Tim. 5:12); of "the beginning of our confidence" (Heb. 3:14).

A Word About the Structure

Readers will note that, unlike in modern books, there are no chapter titles—Owen didn't assign any. Furthermore, the location of the chapter breaks can

[7] Readers will note that the Scripture references in this volume do not correspond precisely to any particular translation. The reason for this is twofold: (1) Owen did not rely upon one translation. His use of Scripture often involves his own combination of translation and paraphrase. (2) While some of the Scripture passages are similar to the Geneva Bible or to the King James Bible (published just five years before Owen's birth), they do not match precisely due to our updating of archaic components in those translations.

come across as arbitrary. As Packer said, Owen "obviously carries the whole of his design in his head, and expects his readers to do the same. Nor are his chapter divisions reliable pointers to the discourse, for though a change of subject is usually marked by a chapter division, Owen often starts a new chapter where there is no break in the thought at all." In fact, we believe that making the chapter breaks prominent can actually add to the confusion in reading Owen's work. (For example, in the outline for *Of the Mortification of Sin in Believers,* you'll note that chapter 3 begins with Roman numeral II.) One option would have been to dispense with the chapter numbers altogether. We decided to retain the chapter numbers, but to make them less prominent by placing them in brackets and not always at the beginning of a new page. This allows Owen's own outline to receive greater emphasis, and we believe it will aid the reader in following Owen's thought.

As noted above, we have also taken Owen's original intricate numbering system and used it to create our own outlines in the back of the book. We encourage readers to use these outlines, paginated for easy reference, where one can see his main points and the flow of his argument.

Our Prayer

Although we desire to see an increased understanding of and appreciation for Owen's works in our day, our greater desire is to see fellow believers return to the biblical means of sanctification in their battle to overcome sin and temptation. All of us find within ourselves a law to the effect that, when we want to do right, we discover evil within ourselves (Rom. 7:21). Our prayer is that this book will be used of God to help us watch and pray against temptation (Matt. 26:41) so that by the Spirit we would mortify the deeds of the body (Rom. 8:13).[8]

Soli Deo gloria.

[8] Romans 7:21 is the foundational text for Owen's *Indwelling Sin.* Matthew 26:41 is the key text for *Of Temptation: The Nature and Power of It.* And Romans 8:13 stands at the front of *Of the Mortification of Sin in Believers.*

ACKNOWLEDGMENTS

WHILE AS EDITORS we have written relatively little of this volume, the amount of time we have spent on it has been considerable. Consequently, a project of this kind simply does not work without the help, kindness, and love of many people. We would therefore like to acknowledge some who have been so important to this process.

It is appropriate to begin by expressing our genuine gratitude to our covenant Lord, in whose love and compassion we find ourselves. We have felt his enabling grace even as we have worked on this project of reintroducing the church to his servant, John Owen.

Cameron Moran, Kelly's research assistant, provided invaluable assistance in tracking down references and helping us to get the manuscript in shape. Others who have given support, insight, and sometimes acted as guinea pigs include Daniel Hill, Jay Green, Jeff Morton, J. I. Packer, Tim Cooper, Ivor J. Davidson, Frank A. James III, John Holberg, Tad Mindemann, Brian Hecker, Andrea Long, Rebecca Sasscer, and Joshua Sowin (who helped Justin create www.johnowen.org).

We would like to acknowledge the generous support received from the Kaleo Center at Covenant College, which is funded through Lilly Endowment Inc.

We are especially thankful to John Piper for interrupting his own writing projects to pen the foreword for this book.

We are grateful to Crossway Books for sharing our vision for this project, and for Bill Deckard in particular, whose excellent edits have made the manuscript better.

We profoundly appreciate our wives, Tabitha Kapic and Lea Taylor, who have patiently and selflessly encouraged us during countless hours of editing. There can be no doubt that without your sacrificial love and support this volume would never have reached completion. And more than that, thank you for always reminding us that life is bigger than books read or written.

Finally, we dedicate this edited volume to our children, Jonathan and Margot Kapic, and Claira and Malachi Taylor. Even though it will be years before you can understand this book—if you ever read it in the first place!—we do pray that by God's Spirit you will always know the freedom and hope that comes in the gospel. We stand in awe of the incredible gift God gave when he gave us you.

—Kelly Kapic and Justin Taylor
July 2006

INTRODUCTION

LIFE IN THE MIDST OF BATTLE: JOHN OWEN'S APPROACH TO SIN, TEMPTATION, AND THE CHRISTIAN LIFE

KELLY M. KAPIC

"Be killing sin or it will be killing you."[1]

WHY READ JOHN OWEN?

Sitting across from me in our London flat with warm tea in her hand and shortbread on the table, my wife had a revelation. During recent conversations we had been praying that God would provide a mentor for me while I was working on my Ph.D.—someone who would ask the hard questions, challenge my thinking and living, and consistently point me to the love of the Father. As we sat talking that morning, in what had become normal language around our home, I began another sentence with, "Do you know what Owen said yesterday . . . ?" Stopping me, Tabitha interjected, "You *are* being mentored. Listen to how you refer to John Owen, as if he were still alive. He is your mentor."

She was right. Although Owen had been dead for centuries, I found myself in almost daily dialogue with this prominent Puritan whose thought was serving as the object of my doctoral studies. While recognizing the cultural and historical differences between Owen's time and my own was of vital importance for my academic research, still I was often drawn into a living dialogue with this intriguing man. Sometimes I found myself frustrated with his methods or conclusions, but very often his insights simply captured me. His words would stir me to the point of honest self-examination and an

[1] John Owen, *The Works of John Owen*, ed. William H. Goold, 24 vols. (Edinburgh: Johnstone & Hunter, 1850-1855; reprint by Banner of Truth Trust, 1965, 1991) (hereafter cited as *Works*), 6:9.

ever-growing appreciation for the glory and love of God. I can recall many a time when I would have to stop reading, stand up, and just walk around for awhile, trying to digest a profound sentence. While a person from another century cannot serve as a replacement for living and breathing fellowship, I have learned the value of listening to the saints of old, and this Puritan theologian is certainly a voice worth hearing. I sometimes think of Dr. John Owen as a perceptive physician who delivers both a terrifying diagnosis and the means of a miraculous cure.

◇ ◇ ◇

John Owen was born in the year of William Shakespeare's death, 1616, and his life paralleled an exciting and tumultuous century in Britain.[2] Before he died in 1683, Owen had experienced life as an army chaplain, a political insider, Vice Chancellor of Oxford, a leading Puritan theologian, faithful pastor, father, and husband. He had also known great personal loss. Though he had eleven children with his first wife, only one of them survived beyond adolescence; the one girl who did survive ended up returning to live with her father after her marriage collapsed, and while in his home she died of consumption.[3] Such painful experience cannot help but leave a deep imprint on a person. On the professional level Owen's career had reached great heights, such as preaching before Parliament, leading Oxford University, and having friendships with those in the highest positions of authority, including Oliver Cromwell. Yet he also lived through the loss of power and position, as his country moved away from a Puritan-influenced government back to a country led by a King who was less than excited about the Puritan ideals.[4]

---

[2] The best published biography on Owen remains Peter Toon, *God's Statesman: The Life and Work of John Owen: Pastor, Educator, Theologian* (Exeter, UK: Paternoster, 1971). See also Peter Toon, ed., *The Correspondence of John Owen* (Cambridge: James Clarke & Co., 1970); idem, ed., *The Oxford Orations of Dr. John Owen* (Cornwall: Gospel Communications, 1971). Some recent book-length studies on Owen's thought deserve mention: Richard W. Daniels, *The Christology of John Owen* (Grand Rapids, Mich.: Reformation Heritage, 2004); Sinclair B. Ferguson, *John Owen on the Christian Life* (Edinburgh: Banner of Truth, 1987); Robert W. Oliver, ed., *John Owen: The Man and His Theology* (Phillipsburg, N.J.: Presbyterian & Reformed, 2002); Steve Griffiths, *Redeem the Time: The Problem of Sin in the Writings of John Owen* (Fearn, UK: Mentor, 2001); Jon D. Payne, ed., *John Owen on the Lord's Supper* (Edinburgh: Banner of Truth, 2004); Sebastian Rehnman, *Divine Discourse: The Theological Methodology of John Owen,* Texts and Studies in Reformation and Post-Reformation Thought (Grand Rapids, Mich.: Baker, 2002); Carl R. Trueman, *The Claims of Truth: John Owen's Trinitarian Theology* (Carlisle, UK: Paternoster, 1998). Kelly M. Kapic, *Communion with God: The Divine and the Human in the Theology of John Owen* (Grand Rapids, Mich.: Baker Academic, forthcoming, 2007).

[3] Dewey D. Wallace, "The Life and Thought of John Owen to 1660: A Study of the Significance of Calvinist Theology in English Puritanism" (Ph.D. thesis, Princeton University, 1965), 124. Sarah Gibbord Cook also writes of the difficult time after the Restoration, when Dr. and Mrs. Owen were separated from their children for long periods of time because of various circumstances ("A Political Biography of a Religious Independent: John Owen, 1616–83" [Ph.D. thesis, Harvard University, 1972], 290).

[4] Cf. Christopher Hill, *The Experience of Defeat: Milton and Some Contemporaries* (London: Faber & Faber, 1984), 170-178.

Throughout the various seasons of his life Owen proved himself a most able author: the authoritative nineteenth-century edition of his works fill twenty-four tightly printed volumes.[5] Amid his extensive writings, which include biblical commentaries and exhaustive (and exhausting!) treatments of doctrines like justification and the atonement, Owen also produced devotional literature that quickly became beloved. In the volume you are reading we have selected three of his classics on spirituality—although it needs to be said that he viewed all of his discourses as spiritual exercises and not as something void of practical import. In these three particular works we find Owen's detailed reflections on sin, temptation, and the believer's call to holiness.

In 1656 Owen first published *Of the Mortification of Sin in Believers*. In 1658 that volume was slightly revised and another short treatise, *Of Temptation: The Nature and Power of It,* was also printed. During the time that these two books were published, Owen was still serving as Dean of Christ Church, Oxford University, and the substance of both discourses grew out of brief sermons that Owen delivered during his tenure there. Young students were most likely the bulk of his original audience—Owen had entered Queen's College Oxford as a student at the age of twelve, which was not uncommon for the time.[6] One consequence of addressing this youthful audience seems to be that his reflections tend toward the concrete and practical, emphasizing the particular rather than lingering too long on the abstract. Here were young people who were beginning to experience the complexity of sin and self, and Owen was compelled to help.

Crucial to resisting sin and temptation, according to Owen, was an understanding of what you were fighting. Although written a decade later, Owen's explorations on these practical subjects are further unpacked in his book, *The Nature, Power, Deceit, and Prevalency of Indwelling Sin* (1667). Here Owen focuses on the power of sin not as it exists "out there," but as it exists "within" a person. By the time this volume was published, Owen's context had significantly changed: he had been removed from the academic setting, had watched the return of Charles II, and had personally witnessed the governmental crackdown on nonconformist Puritan preachers. But for Owen, circumstances—whether amiable or painful—were not an excuse to

[5] Besides the standard printed 24-volume set noted above, an electronic version has recently been produced: "The Works of John Owen" (Rio, Wis.: Ages Software, 2000). Owen's Latin writings have also recently been translated and made available in English: John Owen, *Biblical Theology, or, the Nature, Origin, Development, and Study of Theological Truth, in Six Books,* trans. Stephen Westcott (Morgan, Pa.: Soli Deo Gloria, 1994).

[6] Toon, *God's Statesman,* 5.

stop resisting sin. The call of holiness was a call from God himself, and thus not contingent upon the state of affairs in which one finds oneself.

Christians are called to war against sin. According to Owen, this means they are called to learn the art of battle, which includes understanding the nature of sin, the complexity of the human heart, and the goodness and provision of God. Following a classic stream of orthodox theology, Owen argues that humility is crucial to growth in the Christian life, and proper humility comes from "a due consideration" both of God and of oneself.[7] Only from this perspective can one be in a right position to approach the call to holiness.

Knowing Yourself

Owen's varied experiences, such as working with students (not to mention faculty) and providing pastoral care, gave him ample opportunity for reflection on the way that sin weaves its way into every aspect of people's lives. Two particular challenges about human nature that appear in these volumes deserve brief comment: his attempt to present a holistic view of the human person, and his belief that personality differences must be considered when dealing with sin.

Engaging the Whole Person

Contemporary readers may at first glance struggle with Owen's detailed parsing of human nature and sin, believing that his reflections are dated and irrelevant. However, upon closer examination the reader may begin to recognize that although Owen does not use current labels, he is dealing with very contemporary issues, such as depression, addiction, apathy, and lust.

One of Owen's concerns was that some people reduced the struggle with sin to a problem centered on the physical body. They had taken the biblical language of the "body of sin" (Rom 6:6, ESV) and inappropriately treated it as a literal reference to physicality. This misunderstanding leads to what Owen considers the monastic "mistake": believing that rigid regiments that yield greater physiological control will eventually diminish the sin that lies in a person.[8] For Owen, while the body is important, it is but the instrument for the real problem.

Using classic faculty-psychology categories of the mind, the will, and the affections, Owen consistently attempts to present a holistic perspective of the

---

[7] *Works*, 6:200.

[8] *Works*, 6:7, 18.

human person, and this informs his view of sin and sanctification.[9] Originally humanity was created without sin, and thus their mind rightly reflected on the Creator and his creation, their affections properly loved God, and their will followed after the good. However, with the fall these faculties became disordered. Even after believers are redeemed by God they will continue to struggle with the abiding vestiges of sin that disorient the faculties, a condition that remains throughout their earthly life.[10]

Sin moves by drawing the mind away from God, enticing the affections and twisting desires and paralyzing the will, thus stunting any real Christian growth.[11] One of the most frightening truths that Owen wants the believer to recognize is that "Your enemy is not only *upon* you . . . but is *in* you also."[12] Part of understanding the battle against sin is seeing that the enemy, so to speak, is not only external, but internal, which is why Christians often have conflicting desires within them.[13] Most Christians seem unaware of or apathetic about the sin that remains in them, but whether they recognize it or not there is a "living coal continually in their houses," which, if not properly attended to, will catch their home on fire.[14]

As the Scriptures often call attention to the "heart" or "soul" of a person, Owen argues that such references tend to be shorthand for the various faculties, and thus to deal with sin the whole person must be engaged.[15] Although Owen gives ample attention to each of the faculties, let us focus on the affections as a test case to show the nature of sin and temptation. Far too often Christians working within the Reformed tradition have been guilty of confusing stoic ideals of emotional detachment with maturity in the Christian life. But this Reformed tradition, which Owen self-consciously grows out of, has at its best made significant space for the importance of the affections. As early as the sixteenth century John Calvin, one of the great fathers of the Reformed tradition, saw this confusion and warned against it. Calvin chided those Christians who acted like "new stoics," because they believed that groaning, weeping, sadness, and having deep concerns were signs of sinfulness. According to Calvin such comments tend to grow from "idle men who, exercising themselves more in speculation than in action," do not understand

[9] For a discussion of Owen's anthropology and his use of faculty psychology, see Kapic, *Communion with God: The Divine and the Human in the Theology of John Owen*, especially chapter 2.
[10] *Works*, 6:165.
[11] *Works*, 6:97, 167, 245, 252.
[12] *Works*, 6:162.
[13] Cf. Romans 7:7-25. Owen's whole treatise *Indwelling Sin* builds off of this chapter, especially Romans 7:21.
[14] *Works*, 6:166.
[15] *Works*, 6:170.

the pain of this world and the ravages of sin, which the Savior who wept and mourned knew so well.[16] The goal of Calvin and of others after him, like Owen, was not the absence of affections, but rightly informed and directed affections.

Affections are a gift from God to all humanity. Far too often the faculties have been "gendered" in the church, for example, when people lump "rationality" with men and "emotions" with women. In addition to empirical evidence that easily contradicts such hastily drawn stereotypes, one should reject such schemas because *all* Christians are called to love God with their mind, will, and affections. Healthy affections are crucial to the life of faith, and numbing them cannot be the answer. In Owen's estimation, because the affections are so important to faithful obedience, Scripture often interchanges the language of heart and affections, for here is "the principal thing which God requires in our walking before him. . . . Save all other things and lose the heart, and all is lost—lost unto all eternity."[17]

The goal of the Christian life is not external conformity or mindless action, but a passionate love for God informed by the mind and embraced by the will. So the path forward is not to decrease one's affections but rather to enlarge them and fill them with "heavenly things." Here one is not trying to escape the painful realities of this life but rather endeavoring to reframe one's perspective of life around a much larger canvas that encompasses *all* of reality. To respond to the distorting nature of sin you must set your affections on the beauty and glory of God, the loveliness of Christ, and the wonder of the gospel: "Were our affections filled, taken up, and possessed with these things . . . what access could sin, with its painted pleasures, with its sugared poisons, with its envenomed baits, have unto our souls?"[18] Resisting sin, according to this Puritan divine, comes not by deadening your affections but by awakening them to God himself. Do not seek to empty your cup as a way to avoid sin, but rather seek to fill it up with the Spirit of life, so there is no longer room for sin.

Considering Personalities

Part of treating persons as holistic beings is recognizing the similarities and differences among them. With this in mind, it seems strange that "psychology" is so often a negative term among Christians. Certainly people have

---

[16] John Calvin, *Institutes of the Christian Religion*, 2 vols., The Library of Christian Classics (Philadelphia: Westminster Press, 1960), 1:709 (III.viii.9).

[17] *Works*, 6:249.

[18] *Works*, 6:250; cf. 6:188.

used this science in a problematic manner at times, reducing human persons to mechanistic behavioral responses without any reference to God. However, many Christians have created problems on the other end by their overly simplistic view of human persons, failing to account for such important factors as physiological distinctions, diverse backgrounds, and deep-seated socioeconomic impulses. While it is true that all humans are made in God's image, and that everyone is called to resist sin and seek righteousness, these commonalities do not cancel out undeniable particularities. In other words, what does righteousness look like in the lives of concrete individuals? How does sin tempt people in different ways? In many respects Owen's three treatises can be read as early modern attempts to explore human psychology as affected by sin and renewed by the Spirit.[19]

Faithful living does not always look the same. Sensitive pastors have long recognized this, learning the art of taking the wisdom of Scripture and applying it with care to the lives of those they counsel. Cookie-cutter molds simply will not work. In this vein, one reason that Owen consistently calls his readers to understand their own temperaments is because this will help them better appreciate how sin and temptation arise in their own lives. He recognizes that some people are by birth and experience "earthy," while others are "naturally gentle," and still others tend to have "passionate" dispositions. The challenge for all is to learn about their own constitution: "He who watches not this thoroughly, who is not exactly skilled in the knowledge of himself, will never be disentangled from one temptation or another all his days."[20]

According to this Puritan pastor, there is no temperament that is free from temptation, and the trick is to be aware of the threats that are easily overlooked. For example, those who are naturally gentle and pleasant may be surprised to find themselves far down a path that they should have courageously departed from long ago. Such a person may, for instance, turn a deaf ear to slander or a blind eye to injustice because acknowledging these wrongs might require the person to act courageously. Although it would be easier to mind his own business, he may need to risk discomfort by standing up for those mocked or being willing to express righteous anger in the face of discrimination. Others who tend toward the "earthy" may rightly uphold what is now commonly called authenticity, but in the process they foster "selfishness" and "harsh thoughts of others." We all have "peculiar lusts" due to our particular constitution, education, or prejudice, and such things have "deep rooting and strength in

---

[19] Cf. Timothy J. Keller, "Puritan Resources for Biblical Counseling," *Journal of Pastoral Practice* 9/3 (1988): 11-43.
[20] *Works,* 6:132.

them."[21] Satan tends to attack us according to our particular personalities, moving against a confident person much differently than an anxious one, but tempting both nonetheless. Thus, we must learn our dispositions, for in so doing we are more prepared to avoid the stealthy arrows directed at us.

A persistent danger among Christians is that we confuse certain personalities with sanctification, creating an inaccurate hierarchy within the kingdom of God. In fact, Owen believes that because of our various backgrounds and temperaments, it is very hard to discern the most faithful Christians, since looks can be deceiving:

> Remember that of many of *the best Christians, the worst* is known and seen. Many who keep up precious communion with God do yet oftentimes, by their *natural tempers* of freedom or passion, not carry so glorious appearances as others who perhaps come short of them in grace and the power of godliness.[22]

Not only can appearances be misleading, but people in positions of leadership in the church often suffer greater falls than the average congregation member. When considering countless examples of the saints in Scripture (e.g., Noah, David, Hezekiah), Owen concludes that great "eruptions of actual sin" often occur not in "the lowest form or ordinary sort of believers," but in people who have in the past "had a peculiar eminency in them on the account of their walking with God in their generation."[23] Past faithfulness is not a protection against present dangers.

In this life there is no escaping the challenges of temptation, and thus all—young and old, pastor and parishioner, poor and rich, wise and simple—must commit themselves to battle against sin. "Be acquainted, then, with thine own heart: though it be deep, search it; though it be dark, inquire into it; though it give all its distempers other names than what are their due, believe it not."[24] Do not justify your own particular sin, but seek to recognize it so that you might fight against it with all your strength. Although sin and temptation affect everyone differently, none can escape the constant onslaught. Christians are called to wage war against this enemy, knowing that there are only two options: "Be killing sin or it will be killing you."[25] While battlefield

[21] *Works,* 6:132.
[22] *Works,* 6:298, emphasis original.
[23] *Works,* 6:279.
[24] *Works,* 6:132.
[25] *Works,* 6:9.

language may sound extreme to our ears, that is how Owen—following the Bible—conceives of this struggle. With this in mind, the only hope Owen can promise comes not through further self-examination but by embracing the love and provision of God.

Knowing Your God

Affirming the importance of honest introspection does not blind Owen to the fact that this exercise will lead a person to despair if it is not also paralleled with a study of the grace of God. Since sin entered the world, it has become challenging for people to rightly view themselves, God, and his work. We are prone to have "hard thoughts" of God that tend to keep us from turning to him.[26] Owen's goal is not to have people remain focused on their sin but rather to embrace the redemption accomplished in Christ. The aim is not despair but freedom for what Owen often calls "gospel obedience."[27] Obedience rightly understood is always a response to God's love.

A crucial work of the mind in the process of sanctification is the consistent consideration of God and his amazing grace.[28] This does not mean considering God as an abstract metaphysical principle. Rather, the Christian meditates *upon* him and *with* him. This distinction makes all the difference, placing the discussion within the framework of *relationality,* rather than mere rationality. Owen's challenge is most instructive: "when we would undertake thoughts and meditations of God, his excellencies, his properties, his glory, his majesty, his love, his goodness, let it be done in a way of speaking unto God, in a deep humiliation . . . in a way of prayer and praise—speaking unto God."[29] The invitation here is not to impersonal theological studies but rather to life-changing encounters with Yahweh.

One of the great promises of God is that he will preserve his people. In fact, the idea of the "perseverance of the saints" is frequently misunderstood, according to Owen, for so often discussion about remaining in the faith focuses on human efforts, as if it is up to us to avoid losing our salvation. In truth, the Christian hope rests not ultimately upon our own diligence, but on God's faithfulness.[30] It is *God,* not us, who will ultimately persevere, and that is why he is able to promise us eternal life: "where the promise is, there is all

---

[26] E.g., *Works,* 2:34-35; 6:377, 570-72; 7:521; 9:37-39; 11:389-390, 581, etc.

[27] E.g., *Works,* 1:441; 2:180-181; 3:323, 634; 8:536; 11:379-424, etc.

[28] *Works,* 6:222.

[29] *Works,* 6:225.

[30] This is the argument made at great length in Owen's massive book, *The Doctrine of the Saints' Perseverance* (1654), *Works,* 11:1-666.

this assistance. The faithfulness of the Father, the grace of the Son, and the power of the Spirit, all are engaged in our preservation."[31] Christians can be confident about their growth in sanctification and eternal security because they are confident in the God who promises it.

Ever deepening communion with God occurs as the Spirit draws us to the Father through the Son.[32] The Father will allow none to be snatched from his hand, the Son incarnate is a truly sympathetic high priest who is the lover of our souls, and the Spirit applies the atoning work of Christ to us. Thus, Owen reminds believers to keep these truths in mind as they face temptation, bringing their "lust to the gospel," lest they lose sight of the sufficient sacrifice and restorative grace found in God's work. "What love, what mercy, what blood, what grace have I despised and trampled on! Is this the return I make to the Father for his love, to the Son for his blood, to the Holy Ghost for his grace?"[33] Notice that the love is preexistent, the blood shed, and the grace extended. The believer is *not* working to secure these realities, but seeking to live in light of them. Christians stand in the shadow of the cross, having experienced the tender mercy of God. They aim not to convince God that they are worthy of his love, but to grow in their knowledge and fellowship with him. It is through this ever-growing communion with the Father, Son, and Spirit that the believer is most able to resist sin and temptation. "Let a soul exercise itself to a communion with Christ in the good things of the gospel—pardon of sin, fruits of holiness, hope of glory, peace with God, joy in the Holy Ghost, dominion over sin—and he shall have a mighty preservative against all temptations."[34]

The Work of Sanctification

How should the Christian understand the work of sanctification? Is the call of believers to holiness God's work or their own? There are two extremes often found in the church when dealing with these questions. On the one hand, there are those who seem to believe that we are saved by grace and sanctified by works: here grace is problematically reduced to the initial work of salvation. On the other hand, in an effort to avoid "works righteousness," others tend to collapse justification and sanctification; the danger here is that

[31] *Works*, 6:142.
[32] Owen unpacks the idea of fellowship with God within a Trinitarian framework in his *Of Communion with God the Father, Son, and Holy Ghost* (1657; *Works*, 2:1-274). To place Owen's approach within the larger context of his thought, see Kapic, *Communion with God: The Divine and the Human in the Theology of John Owen*, especially chapter 5.
[33] *Works*, 6:58.
[34] *Works*, 6:144.

the biblical call to active, faithful obedience by the believer can be nullified, and inappropriate passivity can set in. Rather than these two extremes, Owen follows the more traditional Reformed perspective that upholds another model of sanctification.[35]

True and lasting resistance to sin comes not through willpower and self-improvement but through the Spirit who empowers believers with a knowledge and love of God. Throughout his writings Owen is always quick to highlight the continuing work of the Holy Spirit in the life of the believer.[36] Not only does the Spirit of God bring life to those who are dead in sin, thus causing a new birth, but he also continues the work of God in the renewing of that person in the image of Christ. The fundamental difference between Owen's proposal and self-help programs is that he believes that only as the Spirit communicates the grace and love of the Father to us can we experience genuine relief.[37] Mortification of sin is "the gift of Christ" to believers, and this is given by the Spirit of the Son.[38] Efforts apart from the Spirit do not bring sanctification, even if they do produce changed behavior. Although the Spirit often uses beneficial activities such as "fasting and watching," rituals and human effort without the Spirit cannot ultimately bring liberation from sin and temptation.[39]

So is the work of sanctification God's work or our work? Or is it some combination of the two? Maybe such questions are themselves problematic. John Murray, writing several centuries after Owen, fairly communicates the kind of approach Owen employs, although Murray here states it more concisely:

> God's working in us [in sanctification] is not suspended because we work, nor our working suspended because God works. Neither is the relation strictly one of co-operation as if God did his part and we did ours so that the conjunction or coordination of both produced the required result. God works in us and we also work. But the relation is that *because* God works we work.[40]

---

[35] Owen warns, for example, against the extremes of rigid legalism on the one hand and false liberty on the other (*Works*, 6:14).

[36] Owen's fullest exploration of the person and work of the Spirit is found in volumes 3 and 4 of his works. Volume 3 contains a massive treatise on the Holy Spirit, and volume 4 contains four shorter explorations of aspects of the work of the Spirit (e.g., the Spirit and prayer, or spiritual gifts).

[37] *Works*, 6:7, 10, 16.

[38] *Works*, 6:19.

[39] *Works*, 6:61, 224-232.

[40] John Murray, *Redemption, Accomplished and Applied* (Grand Rapids, Mich.: Eerdmans, 1955; reprint, 1992), 148-149, emphasis original.

Owen's own view is similar, seeing sanctification as the work of God in and through the life of the believer. This is not passivity, but active living empowered by the Spirit of life.[41]

Two concepts commonly appear in early Reformed approaches to sanctification: mortification and vivification. Building on the language and imagery of Colossians 3:9-10, the idea of *mortification* was understood as a putting off of the "old man," and *vivification* was conceived as the reality of being made alive by the Spirit.[42] Although the actual language of "vivification" is found less often in Owen than in earlier theologians like John Calvin or the renowned Puritan Thomas Goodwin, the idea is clearly present.[43] These twin ideas of sanctification require not only the shedding of sin but also renewal in grace. A practical example of how this works out may prove helpful.

Consider a man who is struggling with inappropriate sexual thoughts about one of his female coworkers. What does holiness look like in this case? Very often Christians have a truncated view of sanctification, which stops far too short of true righteousness. Although it would be a good thing for this man to get to the point that he no longer looks at this women as an object of lust, that is not all that is hoped for in sanctification. Rather, in the power of the Spirit the goal is to move to a life-affirming position. Thus, the objective is not the absence of thoughts about this woman but the presence of a godly appreciation for her. Under normal circumstances this man should not simply try to deny her existence by avoiding her, but rather begin treating her with dignity, offering words that build her up instead of dehumanizing her with his thoughts. Ultimately lust will be replaced by genuine and appropriate respect and love. Similarly, the goal of dealing with gossip is not merely the absence of slander (which is the good work of mortification), but eventually the creating of an environment of encouragement, peace, and trust (further fruits of the Spirit's enlivening presence and work). Following

---

[41] Owen puts it thus: "The Holy Spirit works in us and upon us, as we are fit to be wrought in and upon; that is, so as to preserve our own liberty and free obedience. He works upon our understandings, wills, consciences, and affections, agreeably to their own natures; he works in us and with us, not against us or without us" (*Works,* 6:20).

[42] See Richard A. Muller, *Dictionary of Latin and Greek Theological Terms: Drawn Principally from Protestant Scholastic Theology* (Grand Rapids, Mich.: Baker, 1985), 196, 328-329.

[43] For a helpful comparison between Calvin and Owen on these topics, see Randall C. Gleason, *John Calvin and John Owen on Mortification: A Comparative Study in Reformed Spirituality,* Studies in Church History (New York: Peter Lang, 1995). Calvin employs this language more often than Owen, but Owen does use it for bringing and sustaining life to people who are spiritually dead (e.g., *Works,* 3:209, 282, 329, 334; 15:585). Thomas Goodwin, a friend of Owen, would be an example of a Puritan who employs the language much more frequently, in his slightly older treatise, *The Trial of a Christian's Growth in Mortification, or Purging Out Corruption; and Vivification, or Bringing Forth More Fruit . . .* (1643), *The Works of Thomas Goodwin,* 12 vols. (James Nichol: 1861–1866; reprint, Eureka, Calif.: Tanski, 1996), 3:432-506.

the trajectory of thought of theologians like Calvin and Owen, sanctification involves both putting sin to death and becoming free to love and obey.

Conclusion

We have briefly explored a few themes from Owen's thought that might help prepare readers for what they are about to encounter in his writings on sin, mortification, and temptation. Several things will quickly become apparent, such as recognizing that the language, sentence structure, and sometimes his sensitivities are not modern. As you read, do not be surprised to feel a certain amount of historical distance between yourself and Owen—to deny such differences would be naïve and problematic. The goal is not to create romantic views of the past, hoping to usher Christians back to some sort of "pure" seventeenth-century setting. Owen makes it perfectly clear that the power of sin and Satan were just as real then as now. Believers should read Owen not to return to the past but to gain insight into how they might more faithfully live in the present and prepare for the future.

"Be killing sin or it will be killing you." Culture has changed, but sinful human nature has not. For centuries Owen's works have challenged Christians to think afresh about how they face the reality of sin and temptation. Now Owen serves yet another generation of believers, calling us to wake from sleepy and apathetic attitudes toward holiness, demanding that we engage in honest self-reflection. But he doesn't stop there, for he intends to excite in us a renewed sense of the tender mercy of God who delights to commune with his people. Owen's thoughts are before you. You stand at the threshold of Dr. John Owen's office. Will you enter and receive the diagnosis, and stay to hear your cure?

Overview of John Owen's

Of the Mortification of Sin in Believers

Justin Taylor

John Owen's *Of the Mortification of Sin in Believers* is divided into three parts.[1] Part 1 begins by explaining the necessity of mortification through an exposition of Romans 8:13—"If you through the Spirit do mortify the deeds of the body you shall live"—a foundational text in Owen's theology of mortification. Owen then sets forth three foundational principles for the mortification of sin: first, believers, who are free from the *condemning* power of sin, ought to make it their daily work to mortify the *indwelling* power of sin; second, only the Holy Spirit is sufficient for this work; and third, the life, vigor, and comfort of the believer's spiritual life depends much upon this work of mortifying sin.

In Part 2 Owen seeks to define the mortification of sin and to set forth directions for this duty. He begins by explaining what mortification is *not*. Mortification is not the utter destruction of sin, nor is it the concealing of sin. Mortification has not occurred just because one's disposition has been improved, or because the sin has been diverted, or because the believer experiences an occasional conquest. So what *is* mortification? Owen argues that mortification is a habitual, successful weakening of sin that involves constant warfare and contention against the flesh.

Having defined mortification, Owen then turns to pastoral counsel on *how* to mortify sin. But first he sets forth some necessary conditions for mortification, namely, that one must be a believer, and that one must seek for universal mortification, before a single sin will be mortified.

Owen then offers nine particular directions for the soul with regard to

[1] A detailed outline of this book is found at the end of this volume.

mortification: (1) consider whether the sin you are contending with has any dangerous symptoms attending it; (2) get a clear and abiding sense upon your mind and conscience of the guilt, danger, and evil of that sin; (3) load your conscience with the guilt of it; (4) get a constant longing for deliverance from the power of it; (5) consider whether the sin is rooted in your nature and exacerbated by your temperament; (6) consider what occasions and advantages your sin has taken to exert and put forth itself, and watch against them all; (7) rise mightily against the first actings and conceptions of your sin; (8) meditate in such a way that you are filled at all times with self-abasement and thoughts of your own vileness; (9) listen to what God says to your soul and do not speak peace to yourself before God speaks it, but hearken what he says to your soul.

Finally, in Part 3 Owen explains that the foregoing is really *preparation* for the work of mortification. When we turn to the work of mortification itself, Owen offers two exhortations: first, we must set our faith on the cross-work of Christ for the killing of sin; second, the entire work of mortification must be done in the power of the Spirit.

Of The

MORTIFICATION of SINNE in BELIEVERS:

The { 1. NECESSITY
2. NATURE, and
3. MEANES of it.

With a Resolution of sundry cases of Conscience, thereunto belonging.

By

JOHN OWEN D. D. *a Servant of Jesus Christ in the worke of the Gospell.*

OXFORD,
Printed by L. LICHFIELD, Printer to the University, for T. ROBINSON, 1656.

Preface

Christian Reader,

I shall in a few words acquaint you with the reasons that obtained my consent to the publishing of the ensuing discourse. The consideration of the pres-ent state and condition of the generality of professors[1]—the visible evidences of the frame of their hearts and spirits—manifesting a great disability of dealing with the temptations, from the peace they have in the world and the divisions that they have among themselves, they are encompassed—holds the chief place among them. This I am assured is of so great importance, that if hereby I only occasion others to press more effectually on the consciences of men the work of considering their ways, and to give more clear direction for the compassing[2] of the end proposed, I shall well esteem of my lot in this undertaking. This was seconded by an observation of some men's dangerous mistakes, who of late days have taken upon them to give directions for the mortification of sin, who, being unacquainted with the mystery of the gospel and the efficacy of the death of Christ, have anew imposed the yoke of a self-wrought-out mortification on the necks of their disciples, which neither they nor their forefathers were ever able to bear [cf. Acts 15:10]. A mortification they cry up and press, suitable to that of the gospel neither in respect of nature, subject, causes, means, nor effects; which constantly produces the deplorable issues[3] of superstition, self-righteousness, and anxiety of conscience in them who take up the burden which is so bound for them.

What is here proposed in weakness, I humbly hope will answer the spirit and letter of the gospel, with the experiences of them who know what it is to walk with God, according to the tenor of the covenant of grace. So that if not this, yet certainly something of this kind, is very necessary at this season for the promotion and furtherance of this work of gospel mortification in the hearts of believers, and their direction in paths safe, and wherein they may find rest to their souls. Something I have to add as to what in particular relates unto myself. Having preached on this subject unto some comfortable success, through the grace of him that administers seed to the sower, I was pressed by sundry[4] persons, in whose hearts are the ways of God, thus to publish

[1] those who make a religious confession; professing Christians
[2] attaining, achieving
[3] results, outcomes
[4] various

what I had delivered, with such additions and alterations as I should judge necessary. Under the inducement of their desires, I called to remembrance the debt, wherein I have now, for some years, stood engaged unto sundry noble and worthy Christian friends, as to a treatise of *Communion with God,* some while since promised to them;[5] and thereon apprehended, that if I could not hereby compound for the greater debt, yet I might possibly tender[6] them this discourse of variance[7] with themselves, as interest for their forbearance of that of peace and communion with God. Besides, I considered that I had been providentially engaged in the public debate of sundry controversies in religion, which might seem to claim something in another kind of more general use, as a fruit of choice, not necessity. On these and the like accounts is this short discourse brought forth to public view, and now presented unto you. I hope I may own[8] in sincerity that my heart's desire unto God, and the chief design of my life in the station wherein the good providence of God has placed me, are that mortification and universal holiness may be promoted in my own and in the hearts and ways of others, to the glory of God; that so the gospel of our Lord and Savior Jesus Christ may be adorned in all things: for the compassing of which end, if this little discourse (of the publishing whereof this is the sum of the account I shall give) may in anything be useful to the least of the saints, it will be looked on as a return of the weak prayers wherewith it is attended by its unworthy author,

—John Owen

---

[5] See John Owen, *Communion with God,* in *The Works of John Owen,* vol. 2, ed. William H. Goold (1850–1855; reprint Edinburgh: Banner of Truth, 1965–1968). *Communion with God* was published in 1657, one year after the publication of *Of the Mortification of Sin in Believers.*

[6] offer

[7] dissent, discord

[8] admit, acknowledge, confess to be true

PART 1:

THE NECESSITY OF MORTIFICATION

[Chapter 1]

The Foundation of Mortification: Romans 8:13

[So] that what I have of direction to contribute to the carrying on of the work of mortification in believers may receive order and perspicuity,[1] I shall lay the foundation of it in those words of the apostle, "If you through the Spirit do mortify the deeds of the body you shall live" (Rom. 8:13), and reduce the whole to an improvement[2] of the great evangelical truth and mystery contained in them.

The apostle having made a recapitulation of his doctrine of justification by faith, and the blessed estate and condition of them who are made by grace partakers thereof, verses 1-3 of this chapter proceed to improve it to the holiness and consolation of believers.

Among his arguments and motives unto holiness, the verse mentioned contains one from the contrary events and effects of holiness and sin: "If you live after the flesh, you shall die." What it is to "live after the flesh," and what it is to "die," that being not my present aim and business, I shall not otherwise explain than as they will fall in with the sense of the latter words of the verse, as before proposed.

In the words peculiarly[3] designed for the foundation of the ensuing discourse, there is:

1. A duty prescribed: "Mortify the deeds of the body."
2. The persons denoted to whom it is prescribed: "You"—"if you mortify."
3. A promise annexed to that duty: "You shall live."
4. The cause or means of the performance of this duty—the Spirit: "If you through the Spirit."
5. The conditionality of the whole proposition, wherein duty, means, and promise are contained: "If you," etc.

The Conditionality: A Certain Connection

The first thing occurring in the words as they lie in the entire proposition is the conditional note, *ei de:* "but if." Conditionals in such propositions may denote two things—

---

[1] clarity
[2] exposition, application
[3] particularly, characteristically

The *uncertainty* of the event or thing promised, in respect of them to whom the duty is prescribed. And this takes place where the condition is absolutely necessary unto the issue,[4] and depends not itself on any determinate[5] cause known to him to whom it is prescribed. So we say, "If we live, we will do such a thing." This cannot be the intention of the conditional expression in this place. Of the persons to whom these words are spoken, it is said (verse 1 of the same chapter), "There is no condemnation to them."

The *certainty* of the coherence and connection that is between the things spoken of; as we say to a sick man, "If you will take such a potion, or use such a remedy, you will be well." The thing we solely intend to express is the certainty of the connection that is between the potion or remedy and health. And this is the use of it here. The certain connection that is between the *mortifying* of the deeds of the body and *living* is intimated in this conditional particle.

Now, the connection and coherence of things being manifold, as of cause and effect, of way and means and the end, this between mortification and life is not of cause and effect properly and strictly—for "eternal life is the gift of God through Jesus Christ" (Rom. 6:23)—but of means and end. God has appointed this means for the attaining of that end, which he has freely promised. Means, though necessary, have a fair subordination to all end of free promise. A gift, and procuring cause in him to whom it is given, are inconsistent. The intention, then, of this proposition as conditional is that *there is a certain infallible connection and coherence between true mortification and eternal life:* if you use this means, you shall obtain that end; if you do mortify, you shall live. And herein lies the main motive unto and enforcement of the duty prescribed.

The Persons: Believers

The next thing we meet with in the words [of Rom. 8:13] is the persons to whom this duty is prescribed, and that is expressed in the word "you," in the original included in the verb, *thanatoute,* "if you mortify"—that is, you believers; you to whom "there is no condemnation" (v. 1); you that are "not in the flesh, but in the Spirit" (v. 9); who are "quickened by the Spirit of Christ" (vv. 10-11); to you is this duty prescribed. The pressing of this duty immediately on any other is a notable fruit of that superstition and self-righteousness that the world is full of—the great work and design of devout men ignorant of the gospel (Rom. 10:3-4; John 15:5). Now, this description

[4] result, outcome

[5] resolved, settled

of the persons, in conjunction with the prescription of the duty, is the main foundation of the ensuing discourse, as it lies in this thesis or proposition:

The choicest believers,
who are assuredly freed from the condemning power of sin,
ought yet to make it their business all their days
to mortify the indwelling power of sin.

The Cause and Means: The Holy Spirit

The principal efficient cause[6] of the performance of this duty is the Spirit: *ei de pneumati*—"if by the Spirit." The Spirit here is the Spirit mentioned [in Rom. 8] verse 11, the Spirit of Christ, the Spirit of God, that "dwells in us" (v. 9), that "quickens us" (v. 11); "the Holy Ghost" (v. 14); the "Spirit of adoption" (v. 15); the Spirit "that makes intercession for us" (v. 26). All other ways of mortification are vain, all helps leave us helpless; it must be done by the Spirit. Men, as the apostle intimates (Rom. 9:30-32), may attempt this work on other principles, by means and advantages administered on other accounts, as they always have done, and do; but, says he, "This is the work of the Spirit; by him alone is it to be wrought,[7] and by no other power is it to be brought about." Mortification from a self-strength, carried on by ways of self-invention, unto the end of a self-righteousness, is the soul and substance of all false religion in the world. And this is a second principle of my ensuing discourse.

The Duty: Mortify the Deeds of the Body

The duty itself, "Mortify the deeds of the body," is next to be remarked upon. Three things are here to be inquired into: (1) What is meant by the body? (2) What by the deeds of the body? (3) What by mortifying of them?

The body. "The body" at the close of the verse is the same with "the flesh" in the beginning: "If you live after the flesh you shall die; but if you . . . mortify the deeds of the body"—that is, of the flesh. It is that which the apostle has all along discoursed of under the name of "the flesh," which is evident from the prosecution[8] of the antithesis between the Spirit and the flesh, before and after. "The body," then, here is taken for that corruption and depravity of our natures whereof the body, in a great part, is the seat and instrument,

---

[6] Aristotle (384–322 B.C.) classified four distinct types of causes, each of which answers a different question: (1) *material cause* (What is it made from?); (2) *formal cause* (What is its form or essence?); (3) *efficient cause* (Who made it?); (4) *final cause* (For what purpose?).

[7] shaped, molded, fashioned

[8] carrying out, execution

the very members of the body being made servants unto unrighteousness thereby (Rom. 6:19). It is *indwelling sin, the corrupted flesh or lust,* that is intended. Many reasons might be given of this metonymical expression[9] that I shall not now insist on. The "body" here is the same with *palaios anthrōpos* and *sōma tēs hamartias,* the "old man" and the "body of sin" (Rom. 6:6); or it may synecdochically[10] express the whole person considered as corrupted, and the seat of lusts and distempered affections.

The deeds of the body. The word is *praxeis,* which, indeed, denotes the outward actions chiefly, "the works of the flesh," as they are called, *ta erga tēs sarkos* (Gal. 5:19); which are there said to be "manifest" and are enumerated. Now, though the outward deeds are here only expressed, yet the inward and next causes are chiefly intended; the "axe is to be laid to the root of the tree" [Matt. 3:10]—the deeds of the flesh are to be mortified in their causes, from whence they spring. The apostle calls them *deeds,* as that which every lust tends unto; though they do but conceive and prove abortive, they aim to bring forth a perfect sin.

Having, both in the seventh and the beginning of this chapter, treated indwelling lust and sin as the fountain and principle of all sinful actions, he here mentions its destruction under the name of the effects which it does produce. *Praxeis tou sōmatos* [works of the body] are, as much as *phronēma tēs sarkos* [mind of the flesh] (Rom. 8:6), the "wisdom of the flesh," by a metonymy of the same nature with the former; or as the *pathēmata* and *epithumiai,* the "passions and lusts of the flesh" (Gal. 5:24), whence the deeds and fruits of it do arise; and in this sense is "the body" used: "The body is dead because of sin" (Rom. 8:10).

To mortify. Ei thanatoute—"if you put to death"—[is] a metaphorical expression, taken from the putting of any living thing to death. To kill a man, or any other living thing, is to take away the principle of all his strength, vigor, and power, so that he cannot act or exert or put forth any proper actings of his own; so it is in this case. Indwelling sin is compared to a person, a living person, called "the old man," with his faculties and properties, his wisdom, craft, subtlety, strength; this, says the apostle, must be killed, put to death, mortified—that is, have its power, life, vigor, and strength to produce its effects taken away by the Spirit. It is, indeed, meritoriously, and by way of

---

[9] A metonymical expression is a figure of speech in which one term is substituted for another term closely associated with it. For example, we might say "wheels" to refer to an automobile, "crown" to refer to a monarchy, or "Washington" to refer to the U.S. government.

[10] Similar to a metonymical expression, a synecdoche is a figure of speech in which—among other uses—the part stands for the whole or the whole stands for the part. In this case, Owen is suggesting that "body" stands for the whole person.

example, utterly mortified and slain by the cross of Christ; and the "old man" is thence said to be "crucified with Christ" (Rom. 6:6), and ourselves to be "dead" with him (Rom. 6:8), and really initially in regeneration (Rom. 6:3-5), when a principle contrary to it and destructive of it (Gal. 5:17) is planted in our hearts; but the whole work is by degrees to be carried on toward perfection all our days. Of this more in the process of our discourse. The intention of the apostle in this prescription of the duty mentioned is that:

The mortification of indwelling sin remaining in our mortal bodies,
that it may not have life and power
to bring forth the works or deeds of the flesh,
is the constant duty of believers.

The Promise: You Shall Live

The promise unto this duty is life: "you shall live." The life promised is opposed to the death threatened in the clause foregoing, "If you live after the flesh, you shall die"; which the same apostle expresses, "You shall of the flesh reap corruption" (Gal. 6:8), or destruction from God. Now, perhaps the word may not only intend eternal life, but also the spiritual life in Christ, which here we have; not as to the essence and being of it, which is already enjoyed by believers, but as to the joy, comfort, and vigor of it: as the apostle says in another case, "now we live, if you stand fast" (1 Thess. 3:8)—"Now my life will do me good; I shall have joy and comfort with my life"—"You shall live, lead a good, vigorous, comfortable, spiritual life while you are here, and obtain eternal life hereafter."

Supposing what was said before of the connection between mortification and eternal life, as of means and end, I shall add only, as a second motive to the duty prescribed, that:

The vigor, and power, and comfort of our spiritual life
depends on the mortification of the deeds of the flesh.

[Chapter 2]

Believers Ought to Make the Mortification of Indwelling Sin Their Daily Work

Having laid this foundation, a brief confirmation of the aforementioned principal deductions will lead me to what I chiefly intend, that:

The choicest believers, who are assuredly freed from the condemning power of sin, ought yet to make it their business all their days to mortify the indwelling power of sin. So the apostle, "Mortify therefore your members which are upon the earth" (Col. 3:5). To whom does he speak? Such as were "risen with Christ" (v. 1); such as were "dead" with him (v. 3); such as whose life Christ was and who should "appear with him in glory" (v. 4).

Do you mortify;
do you make it your daily work;
be always at it while you live;
cease not a day from this work;
be killing sin or it will be killing you.

Your being dead with Christ virtually, your being quickened with him, will not excuse you from this work. And our Savior tells us how his Father deals with every branch in him that bears fruit, every true and living branch. "He purges it, that it may bring forth more fruit" (John 15:2). He prunes it, and that not for a day or two, but while it is a branch in this world. And the apostle tells you what was his practice: "I keep under my body, and bring it into subjection" (1 Cor. 9:27). "I do it," says he, "daily; it is the work of my life: I omit it not; this is my business." And if this were the work and business of Paul, who was so incomparably exalted in grace, revelations, enjoyments, privileges, consolations, above the ordinary measure of believers, where may we possibly bottom[11] an exemption from this work and duty while we are in this world? Some brief account of the reasons hereof may be given.

Indwelling Sin Always Abides, Therefore It Must Always Be Mortified

Indwelling sin always abides while we are in this world; therefore it is always to be mortified. The vain, foolish, and ignorant disputes of men about perfectly keeping the commands of God, of perfection in this life, of being wholly and perfectly dead to sin, I meddle not now with. It is more than probable that the men of those abominations never knew what belonged to the keeping of any one of God's commands and are so much below perfection of degrees that they never attained to a perfection of parts in obedience or universal obedience in sincerity. And, therefore, many in our days who have talked

[11] found, base (find a basis for)

of perfection have been wiser and have affirmed it to consist in knowing no difference between good and evil. Not that they are perfect in the things we call good, but that all is alike to them, and the height of wickedness is their perfection. Others who have found out a new way to it, by denying original, indwelling sin, and tempering the spirituality of the law of God unto men's carnal hearts, as they have sufficiently discovered themselves to be ignorant of the life of Christ and the power of it in believers, so they have invented a new righteousness that the gospel knows not of, being vainly puffed up by their fleshly minds. For us, who dare not be wise above what is written, nor boast by other men's lines of what God has not done for us, we say that indwelling sin lives in us, in some measure and degree, while we are in this world. We dare not speak as "though we had already attained, or were already perfect" (Phil. 3:12). Our "inward man is to be renewed day by day" while here we live (2 Cor. 4:16), and according to the renovations of the new are the breaches[12] and decays of the old. While we are here we "know but in part" (1 Cor. 13:12), having a remaining darkness to be gradually removed by our "growth in the knowledge of our Lord Jesus Christ" (2 Pet. 3:18); and "the flesh lusts against the Spirit . . . so that we cannot do the things that we would" (Gal. 5:17), and are therefore defective in our obedience as well as in our light (1 John 1:8). We have a "body of death" (Rom. 7:24), from whence we are not delivered but by the death of our bodies (Phil. 3:20). Now, it being our duty to mortify, to be killing of sin while it is in us, we must be at work. He that is appointed to kill an enemy, if he leave[13] striking before the other ceases living, does but half his work (Gal. 6:9; Heb. 12:1; 2 Cor. 7:1).

Indwelling Sin Not Only Abides, But Is Still Acting

Sin does not only still abide in us, but is still acting, still laboring to bring forth the deeds of the flesh. When sin lets us alone we may let sin alone; but as sin is never less quiet than when it seems to be most quiet, and its waters are for the most part deep when they are still, so ought our contrivances against it to be vigorous at all times and in all conditions, even where there is least suspicion. Sin does not only abide in us, but "the law of the members is still rebelling against the law of the mind" (Rom. 7:23); and "the spirit that dwells in us lusts to envy" (James 4:5). It is always in continual work; "the flesh lusts against the Spirit" (Gal. 5:17); lust is still tempting and conceiving sin (James 1:14); in every moral action it is always either inclining to evil, or

[12] gaps, broken areas
[13] cease

hindering from that which is good, or disframing[14] the spirit from communion with God. It inclines to evil. "The evil which I would not, that I do," says the apostle (Rom. 7:19). Whence is that? Why, "Because in me (that is, in my flesh) dwells no good thing." And it hinders from good: "The good that I would do, that I do not" (v. 19)—"Upon the same account, either I do it not, or not as I should; all my holy things being defiled by this sin." "The flesh lusts against the Spirit . . . so that you cannot do the things that you would" (Gal. 5:17). And it unframes our spirit, and thence is called "the sin that so easily besets us" (Heb. 12:1); on which account are those grievous complaints that the apostle makes of it (Romans 7). So that sin is always acting, always conceiving, always seducing and tempting. Who can say that he had ever anything to do with God or for God, that indwelling sin had not a hand in the corrupting of what he did? And this trade[15] will it drive more or less all our days. If, then, sin will be always acting, if we be not always mortifying, we are lost creatures. He that stands still and suffers[16] his enemies to double blows upon him without resistance will undoubtedly be conquered in the issue. If sin be subtle, watchful, strong, and always at work in the business of killing our souls, and we be slothful, negligent, foolish, in proceeding to the ruin thereof, can we expect a comfortable event?[17] There is not a day but sin foils or is foiled, prevails or is prevailed on; and it will be so while we live in this world.

I shall discharge him from this duty who can bring sin to a composition,[18] to a cessation of arms in this warfare; if it will spare him any one day, in any one duty (provided he be a person that is acquainted with the spirituality of obedience and the subtlety of sin), let him say to his soul, as to this duty, "Soul, take your rest." The saints, whose souls breathe after deliverance from its [i.e., sin's] perplexing rebellion, know there is no safety against it but in a constant warfare.

Indwelling Sin Is Not Only Active, But Will Produce Soul-Destroying Sins If Not Mortified

Sin will not only be striving, acting, rebelling, troubling, disquieting, but if let alone, if not continually mortified, it will bring forth great, cursed, scandalous, soul-destroying sins. The apostle tells us what the works and fruits of it

---

[14] dismantling, undoing
[15] course, path, way or manner of life
[16] allows, permits, tolerates
[17] result, outcome
[18] truce, cessation of hostilities

are. "The works of the flesh are manifest, which are, adultery, fornication, uncleanness, lasciviousness,[19] idolatry, witchcraft, hatred, variance, emulations,[20] wrath, strife, seditions, heresies, envyings, murders, drunkenness, revelings, and such like" (Gal. 5:19-21). You know what it did in David and sundry[21] others. Sin aims always at the utmost; every time it rises up to tempt or entice, might it have its own course, it would go out to the utmost sin in that kind. Every unclean thought or glance would be adultery if it could; every covetous desire would be oppression, every thought of unbelief would be atheism, might it grow to its head.[22] Men may come to that, that sin may not be heard speaking a scandalous word in their hearts—that is, provoking to any great sin with scandal in its mouth; but yet every rise of lust, might it have its course, would come to the height of villainy: it is like the grave that is never satisfied. And herein lies no small share of the deceitfulness of sin, by which it prevails to the hardening of men, and so to their ruin (Heb. 3:13)—it is modest, as it were, in its first motions and proposals, but having once got footing in the heart by them, it constantly makes good its ground, and presses on to some farther degrees in the same kind. This new acting and pressing forward makes the soul take little notice of what an entrance to a falling off from God is already made; it thinks all is indifferently well if there be no further progress; and so far as the soul is made insensible[23] of any sin—that is, as to such a sense as the gospel requires—so far it is hardened: but sin is still pressing forward, and that because it has no bounds but utter relinquishment of God and opposition to him; that it proceeds toward its height by degrees, making good the ground it has got by hardness, is not from its nature, but its deceitfulness. Now nothing can prevent this but mortification; that withers the root and strikes at the head of sin every hour, so that whatever it aims at, it is crossed in. There is not the best saint in the world but, if he should give over this duty, would fall into as many cursed sins as ever any did of his kind.

Indwelling Sin Is to Be Opposed by the Spirit and the New Nature

This is one main reason why the Spirit and the new nature are given unto us—that we may have a principle within us whereby to oppose sin and lust. "The flesh lusts against the Spirit." Well! and what then? Why, "the Spirit also lusts

---

[19] wantonness, inclination to lust
[20] jealousies, especially of power and position
[21] various
[22] ultimate outcome
[23] apathetic, callous, uncomprehending

against the flesh" (Gal. 5:17). There is a propensity in the Spirit, or spiritual new nature, to be acting against the flesh, as well as in the flesh to be acting against the Spirit (2 Pet. 1:4-5). It is our participation of the divine nature that gives us an escape from the pollutions that are in the world through lust; and there is a law of the mind (Rom. 7:23), as well as a law of the members. Now this is, first, the most unjust and unreasonable thing in the world, when two combatants are engaged, to bind one and keep him up from doing his utmost and to leave the other at liberty to wound him at his pleasure; and, secondly, the most foolish thing in the world to bind him who fights for our eternal condition and to let him alone who seeks and violently attempts our everlasting ruin. The contest is for our lives and souls. Not to be daily employing the Spirit and new nature for the mortifying of sin is to neglect that excellent succor[24] which God has given us against our greatest enemy. If we neglect to make use of what we have received, God may justly hold his hand from giving us more. His graces, as well as his gifts, are bestowed on us to use, exercise, and trade with. Not to be daily mortifying sin is to sin against the goodness, kindness, wisdom, grace, and love of God, who has furnished us with a principle of doing it.

The Results of Neglecting the Mortification of Indwelling Sin

Negligence in this duty casts the soul into a perfect contrary condition to that which the apostle affirms was his: "Though our outward man perish, yet the inward man is renewed day by day" (2 Cor. 4:16). In these the inward man perishes, and the outward man is renewed day by day. Sin is as the house of David, and grace as the house of Saul. *Exercise* and *success* are the two main cherishers of grace in the heart; when it is suffered to lie still, it withers and decays: the things of it are ready to die (Rev. 3:2); and sin gets ground toward the hardening of the heart (Heb. 3:13). This is that which I intend: by the omission of this duty grace withers, lust flourishes, and the frame of the heart grows worse and worse; and the Lord knows what desperate and fearful issues it has had with many. Where sin, through the neglect of mortification, gets a considerable victory, it breaks the bones of the soul (Ps. 31:10; 51:8), and makes a man weak, sick, and ready to die (Ps. 38:3-5), so that he cannot look up (Ps. 40:12; Isa. 33:24); and when poor creatures will take blow after blow, wound after wound, foil after foil, and never rouse up themselves to a vigorous opposition, can they expect anything but to be hardened through the deceitfulness of sin, and that their souls should bleed to death (2 John 8)? Indeed, it is

---

[24] assistance, relief

a sad thing to consider the fearful issues of this neglect, which lie under our eyes every day. See we not those, whom we knew humble, melting, broken-hearted Christians, tender and fearful to offend, zealous for God and all his ways, his Sabbaths and ordinances, grown, through a neglect of watching unto this duty, earthly, carnal, cold, wrathful, complying with the men of the world and things of the world, to the scandal of religion and the fearful temptation of them that know them? The truth is, what between placing mortification in a rigid, stubborn frame of spirit—which is for the most part earthly, legal, censorious,[25] partial, consistent with wrath, envy, malice, pride—on the one hand, and pretenses of liberty, grace, and I know not what, on the other, true evangelical mortification is almost lost among us: of which afterward.

It Is Our Duty to Perfect Holiness in the Fear of God and Grow in Grace Every Day

It is our duty to be "perfecting holiness in the fear of God" (2 Cor. 7:1); to be "growing in grace" every day (1 Pet. 2:2; 2 Pet. 3:18); to be "renewing our inward man day by day" (2 Cor. 4:16). Now, this cannot be done without the daily mortifying of sin. Sin sets its strength against every act of holiness and against every degree we grow to. Let not that man think he makes any progress in holiness who walks not over the bellies of his lusts. He who does not kill sin in his way takes no steps toward his journey's end. He who finds not opposition from it, and who sets not himself in every particular to its mortification, is at peace with it, not dying to it.

This, then, is the first general principle of our ensuing discourse: Notwithstanding the meritorious mortification, if I may so speak, of all and every sin in the cross of Christ; notwithstanding the real foundation of universal mortification laid in our first conversion, by conviction of sin, humiliation for sin, and the implantation of a new principle opposite to it and destructive of it—yet *sin does so remain, so act and work in the best of believers, while they live in this world, that the constant daily mortification of it is all their days incumbent on them.* Before I proceed to the consideration of the next principle, I cannot but by the way complain of many professors[26] of these days, who, instead of bringing forth such great and evident fruits of mortification as are expected, scarce bear any leaves of it. There is, indeed, a broad light fallen upon the men of this generation, and together therewith many spiritual gifts communicated, which, with some other considerations, have

[25] critical
[26] those who make a religious confession; professing Christians

wonderfully enlarged the bounds of professors and profession; both they and it are exceedingly multiplied and increased. Hence there is a noise of religion and religious duties in every corner, preaching in abundance—and that not in an empty, light, trivial, and vain manner, as formerly, but to a good proportion of a spiritual gift—so that if you will measure the number of believers by light, gifts, and profession, the church may have cause to say, "Who has born me all these?" But now if you will take the measure of them by this great discriminating grace of Christians, perhaps you will find their number not so multiplied. Where almost is that professor[27] who owes his conversion to these days of light, and so talks and professes at such a rate of spirituality as few in former days were, in any measure, acquainted with (I will not judge them, but perhaps boasting what the Lord has done in them), that does not give evidence of a miserably unmortified heart? If vain spending of time, idleness, unprofitableness in men's places, envy, strife, variance, emulations, wrath, pride, worldliness, selfishness (1 Corinthians 1) be badges of Christians, we have them on us and among us in abundance. And if it be so with them who have much light, and which, we hope, is saving, what shall we say of some who would be accounted religious and yet despise gospel light, and for the duty we have in hand, know no more of it but what consists in men's denying themselves sometimes in outward enjoyments, which is one of the outmost branches of it, which yet they will seldom practice? The good Lord send out a spirit of mortification to cure our distempers, or we are in a sad condition!

There are two evils which certainly attend every unmortified professor—the first, in himself; the other, in respect of others.

In himself. Let him pretend what he will, he has *slight thoughts of sin;* at least, of sins of daily infirmity. The root of an unmortified course is the digestion of sin without bitterness in the heart. When a man has confirmed his imagination to such an apprehension of grace and mercy as to be able, without bitterness, to swallow and digest daily sins, that man is at the very brink of turning the grace of God into lasciviousness and being hardened by the deceitfulness of sin. Neither is there a greater evidence of a false and rotten heart in the world than to drive such a trade. To use the blood of Christ, which is given to *cleanse* us (1 John 1:7; Titus 2:14); the exaltation of Christ, which is to give us *repentance* (Acts 5:31); the doctrine of grace, which teaches us to *deny all ungodliness* (Titus 2:11-12), to countenance[28] sin is a rebellion that in the issue[29] will break the bones. At this door have gone out

[27] Where, I wonder, is that professor
[28] approve, condone
[29] outcome

from us most of the professors that have apostatized in the days wherein we live. For a while most of them were under convictions; these kept them unto duties, and brought them to profession; so they "escaped the pollutions that are in the world, through the knowledge of our Lord Jesus Christ" (2 Pet. 2:20): but having got an acquaintance with the doctrine of the gospel, and being weary of duty, for which they had no principle, they began to countenance themselves in manifold neglects from the doctrine of grace. Now, when once this evil had laid hold of them, they speedily tumbled into perdition.[30]

To others. It has an evil influence on them on a twofold account: It *hardens* them, by begetting in them a persuasion that they are in as good condition as the best professors. Whatever they see in them is so stained for want[31] of this mortification that it is of no value with them. They have a zeal for religion; but it is accompanied with want of forbearance and universal righteousness. They deny prodigality,[32] but with worldliness; they separate from the world, but live wholly to themselves, taking no care to exercise lovingkindness in the earth; or they talk spiritually, and live vainly; mention communion with God, and are every way conformed to the world; boasting of forgiveness of sin, and never forgiving others. And with such considerations do poor creatures harden their hearts in their unregeneracy.

They *deceive* them, in making them believe that if they can come up to their condition it shall be well with them; and so it grows an easy thing to have the great temptation of repute in religion to wrestle with, when they may go far beyond them as to what appears in them, and yet come short of eternal life. But of these things and all the evils of unmortified walking, afterward.

[Chapter 3]

The Holy Spirit Is the Great Sovereign Cause of the Mortification of Indwelling Sin

The next principle relates to the great sovereign cause of the mortification treated of; which, in the words laid for the foundation of this discourse [Rom. 8:13], is said to be the Spirit—that is, the Holy Ghost, as was evinced.[33]

He only is sufficient for this work; all ways and means without him are

---

[30] ruin, damnation, destruction
[31] lack
[32] reckless extravagance, especially with money
[33] proven, evidenced, made manifest

as a thing of naught; and he is the great efficient[34] of it—he works in us as he pleases.

Other Remedies Are Sought in Vain

In vain do men seek other remedies; they shall not be healed by them. What several ways have been prescribed for this, to have sin mortified, is known. The greatest part of popish[35] religion, of that which looks most like religion in their profession, consists in mistaken ways and means of mortification. This is the pretense of their rough garments, whereby they deceive.[36] Their vows, orders, fastings, penances, are all built on this ground; they are all for the mortifying of sin. Their preachings, sermons, and books of devotion, they look all this way. Hence, those who interpret the locusts that came out of the bottomless pit (Rev. 9:3), who are said to torment men so "that they should seek death and not find it" (Rev. 9:6), to be the friars of the Romish[37] church, think that they did it by their stinging sermons, whereby they convinced them of sin, but being not able to discover the remedy for the healing and mortifying of it, they kept them in such perpetual anguish and terror, and such trouble in their consciences, that they desired to die. This, I say, is the substance and glory of their religion; but what with their laboring to mortify dead creatures, ignorant of the nature and end of the work—what with the poison they mixed with it, in their persuasion of its merit, yea, supererogation[38] (as they style their unnecessary merit, with a proud, barbarous[39] title)—their glory is their shame [cf. Phil. 3:19]: but of them and their mortification more afterward (chapter 7).

That the ways and means to be used for the mortification of sin invented by them are still insisted on and prescribed, for the same end, by some who should have more light and knowledge of the gospel, is known. Such directions to this purpose have of late been given by some, and are greedily catched at[40] by others professing themselves Protestants, as might have become popish devotionists three or four hundred years ago. Such outside endeavors, such

[34] i.e., efficient cause (see note 6, above)

[35] negative label for Roman Catholicism, relating to belief in papal supremacy

[36] an allusion to Zechariah 13:4, where rough garments, or hairy cloaks, were deceptively used by false prophets in order to fool the people into thinking they were true prophets

[37] of or relating to the Roman Catholic Church

[38] According to the Roman Catholic doctrine of *opera supererogationis,* supererogatory acts—that is, actions that go beyond the call of duty and the requirements for salvation—produce a superabundance of merit that is deposited in a spiritual treasury of the Church and can be used by ordinary sinners for the remission of their sins.

[39] uncivilized

[40] grasped, sought

bodily exercises, such self-performances, such merely legal duties, without the least mention of Christ or his Spirit, are varnished over with swelling words of vanity, for the only means and expedients for the mortification of sin, as discover[41] a deep-rooted unacquaintedness with the power of God and mystery of the gospel. The consideration hereof was one motive to the publishing of this plain discourse.

Now, the reasons why the papists[42] can never, with all their endeavors, truly mortify any one sin, among others, are:

Because many of the ways and means they use and insist upon for this end were never appointed of God for that purpose. (Now, there is nothing in religion that has any efficacy for compassing[43] an end, but it has it from God's appointment of it to that purpose.) Such as these are their rough garments, their vows, penances, disciplines, their course of monastical life, and the like; concerning all which God will say, "Who has required these things at your hand?" [Isa. 1:12] and, "In vain do you worship me, teaching for doctrines the traditions of men" [Matt. 15:9]. Of the same nature are sundry self-vexations[44] insisted on by others.

Because those things that are appointed of God as means are not used by them in their due place and order—such as are praying, fasting, watching, meditation, and the like. These have their use in the business at hand; but whereas they are all to be looked on as streams, they look on them as the fountain. Whereas they effect and accomplish the end as means only, subordinate to the Spirit and faith, they look on them to do it by virtue of the work wrought. If they fast so much, and pray so much, and keep their hours and times, the work is done. As the apostle says of some in another case, "They are always learning, never coming to the knowledge of the truth" [2 Tim. 3:7]; so they are always mortifying, but never come to any sound mortification. In a word, they have sundry means to mortify the natural man, as to the natural life here we lead; none to mortify lust or corruption.

This is the general mistake of men ignorant of the gospel about this thing; and it lies at the bottom of very much of that superstition and will-worship that has been brought into the world. What horrible self-macerations[45] were practiced by some of the ancient authors of monastical devotion! What violence did they offer to nature! What extremity of sufferings did they put

41 uncover, reveal, demonstrate
42 negative label for Roman Catholics, relating to belief in papal supremacy; from the Latin *papa* ("pope")
43 attaining, achieving
44 annoyances
45 self-inflicted starvation, emaciation

themselves upon! Search their ways and principles to the bottom, and you will find that it had no other root but this mistake, namely, that attempting rigid mortification, they fell upon the natural man instead of the corrupt old man—upon the body wherein we live instead of the body of death.

Neither will the natural popery that is in others do it. Men are galled with the guilt of a sin that has prevailed over them; they instantly[46] promise to themselves and God that they will do so no more; they watch over themselves and pray for a season until this heat waxes[47] cold and the sense of sin is worn off—and so mortification goes also, and sin returns to its former dominion. Duties are excellent food for an unhealthy soul; they are no physic[48] for a sick soul. He that turns his meat into his medicine must expect no great operation. Spiritually sick men cannot sweat out their distemper with working. But this is the way of men who deceive their own souls; as we shall see afterward.

That none of these ways are sufficient is evident from the nature of the work itself that is to be done; it is a work that requires so many concurrent actings in it as no self-endeavor can reach unto, and is of that kind that an almighty energy is necessary for its accomplishment; as shall be afterward manifested.

Why Mortification Is the Work of the Spirit

It is, then, the work of the Spirit. For—

He is promised of God to be given unto us to do this work. The taking away of the stony heart—that is, the stubborn, proud, rebellious, unbelieving heart—is in general the work of mortification that we treat of. Now this is still promised to be done by the Spirit, "I will give my Spirit, and take away the stony heart" (Ezek. 11:19; 36:26), and by the Spirit of God is this work wrought when all means fail (Isa. 57:17-18).

We have all our mortification from the gift of Christ, and all the gifts of Christ are communicated to us and given us by the Spirit of Christ: "Without Christ we can do nothing" (John 15:5). All communications of supplies and relief, in the beginnings, increasings, actings of any grace whatsoever, from him, are by the Spirit, by whom he alone works in and upon believers. From him we have our mortification: "He is exalted and made a Prince and a Savior, to give repentance unto us" (Acts 5:31); and of our repentance our mortification is no small portion. How does he do it? Having "received . . .

---

[46] insistently, constantly, faithfully
[47] grows, becomes
[48] remedy, relief, medicine

the promise of the Holy Ghost," he sends him abroad for that end (Acts 2:33). You know the manifold promises he made of sending the Spirit, as Tertullian speaks, "*Vicariam navare operam,*"[49] to do the works that he had to accomplish in us.

The resolution of one or two questions will now lead me nearer to what I principally intend.

How the Spirit Mortifies Sin

The first [question] is: How does the Spirit mortify sin? I answer, in general, three ways.

By causing our hearts to abound in grace and the fruits that are contrary to the flesh, and the fruits thereof and principles of them. So the apostle opposes the fruits of the flesh and of the Spirit: "The fruits of the flesh," says he, "are so and so" (Gal. 5:19-21); "but," says he, "the fruits of the Spirit are quite contrary, quite of another sort" (vv. 22-23). Yea; but what if these are in us and do abound, may not the other abound also? No, says he, "They that are Christ's have crucified the flesh with the affections and lusts" (v. 24). But how? Why, "by living in the Spirit and walking after the Spirit" (v. 25)—that is, by the abounding of these graces of the Spirit in us and walking according to them. For, says the apostle, "these are contrary one to another" (v. 17); so that they cannot both be in the same subject in any intense or high degree. This "renewing of us by the Holy Ghost," as it is called (Titus 3:5), is one great way of mortification; he causes us to grow, thrive, flourish, and abound in those graces which are contrary, opposite, and destructive to all the fruits of the flesh, and to the quiet or thriving of indwelling sin itself.

By a real physical efficiency on the root and habit of sin, for the weakening, destroying, and taking it away. Hence he is called a "spirit of judgment and . . . burning" (Isa. 4:4), really consuming and destroying our lusts. He takes away the stony heart by an almighty efficiency; for as he begins the work as to its kind, so he carries it on as to its degrees. He is the fire which burns up the very root of lust.

He brings the cross of Christ into the heart of a sinner by faith, and gives us communion with Christ in his death and fellowship in his sufferings: of the manner whereof more afterward.

---

[49] May be translated: "to perform the work on his behalf." This quote is also found in Owen's *Communion with God* (*Works,* 2:148). Owen may be quoting Tertullian's "De Praescriptionibus Haereticos (On Prescription Against Heretics)," found in *Anti-Nicene Fathers: Volume 3* (Peabody, Mass.: Hendrickson, 2004), 249. For similar uses of the "vicariam" in connection with Tertullian and the Holy Spirit see Richard Baxter's *The Practical Works of Richard Baxter* (London, 1838), 2:266; and Thomas Manton's *Eighteen Sermons on the Second Chapter of the Second Epistle to the Thessalonians* (Achill, 1842 [1679]), 49.

If the Spirit Alone Mortifies Sin, Why Are We Exhorted to Mortify It?

Secondly, if this be the work of the Spirit alone, how is it that we are exhorted to it?—seeing the Spirit of God only can do it, let the work be left wholly to him.

It is no otherwise the work of the Spirit but as all graces and good works which are in us are his. He "works in us to will and to do of his own good pleasure" (Phil. 2:13); he works "all our works in us" (Isa. 26:12)—"the work of faith with power" (2 Thess. 1:11; Col. 2:12); he causes us to pray, and is a "spirit of supplication" (Rom. 8:26; Zech. 12:10); and yet we are exhorted, and are to be exhorted, to all these.

He does not so work our mortification in us as not to keep it still an act of our obedience. The Holy Ghost works in us and upon us, as we are fit to be wrought in and upon; that is, so as to preserve our own liberty and free obedience. He works upon our understandings, wills, consciences, and affections, agreeably to their own natures; he works in us and with us, not against us or without[50] us; so that his assistance is an encouragement as to the facilitating of the work, and no occasion of neglect as to the work itself. And, indeed, I might here bewail the endless, foolish labor of poor souls, who, being convinced of sin and not able to stand against the power of their convictions, do set themselves, by innumerable perplexing ways and duties, to keep down sin, but, being strangers to the Spirit of God, all in vain. They combat without victory, have war without peace, and are in slavery all their days. They spend their strength for that which is not bread, and their labor for that which profits not [Isa. 55:2].

This is the saddest warfare that any poor creature can be engaged in. A soul under the power of conviction from the law is pressed to fight against sin, but has no strength for the combat. They cannot but fight, and they can never conquer; they are like men thrust on the sword of enemies on purpose to be slain. The *law* drives them on, and sin beats them back. Sometimes they think, indeed, that they have foiled sin, when they have only raised a dust that they see it not; that is, they distemper their natural affections of fear, sorrow, and anguish, which makes them believe that sin is conquered when it is not touched. By that time they are cold, they must go to the battle again; and the lust which they thought to be slain appears to have had no wound.

And if the case be so sad with them who do labor and strive, and yet enter not into the kingdom, what is their condition who despise all this; who

---

[50] outside of

are perpetually under the power and dominion of sin and love to have it so; and are troubled at nothing, but that they cannot make sufficient provision for the flesh, to fulfill the lusts thereof [cf. Rom. 13:14]?

[Chapter 4]

The Life, Vigor, and Comfort of Our Spiritual Life Depend Much on Our Mortification of Sin

The last principle I shall insist on (omitting, first, the necessity of mortification unto life, and, secondly, the certainty of life upon mortification) is that the life, vigor, and comfort of our spiritual life depend much on our mortification of sin. Strength and comfort, and power and peace, in our walking with God, are the things of our desires. Were any of us asked seriously what it is that troubles us, we must refer it to one of these heads[51]—either we want strength or power, vigor and life, in our obedience, in our walking with God; or we want peace, comfort, and consolation therein. Whatever it is that may befall a believer that does not belong to one of these two heads does not deserve to be mentioned in the days of our complaints.

Now, all these do much depend on a constant course of mortification, about which observe:

Life, Vigor, and Comfort Are Not Necessarily Connected to Mortification

I do not say they proceed from it, as though they were necessarily tied to it. A man may be carried on in a constant course of mortification all his days; and yet perhaps never enjoy a good day of peace and consolation. So it was with Heman (Psalm 88); his life was a life of perpetual mortification and walking with God, yet terrors and wounds were his portion all his days. But God singled out Heman, a choice friend, to make him an example to them that afterward should be in distress. Can you complain if it be no otherwise with you than it was with Heman, that eminent servant of God? And this shall be his praise to the end of the world. God makes it his prerogative to speak peace and consolation (Isa. 57:18-19). "*I* will do that work," says God, "I will comfort him" (v. 18). But how? By an immediate work of the new cre-

[51] headings, categories

ation: "I create it," says God (v. 19). The *use of means* for the obtaining of peace is ours; the *bestowing* of it is God's prerogative.

Adoption and Justification, Not Mortification, Are the Immediate Causes of Life, Vigor, and Comfort

In the ways instituted by God to give us life, vigor, courage, and consolation, mortification is not one of the immediate causes of it. They are the privileges of our adoption made known to our souls that give us immediately these things. "The Spirit bearing witness with our spirits that we are the children of God" [Rom. 8:16], giving us a new name and a white stone, adoption and justification, that is, as to the sense and knowledge of them—are the immediate causes (in the hand of the Spirit) of these things. But this I say:

In the Ordinary Relationship with God, the Vigor and Comfort of Our Spiritual Lives Depend Much on Our Mortification of Sin

In our ordinary walking with God, and in an ordinary course of his dealing with us, the vigor and comfort of our spiritual lives depend much on our mortification, not only as a *causa sine qua non,*[52] but as a thing that has an effectual influence thereinto. For:

This alone keeps sin from depriving us of the one and the other. Every unmortified sin will certainly do two things: It will *weaken the soul* and deprive it of its vigor. It will *darken the soul* and deprive it of its comfort and peace.

It weakens the soul and deprives it of its strength. When David had for a while harbored an unmortified lust in his heart, it broke all his bones and left him no spiritual strength; hence he complained that he was sick, weak, wounded, faint. "There is," says he, "no soundness in me" (Ps. 38:3); "I am feeble and sore broken" (v. 8); "yea, I cannot so much as look up" (Ps. 40:12). An unmortified lust will drink up the spirit and all the vigor of the soul, and weaken it for all duties. For:

It untunes and unframes the heart itself by entangling its affections. It diverts the heart from the spiritual frame that is required for vigorous communion with God; it lays hold on the affections, rendering its object beloved and desirable, so expelling the love of the Father (1 John 2:15; 3:17); so that the soul cannot say uprightly and truly to God, "You are my portion," having something else that it loves. Fear, desire, hope, which are the choice

[52] a necessary cause or an essential condition—lit., "a cause without which not"

affections of the soul, that should be full of God, will be one way or other entangled with it.

It fills the thoughts with contrivances about it. Thoughts are the great purveyors of the soul to bring in provision to satisfy its affections; and if sin remain unmortified in the heart, they must ever and anon[53] be making provision for the flesh, to fulfill the lusts thereof. They must glaze, adorn, and dress the objects of the flesh, and bring them home to give satisfaction; and this they are able to do, in the service of a defiled imagination, beyond all expression.

It breaks out and actually hinders duty. The ambitious man must be studying, and the worldling must be working or contriving, and the sensual,[54] vain person providing himself for vanity, when they should be engaged in the worship of God.

Were this my present business, to set forth the breaches, ruin, weakness, desolations, that one unmortified lust will bring upon a soul, this discourse must be extended much beyond my intention.

As sin weakens, so it darkens the soul. It is a cloud, a thick cloud, that spreads itself over the face of the soul, and intercepts all the beams of God's love and favor. It takes away all sense of the privilege of our adoption; and if the soul begins to gather up thoughts of consolation, sin quickly scatters them: of which afterward.

Now, in this regard does the vigor and power of our spiritual life depend on our mortification: It is the only means of the removal of that which will allow us neither the one nor the other. Men that are sick and wounded under the power of lust make many applications for help; they cry to God when the perplexity of their thoughts overwhelms them, even to God do they cry, but are not delivered; in vain do they use many remedies—"they shall not be healed." So, "Ephraim saw his sickness, and Judah saw his wound" (Hos. 5:13), and attempted sundry remedies: nothing will do until they come to "acknowledge their offense" (v. 15). Men may see their sickness and wounds, but yet, if they make not due applications, their cure will not be effected.

Mortification prunes all the graces of God and makes room for them in our hearts to grow. The life and vigor of our spiritual lives consists in the vigor and flourishing of the plants of grace in our hearts. Now, as you may see in a garden, let there be a precious herb planted, and let the ground be untilled, and weeds grow about it, perhaps it will live still, but be a poor,

[53] again, i.e., reoccurring
[54] perceived by the senses (not necessarily sexual)

withering, unuseful thing. You must look and search for it, and sometimes can scarce find it; and when you do, you can scarce know it, whether it be the plant you look for or not; and suppose it be, you can make no use of it at all. When, let another of the same kind be set in the ground, naturally as barren and bad as the other, but let it be well weeded, and everything that is noxious[55] and hurtful removed from it—it flourishes and thrives; you may see it at first look into the garden, and have it for your use when you please. So it is with the graces of the Spirit that are planted in our hearts. That is true; they are still, they abide in a heart where there is some neglect of mortification; but they are ready to die (Rev. 3:2), they are withering and decaying. The heart is like the sluggard's field—so overgrown with weeds that you can scarce see the good corn. Such a man may search for faith, love, and zeal, and scarce be able to find any; and if he does discover that these graces are there yet alive and sincere, yet they are so weak, so clogged with lusts, that they are of very little use; they remain, indeed, but are ready to die. But now let the heart be cleansed by mortification, the weeds of lust constantly and daily rooted up (as they spring daily, nature being their proper soil), let room be made for grace to thrive and flourish—how will every grace act its part, and be ready for every use and purpose!

As to our peace; as there is nothing that has any evidence of sincerity without it, so I know nothing that has such an evidence of sincerity in it—which is no small foundation of our peace. Mortification is the soul's vigorous opposition to self, wherein sincerity is most evident.

[55] injurious, harmful, unwholesome

PART 2:

The Nature of Mortification

[Chapter 5]

These things being premised, I come to my principal retention,[1] of handling some questions or practical cases that present themselves in this business of mortification of sin in believers.

The first, which is the head of all the rest, and whereunto they are reduced, may be considered as lying under the ensuing proposal: Suppose a man to be a true believer, and yet finds in himself a powerful indwelling sin, leading him captive to the law of it, consuming his heart with trouble, perplexing his thoughts, weakening his soul as to duties of communion with God, disquieting him as to peace, and perhaps defiling his conscience, and exposing him to hardening through the deceitfulness of sin, what shall he do? What course shall he take and insist on for the mortification of this sin, lust, distemper, or corruption, to such a degree as that, though it be not utterly destroyed, yet, in his contest with it, he may be enabled to keep up power, strength, and peace in communion with God?

In answer to this important inquiry, I shall do these things: (1) *Show what it is to mortify any sin,* and that both negatively and positively, that we be not mistaken in the foundation; (2) *Give general directions* for such things as without which it will be utterly impossible for anyone to get any sin truly and spiritually mortified; (3) *Draw out the particulars* whereby this is to be done; in the whole carrying on this consideration, that it is not of the doctrine of mortification in general, but only in reference to the particular case before proposed, that I am treating.

What Mortification Is *Not*

Mortification Is Not the Utter Destruction and Death of Sin

To mortify a sin is not utterly to kill, root it out, and destroy it, that it should have no more hold at all nor residence in our hearts. It is true this is that which is *aimed at;* but this is not in this life to be *accomplished.* There is no man that truly sets himself to mortify any sin, but he aims at, intends, desires its utter destruction, that it should leave neither root nor fruit in the heart or life. He would so kill it that it should never move nor stir anymore, cry or call, seduce or tempt, to eternity. Its *not-being* is the thing aimed at. Now, though doubtless there may, by the Spirit and grace of Christ, a wonderful success and eminency of victory against any sin be attained, so that a man may have

[1] contention, concern

almost constant triumph over it, yet an utter killing and destruction of it, that it should not be, is not in this life to be expected. This Paul assures us of: "Not as though I had already attained, either were already perfect" (Phil. 3:12). He was a *choice saint,* a pattern for believers, who, in faith and love, and all the fruits of the Spirit, had not his fellow in the world, and on that account ascribes perfection to himself in comparison of others (v. 15); yet he had not "attained," he was not "perfect," but was "following after" (v. 12): still a vile body he had, and we have, that must be changed by the great power of Christ at last (v. 21). This we would have; but God sees it best for us that we should be complete in nothing in ourselves, that in all things we must be "complete in Christ," which is best for us (Col. 2:10).

Mortification Is Not the Dissimulation of Sin

I think I need not say it is not the dissimulation[2] of a sin. When a man on some outward respects forsakes the practice of any sin, men perhaps may look on him as a changed man. God knows that to his former iniquity he has added cursed hypocrisy, and is now on a safer path to hell than he was before. He has got another heart than he had, that is more cunning; not a new heart, that is more holy.

Mortification Is Not the Improvement of a Quiet, Sedate Nature

The mortification of sin consists not in the improvement of a quiet, sedate nature. Some men have an advantage by their natural constitution so far as that they are not exposed to such violence of unruly passions and tumultuous affections as many others are. Let now these men cultivate and improve their natural frame and temper[3] by discipline, consideration, and prudence, and they may seem to themselves and others very mortified men, when, perhaps, their hearts are a standing sink of all abominations. Some man is never so much troubled all his life, perhaps, with anger and passion, nor does trouble others, as another is almost every day; and yet the latter has done more to the mortification of the sin than the former. Let not such persons try their mortification by such things as their natural temper gives no life or vigor to. Let them bring themselves to self-denial, unbelief, envy, or some such spiritual sin, and they will have a better view of themselves.

---

[2] making unlike; process of becoming unlike

[3] character, disposition

Mortification Is Not the Diversion of Sin

A sin is not mortified when it is only diverted. Simon Magus for a season left his *sorceries;* but his *covetousness and ambition,* that set him on work, remained still, and would have been acting another way. Therefore Peter tells him, "I perceive you are in the gall of bitterness" [Acts 8:23]—"Notwithstanding the profession you have made, notwithstanding your relinquishment of your sorceries, your lust is as powerful as ever in you; the same lust, only the streams of it are diverted. It now exerts and puts forth itself another way, but it is the old gall of bitterness still." A man may be sensible of a lust, set himself against the eruptions of it, take care that it shall not break forth as it has done, but in the meantime suffer the same corrupted habit to vent itself some other way; as he who heals and skins a running sore thinks himself cured, but in the meantime his flesh festers by the corruption of the same humor,[4] and breaks out in another place. And this diversion, with the alterations that attend it, often befalls men on accounts wholly foreign unto grace: change of the course of life that a man was in, of relations, interests, designs, may effect it; yea, the very alterations in men's constitutions, occasioned by a natural progress in the course of their lives, may produce such changes as these. Men in [old] age do not usually persist in the pursuit of youthful lusts, although they have never mortified any one of them. And the same is the case of bartering of lusts, and leaving to serve one that a man may serve another. He that changes pride for worldliness, sensuality for Pharisaism, vanity in himself to the contempt of others, let him not think that he has mortified the sin that he seems to have left. He has changed his master, but is a servant still.

Mortification Is Not Just Occasional Conquests Over Sin

Occasional conquests of sin do not amount to a mortifying of it. There are two occasions or seasons wherein a man who is contending with any sin may seem to himself to have mortified it:

When it has had some sad *eruption,* to the disturbance of his peace, terror of his conscience, dread of scandal, and evident provocation of God. This awakens and stirs up all that is in the man, and amazes him, fills him with abhorrency of sin and himself for it; sends him to God, makes him cry out as for life, to abhor his lust as hell and to set himself against it. The whole man, spiritual and natural, being now awakened, sin shrinks in its head, appears not, but lies as dead before him: as when one that has drawn nigh[5] to an army

[4] bodily fluid, thought to be the physical root of the passions
[5] near

in the night, and has killed a principal person—instantly the guards awake, men are roused up, and strict inquiry is made after the enemy, who, in the meantime, until the noise and tumult be over, hides himself, or lies like one that is dead, yet with firm resolution to do the like mischief again upon the like opportunity. Upon the sin among the Corinthians, see how they muster up themselves for the surprise and destruction of it (2 Cor. 7:11). So it is in a person when a breach has been made upon his *conscience,* quiet, perhaps credit, by his lust, in some eruption of actual sin—carefulness, indignation, desire, fear, revenge, are all set on work about it and against it, and lust is quiet for a season, being run down before them; but when the hurry is over and the inquest[6] past, the thief appears again alive, and is as busy as ever at his work.

In a time of some *judgment,* calamity, or pressing affliction, the heart is then taken up with thoughts and contrivances of flying from the present troubles, fears, and dangers. This, as a convinced person concludes, is to be done only by relinquishment of sin, which gains peace with God. It is the anger of God in every affliction that galls a convinced person. To be quit of this,[7] men resolve at such times against their sins. Sin shall never more have any place in them; they will never again give up themselves to the service of it. Accordingly, sin is quiet, stirs not, seems to be mortified; not, indeed, that it has received any one wound, but merely because the soul has possessed its faculties, whereby it should exert itself, with thoughts inconsistent with the motions thereof; which, when they are laid aside, sin returns again to its former life and vigor. So they are a full instance and description of this frame of spirit whereof I speak:

> For all this they sinned still, and believed not for his wondrous works. Therefore their days did he consume in vanity, and their years in trouble. When he slew them, then they sought him: and they returned and inquired early after God. And they remembered that God was their rock, and the high God their redeemer. Nevertheless they did flatter him with their mouth, and they lied unto him with their tongues. For their heart was not right with him, neither were they steadfast in his covenant. (Ps. 78:32-37)

I no way doubt but that when they sought, and returned, and inquired early after God, they did it with full purpose of heart as to the relinquishment of their sins; it is expressed in the word "returned." To turn or return to the Lord is by a relinquishment of sin. This they did "early"—with earnestness

[6] inquiry, investigation
[7] to be freed or released from this

and diligence—but yet their sin was unmortified for all this (vv. 36-37). And this is the state of many humiliations in the days of affliction, and a great deceit in the hearts of believers themselves lies oftentimes herein.

These and many other ways there are whereby poor souls deceive themselves, and suppose they have mortified their lusts, when they live and are mighty, and on every occasion break forth, to their disturbance and disquietness.

[Chapter 6]

What it is to mortify a sin in general, which will make further way for particular directions, is next to be considered.

What Mortification Is

Mortification Consists in a Habitual Weakening of Sin

Every lust is a depraved habit or disposition, continually inclining the heart to evil. Thence is that description of him who has no lust truly mortified: "Every imagination of the thoughts of his heart is only evil continually" (Gen. 6:5). He is always under the power of a strong bent and inclination to sin. And the reason why a natural man is not always perpetually in the pursuit of some one lust, night and day, is because he has many to serve, every one crying to be satisfied; thence he is carried on with great variety, but still in general he lies toward the satisfaction of self.

We will suppose, then, the lust or distemper whose mortification is inquired after to be in itself a strong, deeply-rooted, habitual inclination and bent of will and affections unto some actual sin, as to the matter of it, though not, under that formal consideration, always stirring up imaginations, thoughts, and contrivances about the object of it. Hence, men are said to have their "hearts set upon evil" [Eccles. 8:11], the bent of their spirits lies toward it, to make "provision for the flesh" [Rom. 13:14]. And a sinful, depraved habit, as in really other things, so in this, differs from all natural or moral habits whatsoever: for whereas they incline the soul gently and suitably to itself, sinful habits impel with violence and impetuousness;[8] whence lusts are said to fight or wage "war against the soul" (1 Pet. 2:11)—to rebel or rise up in war with that conduct and opposition which is usual therein (Rom. 7:23)—

[8] vehemence

to lead captive, or effectually captivating upon success in battle—all works of great violence and impetuousness.

I might manifest fully, from that description we have of it (Romans 7), how it will darken the mind, extinguish convictions, dethrone reason, interrupt the power and influence of any considerations that may be brought to hamper it, and break through all into a flame. But this is not my present business. Now, the first thing in mortification is the weakening of this habit of sin or lust, that it shall not, with that violence, earnestness, frequency, rise up, conceive, tumultuate,[9] provoke, entice, disquiet, as naturally it is apt to do (James 1:14-15).

I shall desire to give one caution or rule by the way, and it is this: Though every lust does in its own nature equally, universally, incline and impel to sin, yet this must be granted with these two limitations:

One lust, or a lust in one man, may receive many accidental[10] *improvements, heightenings, and strengthenings, which may give it life, power, and vigor, exceedingly above what another lust has, or the same lust (that is, of the same kind and nature) in another man.* When a lust falls in with the natural constitutions and temper, with a suitable course of life, with occasions, or when Satan has got a fit handle to it to manage it, as he has a thousand ways so to do, that lust grows violent and impetuous above others, or more than the same lust in another man; then the steams of it darken the mind so, that though a man knows the same things as formerly, yet they have no power nor influence on the will, but corrupt affections and passions are set by it at liberty.

But especially, lust gets strength by *temptation.* When a suitable temptation falls in with a lust, it gives it a new life, vigor, power, violence, and rage, which it seemed not before to have or to be capable of. Instances to this purpose might be multiplied; but it is the design of some part of another treatise[11] to evince this observation.

Some lusts are far more sensible and discernible in their violent actings than others. Paul puts a difference between uncleanness and all other sins: "Flee fornication. Every sin that a man does is without the body; but he that commits fornication sins against his own body" (1 Cor. 6:18). Hence, the motions of that sin are more sensible, more discernible than of others; when perhaps the love of the world, or the like, is in a person no less habitually predominant than that, yet it makes not so great a combustion[12] in the whole man.

[9] agitate, disturb, stir up
[10] non-essential, incidental
[11] See Owen's *Of Temptation: The Nature and Power of It,* reprinted in this volume.
[12] consuming as by fire; tumult

And on this account some men may go in their own thoughts and in the eyes of the world for mortified men, who yet have in them no less predominancy of lust than those who cry out with astonishment upon the account of its perplexing tumultuatings, yea, than those who have by the power of it been hurried into scandalous sins; only their lusts are in and about things which raise not such a tumult in the soul, about which they are exercised with a calmer frame of spirit, the very fabric of nature being not so nearly concerned in them as in some other.

I say, then, that the first thing in mortification is the *weakening* of this habit, that it shall not impel and tumultuate as formerly; that it shall not entice and draw aside; that it shall not disquiet and perplex the killing of its life, vigor, promptness, and readiness to be stirring. This is called "crucifying the flesh with the lusts thereof" (Gal. 5:24); that is, taking away its blood and spirits that give it strength and power—the wasting of the body of death "day by day" (2 Cor. 4:16).

As a man nailed to the cross he first struggles and strives and cries out with great strength and might, but, as his blood and spirits waste, his strivings are faint and seldom, his cries low and hoarse, scarce to be heard; when a man first sets on a lust or distemper, to deal with it, it struggles with great violence to break loose; it cries with earnestness and impatience to be satisfied and relieved; but when by mortification the blood and spirits of it are let out, it moves seldom and faintly, cries sparingly, and is scarce heard in the heart; it may have sometimes a dying pang, that makes an appearance of great vigor and strength, but it is quickly over, especially if it be kept from considerable success. This the apostle describes, as in the whole chapter, so especially Romans 6:6.

"Sin," says he, "is crucified; it is fastened to the cross." To what end? "That the body of death may be destroyed," the power of sin weakened and abolished by little and little, that "henceforth we should not serve sin," that is, that sin might not incline, impel us with such efficacy as to make us servants to it, as it has done heretofore. And this is spoken not only with respect to carnal and sensual affections, or desires of worldly things—not only in respect of the lust of the flesh, the lust of the eyes, and the pride of life—but also as to the flesh, that is, in the mind and will, in that opposition unto God which is in us by nature. Of whatsoever nature the troubling distemper be, by whatsoever ways it [might] make itself out, either by impelling to evil or hindering from that which is good, the rule is the same; and unless this be done effectually, all after-contention will not compass the end aimed at. A man may beat down the bitter fruit from an evil tree until he is weary; while the root abides in strength and vigor, the beating down of the present fruit will not hinder it from bringing forth more. This is the folly of some men; they set themselves with all earnestness and diligence against the appearing eruption of lust, but, leaving the principle and root untouched, perhaps unsearched out, they make but little or no progress in this work of mortification.

Mortification Consists in Constant Fighting and Contending Against Sin

To be able always to be laying load on sin is no small degree of mortification. When sin is strong and vigorous, the soul is scarce able to make any head against it; it sighs, and groans, and mourns, and is troubled, as David speaks of himself, but seldom has sin in the pursuit. David complains that his sin had "taken fast hold upon him, that he could not look up" (Ps. 40:12). How little, then, was he able to fight against it! Now, sundry things are required unto and comprised in this fighting against sin:

To know that a man has such an enemy to deal with it, to take notice of it, to consider it as an enemy indeed, and one that is to be destroyed by all means possible, is required hereunto. As I said before, the contest is vigorous and hazardous—it is about the things of eternity. When, therefore, men have slight and transient thoughts of their lusts, it is no great sign that they are mortified, or that they are in a way for their mortification. This is every man's "knowing the plague of his own heart" (1 Kings 8:38), without which no other work can be done. It is to be feared that very many have little knowledge of the main enemy that they carry about with them in their bosoms. This makes them ready to justify themselves and to be impatient of reproof or admonition, not knowing that they are in any danger (2 Chron. 16:10).

To labor to be acquainted with the ways, wiles, methods, advantages, and occasions of its success is the beginning of this warfare. So do men deal with enemies. They inquire out their counsels and designs, ponder their ends, consider how and by what means they have formerly prevailed, that they may be prevented. In this consists the greatest skill in conduct. Take this away, and all waging of war, wherein is the greatest improvement of human wisdom and industry, would be brutish. So do they deal with lust who mortify it indeed. Not only when it is actually vexing, enticing, and seducing, but in their retirements[13] they consider, "This is our enemy; this is his way and progress, these are his advantages, thus has he prevailed, and thus he will do, if not prevented." So David, "My sin is ever before me" (Ps. 51:3). And,

[13] privacy, seclusion, leisure

indeed, one of the choicest and most eminent parts of practically spiritual wisdom consists in finding out the subtleties, policies, and depths of any indwelling sin; to consider and know wherein its greatest strength lies—what advantage it uses to make of occasions, opportunities, temptations—what are its pleas, pretenses, reasonings—what its stratagems, colors,[14] excuses; to set the wisdom of the Spirit against the craft of the *old man;* to trace this serpent in all its turnings and windings; to be able to say, at its most secret and (to a common frame of heart) imperceptible actings, "This is your old way and course; I know what you aim at"—and so to be always in readiness is a good part of our warfare.

To load it daily with all the things which shall after be mentioned, that are grievous, killing, and destructive to it is the height of this contest. Such a one never thinks his lust dead because it is quiet, but labors still to give it new wounds, new blows every day. (So the apostle, Col. 3:5.)

Now, while the soul is in this condition, while it is thus dealing, it is certainly uppermost; sin is under the sword and dying.

Mortification Consists in Frequent Success

Frequent success against any lust is another part and evidence of mortification. By success I understand not a mere disappointment[15] of sin, that it be not brought forth nor accomplished, but a victory over it and pursuit of it to a complete conquest. For instance, when the heart finds sin at any time at work, seducing, forming imaginations to make provision for the flesh, to fulfill the lusts thereof, it instantly apprehends sin and brings it to the law of God and love of Christ, condemns it, follows it with execution to the uttermost.

Now, I say, when a man comes to this state and condition, that lust is weakened in the root and principle, that its motions and actions are fewer and weaker than formerly, so that they are not able to hinder his duty nor interrupt his peace—when he can, in a quiet, sedate frame of spirit, find out and fight against sin, and have success against it—then sin is mortified in some considerable measure, and, notwithstanding all its opposition, a man may have peace with God all his days.

Unto these heads, then, do I refer the mortification aimed at; that is, of any one perplexing distemper, whereby the general depravity and corruption of our nature attempts to exert and put forth itself:

First, the weakening of its indwelling disposition, whereby it inclines,

[14] embellishments concealing the truth

[15] undoing of an intended end or use

entices, impels to evil, rebels, opposes, fights against God, by the implanting, habitual residence, and cherishing of a principle of grace that stands in direct opposition to it and is destructive of it, is the foundation of it. So, by the implanting and growth of humility is pride weakened, passion by patience, uncleanness by purity of mind and conscience, love of this world by heavenly-mindedness: which are graces of the Spirit, or the same habitual grace variously acting itself by the Holy Ghost, according to the variety or diversity of the objects about which it is exercised; as the other are several lusts, or the same natural corruption variously acting itself, according to the various advantages and occasions that it meets with.

The promptness, alacrity,[16] vigor of the Spirit, or new man, in contending with, cheerful fighting against, the lust spoken of, by all the ways and with all the means that are appointed thereunto, constantly using the succors provided against its motions and actings, is a second thing hereunto required.

Success unto several degrees attends these two. Now this, if the distemper has not an unconquerable advantage from its natural situation, may possibly be to such a universal conquest as the soul may never more sensibly feel its opposition, and shall, however, assuredly arise to an allowance of peace to the conscience, according to the tenor of the covenant of grace.

[Chapter 7]

General Directions for Mortification

The *ways* and *means* whereby a soul may proceed to the mortification of any particular lust and sin, which Satan takes advantage by to disquiet and weaken him, come next under consideration.

Now, there are some general considerations to be premised, concerning some principles and foundations of this work, without which no man in the world, be he never so much raised by convictions, and resolved for the mortification of any sin, can attain thereunto.

General rules and principles, without which no sin will be ever mortified, are these:

---

[16] eagerness, liveliness, speed

There Will Be No Mortification Unless a Man Be a Believer

Unless a man be a believer—that is, one that is truly ingrafted into Christ—he can never mortify any one sin; I do not say, unless he *know* himself to be so, but unless indeed he *be* so.

Mortification is the work of believers: "If you through the Spirit" (Rom. 8:13), etc.—you *believers,* to whom there is no condemnation (v. 1). They alone are exhorted to it: "Mortify therefore your members which are upon the earth" (Col. 3:5). Who should mortify? You who [are] "risen with Christ" (v. 1); whose "life is hid with Christ in God" (v. 3); who "shall appear with him in glory" (v. 4). An unregenerate man may do something like it; but the work itself, so as it may be acceptable with God, he can never perform. You know what a picture of it is drawn in some of the philosophers—Seneca, Tully, Epictetus[17]—what affectionate discourses they have of contempt of the world and self, of regulating and conquering all exorbitant affections and passions! The lives of most of them manifested that their maxims differed as much from true mortification as the sun painted on a sign-post from the sun in the firmament; they had neither light nor heat. Their own Lucian[18] sufficiently manifests what they all were. There is no death of sin without the death of Christ. You know what attempts there are made after it by the papists, in their vows, penances, and satisfactions. I dare say of them (I mean as many of them as act upon the principles of their church, as they call it) what Paul says of Israel in point of righteousness: They have followed after mortification, but they have not attained to it. Wherefore? "Because they seek it not by faith, but as it were by the works of the law" (Rom. 9:31-32). The same is the state and condition of all among ourselves who, in obedience to their convictions and awakened consciences, do attempt a relinquishment of sin—they follow after it, but they do not attain it.

It is true, it is—it will be—required of every person whatsoever that hears the law or gospel preached, that he mortify sin. It is his duty, but it is not his immediate duty; it is his duty to do it, but to do it in God's way. If you require your servant to pay so much money for you in such a place, but first to go and take it up in another, it is his duty to pay the money appointed, and you will blame him if he does it not; yet it was not his immediate duty—he was first to take it up, according to your direction. So it is in this case: sin is to be mortified, but something is to be done in the first place to enable us thereunto.

---

[17] Seneca (c. 4 B.C.–65 A.D.) was a Roman playwright, orator, and philosopher. "Tully" is an older way of referring to Marcus Tullius Cicero (106–43 B.C.), a Roman statesman, lawyer, and philosopher. Epictetus (c. 55–c. 135 A.D.) was a Greek Stoic philosopher.

[18] Lucian of Samosata (c. 120–c. 190 A.D.) was a Greek satirist who mocked Greek philosophy and mythology.

I have proved that it is the Spirit alone that can mortify sin; he is promised to do it, and all other means without him are empty and vain. How shall he, then, mortify sin that has not the Spirit? A man may easier see without eyes, speak without a tongue, than truly mortify one sin without the Spirit. Now, how is he attained? It is the Spirit of Christ: and as the apostle says, "If we have not the Spirit of Christ, we are none of his" (Rom. 8:9); so, if we are Christ's, have an interest[19] in him, we have the Spirit, and so alone have power for mortification. This the apostle discourses at large, "So then they that are in the flesh cannot please God" (v. 8). It is the inference and conclusion he makes of his foregoing discourse about our natural state and condition, and the enmity we have unto God and his law therein. If we are in the flesh, if we have not the Spirit, we cannot do anything that should please God. But what is our deliverance from this condition? "But you are not in the flesh, but in the Spirit, if so be that the Spirit of God dwell in you" (v. 9)—"You believers, that have the Spirit of Christ, you are not in the flesh." There is no way of deliverance from the state and condition of being in the flesh but by the Spirit of Christ. And what if this Spirit of Christ be in you? Why, then, you are mortified; "the body is dead because of sin" or unto it (v. 10); mortification is carried on; the new man is quickened to righteousness. This the apostle proves from the union we have with Christ by the Spirit (v. 11), which will produce suitable operations in us to what it wrought in him. All attempts, then, for mortification of any lust, without an interest in Christ, are vain. Many men that are galled with and for sin, the arrows of Christ for conviction, by the preaching of the word, or some affliction having been made sharp in their hearts, do vigorously set themselves against this or that particular lust, wherewith their consciences have been most disquieted or perplexed. But, poor creatures! They labor in the fire, and their work consumes. When the Spirit of Christ comes to this work he will be "like a refiner's fire and like fullers' soap," and he will purge men as gold and as silver (Mal. 3:2-3)—take away their dross and tin [Isa. 1:25], their filth and blood (Isa. 4:4); but men must be gold and silver in the bottom, or else refining will do them no good. The prophet gives us the sad issue of wicked men's utmost attempts for mortification, by whatsoever means that God affords them: "The bellows[20] are burned, and the lead is consumed of the fire; the founder melts in vain. . . . Reprobate silver shall men call them, because the Lord has rejected them" (Jer. 6:29-30). And what is the reason hereof? They were "brass and iron"

---

[19] share or stake

[20] blacksmith's device for blowing air into fire

when they were put into the furnace (v. 28). Men may refine brass and iron long enough before they will be good silver.

I say, then, mortification is not the present business of unregenerate men. God calls them not to it as yet; conversion is their work—the conversion of the *whole* soul—not the mortification of this or that particular lust. You would laugh at a man that you should see setting up a great fabric, and never take any care for a foundation; especially if you should see him so foolish as that, having a thousand experiences that what he built one day fell down another, he would yet continue in the same course. So it is with convinced persons; though they plainly see that what ground they get against sin one day they lose another, yet they will go on in the same road still without inquiring where the destructive flaw in their progress lies. When the Jews, upon the conviction of their sin, were cut to the heart and cried out, "What shall we do?" (Acts 2:37), what does Peter direct them to do? Does he bid them go and mortify their pride, wrath, malice, cruelty, and the like? No; he knew that was not their present work, but he calls them to conversion and faith in Christ in general (v. 38). Let the soul be first thoroughly converted, and then, "looking on him whom they had pierced" [Zech. 12:10; John 19:37], humiliation and mortification will ensue. Thus, when John came to preach repentance and conversion, he said, "The axe is now laid to the root of the tree" (Matt. 3:10). The Pharisees had been laying heavy burdens, imposing tedious duties, and rigid means of mortification, in fastings, washings, and the like, all in vain. Says John, "The doctrine of conversion is for you; the axe in my hand is laid to the root." And our Savior tells us what is to be done in this case; says he, "Do men gather grapes of thorns?" (Matt. 7:16). But suppose a thorn be well pruned and cut, and have pains taken with him? "Yea, but he will never bear figs" (vv. 17-18 [cf. also James 3:12]); it cannot be but every tree will bring forth fruit according to its own kind. What is then to be done, he tells us, "Make the tree good, and his fruit will be good" (Matt. 12:33). The root must be dealt with, the nature of the tree changed, or no good fruit will be brought forth.

This is that I aim at: unless a man be regenerate, unless he be a believer, all attempts that he can make for mortification, be they never so specious and promising—all means he can use, let him follow them with never so much diligence, earnestness, watchfulness, and intention of mind and spirit—are to no purpose. In vain shall he use many remedies; he shall not be healed. Yea, there are sundry desperate evils attending an endeavor in convinced persons, that are no more but so, to perform this duty:

The mind and soul is taken up about that which is not the man's proper business, and so he is diverted from that which is so. God lays hold by his word and judgments on some sin in him, galls his conscience, disquiets his heart, deprives him of his rest; now other diversions will not serve his turn; he must apply himself to the work before him. The business in hand being to awaken the whole man unto a consideration of the state and condition wherein he is, that he might be brought home to God, instead hereof he sets himself to mortify the sin that galls him—which is a pure issue of self-love, to be freed from his trouble, and not at all to the work he is called unto—and so is diverted from it. Thus God tells us of Ephraim, when he "spread his net upon them, and brought them down as the fowls of heaven, and chastised them" (Hos. 7:12), caught them, entangled them, convinced them that they could not escape; says he of them, "They return, but not to the Most High" [Hos. 7:16]—they set themselves to a relinquishment of sin, but not in that manner, by *universal conversion,* as God called for it. Thus are men diverted from coming unto God by the most glorious ways that they can fix upon to come to him by. And this is one of the most common deceits whereby men ruin their own souls. I wish that some whose trade it is to daub[21] with untempered mortar in the things of God did not teach this deceit and cause the people to err by their ignorance. What do men do, what oftentimes are they directed unto, when their consciences are galled by sin and disquietment from the Lord, who has laid hold upon them? Is not a relinquishment of the sin, as to practice, that they are, in some fruits of it, perplexed with, and making head against it, the sum of what they apply themselves unto? And is not the gospel end of their convictions lost thereby? Here men abide and perish.

This duty being a thing good in itself, in its proper place, a duty evidencing sincerity, bringing home peace to the conscience; a man finding himself really engaged in it, his mind and heart set against this or that sin, with purpose and resolution to have no more to do with it—he is ready to conclude that his state and condition is good, and so to delude his own soul. For—

When his conscience has been made sick with sin, and he could find no rest, when he should go to the great Physician of souls, and get healing in his blood, the man by this engagement against sin pacifies and quiets his conscience, and sits down without going to Christ at all. Ah! How many poor souls are thus deluded to eternity! "When Ephraim saw his sickness, he sent to king Jareb" (Hos. 5:13), which kept him off from God. The whole

[21] cover, as with plaster

bundle of the popish religion is made up of designs and contrivances to pacify conscience without Christ; all described by the apostle (Rom. 10:3). By this means men satisfy themselves that their state and condition is good, seeing they do that which is a work good in itself, and they do not do it to be seen. They know they would have the work done in sincerity, and so are hardened in a kind of self-righteousness.

When a man has thus for a season been deluded, and has deceived his own soul, and finds in a long course of life that indeed his sin is not mortified, or if he has changed one [but] he has gotten another, he begins at length to think that all contending is in vain—he shall never be able to prevail; he is making a dam against water that increases on him. Hereupon *he gives over,* as one despairing of any success, and yields up himself to the power of sin and that habit of formality that he has gotten.

And this is the usual issue with persons attempting the mortification of sin without an interest in Christ first obtained. It deludes them, hardens them—destroys them. And therefore we see that there are not usually more vile and desperate sinners in the world than such as, having by conviction been put on this course, have found it fruitless and deserted it without a discovery of Christ. And this is the substance of the religion and godliness of the choicest formalists in the world, and of all those who in the Roman[22] synagogue are drawn to mortification, as they drive Indians to baptism or cattle to water. I say, then, that mortification is the work of believers, and believers only. To kill sin is the work of living men; where men are *dead* (as all unbelievers, the best of them, are dead), sin is *alive,* and will live.

It is the work of *faith,* the *peculiar* work of faith. Now, if there be a work to be done that will be effected by only one instrument, it is the greatest madness for any to attempt the doing of it that has not that instrument. Now, it is faith that purifies the heart (Acts 15:9); or, as Peter speaks, we "purify our souls in obeying the truth through the Spirit" (1 Pet. 1:22); and without it, it will not be done.

What has been spoken I suppose is sufficient to make good my first general rule:

Be sure to get an interest in Christ—
if you intend to mortify any sin without it,
it will never be done.

---

[22] Roman Catholic

Objection

You will say, "What, then, would you have unregenerate men that are convinced of the evil of sin do? Shall they cease striving against sin, live dissolutely, give their lusts their swing,[23] and be as bad as the worst of men? This were a way to set the whole world into confusion, to bring all things into darkness, to set open the floodgates of lust, and lay the reins upon the necks of men to rush into all sin with delight and greediness, like the horse into the battle."

Answers

God forbid! It is to be looked on as a great issue of the wisdom, goodness, and love of God, that by manifold ways and means he is pleased to restrain the sons of men from running forth into that compass of excess and riot which the depravity of their nature would carry them out unto with violence. By whatsoever way this is done, it is an issue of the care, kindness, and goodness of God, without which the whole earth would be a hell of sin and confusion.

There is a peculiar *convincing* power in the word, which God is oftentimes pleased to put forth, to the wounding, amazing, and, in some sort, humbling of sinners, though they are never converted. And the word is to be preached though it has this end, yet not *with* this end. Let, then, the word be preached and the sins of men rebuked, [and] lust will be restrained, and some oppositions will be made against sin; though that be not the effect aimed at.

Though this be the work of the word and Spirit, and it be good in itself, yet it is not profitable nor available as to the main end in them in whom it is wrought; they are still in the gall of bitterness and under the power of darkness.

Let men know it is their *duty,* but in its proper place; I take not men from mortification, but put them upon conversion. He that shall call a man from mending a hole in the wall of his house, to quench a fire that is consuming the whole building, is not his enemy. Poor soul! It is not your sore finger but your hectic fever that you are to apply yourself to the consideration of. You set yourself against *a particular* sin and do not consider that you are *nothing* but sin.

Let me add this to those who are preachers of the word, or intend, through the good hand of God, that employment: It is their duty to plead with men about their sins, to lay load on particular sins, but always remember that

[23] liberty, sway

it be done with that which is the proper end of law and gospel—that is, that they make use of the sin they speak against to the discovery of the state and condition wherein the sinner is; otherwise, haply,[24] they may work men to formality and hypocrisy, but little of the true end of preaching the gospel will be brought about. It will not avail to beat a man off from his drunkenness into a sober formality. A skillful master of the assemblies lays his axe at the root, drives still at the heart. To inveigh[25] against particular sins of ignorant, unregenerate persons, such as the land is full of, is a good work; but yet, though it may be done with great efficacy, vigor, and success, if this be all the effect of it, that they are set upon the most sedulous[26] endeavors of mortifying their sins preached down, all that is done is but like the beating of an enemy in an open field, and driving him into an impregnable castle, not to be prevailed against. Get you at any time a sinner at the advantage, on the account of any one sin whatsoever? have you anything to take hold of him by?—bring it to his state and condition, drive it up to the head, and there deal with him. To break men off particular sins, and not to break their hearts, is to deprive ourselves of advantages of dealing with them.

And herein is the Roman mortification grievously peccant;[27] they drive all sorts of persons to it, without the least consideration whether they have a principle for it or no. Yea, they are so far from calling on men to believe, that they may be able to mortify their lusts, that they call men to mortification instead of believing. The truth is, they neither know what it is to believe nor what mortification itself intends. Faith with them is but a general assent to the doctrine taught in their church; and mortification the betaking of a man by a vow to some certain course of life, wherein he denies himself something of the use of the things of this world, not without a considerable compensation. Such men know neither the Scriptures nor the power of God [Mark 12:24]. Their boasting of their mortification is but their glorying in their shame. Some casuists[28] among ourselves, who, overlooking the necessity of regeneration, do avowedly give this for direction to all sorts of persons that complain of any sin or lust, that they should vow against it, at least for a season, a month or so, seem to have a scantling of light in the mystery of the gospel, much like that of Nicodemus when he came first to Christ [John 3:1-21]. They bid men vow to abstain from their sin for a season. This commonly

[24] by chance
[25] denounce, censure
[26] constant, persistent
[27] offending, faulty
[28] those who rigidly apply ethical rules

makes their lust more impetuous. Perhaps with great perplexity they keep their word; perhaps not, which increases their guilt and torment. Is their sin at all mortified hereby? Do they find a conquest over it? Is their condition changed, though they attain a relinquishment of it? Are they not still in the gall of bitterness? Is not this to put men to make brick, if not without *straw*, yet, which is worse, without *strength?* What promise has any unregenerate man to countenance him in this work? What assistance for the performance of it? Can sin be killed without an interest in the death of Christ, or mortified without the Spirit? If such directions should prevail to change men's lives, as seldom they do, yet they never reach to the change of their hearts or conditions. They may make men self-justiciaries[29] or hypocrites, not Christians. It grieves me oftentimes to see poor souls, that have a zeal for God and a desire of eternal welfare, kept by such directors and directions under a hard, burdensome, outside worship and service of God, with many specious endeavors for mortification, in an utter ignorance of the righteousness of Christ and unacquaintedness with his Spirit all their days. Persons and things of this kind I know too many. If ever God shine into their hearts, to give them the knowledge of his glory in the face of his Son Jesus Christ [2 Cor. 4:6], they will see the folly of their present way.

[CHAPTER 8]

There Will Be No Mortification of Any Sin Without Sincerity and Diligence in a Universality of Obedience

The second principle which to this purpose I shall propose is this: *Without sincerity and diligence in a universality of obedience, there is no mortification of any one perplexing lust to be obtained.* The other [principle] was to the person; this to the thing itself. I shall a little explain this position.

A man finds any lust to bring him into the condition formerly described; it is powerful, strong, tumultuating, leads captive, vexes, disquiets, takes away peace; he is not able to bear it; wherefore he sets himself against it, prays against it, groans under it, sighs to be delivered: but in the meantime, perhaps, in other duties—in constant communion with God—in reading, prayer, and meditation—in other ways that are not of the same kind with the lust wherewith he is troubled—he is loose and negligent. Let not that man think that ever he shall arrive to the mortification of the lust he is perplexed

[29] those who believe they can attain righteousness by their own action or nature

with. This is a condition that not seldom befalls men in their pilgrimage. The Israelites, under a sense of their sin, drew nigh to God with much diligence and earnestness, with fasting and prayer (Isaiah 58); many expressions are made of their earnestness in the work: "They seek me daily, and delight to know my ways; they ask of me the ordinances of justice; they take delight in approaching to God" (v. 2). But God rejects all. Their fast is a remedy that will not heal them, and the reason given of it is because they were particular in this duty (vv. 5-7). They attended diligently to that, but in others were negligent and careless. He that has a "running sore"[30] (it is the Scripture expression) upon him, arising from an ill habit of body, contracted by intemperance[31] and ill diet, let him apply himself with what diligence and skill he can to *the cure of his sore,* if he leave *the general habit of his body* under distempers, his labor and travail will be in vain. So will his attempts be that shall endeavor to stop a bloody issue of sin and filth in his soul, and is not equally careful of his universal spiritual temperature and constitution. For—

This kind of endeavor for mortification proceeds from a *corrupt principle,* ground, and foundation; so that it will never proceed to a good issue. The true and acceptable principles of mortification shall be afterward insisted on. Hatred of sin as sin, not only as galling or disquieting, a sense of the love of Christ in the cross, lies at the bottom of all true spiritual mortification. Now, it is certain that that which I speak of proceeds from *self-love.* You set yourself with all diligence and earnestness to mortify such a lust or sin; what is the reason of it? It disquiets you, it has taken away your peace, it fills your heart with sorrow and trouble and fear; you have no rest because of it. Yea, but friend, you have neglected prayer or reading; you have been vain and loose in your conversation in other things, that have not been of the same nature with that lust wherewith you are perplexed. These are no less sins and evils than those under which you groan. Jesus Christ bled for them also. Why do you not set yourself against them also? If you hate sin as sin, every evil way, you would be no less watchful against everything that grieves and disquiets the Spirit of God, than against that which grieves and disquiets your own soul. It is evident that you contend against *sin* merely because of your own *trouble* by it. Would your conscience be quiet under it, you would let it alone. Did it not disquiet you, it should not be disquieted by you. Now, can you think that God will set in with such hypocritical endeavors—that ever his Spirit will bear witness to the treachery and falsehood of your spirit?

---

30 discharge associated with illness or uncleanness

31 lack of moderation; indulgence, especially of intoxicating drink

Do you think he will ease you of that which perplexes you, that you may be at liberty to that which no less grieves him? No. God says, "Here is one, if he could be rid of this lust I should never hear of him more; let him wrestle with this, or he is lost." Let not any man think to do his own work that will not do God's. God's work consists in *universal obedience;* to be freed of the present perplexity is their own only. Hence is that of the apostle: "Cleanse yourselves from all pollution of the flesh and spirit, perfecting holiness in the fear of God" (2 Cor. 7:1). If we will do anything, we must do all things. So, then, it is not only an intense opposition to this or that peculiar lust, but a universal humble frame and temper of heart, with watchfulness over every evil and for the performance of every duty, that is accepted.

Question

How do you know but that God has suffered[32] the lust wherewith you have been perplexed to get strength in you, and power over you, to chasten you for your other negligences and common lukewarmness in walking before him; at least to awaken you to the consideration of your ways, that you may make a thorough work and change in your course of walking with him?

Answers

The rage and predominancy of a particular lust is commonly the fruit and issue of a careless, negligent course in general, and that upon a double account:

As its natural effect, if I may so say. Lust, as I showed in general, lies in the heart of everyone, even the best, while he lives; and think not that the Scripture speaks in vain, that it is subtle, cunning, crafty—that it seduces, entices, fights, rebels. While a man keeps a diligent watch over his heart, its root and fountain—while above all keepings he keeps his heart, whence are the issues of life and death—lust withers and dies in it. But if, through negligence, it makes an eruption any particular way, gets a passage to the thoughts by the affections, and from them and by them perhaps breaks out into open sin in the conversation, the strength of it bears that way it has found out, and that way mainly it urges, until, having got a passage, it then vexes and disquiets and is not easily to be restrained: thus, perhaps, a man may be put to wrestle all his days in sorrow with that which, by a strict and universal watch, might easily have been prevented.

As I said, *God oftentimes suffers it to chasten our other negligences:* for as with wicked men, he gives them up to *one* sin as the judgment of another,

[32] permitted, allowed

a greater for the punishment of a less, or one that will hold them more firmly and securely for that which they might have possibly obtained a deliverance from [Rom. 1:26]; so even with his own, he may, he does, leave them sometimes to some vexatious distempers, either to prevent or cure some other evil. So was the messenger of Satan let loose on Paul, that he "might not be lifted up through the abundance of spiritual revelations" [2 Cor. 12:7]. Was it not a correction to Peter's vain confidence that he was left to deny his Master? Now, if this be the state and condition of lust in its prevalency, that God oftentimes suffers it so to prevail, at least to admonish us, and to humble us, perhaps to chasten and correct us for our general loose and careless walking, is it possible that the *effect* should be removed and the *cause* continued, that the *particular* lust should be mortified and the *general* course be unreformed? He, then, that would really, thoroughly, and acceptably mortify any disquieting lust, let him take care to be equally diligent in all parts of obedience, and know that every lust, every omission of duty, is burdensome to God [Isa. 43:24], though but one is so to him. While there abides a treachery in the heart to indulge to any negligence in not pressing universally to all perfection in obedience, the soul is *weak,* as not giving faith its whole work; and *selfish,* as considering more the trouble of sin than the filth and guilt of it; and lives under a constant *provocation* of God: so that it may not expect any comfortable issue in any spiritual duty that it does undertake, much less in this under consideration, which requires another principle and frame of spirit for its accomplishment.

[Chapter 9]

Particular Directions for Mortification

The foregoing *general rules* being supposed, *particular directions* to the soul for its guidance under the sense of a disquieting lust or distemper, being the main thing I aim at, come next to be proposed. Now, of these some are previous and preparatory, and in some of them the work itself is contained. Of the *first sort* are these ensuing:

Consider Whether Your Lust Has These Dangerous Symptoms Accompanying It

Consider what dangerous symptoms your lust has attending or accompanying it—whether it has any deadly mark on it or no; if it has, extraordinary remedies are to be used; an ordinary course of mortification will not do it.

You will say, "What are these dangerous marks and symptoms, the desperate attendancies of an indwelling lust, that you intend?" Some of them I shall name:

Inveterateness.[33] If it has lain long corrupting in your heart, if you have suffered it to abide in power and prevalency, without attempting vigorously the killing of it and the healing of the wounds you have received by it for some long season, your distemper is dangerous. Have you permitted worldliness, ambition, greediness of study to eat up other duties, the duties wherein you ought to hold constant communion with God, for some long season? Or uncleanness to defile your heart with vain and foolish and wicked imaginations for many days? Your lust has a dangerous symptom. So was the case with David: "My wounds stink and are corrupt because of my foolishness" (Ps. 38:5). When a lust has lain long in the heart, corrupting, festering, cankering,[34] it brings the soul to a woeful condition. In such a case an ordinary course of humiliation will not do the work: whatever it be, it will by this means insinuate itself more or less into all the faculties of the soul, and habituate the affections to its company and society; it grows familiar to the mind and conscience, that they do not startle at it as a strange thing, but are bold with it as that which they are wonted[35] unto; yea, it will get such advantage by this means as oftentimes to exert and put forth itself without having any notice taken of it at all, as it seems to have been with Joseph in his swearing by the life of Pharaoh [Gen. 42:15-16]. Unless some extraordinary course be taken, such a person has no ground in the world to expect that his latter end shall be peace.

For, first, how will he be able to distinguish between the long abode of an unmortified lust and the dominion of sin, which cannot befall a regenerate person? Secondly, how can he promise himself that it shall ever be otherwise with him, or that his lust will cease tumultuating and seducing, when he sees it fixed and abiding, and has done so for many days, and has gone through a variety of conditions with him? It may be it has tried *mercies* and *afflictions,* and those possibly so remarkable that the soul could not avoid taking special notice of them; it may be it has weathered out many a storm, and passed under much variety of gifts in the administration of the word; and will it prove an easy thing to dislodge an inmate pleading a title by prescription? Old neglected wounds are often mortal, always dangerous. Indwelling

[33] the state of being hardened, habitual, deep-rooted
[34] festering, corroding, infecting
[35] accustomed

distempers grow rusty and stubborn by continuance in ease and quiet. Lust is such an inmate as, if it can plead time and some prescription, will not easily be ejected. As it never dies of itself, so if it be not daily killed it will always gather strength.

Secret pleas of the heart for the countenancing[36] *of itself,* and keeping up its peace, notwithstanding the abiding of a lust, *without a vigorous gospel attempt for its mortification,* is another dangerous symptom of a deadly distemper in the heart. Now, there be several ways whereby this may be done. I shall name some of them; as—

When upon thoughts, perplexing thoughts about sin, instead of applying himself to the destruction of it, a man searches his heart to see what evidences he can find of a good condition, notwithstanding that sin and lust, so that it may go well with him. For a man to gather up his experiences of God, to call them to mind, to collect them, consider, try, improve them, is an excellent thing—a duty practiced by all the saints, commended in the Old Testament and the New. This was David's work when he "communed with his own heart," and called to remembrance the former lovingkindness of the Lord [Ps. 77:6-9, 10, 11]. This is the duty that Paul sets us to practice (2 Cor. 13:5). And as it is in itself excellent, so it has beauty added to it by a proper season, a time of trial or temptation, or disquietness of the heart about sin, it is a picture of silver to set off this golden apple, as Solomon speaks [Prov. 25:11]. But now to do it for this end, to satisfy conscience, which cries and calls for another purpose, is a desperate device of a heart in love with sin. When a man's conscience shall deal with him, when God shall rebuke him for the sinful distemper of his heart, if he, instead of applying himself to get that sin pardoned in the blood of Christ and mortified by his Spirit, shall relieve himself by any such other evidences as he has, or thinks himself to have, and so disentangle himself from under the yoke that God was putting on his neck, his condition is very dangerous, his wound hardly curable. Thus the Jews, under the gallings of their own consciences and the convincing preaching of our Savior, supported themselves with this, that they were "Abraham's children," and on that account accepted with God; and so countenanced themselves in all abominable wickedness, to their utter ruin.

This is, in some degree, a blessing of a man's self, and saying that upon one account or other he shall have peace, "*although* he adds drunkenness to thirst" [Deut. 29:19]. Love of sin, undervaluation of peace and of all tastes of love from God, are enwrapped in such a frame. Such a one plainly shows

[36] sanctioning, approving

that if he can but keep up hope of escaping the "wrath to come," he can be well content to be unfruitful in the world, at any distance from God that is not final separation. What is to be expected from such a heart?

By applying grace and mercy to an unmortified sin, or one not sincerely endeavored to be mortified, is this deceit carried on. This is a sign of a heart greatly entangled with the love of sin. When a man has secret thoughts in his heart, not unlike those of Naaman about his worshipping in the house of Rimmon—"In all other things I will walk with God, but in this thing, God be merciful unto me" [2 Kings 5:18]—his condition is sad. It is true, indeed, a resolution to this purpose, to indulge a man's self in any sin on the account of mercy, seems to be, and doubtless in any course is, altogether inconsistent with Christian sincerity, and is a badge of a hypocrite, and is the "turning of the grace of God into wantonness"[37] [Jude 4], yet I doubt not but, through the craft of Satan and their own remaining unbelief, the children of God may themselves sometimes be ensnared with this deceit of sin, or else Paul would never have so cautioned them against it as he does (Rom. 6:1-2). Yea, indeed, there is nothing more natural than for fleshly reasonings to grow high and strong upon this account. The flesh would fain[38] be indulged unto upon the account of grace, and every word that is spoken of mercy, it stands ready to catch at and to pervert it, to its own corrupt aims and purposes. To apply mercy, then, to a sin not vigorously mortified is to fulfill the end of the flesh upon the gospel.

These and many other ways and wiles a deceitful heart will sometimes make use of to countenance itself in its abominations. Now, when a man with his sin is in this condition, that there is a secret liking of the sin prevalent in his heart, and though his will be not wholly set upon it, yet he has an imperfect velleity[39] toward it, he would practice it were it not for such and such considerations, and hereupon relieves himself other ways than by the mortification and pardon of it in the blood of Christ; that man's "wounds stink and are corrupt" [Ps. 38:5], and he will, without speedy deliverance, be at the door of death.

Frequency of success in sin's seduction, in obtaining the prevailing consent of the will unto it, is another dangerous symptom. This is that I mean: When the sin spoken of gets the consent of the will with some delight, though it be not actually outwardly perpetrated, yet it has success. A man may not be

[37] lack of discipline
[38] eagerly, gladly
[39] inclination, desire

able, upon outward considerations, to go along with sin to that which James calls the "finishing" of it [1:14-15], as to the outward acts of sin, when yet the will of sinning may be actually obtained; then has it, I say, success. Now, if any lust be able thus far to prevail in the soul of any man, as his condition may possibly be very bad and himself be unregenerate, so it cannot possibly be very good, but dangerous; and it is all one upon the matter whether this be done by the choice of the will or by inadvertency,[40] for that inadvertency itself is in a manner chosen. When we are inadvertent and negligent, where we are bound to watchfulness and carefulness, that inadvertency does not take off from the voluntariness of what we do thereupon; for although men do not choose and resolve to be negligent and inadvertent, yet if they choose the things that will make them so, they choose inadvertency itself as a thing may be chosen in its cause.

And let not men think that the evil of their hearts is in any measure extenuated[41] because they seem, for the most part, to be surprised into that consent which they seem to give unto it; for it is negligence of their duty in watching over their hearts that betrays them into that surprise.

When a man rights[42] *against his sin only with arguments from the issue or the punishment due unto it,* this is a sign that sin has taken great possession of the will, and that in the heart there is a superfluity of naughtiness [James 1:21]. Such a man as opposes nothing to the seduction of sin and lust in his heart but fear of shame among men or hell from God, is sufficiently resolved to do the sin if there were no punishment attending it; which, what it differs from living in the practice of sin, I know not. Those who are Christ's, and are acted[43] in their obedience upon gospel principles, have the death of Christ, the love of God, the detestable nature of sin, the preciousness of communion with God, a deep-grounded abhorrency of sin *as sin,* to oppose to any seduction of sin, to all the workings, strivings, rightings of lust in their hearts. So did Joseph. "How shall I do this great evil," says he, "and sin against the LORD," my good and gracious God? [Gen. 39:9]. And Paul, "The love of Christ constrains us" [2 Cor. 5:14]; and, "Having received these promises, let us cleanse ourselves from all pollution of the flesh and spirit" (2 Cor. 7:1). But now if a man be so under the power of his lust that he has nothing but law to oppose it with, if he cannot fight against it with gospel weapons, but deals with it altogether with hell and judgment, which are the

40 negligence
41 made less serious
42 seeks to correct or amend
43 activated

proper arms of the law, it is most evident that sin has possessed itself of his will and affections to a very great prevalency and conquest.

Such a person has cast off, as to the particular spoken of, the conduct of *renewing* grace and is kept from ruin only by *restraining* grace; and so far is he fallen from grace and returned under the power of the law. And can it be thought that this is not a great provocation to Christ, that men should cast off his easy, gentle yoke and rule, and cast themselves under the iron yoke of the law, merely out of indulgence unto their lusts?

Try yourself by this also: When you are by sin driven to make a stand, so that you must either serve it and rush at the command of it into folly, like the horse into the battle, or make head against it to suppress it, what do you say to your soul? What do you expostulate[44] with yourself? Is this all—"Hell will be the end of this course; vengeance will meet with me and find me out"? It is time for you to look about you; evil lies at the door [Gen. 4:7]. Paul's main argument to evince that sin shall not have dominion over believers is that they "are not under the law, but under grace" (Rom. 6:14). If your contendings against sin be all on legal accounts, from legal principles and motives, what assurance can you attain unto that sin shall not have dominion over you, which will be your ruin?

Yea, know that this reserve will not long hold out. If your lust has driven you from stronger gospel forts, it will speedily prevail against this also. Do not suppose that such considerations will deliver you, when you have voluntarily given up to your enemy those helps and means of preservation which have a thousand times their strength. Rest assuredly in this, that unless you recover yourself with speed from this condition, the thing that you fear will come upon you. What *gospel principles* do not, *legal motives* cannot do.

When it is probable that there is, or may be, somewhat of *judiciary hardness,* or at least of *chastening punishment,* in your lust as disquieting—this is another dangerous symptom. That God does sometimes leave even those of his own under the perplexing power at least of some lust or sin, to correct them for former sins, negligence, and folly, I no way doubt. Hence was that complaint of the church, "Why have you hardened us from the fear of your name?" (Isa. 63:17). That this is his way of dealing with unregenerate men, no man questions. But how shall a man know whether there be anything of God's chastening hand in his being left to the disquietment of his distemper?

---

[44] discuss earnestly

Examine your heart and ways. What was the state and condition of your soul before you fell into the entanglements of that sin which now you so complain of? Have you been negligent in duties? Have you lived inordinately to yourself? Is there the guilt of any great sin lying upon you unrepented of? A new sin may be permitted, as well as a new affliction sent, to bring an old sin to remembrance.

Have you received any eminent mercy, protection, deliverance, which you did not improve in a due manner, nor were thankful for? Or have you been exercised with any affliction without laboring for the appointed end of it? Or have you been wanting of the opportunities of glorifying God in your generation, which, in his good providence, he had graciously afforded unto you? Or have you conformed yourself unto the world and the men of it, through the abounding of temptations in the days wherein you live? If you find this to have been your state, awake, call upon God; you are fast asleep in a storm of anger round about you.

When your lust has already withstood particular dealings from God against it. This condition is described, "For the iniquity of his covetousness I was angry and struck him; I hid and was angry, and he went on backsliding in the way of his heart" (Isa. 57:17). God had dealt with them about their prevailing lust, and that several ways—by affliction and desertion; but they held out against all. This is a sad condition, which nothing but mere sovereign grace (as God expresses it in the next verse) can relieve a man in, and which no man ought to promise himself or bear himself upon. God oftentimes, in his providential dispensations,[45] meets with a man, and speaks particularly to the evil of his heart, as he did to Joseph's brethren in their selling of him into Egypt. This makes the man reflect on his sin, and judge himself in particular for it. God makes it to be the voice of the danger, affliction, trouble, sickness that he is in or under. Sometimes in reading of the word God makes a man stay on something that cuts him to the heart, and shakes him as to his present condition. More frequently in the hearing of the word preached—his great ordinance for conviction, conversion, and edification—does he meet with men. God often hews men by the sword of his word in that ordinance, strikes directly on their bosom-beloved lust, startles the sinner, makes him engage unto the mortification and relinquishment of the evil of his heart. Now, if his lust has taken such hold on him as to enforce him to break these bands of the Lord and to cast these cords from him—if it

[45] provisions, orderings

overcomes these convictions and gets again into its old posture; if it can cure the wounds it so receives—that soul is in a sad condition.

Unspeakable are the evils which attend such a frame of heart. Every particular warning to a man in such an estate is an inestimable mercy; how then does he despise God in them who holds out against them! And what infinite patience is this in God, that he does not cast off such a one, and swear in his wrath that he shall never enter into his rest [cf. Heb. 4:3]!

These and many other evidences are there of a lust that is dangerous, if not mortal. As our Savior said of the evil spirit, "This kind goes not out but by fasting and prayer" [Matt. 17:21], so say I of lusts of this kind. An ordinary course of mortification will not do it; extraordinary ways must be fixed upon.

This is the first particular direction: *Consider whether the lust or sin you are contending with has any of these dangerous symptoms attending of it.*

Before I proceed I must give you one caution by the way, lest any be deceived by what has been spoken. Whereas I say the things and evils abovementioned may befall true believers, let not any that finds the same things in himself thence or from thence conclude that he is a true believer. These are the evils that believers may fall into and be ensnared with, not the things that constitute a believer. A man may as well conclude that he is a believer because he is an adulterer, because David that was so fell into adultery, as conclude it from the signs foregoing, which are the evils of sin and Satan in the hearts of believers. The seventh chapter of the [book of] Romans contains the description of a regenerate man. He that shall consider what is spoken of his dark side, of his unregenerate part, of the indwelling power and violence of sin remaining in him, and, because he finds the like in himself, conclude that he is a regenerate man, will be deceived in his reckoning. It is all one as if you should argue: A wise man may be sick and wounded, yea, do some things foolishly; therefore, everyone who is sick and wounded and does things foolishly is a wise man. Or as if a silly, deformed creature, hearing one speak of a beautiful person, saying that he had a mark or a scar that much disfigured him, should conclude that because he has himself scars, and moles, and warts, he also is beautiful. If you will have evidences of your being believers, it must be from those things that constitute men believers. He that has these things in himself may safely conclude, "If I am a believer, I am a most miserable one." But that any man is so, he must look for other evidences if he will have peace.

[Chapter 10]

Get a Clear and Abiding Sense Upon Your Mind and Conscience of the Guilt, Danger, and Evil of Your Sin

The second direction is this: Get a clear and abiding sense upon your mind and conscience of the guilt, danger, and evil of that sin wherewith you are perplexed.

Of the guilt of it. It is one of the deceits of a prevailing lust to extenuate its own guilt. "Is it not a little one?" "When I go and bow myself in the house of Rimmon, God be merciful to me in this thing" [2 Kings 5:18]. "Though this be bad, yet it is not so bad as such and such an evil; others of the people of God have had such a frame; yea, what dreadful actual sins have some of them fallen into!" Innumerable ways there are whereby sin diverts the mind from a right and due apprehension of its guilt. Its noisome[46] exhalations darken the mind, that it cannot make a right judgment of things. Perplexing reasonings, extenuating promises, tumultuating desires, treacherous purposes of relinquishment, hopes of mercy, all have their share in disturbing the mind in its consideration of the guilt of a prevailing lust. The prophet tells us that lust will do thus wholly when it comes to the height: "Whoredom and wine and new wine take away the heart" [Hos. 4:11]—the heart, that is the understanding, as it is often used in the Scripture. And as they accomplish this work to the height in unregenerate persons, so in part in regenerate also. Solomon tells you of him who was enticed by the lewd woman, that he was "among the simple ones," he was "a young man void of understanding" (Prov. 7:7). And wherein did his folly appear? Why, says he (v. 23), "he knew not that it was for his life," he considered not the guilt of the evil that he was involved in. And the Lord, rendering a reason why his dealings with Ephraim took no better effect, gives this account: "Ephraim is like a silly dove without heart" (Hos. 7:11)—had no understanding of his own miserable condition. Had it been possible that David should have lain so long in the guilt of that abominable sin, but that he had innumerable corrupt reasonings, hindering him from taking a clear view of its ugliness and guilt in the glass of the law? This made the prophet that was sent for his awaking, in his dealings with him, to shut up all subterfuges and pretenses by his parable, that so he might fall fully under a sense of the guilt of it. This is the proper issue of lust in the heart—it darkens the mind that it shall not

[46] dangerous, offensive, foul

judge aright of its guilt; and many other ways it has for its own extenuation that I shall not now insist on.

Let this, then, be the first care of him that would mortify sin—to fix a right judgment of its guilt in his mind. To which end take these considerations to your assistance:

Though the power of sin be weakened by inherent grace in them that have it, [so] that sin shall not have dominion over them as it has over others, yet the guilt of sin that does yet abide and remain is aggravated and heightened by it [i.e., sin's power]: "What shall we say then? Shall we continue in sin, that grace may abound? God forbid. How shall we, that are dead to sin, live any longer therein?" (Rom. 6:1-2)—"How shall we, that are dead?" The emphasis is on the word "we." How shall *we* do it, who, as he afterward describes it, have received grace from Christ to the contrary? We, doubtless, are more evil than any, if we do it. I shall not insist on the special aggravations of the sins of such persons—how they sin against more love, mercy, grace, assistance, relief, means, and deliverances than others. But let this consideration abide in your mind—there is inconceivably more evil and guilt in the evil of your heart that does remain, than there would be in so much sin if you had no grace at all. Observe:

That as God sees abundance of beauty and excellency in the desires of the heart of his servants, more than in any [of] the most glorious works of other men, yea, more than in most of their own outward performances, which have a greater mixture of sin than the desires and pantings of grace in the heart have; so *God sees a great deal of evil in the working of lust in their hearts, yea, and more than in the open, notorious acts of wicked men,* or in many outward sins whereinto the saints may fall, seeing against them there is more opposition made, and more humiliation generally follows them. Thus Christ, dealing with his decaying children, goes to the root with them, lays aside their profession: "I know you" (Rev. 3:15)—"You are quite another thing than you profess; and this makes you abominable."

So, then, let these things, and the like considerations, lead you to a clear sense of the guilt of your indwelling lust, that there may be no room in your heart for extenuating or excusing thoughts, whereby sin insensibly will get strength and prevail.

Consider the danger of it, which is manifold:

Of being hardened by the deceitfulness. This the apostle sorely charges on the Hebrews (3:12-13), "Take heed, brethren, lest there be in any of you an evil heart of unbelief, in departing from the living God. But exhort one another daily, while it is called Today; lest any of you be hardened through the deceitfulness of sin." "Take heed," says he, "use all means, consider your temptations, watch diligently; there is a treachery, a deceit in sin, that tends to the hardening of your hearts from the fear of God." The hardening here mentioned is to the utmost—utter obduration[47]; sin tends to it, and every distemper and lust will make at least some progress toward it. You that were tender, and used to melt under the word, under afflictions, will grow as some have profanely spoken, "sermon-proof and sickness-proof." You that did tremble at the presence of God, thoughts of death, and appearance before him, when you had more assurance of his love than now you have, shall have a stoutness upon your spirit not to be moved by these things. Your soul and your sin shall be spoken of and spoken to, and you shall not be at all concerned, but shall be able to pass over duties, praying, hearing, reading, and your heart not in the least affected. Sin will grow a light thing to you; you will pass it by as a thing of naught; this it will grow to. And what will be the end of such a condition? Can a sadder thing befall you? Is it not enough to make any heart to tremble, to think of being brought into that estate wherein he should have slight thoughts of sin? Slight thoughts of grace, of mercy, of the blood of Christ, of the law, heaven, and hell, come all in at the same season. Take heed, this is that [which] your lust is working toward—the hardening of the heart, searing of the conscience, blinding of the mind, stupifying of the affections, and deceiving of the whole soul.

The danger of some great temporal correction, which the Scripture calls "vengeance," "judgment," and "punishment." Though God should not utterly cast you off for this abomination that lies in your heart, yet he will visit you with the rod; though he pardon and forgive, he will take vengeance of your inventions (Ps. 89:30-33). Oh, remember David and all his troubles! Look on him flying into the wilderness, and consider the hand of God upon him. Is it nothing to you that God should kill your child in anger, ruin your estate in anger, break your bones in anger, suffer you to be a scandal and reproach in anger, kill you, destroy you, make you lie down in darkness, in anger? Is it nothing that he should punish, ruin, and undo others for your sake? Let me not be mistaken. I do not mean that God does send all these things always on *his* in anger; God forbid! But this I say, that when he does so deal with you, and your conscience bears witness with him what your provocations have been, you will find his dealings full of bitterness to your soul. If you fear not these things, I fear you are under hardness.

Loss of peace and strength all a man's days. To have peace with God,

[47] hardening

to have strength to walk before God, is the sum of the great promises of the covenant of grace. In these things is the life of our souls. Without them in some comfortable measure, to live is to die. What good will our lives do us if we see not the face of God sometimes in peace? If we have not some strength to walk with him? Now, [of] both these will an unmortified lust certainly deprive the souls of men. This case is so evident in David, as that nothing can be more clear. How often does he complain that his bones were broken, his soul disquieted, his wounds grievous, on this account! Take other instances: "For the iniquity of his covetousness I was angry, and hid myself" (Isa. 57:17). What peace, I pray, is there to a soul while God hides himself, or strength while he smites? "I will go and return to my place, till they acknowledge their offense, and seek my face" (Hos. 5:15)—"I will leave them, hide my face, and what will become of their peace and strength?" If ever, then, you have enjoyed peace with God, if ever his terrors have made you afraid, if ever you have had strength to walk with him, or ever have mourned in your prayer, and been troubled because of your weakness, think of this danger that hangs over your head. It is perhaps but a little while and you shall see the face of God in peace no more. Perhaps by tomorrow you shall not be able to pray, read, hear, or perform any duties with the least cheerfulness, life, or vigor; and possibly you may never see a quiet hour while you live—that you may carry about you broken bones, full of pain and terror, all the days of your life. Yea, perhaps God will shoot his arrows at you, and fill you with anguish and disquietness, with fears and perplexities; make you a terror and an astonishment to yourself and others; show you hell and wrath every moment; frighten and scare you with sad apprehensions of his hatred; so that your sore shall run in the night season, and your soul shall refuse comfort; so that you shall wish death rather than life, yea, your soul may choose strangling. Consider this a little—though God should not utterly destroy you, yet he might cast you into this condition, wherein you shall have quick and living apprehensions of your destruction. Wont[48] your heart to thoughts hereof; let it know what [it] is like to be the issue of its state. Leave not this consideration until you have made your soul to tremble within you.

There is *the danger of eternal destruction.* For the due management of this consideration, observe—

That there is such a connection between a continuance in sin and eternal destruction that though God does resolve to deliver some from a continuance in sin that they may not be destroyed, yet he will deliver none from destruc-

---

[48] accustom

tion that continue in sin; so that while anyone lies under an abiding power of sin, the threats of destruction and everlasting separation from God are to be held out to him (so Heb. 3:12; to which add Heb. 10:38). This is the rule of God's proceeding: If any man "depart" from him [Heb. 3:12], "draw back" through unbelief, "God's soul has no pleasure in him" [Heb. 10:38]—"that is, his indignation shall pursue him to destruction" (so evidently Gal. 6:8).

That he who is so entangled, as above described, under the power of any corruption, can have at that present no clear prevailing evidence of his interest in the covenant, by the efficacy whereof he may be delivered from fear of destruction; so that destruction from the Lord may justly be a terror to him; and he may, he ought to look upon it, as that which will be the end of his course and ways. "There is no condemnation to them that are in Christ Jesus" (Rom. 8:1). True; but who shall have the comfort of this assertion? Who may assume it to himself? "They that walk after the Spirit, and not after the flesh." But you will say, "Is not this to persuade men to unbelief?" I answer, "No." There is a twofold judgment that a man may make of himself: first, *of his person;* and, secondly, *of his ways.* It is the judgment of his ways, not his person, that I speak of. Let a man get the best evidence for his person that he can, yet to judge that an evil way will end in destruction is his duty; not to do it is atheism. I do not say that in such a condition a man ought to throw away the evidence of his personal interest in Christ; but I say, he cannot keep them. There is a twofold condemnation of a man's self:

First, in respect of desert,[49] when the soul concludes that it deserves to be cast out of the presence of God; and this is so far from a business of unbelief that it is an effect of faith. Secondly, with respect to the issue and event, when the soul concludes it shall be damned. I do not say this is the duty of anyone, nor do I call them to it. But this I say, that the end of the way may be provoked to fly from it. And this is another consideration that ought to dwell upon such a soul, if it desire to be freed from the entanglement of its lusts.

Consider the evils of it; I mean its present evils. Danger respects what is to come; evil, what is present. Some of the many evils that attend an unmortified lust may be mentioned:

It grieves the holy and blessed Spirit, which is given to believers to dwell in them and abide with them. So the apostle, dehorting[50] them from many lusts and sins (Eph. 4:25-29), gives this as the great motive of it: "Grieve not the Holy Spirit, whereby you are sealed unto the day of redemption" (v. 30).

---

[49] that which is deserved (such as punishment)
[50] exhorting, in an effort to dissuade

"Grieve not that Spirit of God," says he, "whereby you receive so many and so great benefits," of which he instances in one signal[51] and comprehensive one—"sealing to the day of redemption." He is grieved by it. As a tender and loving friend is grieved at the unkindness of his friend, of whom he has well deserved, so is it with this tender and loving Spirit, who has chosen our hearts for a habitation to dwell in, and there to do for us all that our souls desire. He is grieved by our harboring his enemies, and those whom he is to destroy, in our hearts with him. "He does not afflict willingly, nor grieve us" (Lam. 3:33); and shall we daily grieve him? Thus is he said sometimes to be "vexed," sometimes "grieved at his heart," to express the greatest sense of our provocation. Now, if there be anything of gracious ingenuity left in the soul, if it be not utterly hardened by the deceitfulness of sin, this consideration will certainly affect it. Consider who and what you are; who the Spirit is that is grieved, what he has done for you, what he comes to your soul about, what he has already done in you; and be ashamed. Among those who walk with God, there is no greater motive and incentive unto universal holiness, and the preserving of their hearts and spirits in all purity and cleanness, than this, that the blessed Spirit, who has undertaken to dwell in them, is continually considering what they give entertainment in their hearts unto, and rejoices when his temple is kept undefiled. That was a high aggravation of the sin of Zimri, that he brought his adulteress into the congregation in the sight of Moses and the rest, who were weeping for the sins of the people (Num. 25:6). And is it not a high aggravation of the countenancing of a lust, or suffering it to abide in the heart, when it is (as it must be, if we are believers) entertained under the peculiar eye and view of the Holy Ghost, taking care to preserve his tabernacle pure and holy?

The Lord Jesus Christ is wounded afresh by it; his new creature in the heart is wounded; his love is foiled; his adversary gratified. As a total relinquishment of him, by the deceitfulness of sin, is the "crucifying him afresh, and the putting of him to open shame" (Heb. 6:6), so every harboring of sin that he came to destroy wounds and grieves him.

It will take away a man's usefulness in his generation. His works, his endeavors, his labors seldom receive blessing from God. If he be a preacher, God commonly blows upon his ministry, that he shall labor in the fire, and not be honored with any success or doing any work for God; and the like may be spoken of other conditions. The world is at this day full of poor withering professors. How few are there that walk in any beauty or glory! How bar-

[51] significant, remarkable, out of the ordinary

ren, how useless are they, for the most part! Among the many reasons that may be assigned of this sad estate, it may justly be feared that this is none of the least effectual—many men harbor spirit-devouring lusts in their bosoms, that lie as worms at the root of their obedience, and corrode and weaken it day by day. All graces, all the ways and means whereby any graces may be exercised and improved, are prejudiced by this means; and as to any success, God blasts such men's undertakings.

This, then, is my second direction, and it regards the opposition that is to be made to lust in respect of its habitual residence in the soul:

Keep alive upon your heart these or the like considerations of its guilt,
danger, and evil;
be much in the meditation of these things;
cause your heart to dwell and abide upon them;
engage your thoughts into these considerations;
let them not go off nor wander from them
until they begin to have a powerful influence upon your soul—
until they make it to tremble.

[Chapter 11]

Load Your Conscience with the Guilt of Sin

This is my third direction: *Load your conscience with the guilt of it.* Not only consider that it has a guilt, but load your *conscience* with the guilt of its actual eruptions and disturbances. For the right improvement of this rule I shall give some particular directions:

Take God's method in it, and *begin with generals,* and so *descend to particulars:*

Charge your conscience with that guilt which appears in it from the rectitude and holiness of the law. Bring the holy law of God into your conscience, lay your corruption to it, pray that you may be affected with it. Consider the holiness, spirituality, fiery severity, inwardness, absoluteness of the law, and see how you can stand before it. Be much, I say, in affecting your conscience with the terror of the Lord in the law, and how righteous it is that every one of your transgressions should receive a recompense of reward. Perhaps your conscience will invent shifts and evasions to keep off the power of this consideration—as, that the condemning power of the law does not belong to you,

you are set free from it, and the like; and so, though you be not conformable to it, yet you need not to be so much troubled at it. But—

Tell your conscience that it cannot manage any evidence to the purpose that you are free from the condemning power of sin, while your unmortified lust lies in your heart; so that, perhaps, the law may make good its plea against you for a full dominion, and then you are a lost creature. Wherefore it is best to ponder to the utmost what it has to say.

Assuredly, he that pleads in the most secret reserve of his heart that he is freed from the condemning power of the law, thereby secretly to countenance himself in giving the least allowance unto any sin or lust, is not able, on gospel grounds, to manage any evidence, unto any tolerable spiritual security, that indeed he is in a due manner freed from what he so pretends himself to be delivered.

Whatever be the issue, yet the law has commission[52] from God to seize upon transgressors wherever it find them, and so bring them before his throne, where they are to plead for themselves. This is your present case; the law has found you out, and before God it will bring you. If you can plead a pardon, well and good; if not, the law will do its work.

However, this is the *proper work* of the law, to discover sin in the guilt of it, to awake and humble the soul for it, to be a glass to represent sin in its colors; and if you deny to deal with it on this account, it is not through faith, but through the hardness of your heart and the deceitfulness of sin.

This is a door that too many professors have gone out at unto open apostasy. Such a deliverance from the law they have pretended, as that they would consult its guidance and direction no more; they would measure their sin by it no more. By little and little this principle has insensibly, from the notion of it, proceeded to influence their practical understandings, and, having taken possession there, has turned the will and affections loose to all manner of abominations.

By such ways, I say, then, as these, persuade your conscience to hearken diligently to what the law speaks, in the name of the Lord, unto you about your lust and corruption. Oh! If your ears be open, it will speak with a voice that shall make you tremble, that shall cast you to the ground and fill you with astonishment. If ever you will mortify your corruptions, you must tie up your conscience to the law, shut it from all shifts and exceptions, until it owns its guilt with a clear and thorough apprehension; so that then, as David speaks, your "iniquity may ever be before you" [Ps. 51:3].

[52] authority

Bring your lust to the gospel—not for relief, but for further conviction of its guilt; look on him whom you have pierced [Zech. 12:10; John 19:37], and be in bitterness. Say to your soul:

> What have I done? What love, what mercy, what blood, what grace have I despised and trampled on! Is this the return I make to the Father for his *love,* to the Son for his *blood,* to the Holy Ghost for his *grace?* Do I thus requite[53] the Lord? Have I defiled the heart that Christ died to wash, that the blessed Spirit has chosen to dwell in? And can I keep myself out of the dust? What can I say to the dear Lord Jesus? How shall I hold up my head with any boldness before him? Do I account communion with him of so little value, that for this vile lust's sake I have scarce left him any room in my heart? How shall I escape if I neglect so great salvation? In the meantime, what shall I say to the Lord? Love, mercy, grace, goodness, peace, joy, consolation—I have despised them all, and esteemed them as a thing of naught, that I might harbor a lust in my heart. Have I obtained a view of God's fatherly countenance, that I might behold his face and provoke him to his face? Was my soul washed, that room might be made for new defilements? Shall I endeavor to disappoint the end of the death of Christ? Shall I daily grieve that Spirit whereby I am sealed to the day of redemption?

Entertain your conscience daily with this treaty. See if it can stand before this aggravation of its guilt. If this make it not sink in some measure and melt, I fear your case is dangerous.

Descend to particulars. As under the general head of the gospel all the benefits of it are to be considered, as redemption, justification, and the like; so, in particular, consider the management of the love of them toward your own soul, for the aggravation of the guilt of your corruption. As—

Consider the infinite patience and forbearance of God toward you in particular. Consider what advantages he might have taken against time, to have made you a shame and a reproach in this world, and an object of wrath forever; how you have dealt treacherously and falsely with him from time to time, flattered him with your lips, but broken all promises and engagements, and that by the means of that sin you are now in pursuit of; and yet he has spared you from time to time, although you seem boldly to have put it to the trial how long he could hold out. And will you yet sin against him? Will you yet weary him, and make him to serve with your corruptions?

Have you not often been ready to conclude yourself that it was utterly

[53] repay

impossible that he should bear any longer with you; that he would cast you off, and be gracious no more; that all his forbearance was exhausted, and hell and wrath was even ready prepared for you? And yet, above all your expectation, he has returned with visitations of love. And will you yet abide in the provocation of the eyes of his glory?

How often have you been at the door of being hardened by the deceitfulness of sin, and by the infinite rich grace of God have been recovered to communion with him again? Have you not found grace decaying; delight in duties, ordinances, prayer and meditation, vanishing; inclinations to loose careless walking, thriving; and they who before were entangled, almost beyond recovery? Have you not found yourself engaged in such ways, societies, companies, and that with delight, as God abhors? And will you venture any more to the brink of hardness?

All God's gracious dealings with you, in providential dispensations, deliverances, afflictions, mercies, enjoyments, all ought here to take place. By these, I say, and the like means, load your conscience; and leave it not until it be thoroughly affected with the guilt of your indwelling corruption, until it is sensible of its wound, and lie in the dust before the Lord. Unless this be done to the purpose, all other endeavors are to no purpose. While the *conscience* has any means to alleviate the guilt of sin, the soul will never vigorously attempt its mortification.

Constantly Long and Breathe After Deliverance from the Power of Sin

Fourthly, being thus affected with your sin, in the next place get a constant longing, breathing after deliverance from the power of it. Suffer not your heart one moment to be contented with your present frame and condition. Longing desires after anything, in things natural and civil, are of no value or consideration, any further but as they incite and stir up the person in whom they are to a diligent use of means for the bringing about the thing aimed at. In spiritual things it is otherwise. Longing, breathing, and panting after deliverance is a grace in itself, that has a mighty power to conform the soul into the likeness of the thing longed after. Hence the apostle, describing the repentance and godly sorrow of the Corinthians, reckons this as one eminent grace that was then set on work, "vehement desire" (2 Cor. 7:11). And in this case of indwelling sin and the power of it, what frame does he express himself to be in? His heart breaks out with longings into a most passionate expression of desire of deliverance (Rom. 7:24). Now, if this be the frame of saints upon the general consideration of indwelling sin, how is it to be heightened and increased when thereunto is added the perplexing rage and power of any particular lust and corruption! Assure yourself, unless you *long* for deliverance you shall not have it.

This will make the heart watchful for all opportunities of advantage against its enemy, and ready to close with any assistances that are afforded for its [enemy's] destruction. Strong desires are the very life of that "praying always" [Luke 21:36] which is enjoined us in all conditions, and in none is more necessary than in this; they set faith and hope on work, and are the soul's moving after the Lord.

Get your heart, then, into a panting and breathing frame; long, sigh, cry out. You know the example of David [Psalm 38 and 42]; I shall not need to insist on it.

Consider Whether the Distemper Is Rooted in Your Nature and Increased by Your Constitution

The fifth direction is: Consider whether the distemper with which you are perplexed be not rooted in your nature, and cherished, fomented,[54] and heightened from your *constitution.* A proneness to some sins may doubtless lie in the natural temper and disposition of men. In this case consider—

This is not in the least an extenuation of the guilt of your sin. Some, with an open profaneness, will ascribe gross enormities to their temper and disposition; and whether others may not relieve themselves from the pressing guilt of their distempers by the same consideration, I know not. It is from the fall, from the original depravation of our natures, that the fomes[55] and nourishment of any sin abides in our natural temper. David reckons his being shapen in iniquity and conception in sin as an aggravation of his following sin, not a lessening or extenuation of it [Ps. 51:5]. That you are peculiarly inclined unto any sinful distemper is but a peculiar breaking out of original lust in your nature, which should peculiarly abase and humble you.

That you have to fix upon on this account, in reference to your walking with God, is, that so great an advantage is given to sin, as also to Satan, by this your temper and disposition, that without extraordinary watchfulness, care, and diligence, they will assuredly prevail against your soul. Thousands have been on this account hurried headlong to hell, who otherwise, at least, might have gone at a more gentle, less provoking, less mischievous rate.

---

[54] incited, agitated
[55] diseased material

For the mortification of any distemper so rooted in the nature of a man, unto all other ways and means already named or further to be insisted on, there is one expedient peculiarly suited; this is that of the apostle, "*I discipline my body, and bring it into subjection*" (1 Cor. 9:27). The bringing of the very body into subjection is an ordinance of God tending to the mortification of sin. This gives check unto the natural root of the distemper and withers it by taking away its fatness[56] of soil. Perhaps, because the papists—men ignorant of the righteousness of Christ, the work of his Spirit, and [the] whole business in hand—have laid the whole weight and stress of mortification in voluntary services and penances, leading to the subjection of the body, knowing indeed the true nature neither of sin nor [of] mortification, it may, on the other side, be a temptation to some to neglect some means of humiliation which by God himself are owned and appointed. The bringing of the body into subjection in the case insisted on, by cutting short the natural appetite, by fasting, watching, and the like, is doubtless acceptable to God, so it be done with the ensuing limitations:

The outward weakening and impairing of the body should not be looked upon as a thing good in itself, or that any mortification does consist therein—which were again to bring us under carnal ordinances; but only as a means for the end proposed—the weakening of any distemper in its natural root and seat. A man may have leanness of body and soul together.

The means whereby this is done—namely, by fasting and watching, and the like—*should not be looked on as things that in themselves, and by virtue of their own power, can produce true mortification of any sin;* for if they would, sin might be mortified without any help of the Spirit in any unregenerate person in the world. They are to be looked on only as ways whereby the Spirit may, and sometimes does, put forth strength for the accomplishing of his own work, especially in the case mentioned. Want of a right understanding and due improvement of these and the like considerations has raised a mortification among the papists that may be better applied to horses and other beasts of the field than to believers.

This is the sum of what has been spoken: When the distemper complained of seems to be rooted in the natural temper and constitution, in applying our souls to a participation of the blood and Spirit of Christ, an endeavor is to be used to give *check* in the way of God to the natural root of that distemper.

---

[56] richness, fertility

Consider the Occasions and Advantages Your Distemper Has Taken to Exert and Put Forth Itself, and Watch Against Them All

The sixth direction is: Consider what occasions, what advantages your distemper has taken to exert and put forth itself, and watch against them all.

This is one part of that duty which our blessed Savior recommends to his disciples under the name of *watching:* "I say unto you all, Watch" (Mark 13:37); which, in Luke 21:34, is: "Take heed lest your hearts be overcharged." Watch against all eruptions of your corruptions. I mean that duty which David professed himself to be exercised unto. "I have," says he, "kept myself from mine iniquity" [Ps. 18:23]. He watched all the ways and workings of his iniquity, to prevent them, to rise up against them. This is that which we are called unto under the name of "considering our ways." Consider what ways, what companies, what opportunities, what studies, what businesses, what conditions, have at any time given, or do usually give, advantages to your distempers, and set yourself heedfully against them all. Men will do this with respect unto their bodily infirmities and distempers. The seasons, the diet, the air that have proved offensive shall be avoided. Are the things of the soul of less importance? Know that he that dares to dally with occasions of sin will dare to sin. He that will venture upon temptations unto wickedness will venture upon wickedness. Hazael thought he should not be so wicked as the prophet told him he would be. To convince him, the prophet tells him no more but, "You shall be king of Syria" [2 Kings 8:13]. If he will venture on temptations unto cruelty, he will be cruel. Tell a man he shall commit such and such sins, he will startle at it. If you can convince him that he will venture on such occasions and temptations of them, he will have little ground left for his confidence.

Particular directions belonging to this head are many, not now to be insisted on. But because this head is of no less importance than the whole doctrine here handled, I have at large in another treatise, about entering into temptations, treated of it.[57]

Rise Mightily Against the First Actings and Conceptions of Your Distemper

The seventh direction is: Rise mightily against the first actings of your distemper, its first conceptions; suffer it not to get the least ground. Do not say, "Thus far it shall go, and no farther." If it have allowance for one step, it will

---

[57] See Owen's *Of Temptation: The Nature and Power of It,* reprinted in this volume.

take another. It is impossible to fix bounds to sin. It is like water in a channel—if it once break out, it will have its course. Its not acting is easier to be compassed than its bounding. Therefore does James give that gradation and process of lust (1:14-15), that we may stop at the entrance. Do you find your corruption to begin to entangle your thoughts? Rise up with all your strength against it, with no less indignation than if it had fully accomplished what it aims at. Consider what an unclean thought would have; it would have you roll yourself in folly and filth. Ask envy what it would have—murder and destruction is at the end of it. Set yourself against it with no less vigor than if it had utterly debased you to wickedness. Without this course you will not prevail. As sin gets ground in the affections to delight in, it gets also upon the understanding to slight it.

[Chapter 12]

Use and Exercise Yourself to Such Meditations as May Serve to Fill You at All Times with Self-Abasement and Thoughts of Your Own Vileness

Eighthly, use and exercise yourself to such meditations as may serve to fill you at all times with self-abasement and thoughts of your own vileness, as:

Be much in thoughtfulness of the excellency of the majesty of God and your infinite, inconceivable distance from him. Many thoughts of it cannot but fill you with a sense of your own vileness, which strikes deep at the root of any indwelling sin. When Job comes to a clear discovery of the greatness and the excellency of God, he is filled with self-abhorrence and is pressed to humiliation (Job 42:5-6). And in what state does the prophet Habakkuk affirm himself to be cast upon the apprehension of the majesty of God [Hab. 3:16]? "With God," says Job, "is terrible majesty" [Job 37:22]. Hence were the thoughts of them of old, that when they had seen God they should die. The Scripture abounds in this self-abasing consideration, comparing the men of the earth to "grasshoppers," to "vanity," the "dust of the balance," in respect of God [Isa. 40:12-25]. Be much in thoughts of this nature, to abase the pride of your heart, and to keep your soul humble within you. There is nothing [that] will render you a greater indisposition[58] to be imposed on by the deceits of sin than such a frame of heart. Think greatly of the greatness of God.

---

[58] disinclination, unwillingness

Think much of your unacquaintedness with him. Though you know enough to keep you low and humble, yet how little a portion is it that you know of him! The contemplation hereof cast that wise man into that apprehension of himself which he expresses:

> Surely I am more brutish than any man, and have not the understanding of a man. I neither learned wisdom, nor have the knowledge of the holy. Who has ascended up into heaven, or descended? Who has gathered the wind in his fists? Who has bound the waters in a garment? Who has established the ends of the earth? What is his name, and what is his Son's name, if you can tell? (Prov. 30:2-4)

Labor with this also to take down the pride of your heart. What do you know of God? How little a portion is it! How immense is he in his nature! Can you look without terror into the abyss of eternity? You cannot bear the rays of his glorious being.

Because I look on this consideration of great use in our walking with God, so far as it may have a consistency with that filial[59] boldness which is given us in Jesus Christ to draw nigh to the throne of grace [Heb. 4:16], I shall further insist upon it, to give an abiding impression of it to the souls of them who desire to walk humbly with God.

Consider, then, I say, to keep your heart in continual awe of the majesty of God, that persons of the most high and eminent attainment, of the nearest and most familiar communion with God, do yet in this life know but a very little of him and his glory. God reveals his name to Moses—the most glorious attributes that he has manifested in the covenant of grace (Ex. 34:5-6); yet all are but the "back parts" of God. All that he knows by it is but little, low, compared to the perfections of his glory. Hence it is with peculiar reference to Moses that it is said, "No man has seen God at any time" (John 1:18); of him in comparison with Christ does he speak (v. 17); and of him it is here said, "No man," no, not Moses, the most eminent among them, "has seen God at any time." We speak much of God, can talk of him, his ways, his works, his counsels, all the day long; the truth is, we know very little of him. Our thoughts, our meditations, our expressions of him are low, many of them unworthy of his glory, none of them reaching his perfections.

[59] pertaining to a son or daughter

Objection

You will say that "Moses was under the law when God wrapped up himself in darkness, and his mind in types and clouds and dark institutions—under the glorious shining of the gospel, which has brought life and immortality to light, God being revealed from his own bosom, we now know him much more clearly, and as he is; we see his face now, and not his back parts only, as Moses did."

Answers

I acknowledge a vast and almost inconceivable difference between the acquaintance we now have with God, after his speaking to us by his own Son [Heb. 1:2], and that which the generality of the saints had under the law; for although their eyes were as good, sharp, and clear as ours, their faith and spiritual understanding not behind ours, the object as glorious unto them as unto us, yet our day is more clear than theirs was, the clouds are blown away and scattered [Song 4:6], the shadows of the night are gone and fled away, the sun is risen, and the means of sight is made more eminent and clear than formerly. Yet—

That peculiar sight which Moses had of God (Exodus 34), was *a gospel-sight,* a sight of God as "gracious," etc., and yet it is called but his "back parts," that is, but low and mean[60] in comparison of his excellencies and perfections.

The apostle, exalting to the utmost this glory of light above that of the law, manifesting that now the "veil" causing darkness is taken away [2 Cor. 3:13-16], so that with "open" or uncovered "face we behold the glory of the Lord" (2 Cor. 3:18) tells us how: "as in a glass" (1 Cor 13:12). "In a glass"—how is that? Clearly, perfectly? Alas, no! He tells you how that is: "We see through a glass, darkly," says he (1 Cor. 13:12). It is not a telescope that helps us to see things afar off, concerning which the apostle speaks; and yet what poor helps are! How short do we come of the truth of things notwithstanding their assistance! It is a looking-glass whereunto he alludes (where are only obscure species and images of things, and not the things themselves), and a sight therein that he compares our knowledge to. He tells you also that all that we do see, *di esoptrou,* "by" or "through this glass," is in *ainigmati*—in "a riddle," in darkness and obscurity. And speaking of himself, who surely was much more clear-sighted than any now living, he tells us that he saw but *ex merous*—"in part." He saw but the back parts of heavenly things (v. 12),

[60] lowly, insignificant

and compares all the knowledge he had attained of God to that he had of things when he was a child (v. 11). It is a *meros*,[61] short of the *to teleion*,[62] yea, such as *katargēthēsetai*—"it shall be destroyed," or done away. We know what weak, feeble, uncertain notions and apprehensions children have of things of any abstruse[63] consideration; how when they grow up with any improvements of parts and abilities, those conceptions vanish, and they are ashamed of them. It is the commendation of a child to love, honor, believe, and obey his father; but for his science and notions, his father knows his childishness and folly. Notwithstanding all our confidence of high attainments, all our notions of God are but childish in respect of his infinite perfections. We lisp and babble, and say we know not what, for the most part, in our most accurate (as we think) conceptions and notions of God.[64] We may love, honor, believe, and obey our Father; and therewith he accepts our childish thoughts, for they are but childish. We see but his back parts; we know but little of him. Hence is that promise wherewith we are so often supported and comforted in our distress, "We shall see him as he is"; we shall see him "face to face"; "know as we are known; comprehend that for which we are comprehended" (1 Cor. 13:12; 1 John 3:2); and positively, "Now we see him not" [1 Pet. 1:8]—all concluding that here we see but his back parts; not as he is, but in a dark, obscure representation; not in the perfection of his glory.

The queen of Sheba had heard much of Solomon, and framed many great thoughts of his magnificence in her mind thereupon; but when she came and saw his glory, she was forced to confess that the one half of the truth had not been told her [1 Kings 10:7]. We may suppose that we have here attained great knowledge, clear and high thoughts of God; but, alas! when he shall bring us into his presence we shall cry out, "We never knew him as he is; the thousandth part of his glory, and perfection, and blessedness, never entered into our hearts."

The apostle tells us that we know not what we ourselves shall be (1 John 3:2)—what we shall find ourselves in the issue; much less will it enter into our hearts to conceive what God is and what we shall find him to be. Consider either him who is to be known, or the way whereby we know him, and this will further appear:

We know so little of God, because it is God who is thus to be known—

---

[61] part

[62] completion, fulfillment

[63] hard to understand

[64] Cf. Calvin, *Institutes* I.xiii.1: ". . . as nurses commonly do with infants, God is wont to 'lisp' in speaking to us . . . not so much to express clearly what God is like as accommodate the knowledge of him to our slight capacity."

that is, he who has described himself to us very much by this, that we cannot know him. What else does he intend where he calls himself invisible, incomprehensible, and the like?—that is, he whom we do not, cannot, know as he is. And our further progress consists more in knowing what he is not, than what he is. Thus is he described to be immortal, infinite—that is, he is not, as we are, mortal, finite, and limited. Hence is that glorious description of him, "Who only has immortality, dwelling in the light which no man can approach unto; whom no man has seen, nor can see" (1 Tim. 6:16). His light is such as no creature can approach unto. He is not seen, not because he cannot be seen, but because we cannot bear the sight of him. The light of God, in whom is no darkness, forbids all access to him by any creature whatsoever. We who cannot behold the sun in its glory are too weak to bear the beams of infinite brightness. On this consideration, as was said, the wise man professes himself "a very beast, and not to have the understanding of a man" (Prov. 30:2)—that is, he knew nothing in comparison of God, so that he seemed to have lost all his understanding when once he came to the consideration of him, his work, and his ways.

In this consideration let our souls descend to some particulars:

For the *being* of God; we are so far from a knowledge of it, so as to be able to instruct one another therein by words and expressions of it, as that to frame any conceptions in our mind, with such species and impressions of things as we receive the knowledge of all other things by, is to make an idol to ourselves, and so to worship a god of our own making, and not the God that made us. We may as well and as lawfully hew him out of wood or stone as form him a being in our minds, suited to our apprehensions. The utmost of the best of our thoughts of the being of God is that we can have no thoughts of it. Our knowledge of a being is but low when it mounts no higher but only to know that we know it not.

There [may] be *some* things of God which he himself has taught us to speak of, and to regulate our expressions of them; but when we have so done, we see not the things themselves; we know them not. To *believe* and *admire* is all that we attain to. We profess, as we are taught, that God is infinite, omnipotent, eternal; and we know what disputes and notions there are about omnipresence, immensity, infiniteness, and eternity. We have, I say, words and notions about these things; but as to the things themselves what do we know? What do we comprehend of them? Can the mind of man do any more but swallow itself up in an infinite abyss, which is as nothing; give itself up to what it cannot conceive, much less express? Is not our understanding "brutish" in the contemplation of such things, and is as if it were not? Yea, the perfection of our understanding is not to understand, and to rest there. They are but the back parts of eternity and infiniteness that we have a glimpse of. What shall I say of the Trinity, or the subsistence of distinct persons in the same individual essence—a mystery by many denied, because by none understood—a mystery whose every letter is mysterious? Who can declare the generation of the Son, the procession of the Spirit, or the difference of the one from the other? But I shall not further instance in particulars. That infinite and inconceivable distance that is between him and us keeps us in the dark as to any sight of his face or clear apprehension of his perfections.

We know him rather by what he does than by what he is—by his doing us good than by his essential goodness; and how little a portion of him, as Job speaks, is hereby discovered!

We know little of God, because it is faith alone whereby here we know him. I shall not now discourse about the remaining impressions on the hearts of all men by nature that there is a God, nor what they may rationally be taught concerning that God from the works of his creation and providence, which they see and behold. It is confessedly, and that upon the woeful experience of all ages, so weak, low, dark, confused, that none ever on that account glorified God as they ought, but, notwithstanding all their knowledge of God, were indeed "without God in the world" [Eph. 2:12].

The chief, and, upon the matter, almost only acquaintance we have with God, and his dispensations of himself, is by faith. "He that comes to God must believe that he is, and that he is a rewarder of them that diligently seek him" (Heb. 11:6). Our knowledge of him and his rewarding (the bottom[65] of our obedience or coming to him), is believing. "We walk by faith, and not by sight" (2 Cor. 5:7)—*dia pisteōs ou dia eidous* by faith, and so by faith as not to have any express idea, image, or species of that which we believe. Faith is all the argument we have of "things not seen" (Heb. 11:1). I might here insist upon the nature of it; and from all its concomitants[66] and concerns manifest that we know but the back parts of what we know by faith only. As to its rise, it is built purely upon the testimony of him whom we have not seen: as the apostle speaks, "How can you love him whom you have not seen?" [1 Pet. 1:8]—that is, whom you know only by faith that he is. Faith receives all upon *his* testimony, whom it receives to be only on his own testimony. As to its nature, it is an assent upon testimony, not an evidence upon demonstration; and the object of it is, as was said before, above us. Hence our faith, as

[65] basis, foundation
[66] things that accompany

was formerly observed, is called a "seeing darkly, as in a glass." All that we know this way (and all that we know of God we know this way) is but low, and dark, and obscure.

Objection

But you will say, "All this is true, but yet it is only so to them that know not God, perhaps, as he is revealed in Jesus Christ; with them who do so it is otherwise. It is true, 'No man has seen God at any time,' but 'the only-begotten Son, he has revealed him' (John 1:18); and 'the Son of God is come, and has given us an understanding, that we may know him that is true' (1 John 5:20). The illumination of 'the glorious gospel of Christ, who is the image of God,' shines upon believers (2 Cor. 4:4); yea, and 'God, who commanded the light to shine out of darkness, shines into their hearts, to give them the knowledge of his glory in the face of his Son' (v. 6). So that 'though we were darkness,' yet we are now 'light in the Lord' (Eph. 5:8). And the apostle says, 'We all with open face behold the glory of the Lord' (2 Cor. 3:18); and we are now so far from being in such darkness, or at such a distance from God, that 'our communion and our fellowship is with the Father and with his Son' (1 John 1:3). The light of the gospel whereby now God is revealed is glorious; not a star, but the sun in his beauty is risen upon us, and the veil is taken from our faces. So that though unbelievers, yea, and perhaps some weak believers, may be in some darkness, yet those of any growth or considerable attainments have a clear sight and view of the face of God in Jesus Christ."

Answers

To which I answer—

The truth is, we all of us know *enough* of him to love him more than we do, to delight in him and serve him, believe him, obey him, put our trust in him, above all that we have hitherto attained. Our darkness and weakness is no plea for our negligence and disobedience. Who is it that has walked up to the knowledge that he has had of the perfections, excellencies, and will of God? God's end in giving us any knowledge of himself here is that we may "glorify him as God" [Rom. 1:21], that is, love him, serve him, believe and obey him—give him all the honor and glory that is due from poor sinful creatures to a sin-pardoning God and Creator. We must all acknowledge that we were never thoroughly transformed into the image of that knowledge which we have had. And had we used our talents well, we might have been trusted with more.

Comparatively, that knowledge which we have of God by the revelation of Jesus Christ in the gospel is exceeding eminent and glorious. It is so in comparison of any knowledge of God that might otherwise be attained, or was delivered in the law under the Old Testament, which had but the shadow of good things, not the express image of them; this the apostle pursues at large (2 Corinthians 3). Christ has now in these last days revealed the Father from his own bosom, declared his name, made known his mind, will, and counsel in a far more clear, eminent, distinct manner than he did formerly, while he kept his people under the pedagogy of the law; and this is that which, for the most part, is intended in the places before mentioned. The clear, perspicuous delivery and declaration of God and his will in the gospel is expressly exalted in comparison of any other way of revelation of himself.

The difference between believers and unbelievers as to knowledge is not so much in the *matter* of their knowledge as in the *manner* of knowing. Unbelievers, some of them, may know more and be able to say more of God, his perfections, and his will, than many believers; but they know nothing as they ought, nothing in a right manner, nothing spiritually and savingly, nothing with a holy, heavenly light. The excellency of a believer is, not that he has a large apprehension of things, but that what he does apprehend, which perhaps may be very little, he sees it in the light of the Spirit of God, in a saving, soul-transforming light; and this is that which gives us communion with God, and not prying thoughts or curious-raised notions.

Jesus Christ by his word and Spirit reveals to the hearts of all his, God as a Father, as a God in covenant, as a rewarder, every way sufficiently to teach us to obey him here, and to lead us to his bosom, to lie down there in the fruition of him to eternity. But yet now,

Notwithstanding all this, it is but a *little portion* we know of him; we see but his back parts. For—

The intention of all gospel revelation is not to *unveil God's essential glory* that we should see him as he is, but merely to declare so much of him as he knows sufficient to be a bottom of our faith, love, obedience, and coming to him—that is, of the faith which here he expects from us; such services as beseem[67] poor creatures in the midst of temptations. But when he calls us to eternal admiration and contemplation, without interruption, he will make a new manner of discovery of himself, and the whole shape of things, as it now lies before us, will depart as a shadow.

We are dull and slow of heart to receive the things that are in the word

---

[67] suit, become, fit

revealed; God, by our infirmity and weakness, keeping us in continual dependence on him for teachings and revelations of himself out of his word, never in this world bringing any soul to the utmost of what is from the word to be made out and discovered—so that although the way of revelation in the gospel be clear and evident, yet we know little of the things themselves that are revealed. Let us, then, revive the use and intention of this consideration: will not a due apprehension of this inconceivable greatness of God, and that infinite distance wherein we stand from him, fill the soul with a holy and awful fear of him, so as to keep it in a frame unsuited to the thriving or flourishing of any lust whatsoever? Let the soul be continually wonted to reverential thoughts of God's greatness and omnipresence, and it will be much upon its watch as to any undue deportments.[68] Consider him with whom you have to do—even "our God is a consuming fire" [Heb. 12:29]—and in your greatest abashments[69] at his presence and eye, know that your very nature is too narrow to bear apprehensions suitable to his essential glory.

[Chapter 13]

Do Not Speak Peace to Yourself Before God Speaks It, But Hearken to What God Says to Your Soul

Ninthly, in case God disquiet the heart about the guilt of its distempers, either in respect of its root and indwelling, or in respect of any eruptions of it, take heed you speak not peace to yourself before God speaks it; but hearken what he says to your soul. This is our next direction, without the observation whereof the heart will be exceedingly exposed to the deceitfulness of sin.

This is a business of great importance. It is a sad thing for a man to deceive his own soul herein. All the warnings God gives us in tenderness to our souls, to try and examine ourselves, do tend to the preventing of this great evil of speaking peace groundlessly to ourselves; which is upon the issue to bless ourselves in an opposition to God. It is not my business to insist upon the danger of it, but to help believers to prevent it, and to let them know when they do so. To manage this direction aright observe—

That as it is the great prerogative and sovereignty of God to give grace to whom he pleases ("He has mercy on whom he will," Rom. 9:18; and among all the sons of men, he calls whom he will, and sanctifies whom he will), so

[68] behaviors
[69] embarrassment, lack of self-confidence

among those so called and justified, and whom he will save, *he yet reserves this privilege to himself to speak peace to whom he pleases, and in what degree he pleases, even among them on whom he has bestowed grace.* He is the "God of all consolation" [2 Cor. 1:3] in a special manner in his dealing with believers; that is, of the good things that he keeps locked up in his family, and gives out of it to all his children at his pleasure. This the Lord insists on (Isa. 57:16-18). It is the case under consideration that is there insisted on. When God says he will heal their breaches and disconsolations, he assumes this privilege to himself in a special manner: "I create it" (v. 19)—"Even in respect of these poor wounded creatures I create it, and according to my sovereignty make it out as I please."

Hence, as it is with the collation of grace in reference to them that are in the state of nature—God does it in great curiosity, and his proceedings therein in taking and leaving, as to outward appearances, quite besides and contrary oftentimes to all probable expectations; so is it in his communications of peace and joy in reference unto them that are in the state of grace—he gives them out oftentimes quite besides our expectation, as to any appearing grounds of his dispensations.

As God creates it for whom he pleases, so *it is the prerogative of Christ to speak it home to the conscience.* Speaking to the church of Laodicea, who had healed her wounds falsely and spoke peace to herself when she ought not, he takes to himself that title, "*I* am the Amen, the faithful Witness" (Rev. 3:14). He bears testimony concerning our condition as it is indeed. We may possibly mistake, and trouble ourselves in vain, or flatter ourselves upon false grounds, but he is the "Amen, the faithful Witness," and what he speaks of our state and condition, that it is indeed. He is said not to "judge after the sight of his eyes" (Isa. 11:3)—not according to any outward appearance, or anything that may be subject to a mistake, as we are apt to do; but he shall judge and determine every cause as it is indeed.

Take these two previous observations, and I shall give some rules whereby men may know whether God speaks peace to them, or whether they speak peace to themselves only.

Men certainly speak peace to themselves when their so doing is not attended with the greatest detestation imaginable of that sin in reference whereunto they do speak peace to themselves, and abhorrency of themselves for it. When men are wounded by sin, disquieted and perplexed, and knowing that there is no remedy for them but only in the mercies of God, through the blood of Christ, do therefore look to him, and to the promises of the covenant in him, and thereupon quiet their hearts that it shall be well with them, and that God will be exalted, that he may be gracious to them, and yet their souls are not wrought to the greatest detestation of the sin or sins upon the account whereof they are disquieted—this is to heal themselves, and not to be healed of God. This is but a great and strong wind, that the Lord is nigh unto, but the Lord is not in the wind [1 Kings 19:11]. When men do truly "look upon Christ whom they have pierced," without which there is no healing or peace, they will "mourn" (Zech. 12:10); they will mourn for him, even upon this account, and detest the sin that pierced him. When we go to Christ for healing, faith eyes him peculiarly as one pierced. Faith takes several views of Christ, according to the occasions of address to him and communion with him that it has. Sometimes it views his holiness, sometimes his power, sometimes his love, [sometimes] his favor with his Father. And when it goes for healing and peace, it looks especially on the blood of the covenant, on his sufferings; for "with his stripes we are healed, and the chastisement of our peace was upon him" (Isa. 53:5). When we look for healing, his stripes are to be eyed—not in the outward story of them, which is the course of popish devotionists, but in the love, kindness, mystery, and design of the cross; and when we look for peace, his chastisements must be in our eye. Now this, I say, if it be done according to the mind of God, and in the strength of that Spirit which is poured out on believers, it will beget a detestation of that sin or sins for which healing and peace is sought. So Ezekiel 16:60-61: "Nevertheless I will remember my covenant with you in the days of your youth, and I will establish unto you an everlasting covenant." And what then? "Then you shall remember your ways, and be ashamed." When God comes home to speak peace in a sure covenant of it, it fills the soul with shame for all the ways whereby it has been alienated from him. And one of the things that the apostle mentions as attending that godly sorrow which is accompanied with repentance unto salvation, never to be repented of, is revenge: "Yea, what revenge!" (2 Cor. 7:11). They reflected on their miscarriages with indignation and revenge, for their folly in them. When Job comes up to a thorough healing, he cries, "Now I abhor myself" (Job 42:6); and until he did so, he had no abiding peace. He might perhaps have made up himself with that doctrine of free grace which was so excellently preached by Elihu (Job 33:14-30); but he had then but skinned his wounds: he must come to self-abhorrency if he come to healing. So was it with those in Psalm 78:33-35, in their great trouble and perplexity, for and upon the account of sin. I doubt not but upon the address they made to God in Christ (for that so they did is evident from the titles they gave him; they call him their Rock and their Redeemer, two words everywhere pointing out the Lord Christ), they spoke peace to themselves; but was it sound and abiding? No; it passed away as the early dew. God speaks not one word of peace to their souls. But why had they not peace? Why, because in their address to God, they flattered him.

But how does that appear? "Their heart was not right with him, neither were they steadfast" (Ps. 78:37); they had not a detestation nor relinquishment of that sin in reference whereunto they spoke peace to themselves. Let a man make what application he will for healing and peace, let him do it to the true Physician, let him do it the right way, let him quiet his heart in the promises of the covenant; yet, when peace is spoken, if it be not attended with the detestation and abhorrency of that sin which was the wound and caused the disquietment, this is no peace of God's creating, but of our own purchasing. It is but a skinning over the wound, while the core lies at the bottom, which will putrefy, and corrupt, and corrode, until it break out again with noisomeness, vexation, and danger. Let not poor souls that walk in such a path as this, who are more sensible of the trouble of sin than of the pollution of uncleanness that attends it; who address themselves for mercy, yea, to the Lord in Christ they address themselves for mercy, but *yet* will keep the sweet morsel of their sin under their tongue—let them, I say, never think to have true and solid peace. For instance, you find your heart running out after the world, and it disturbs you in your communion with God; the Spirit speaks expressly to you—"He that loves the world, the love of the Father is not in him" [1 John 2:15]. This puts you on dealing with God in Christ for the healing of your soul, the quieting of your conscience; but yet, withal, a thorough detestation of the evil itself abides not upon you; yea, perhaps that is liked well enough, but only in respect of the consequences of it. Perhaps you may be saved, yet as through fire, and God will have some work with you before he has done; but you will have little peace in this life—you will be sick and fainting all your days (Isa. 57:17). This is a deceit that lies at the root of the peace of many professors and wastes it. They deal with all their strength about mercy and pardon, and seem to have great communion with God in their so doing; they lie before him, bewail their sins and follies, that anyone would think, yea, they think themselves, that surely they and their sins are now parted; and so receive in mercy that satisfies their hearts for a little season. But when a thorough search comes to be made, there has been some secret reserve for the folly or follies treated about—at least, there has not been that thorough abhorrency of it which is necessary; and their whole peace is quickly discovered to be weak and rotten, scarce abiding any longer than the words of begging it are in their mouths.

When men measure out peace to themselves upon the conclusions that their convictions and rational principles will carry them out unto, this is a false peace and will not abide. I shall a little explain what I mean hereby. A man has got a wound by sin; he has a conviction of some sin upon his conscience; he has not walked uprightly as becomes the gospel; all is not well and right between God and his soul. He considers now what is to be done. Light he has, and knows what path he must take, and how his soul has been formerly healed. Considering that the promises of God are the outward means of application for the healing of his sores and quieting of his heart, he goes to them, searches them out, finds out some one or more of them whose literal expressions are directly suited to his condition. Says he to himself, "God speaks in this promise; here I will take myself a plaster[70] as long and broad as my wound," and so brings the word of the promise to his condition, and sets him down in peace. This is another appearance upon the mount; the Lord is near, but the Lord is not in it. It has not been the work of the Spirit, who alone can "convince us of sin, and righteousness, and judgment" [John 16:8], but the mere actings of the intelligent, rational soul. As there are three sorts of lives, we say—the vegetative, the sensitive, and the rational or intelligent[71]—some things have only the vegetative; some the sensitive also, and that includes the former; some have the rational, which takes in and supposes both the other. Now, he that has the rational does not only act suitably to that principle, but also to both the others—he grows and is sensible. It is so with men in the things of God. Some are mere *natural* and rational men; some have a *superadded* conviction with illumination; and some are truly *regenerate.* Now, he that has the latter has also both [of] the former; and therefore he acts sometimes upon the principles of the rational, sometimes upon the principles of the enlightened man. His true spiritual life is not the principle of all his motions; he acts not always in the strength thereof, neither are all his fruits from that root. In this case that I speak of, he acts merely upon the principle of conviction and illumination, whereby his first naturals[72] are heightened; but the Spirit breathes not at all upon all these waters. Take an instance: Suppose the wound and disquiet of the soul to be upon the account of relapses—which, whatever the evil or folly be, though for the matter of it never so small, yet there are no wounds deeper than those that are given the soul on that account, nor disquietments greater. In the perturbation[73] of his

---

[70] medicated bandage

[71] Aristotle differentiated three types of the soul, or three different types of living things in distinction from inanimate things: vegetative (plants), sensitive (animals), and rational (human beings). See Aristotle, *Nichomachean Ethics,* book 1.

[72] i.e., natural faculties

[73] disturbance, agitation

mind, he finds out that promise, "The LORD will have mercy, and our God will abundantly pardon" (Isa. 55:7)—he will multiply or add to pardon, he will do it again and again; or that in, "I will heal their backsliding, I will love them freely" (Hos. 14:4). This the man considers, and thereupon concludes peace to himself; whether the Spirit of God make the application or no, whether that gives life and power to the letter or no, that he regards not. He does not hearken whether God the Lord speak peace. He does not wait upon God, who perhaps yet hides his face, and sees the poor creature stealing peace and running away with it, knowing that the time will come when he will deal with him again, and call him to a new reckoning [Hos. 9:9]; when he shall see that it is in vain to go one step where God does not take him by the hand.

Question

I see here, indeed, sundry other questions upon this arising and interposing themselves. I cannot apply myself to them all: one I shall a little speak to. It may be said, then, *"Seeing that this seems to be the path that the Holy Spirit leads us in for the healing of our wounds and quieting of our hearts, how shall we know when we go alone ourselves, and when the Spirit also does accompany us?"*

Answer

If any of you are out of the way upon this account, God will speedily let you know it; for besides that you have his promise, that the "meek he will guide in judgment and teach them his way" (Ps. 25:9), he will not let you always err. He will, I say, not suffer your nakedness to be covered with fig-leaves, but take them away and all the peace you have in them, and will not suffer you to settle on such lees.[74] You shall quickly know your wound is not healed; that is, you shall speedily know whether or not it be thus with you by the event. The peace you thus get and obtain will not abide. While the mind is overpowered by its own convictions, there is no hold for disquietments to fix upon. Stay a little, and all these reasonings will grow cold and vanish before the face of the first temptation that arises. But—

This course is commonly taken without *waiting;* which is the grace, and that peculiar acting of faith which God calls for, to be exercised in such a condition. I know God does sometimes come in upon the soul instantly, in a moment, as it were, wounding and healing it—as I am persuaded it was in

[74] shelters, protections

the case of David, when he cut off the lap of Saul's garment [1 Sam. 24:4]; but ordinarily, in such a case, God calls for waiting and laboring, attending as the eye of a servant upon his master [Ps. 123:2; 130:6]. Says the prophet Isaiah: "I will wait upon the LORD, who hides his face from the house of Jacob" (Isa. 8:17). God will have his children lie a while at his door when they have run from his house, and not instantly rush in upon him; unless he take them by the hand and pluck them in, when they are so ashamed that they dare not come to him. Now, self-healers, or men that speak peace to themselves, do commonly make haste; they will not tarry; they do not hearken what God speaks, but on they will go to be healed [Isa. 28:16].

Such a course, though it may quiet the conscience and the mind, the rational concluding part of the soul, yet it does not *sweeten* the heart with rest and gracious contentation.[75] The answer it receives is much like that [which] Elisha gave Naaman: "Go in peace" [2 Kings 5:19]; it quieted his mind, but I much question whether it sweetened his heart, or gave him any joy in believing, other than the natural joy that was then stirred in him upon his healing. "Do not my words do good?" says the Lord (Mic. 2:7). When God speaks, there is not only truth in his words, that may answer the conviction of our understandings, but also they do good; they bring that which is sweet, and good, and desirable to the will and affections; by them the "soul returns unto its rest" (Ps. 116:7).

Which is worst of all, it *amends not the life,* it heals not the evil, it cures not the distemper. When God speaks peace, it guides and keeps the soul that it "turn not again to folly" [Ps. 85:8]. When we speak it ourselves, the heart is not taken off the evil; nay, it is the readiest course in the world to bring a soul into a trade of backsliding. If, upon your plastering yourself, you find yourself rather animated to the battle again than utterly weaned from it, it is too palpable that you have been at work with your own soul, but Jesus Christ and his Spirit were not there. Yea, and oftentimes nature having done its work, will, ere[76] a few days are over, come for its reward; and, having been active in the work of healing, will be ready to reason for a new wounding. In God's speaking peace there comes along so much sweetness, and such a discovery of his love, as is a strong obligation on the soul no more to deal perversely [Luke 22:32].

We speak peace to ourselves when we do it slightly. This the prophet complains of in some teachers: "They have healed the hurt of the daughter

[75] satisfaction, reassurance
[76] before

of my people slightly" (Jer. 6:14). And it is so with some persons: they make the healing of their wounds a slight work; a look, a glance of faith to the promises does it, and so the matter is ended. The apostle tells us that "the word did not profit" some, because "it was not mixed with faith" (Heb. 4:2)—*mē sugchecherasmenous,* "it was not well tempered" and mingled with faith. It is not a mere look to the word of mercy in the promise, but it must be mingled with faith until it is incorporated into the very nature of it; and then, indeed, it does good unto the soul. If you have had a wound upon your conscience, which was attended with weakness and disquietness, which now you are freed of, how came you so? "I looked to the promises of pardon and healing, and so found peace." Yea, but perhaps you have made too much haste, you have done it overtly, you have not fed upon the promise so as to mix it with faith, to have got all the virtue of it diffused into your soul; only you have done it slightly. You will find your wound, ere it be long, breaking out again; and you shall know that you are not cured.

Whoever speaks peace to himself upon any one account, and at the same time has another evil of no less importance lying upon his spirit, about which he has had no dealing with God, that man cries "Peace" when there is none [Jer. 6:14; 8:11]. A little to explain my meaning: A man has neglected a duty again and again, perhaps, when in all righteousness it was due from him; his conscience is perplexed, his soul wounded, he has no quiet in his bones by reason of his sin; he applies himself for healing, and finds peace. Yet, in the meantime, perhaps, worldliness, or pride, or some other folly, wherewith the Spirit of God is exceedingly grieved, may lie in the bosom of that man, and they neither disturb him nor he them. Let not that man think that any of his peace is from God. Then shall it be well with men, when they have an equal respect to all God's commandments. God will justify us *from* our sins, but he will not justify the least sin *in* us: "He is a God of purer eyes than to behold iniquity" [Hab. 1:13].

When men of themselves speak peace to their consciences, it is seldom that God speaks humiliation to their souls. God's peace is humbling peace, melting peace, as it was in the case of David; never such deep humiliation as when Nathan brought him the tidings of his pardon.

Question

But you will say, "*When may we take the comfort of a promise as our own, in relation to some peculiar wound, for the quieting the heart?*"

Answer

First, in general, *when God speaks it, be it when it will, sooner or later.* I told you before, he may do it in the very instant of the sin itself, and that with such irresistible power that the soul must needs receive his mind in it; sometimes he will make us wait longer: but when he speaks, be it sooner or later, be it when we are sinning or repenting, be the condition of our souls what they please, if God speak, he must be received. There is not anything that, in our communion with him, the Lord is more troubled with us for, if I may so say, than our unbelieving fears, that keep us off from receiving that strong consolation which he is so willing to give to us.

Question

But you will say, "*We are where we were. When God speaks it, we must receive it, that is true; but how shall we know when he speaks?*"

Answer

I would [desire that] we could all practically come up to this, to receive peace when we are convinced that God speaks it, and that it is our duty to receive it. But—

There is, if I may so say, *a secret instinct in faith,* whereby it knows the voice of Christ when he speaks indeed; as the babe leaped in the womb when the blessed Virgin came to Elizabeth [Luke 1:44], faith leaps in the heart when Christ indeed draws nigh to it. "My sheep," says Christ, "know my voice" (John 10:4)—"They know my voice; they are used to the sound of it," and they know when his lips are opened to them and are full of grace. The spouse was in a sad condition (Song 5:2)—asleep in security; but yet as soon as Christ speaks, she cries, "It is the voice of my beloved that speaks!"[77] She knew his voice, and was so acquainted with communion with him, that instantly she discovers him; and so will you also. If you exercise yourselves to acquaintance and communion with him, you will easily discern between his voice and the voice of a stranger. And take this *critērion* with you: When he does speak, he speaks as never man spoke; he speaks with power, and one way or other will make your "hearts burn within you," as he did to the disciples (Luke 24[:32]). He does it by "putting in his hand at the hole of the door" (Song 5:4)—his Spirit into your hearts to seize on you.

[77] Owen—along with most interpreters in the seventeenth century—interpreted the Song of Solomon (or Canticles, as they referred to it) as a "description of the communion that is between the Lord Christ and his saints" (*Works,* 2:46).

He that has his senses exercised to discern good or evil, being increased in judgment and experience by a constant observation of the ways of Christ's intercourse, the manner of the operations of the Spirit, and the effects it usually produces, is the best judge for himself in this case.

Secondly, *if the word of the Lord does good to your souls, he speaks it;* if it humble, if it cleanse, and be useful to those ends for which promises are given—namely, to endear, to cleanse, to melt and bind to obedience, to self-emptiness, etc. But this is not my business; nor shall I further divert in the pursuit of this direction. Without the observation of it, sin will have great advantages toward the hardening of the heart.

PART 3:

The Means of Mortification

[Chapter 14]

Directions for the Work Itself

Now, the considerations which I have hitherto insisted on are rather of things *preparatory* to the work aimed at than such as will *effect* it. It is the heart's due preparation for the work itself, without which it will not be accomplished, that hitherto I have aimed at.

Directions for the work itself are very few; I mean that are peculiar to it. And they are these that follow:

Set faith at work on Christ for the killing of your sin. His blood is the great sovereign remedy for sin-sick souls. Live in this, and you will die a conqueror; yea, you will, through the good providence of God, live to see your lust dead at your feet.

Question

But you will say, "*How shall faith act itself on Christ for this end and purpose?*"

Answer

I say, sundry ways—

By faith fill your soul with a due consideration of that provision which is laid up in Jesus Christ for this end and purpose, that all your lusts, this very lust wherewith you are entangled, may be mortified. By faith ponder on this, that though you are no way able in or by yourself to get the conquest over your distemper, though you are even weary of contending, and are utterly ready to faint, yet that there is enough in Jesus Christ to yield you relief (Phil. 4:13). It staid[1] the prodigal, when he was ready to faint, that yet there was bread enough in his father's house; though he was at a distance from it, yet it relieved him, and staid him, that there it was [Luke 15:17]. In your greatest distress and anguish, consider that fullness of grace, those riches, those treasures of strength, might, and help [Isa. 40:28-31], that are laid up in him for our support (John 1:16; Col. 1:19). Let them come into and abide in your mind. Consider that he is "exalted and made a Prince and a Savior to give repentance unto Israel" (Acts 5:31); and if to give repentance, to give mortification, without which the other is not, nor can be. Christ tells us that we obtain purging grace by abiding in him (John 15:3). To act faith upon the fullness that is in Christ for our supply is an eminent way of abiding in Christ,

[1] steadied, stabilized

for both our insition[2] and abode is by faith (Rom. 11:19-20). Let, then, your soul by faith be exercised with such thoughts and apprehensions as these:

> I am a poor, weak creature; unstable as water, I cannot excel. This corruption is too hard for me, and is at the very door of ruining my soul; and what to do I know not. My soul is become as parched ground, and an habitation of dragons. I have made promises and broken them; vows and engagements have been as a thing of naught. Many persuasions have I had that I had got the victory and should be delivered, but I am deceived; so that I plainly see, that without some eminent succor and assistance, I am lost, and shall be prevailed on to an utter relinquishment of God. But yet, though this be my state and condition, let the hands that hang down be lifted up, and the feeble knees be strengthened. Behold, the Lord Christ, that has all fullness of grace in his heart [John 1:16], all fullness of power in his hand [Matt. 28:18], he is able to slay all these his enemies. There is sufficient provision in him for my relief and assistance. He can take my drooping, dying soul and make me more than a conqueror [Rom. 8:37].
>
>> "Why do you say, O my soul, My way is hid from the LORD, and my judgment is passed over from my God? Have you not known, have you not heard, that the everlasting God, the LORD, the Creator of the ends of the earth, faints not, neither is weary? There is no searching of his understanding. He gives power to the faint; and to them that have no might he increases strength. Even the youths shall faint and be weary, and the young men shall utterly fall: but they that wait upon the LORD shall renew their strength; they shall mount up with wings as eagles; they shall run, and not be weary; they shall walk, and not faint" (Isa. 40:27-31).
>
> He can make the "dry, parched ground of my soul to become a pool, and my thirsty, barren heart as springs of water"; yea, he can make this "habitation of dragons," this heart, so full of abominable lusts and fiery temptations, to be a place for "grass" and fruit to himself (Isa. 35:7).

So God staid Paul, under his temptation, with the consideration of the sufficiency of his grace: "My grace is sufficient for you" (2 Cor. 12:9). Though he were not immediately so far made partaker of it as to be freed from his temptation, yet the sufficiency of it in God, for that end and purpose, was enough to stay his spirit. I say, then, by faith, be much in the consideration

[2] engraftment

of that supply and the fullness of it that is in Jesus Christ, and how he can at any time give you strength and deliverance. Now, if hereby you do not find success to a conquest, yet you will be staid in the chariot, that you shall not fly out of the field until the battle be ended; you will be kept from an utter despondency and a lying down under your unbelief, or a turning aside to false means and remedies, that in the issue will not relieve you. The efficacy of this consideration will be found only in the practice.

Raise up your heart by faith to an expectation of relief from Christ. Relief in this case from Christ is like the prophet's vision: "It is for an appointed time, but at the end it shall speak, and not lie: though it tarry, yet wait for it; because it will surely come, it will not tarry" (Hab. 2:3). Though it may seem somewhat long to you, while you are under your trouble and perplexity, yet it shall surely come in the appointed time of the Lord Jesus; which is the best season. If, then, you can raise up your heart to a settled expectation of relief from Jesus Christ—if your eyes are toward him "as the eyes of a servant to the hand of his master" [Ps. 123:2] when he expects to receive somewhat from him—your soul shall be satisfied, he will assuredly deliver you; he will slay the lust, and your latter end shall be peace. Only look for it at his hand; expect when and how he will do it. "If you will not believe, surely you shall not be established" [Isa. 7:9].

Question

But will you say, "*What ground have I to build such an expectation upon, so that I may expect not to be deceived?*"

Answer

As you have necessity to put you on this course, you must be relieved and saved this way or none. To whom will you go [John 6:68]? So there are in the Lord Jesus innumerable things to encourage and engage you to this expectation.

For the necessity of it, I have in part discovered[3] it before, when I manifested that this is the work of faith and of believers only. "Without me," says Christ, "you can do nothing" (John 15:5), speaking with special relation to the purging of the heart from sin (v. 2). Mortification of any sin must be by a supply of grace. Of ourselves we cannot do it. Now, "it has pleased the Father that in Christ should all fullness dwell" (Col. 1:19); that "of his fullness we might receive grace for grace" (John 1:16). He is the head from whence the

[3] demonstrated

new man must have influences of life and strength, or it will decay every day. If we are "strengthened with might in the inner man" [Eph. 3:16], it is by "Christ's dwelling in our hearts by faith" (Eph. 3:16-17). That this work is not to be done without the Spirit I have also shown before. Whence, then, do we expect the Spirit? From whom do we look for him? Who has promised him to us, having procured[4] him for us? Ought not all our expectations to this purpose to be on Christ alone? Let this, then, be fixed upon your heart, that if you have not relief from him you shall never have any. All ways, endeavors, contendings that are not animated by this expectation of relief from Christ and him only are to no purpose, will do you no good. Yea, if they are anything but supports of your heart in this expectation, or means appointed by himself for the receiving of help from him, they are in vain.

Now, farther to engage you to this expectation:

Consider his mercifulness, tenderness, and kindness, as he is our great High Priest at the right hand of God. Assuredly he pities you in your distress; says he, "As one whom his mother comforts, so will I comfort you" (Isa. 66:13). He has the tenderness of a mother to a sucking child. "Wherefore in all things it behooved him to be made like unto his brethren, that he might be a merciful and faithful high priest in things pertaining to God, to make reconciliation for the sins of the people. For in that he himself has suffered being tempted, he is able to succor them that are tempted" (Heb. 2:17-18). How is the ability of Christ upon the account of his suffering proposed to us? "In that he himself has suffered being tempted, he is able." Did the sufferings and temptations of Christ add to his ability and power? Not, doubtless, considered absolutely and in it itself. But the ability here mentioned is such as has readiness, proneness, willingness to put itself forth, accompanying of it; it is an ability of will against all dissuasions. He is able, having suffered and been tempted, to break through all dissuasions to the contrary, to relieve poor tempted souls: *dunatai boēthēsai*—"He is able to help." It is a metonymy of the effect, for he can now be moved to help, having been so tempted. So Hebrews 4:15-16: "For we have not an high priest which cannot be touched with the feeling of our infirmities; but was in all points tempted like as we are, yet without sin. Let us therefore come boldly unto the throne of grace, that we may obtain mercy, and find grace to help in time of need." The exhortation of verse 16 is the same that I am upon—namely, that we would entertain expectations of relief from Christ, which the apostle there calls *charin eis eukairon boētheian,* "grace for seasonable help." "If ever," says the soul, "help were seasonable, it would be

[4] gained, obtained

so to me in my present condition. This is that which I long for—grace for seasonable help. I am ready to die, to perish, to be lost forever; iniquity will prevail against me, if help come not in." Says the apostle, "Expect this help, this relief, this grace from Christ." Yea, but on what account? That which he lays down (v. 15). And we may observe that the word which we have translated to "obtain" is *labōmen. Hina labōmen eleon,* "That we may receive it" (v. 16); suitable and seasonable help will come in. I shall freely say, this one thing of establishing the soul by faith in expectation of relief from Jesus Christ, on the account of his mercifulness as our high priest, will be more available to the ruin of your lust and distemper, and have a better and speedier issue, than all the rigidest means of self-maceration that ever any of the sons of men engaged themselves unto. Yea, let me add that never any soul did or shall perish by the power of any lust, sin, or corruption, who could raise his soul by faith to an expectation of relief from Jesus Christ.

Consider his faithfulness who has promised; which may raise you up and confirm you in this waiting in an expectation of relief. He has promised to relieve in such cases, and he will fulfill his word to the utmost. God tells us that his covenant with us is like the "ordinances" of heaven, the sun, moon, and stars, which have their certain courses (Jer. 31:36). Thence David said that he watched for relief from God "as one watched for the morning" [Ps. 130:6]—a thing that will certainly come in its appointed season. So will be your relief from Christ. It will come in its season, as the dew and rain upon the parched ground; for faithful is he who has promised. Particular promises to this purpose are innumerable; with some of them, that seem peculiarly to suit his condition, let the soul be always furnished.

Now, there are two eminent advantages which always attend this expectation of succor from Jesus Christ:

It engages him to a full and speedy assistance. Nothing does more engage the heart of a man to be useful and helpful to another than his expectation of help from him, if justly raised and countenanced by him who is to give the relief. Our Lord Jesus has raised our hearts, by his kindness, care, and promises, to this expectation; certainly our rising up unto it must needs be[5] a great engagement upon him to assist us accordingly. This the psalmist gives us as an approved maxim, "You, Lord, never forsake them that put their trust in you" [Ps. 9:10]. When the heart is once won to rest in God, to repose[6] himself on him, he will assuredly satisfy it. He will never be as water that

[5] is of necessity
[6] rest

fails; nor has he said at any time to the seed of Jacob, "Seek you my face in vain" [Isa. 45:19]. If Christ be chosen for the foundation of our supply, he will not fail us.

It engages the heart to attend diligently to all the ways and means whereby Christ is wont to communicate himself to the soul; and so takes in the real assistance of all graces and ordinances whatsoever. He that expects anything from a man, applies himself to the ways and means whereby it may be obtained. The beggar that expects an alms lies at his door or in his way from whom he does expect it. The way whereby and the means wherein Christ communicates himself is, and are, his ordinances ordinarily; he that expects anything from him must attend upon him therein. It is the expectation of faith that sets the heart on work. It is not an idle, groundless hope that I speak of. If now there be any vigor, efficacy, and power in prayer or sacrament to this end of mortifying sin, a man will assuredly be interested in it all by this expectation of relief from Christ. On this account I reduce all particular actings, by prayer, meditation, and the like, to this head; and so shall not farther insist on them, when they are grounded on this bottom and spring from this root. They are of singular use to this purpose, and not [anything] else.

Now, on this direction for the mortification of a prevailing distemper you may have a thousand *probatum est*'s.[7] Who have walked with God under this temptation, and have not found the use and success of it? I dare leave the soul under it, without adding any more. Only some particulars relating thereunto may be mentioned—

First, *act faith peculiarly upon the death, blood, and cross of Christ; that is, on Christ as crucified and slain.* Mortification of sin is peculiarly from the death of Christ. It is one peculiar, yea, eminent end of the death of Christ, which shall assuredly be accomplished by it. He died to destroy the works of the devil [1 John 3:8]. Whatever came upon our natures by his first temptation, whatever receives strength in our persons by his daily suggestions, Christ died to destroy it all. "He gave himself for us, that he might redeem us from all iniquity, and purify unto himself a peculiar people, zealous of good works" (Titus 2:14). This was his aim and intention (wherein he will not fall) in his giving himself for us. That we might be freed from the power of our sins, and purified from all our defiling lusts, was his design. "He gave himself for the church, that he might sanctify and cleanse it; that he might present it to himself a glorious church, not having spot, or wrinkle, or any such thing; but that it should be holy, and without blemish" (Eph. 5:25-27). And this,

[7] *probatum est* means "it is proved"

by virtue of his death, in various and several degrees, shall be accomplished. Hence our washing, purging, and cleansing is everywhere ascribed to his blood (1 John 1:7; Heb. 1:3; Rev. 1:5). That being sprinkled on us "purges our consciences from dead works to serve the living God" (Heb. 9:14). This is that we aim at, this we are in pursuit of—that our consciences may be purged from dead works, that they may be rooted out, destroyed, and have place in us no more. This shall certainly be brought about by the death of Christ; there will virtue go out from thence to this purpose. Indeed, all supplies of the Spirit, all communications of grace and power, are from hence (as I have elsewhere showed[8]). Thus the apostle states it; Romans 6:2 is the case proposed that we have in hand: "How shall we, that are dead to sin, live any longer therein?"—"Dead to sin by profession; dead to sin by obligation to be so; dead to sin by participation of virtue and power for the killing of it; dead to sin by union and interest in Christ, in and by whom it is killed: how shall we live therein?" This he presses by sundry considerations, all taken from the death of Christ, in the ensuing verses. This must not be: "Know you not, that so many of us as were baptized into Jesus Christ were baptized into his death?" (v. 3). We have in baptism an evidence of our implantation into Christ; we are baptized into him. But what of him are we baptized into an interest in? "His death," says he. If indeed we are baptized into Christ, and beyond outward profession, we are baptized into his death. The explication of this, of one being baptized into the death of Christ, the apostle gives us: "Therefore we are buried with him by baptism into death; that like as Christ was raised up from the dead by the glory of the Father, even so we also should walk in newness of life. Knowing this, that our old man is crucified with him, that the body of sin might be destroyed, that henceforth we should not serve sin" (vv. 4, 6). "This is," says he, "our being baptized into the death of Christ, namely, our conformity thereunto; to be dead unto sin, to have our corruptions mortified, as he was put to death for sin: so that as he was raised up to glory, we may be raised up to grace and newness of life." He tells us whence it is that we have this baptism into the death of Christ (v. 6); and this is from the death of Christ itself: "Our old man is crucified with him, that the body of sin might be destroyed"; *sunestaurōthe,* "is crucified with him," not in respect of time, but causality. We are crucified with him *meritoriously,* in that he procured the Spirit for us to mortify sin; *efficiently,* in that from his death virtue comes forth for our crucifying; in the way of a *representation* and *exemplar* we shall assuredly be crucified unto sin, as he was for our sin.

[8] See John Owen, *Communion with God,* chapters 7–8, in *Works,* 2.

This is that [which] the apostle intends: Christ by his death destroying the works of the devil, procuring the Spirit for us, has so killed sin as to its reign in believers, that it shall not obtain its end and dominion.

Secondly, *then act faith on the death of Christ,* and that under these two notions—first, in *expectation of power;* secondly, in *endeavors for conformity.* For the first, the direction given in general may suffice; as to the latter, that of the apostle may give us some light into our direction (Gal. 3:1). Let faith look on Christ in the gospel as he is set forth dying and crucified for us. Look on him under the weight of our sins, praying, bleeding, dying; bring him in that condition into your heart by faith; apply his blood so shed to your corruptions. Do this daily. I might draw out this consideration to a great length, in sundry particulars, but I must come to a close.

I have only, then, to add the heads of the work of the Spirit in this business of mortification, which is so *peculiarly* ascribed to him. In one word: *this whole work, which I have described as our duty, is effected, carried on, and accomplished by the power of the Spirit, in all the parts and degrees of it;* as—

He alone clearly and fully convinces the heart of the evil and guilt and danger of the corruption, lust, or sin to be mortified. Without this conviction, or while it is so faint that the heart can wrestle with it or digest it, there will be no thorough work made. An unbelieving heart (as in part we have all such) will shift with any consideration, until it be overpowered by clear and evident convictions. Now this is the proper work of the Spirit: "He convinces of sin" (John 16:8); he alone can do it. If men's rational considerations, with the preaching of the letter, were able to convince them of sin, we should, it may be, see more convictions than we do. There comes by the preaching of the word an apprehension upon the understandings of men that they are sinners, that such and such things are sins, that themselves are guilty of them; but this light is not powerful, nor does it lay hold on the practical principles of the soul, so as to conform the mind and will unto them, to produce effects suitable to such an apprehension. And therefore it is that wise and knowing men, destitute of the Spirit, do not think those things to be sins at all wherein the chief movings and actings of lust do consist. It is the Spirit alone that can do, that does, this work to the purpose. And this is the first thing that the Spirit does in order to the mortification of any lust whatsoever—it convinces the soul of all the evil of it, cuts off all its pleas, discovers all its deceits, stops all its evasions, answers its pretenses, makes the soul own its abomination and lie down under the sense of it. Unless this be done all that follows is in vain.

The Spirit alone reveals unto us the fullness of Christ for our relief;

which is the consideration that stays the heart from false ways and from despairing despondency (Col. 2:8).[9]

The Spirit alone establishes the heart in expectation of relief from Christ; which is the great sovereign means of mortification, as has been discovered (2 Cor. 1:21).

The Spirit alone brings the cross of Christ into our hearts with its sin-killing power; for by the Spirit are we baptized into the death of Christ [Rom. 6:3; 1 Cor. 12:13].

The Spirit is the author and finisher of our sanctification; gives new supplies and influences of grace for holiness and sanctification, when the contrary principle is weakened and abated[10] (Eph. 3:16-18).

In all the soul's addresses to God in this condition, it has support from the Spirit. Whence is the power, life, and vigor of prayer? Whence its efficacy to prevail with God? Is it not from the Spirit? He is the "Spirit of supplications" promised to them "who look on him whom they have pierced" (Zech. 12:10), enabling them "to pray with sighs and groans that cannot be uttered" (Rom. 8:26). This is confessed to be the great medium or way of faith's prevailing with God. Thus Paul dealt with his temptation, whatever it was: "I besought the Lord that it might depart from me" [2 Cor. 12:8]. What is the work of the Spirit in prayer, whence and how it gives us in assistance and makes us to prevail, what we are to do that we may enjoy his help for that purpose, is not my present intention to demonstrate.

[9] This reference is mistakenly given as 1 Corinthians 2:8 in the original and in the Goold edition.
[10] reduced, diminished

Overview of John Owen's

Of Temptation: The Nature and Power of It

Justin Taylor

John Owen begins this work by citing Christ's instructions to his disciples: "Watch and pray, that you enter not into temptation" (Matt. 26:41). Three elements within this verse constitute the main themes of this work: (1) the evil cautioned against (*temptation*); (2) the means of its prevalency (*by our entering into it*); and (3) the way of preventing it (*watch and pray*).[1]

In Part 1 Owen looks at the nature of temptation itself (chapter 1). In general, temptation is a neutral term that signifies testing something. The special nature of temptation, on the other hand, denotes evil, whether passively (when we are afflicted) or actively (when we enter into temptation). Owen goes on to suggest the reasons and the means for God's tempting, as well as the way in which Satan tempts. His working definition of temptation is "any thing, state, way, or condition that, upon any account whatsoever, has a force or efficacy to seduce, to draw the mind and heart of a man from its obedience, which God requires of him, into any sin, in any degree of it whatsoever."

Part 2 (chapter 2) addresses the danger of entering temptation. He explains what "entering temptation" is and is not. It is neither being tempted nor being conquered by temptation, but rather falling into and being entangled by the snares of temptation. He explains what must happen in order for us to enter this state and how we might know why temptation is "at its hour."

All of this is preparation for Owen to advance his thesis in Part 3 (chap-

[1] Our section divisions don't correspond to this exactly because Owen's actual text is not quite this neat. William Goold, editor of the nineteenth-century editions of Owen's *Works,* wrote: "Slight defects in the arrangement, the renewed discussion of a point after it has been quitted, and the disproportionate space accorded to some parts of the subject, are explained, perhaps, by the circumstances that the treatise was originally a series of discourses" (*Works,* 6:88). A detailed outline of *Of Temptation: The Nature and Power of It* is found at the end of this volume.

ter 3), namely, that "it is the great duty of all believers to use all diligence in the ways of Christ's appointment, that they fall not into temptation." He offers a number of general considerations to demonstrate this thesis, then entertains a series of objections and questions. Part 4 (chapters 4–9) then looks at particular cases arising from this proposed truth. He explains how one knows whether or not he has entered into temptation (chapter 4), how to preserve one's soul from entering into temptation (chapter 5), how to be aware of the seasons wherein people usually enter into temptation (chapter 6), how to watch the heart itself (chapter 7), and how to keep Christ's word about patience. He then closes with some further exhortations related to the duty of believers to watch.

OF

Temptation,

The nature and Povver of it.
The Danger of entring into it.

AND

The meanes of preventing that danger.

WITH

A Resolution of sundry cases there-unto belonging,

By
JOHN OWEN. D.D.

Because thou hast kept the word of my patience, I will also keep thee from the hour of Temptation, which shall come upon all the world, to try them that dwell upon the earth. *Revel.* 3. 10.

OXFORD.
Printed by H. HALL, Printer to the University, for T. ROBINSON. 1658.

Preface

Christian Reader,

If you are in any measure awake in these days wherein we live, and have taken notice of the manifold, great, and various temptations wherewith all sorts of persons that know the Lord and profess his name are beset, and whereunto they are continually exposed, with what success those temptations have obtained, to the unspeakable scandal of the gospel, with the wounding and ruin of innumerable souls, I suppose you will not inquire any further after other reasons of the publishing of the ensuing warnings and directions, being suited to the times that pass over us, and your own concern in them. This I shall only say to those who think [it is] meet[1] to persist in any such inquiry, that though my first engagement for the exposing of these meditations unto public view did arise from the desires of some, whose avouching[2] the interest[3] of Christ in the world by personal holiness and constant adhering to everything that is made precious by its relation to him, have given them power over me to require at any time services of greater importance; yet I dare not lay my doing of it so upon that account, as in the least to intimate that, with respect to the general state of things mentioned, I did not myself esteem it seasonable and necessary. The variety of outward providences and dispensations[4] wherewith I have myself been exercised in this world, with the inward trials they have been attended with, added to the observation that I have had advantages to make of the ways and walkings of others—their beginnings, progresses, and endings, their risings and falls, in profession[5] and conversation, in darkness and light—have left such a constant sense and impression of the power and danger of temptations upon my mind and spirit, that, without other pleas and pretenses, I cannot but own[6] a serious call unto men to beware, with a discovery of some of the most eminent ways and means of

[1] fitting, appropriate
[2] affirming, confessing
[3] share or stake
[4] provisions, orderings
[5] confession
[6] admit, acknowledge, confess to be true

the prevalence of present temptations, to have been, in my own judgment, in this season needful.

But now, reader, if you are among them who takes no notice of these things or cares not for them—who has no sense of the efficacy and dangers of temptations in your own walking and profession, nor has observed the power of them upon others—who discerns not the manifold advantages that they have got in these days, wherein all things are shaken, nor has been troubled or moved by the sad successes they have had among professors;[7] but supposes that all things are well within doors and without, and would be better, could you obtain fuller satisfaction to some of your lusts in the pleasures or profits of the world—I desire you to know that I write not for you, nor do [I] esteem you a fit reader or judge of what is here written. While all the issues[8] of providential dispensations, in reference to the public concerns of these nations, are perplexed and entangled, the footsteps of God lying in the deep, where his paths are not known; while, in particular, unparalleled distresses and strange prosperities are measured out to men, yea, to professors; while a spirit of error, giddiness, and delusion goes forth with such strength and efficacy, as it seems to have received a commission[9] to go and prosper; while there are such divisions, strifes, emulations,[10] attended with such evil surmises, wrath, and revenge, found among brethren; while the desperate issues and products of men's temptations are seen daily in partial and total apostasy, in the decay of love, the overthrow of faith, our days being filled with fearful examples of backsliding, such as former ages never knew; while there is a visible declension[11] from reformation seizing upon the professing party of these nations, both as to personal holiness and zeal for the interest of Christ—he that understands not that there is an "hour of temptation" come upon the world to "try them that dwell upon the earth" [Rev 3:10], is doubtless either himself at present captivated under the power of some woeful lust, corruption, or temptation, or is indeed stark blind and knows not at all what it is to serve God in temptations. With such, then, I have not at present to do. For those who have in general a sense of these things—who also, in some measure, are able to consider that the plague is begun, that they may be further awakened to look about them, lest the infection have

---

[7] those who make a religious confession; professing Christians
[8] results
[9] an authority
[10] jealousies, especially of power and position
[11] moral decline

approached nearer to them, by some secret and imperceptible ways, than they did apprehend; or lest they should be surprised at unawares hereafter by any of those temptations that in these days either waste at noon or else walk in darkness [Ps. 91:6]—is the ensuing warning intended. And for the sake of them that mourn in secret for all the abominations that are found among and upon them that profess the gospel, and who are under the conduct of the Captain of their salvation [Heb 2:10], fighting and resisting the power of temptations, from whatsoever spring they rise in themselves, are the ensuing directions proposed to consideration.

That our faithful and merciful High Priest, who both suffered and was tempted, and is on that account touched with the feeling of our infirmities [Heb 2:17-18], would accompany this small discourse with seasonable supplies of his Spirit and suitable mercy to them that shall consider it, that it may be useful to his servants for the ends whereunto it is designed, is the prayer of him who received this handful of seed from his storehouse and treasure.

—John Owen

PART 1:

The Nature of Temptation

[Chapter 1]

Foundational Text on Temptation: Matthew 26:41

"Watch and pray, that you enter not into temptation" (Matt. 26:41). These words of our Savior are repeated with very little alteration in three evangelists; only, whereas Matthew and Mark have recorded them as above written, Luke reports them thus: "Rise and pray, lest you enter into temptation" [Luke 22:46]; so that the whole of his caution seems to have been, "Arise, watch and pray, that you enter not into temptation."

Solomon tells us of some that "lie down on the top of a mast in the midst of the sea" (Prov. 23:34)—men overborne by security in the mouth of destruction. If ever poor souls lay down on the top of a mast in the midst of the sea, these disciples with our Savior in the garden did so. Their Master, at a little distance from them, was "offering up prayers and supplications, with strong crying and tears" (Heb. 5:7), being then taking into his hand and beginning to taste that cup that was filled with the curse and wrath due to their sins—the Jews, armed for *his* and *their* destruction, being but a little more distant from them, on the other hand. Our Savior had a little before informed them that that night he should be betrayed, and be delivered up to be slain; they saw that he was "sorrowful, and very heavy" (Matt. 26:37); nay, he told them plainly that his "soul was exceeding sorrowful, even unto death" (v. 38), and therefore entreated them to tarry and watch with him, now he was dying, and that for them. In this condition, leaving them but a little space, like men forsaken of all love toward him or care of themselves, they fall fast asleep! Even the best of saints, being left to themselves, will quickly appear to be less than men—to be nothing. All our own strength is weakness, and all our wisdom folly. Peter being one of them—who but a little before had with so much self-confidence affirmed that though all men forsook him, yet he never would so do [v. 35]—our Savior expostulates[1] the matter in particular with him: "He says unto Peter, Could you not watch with me one hour?" (v. 40) as if he should have said, "Are you he, Peter, who but now boasts of your resolution never to forsake me? Is it likely that you should hold out therein, when you cannot watch with me one hour? Is this your dying for me, to be dead in security, when I am dying for you?" And indeed it would be an amazing thing to consider that Peter should make so

[1] discusses earnestly

high a promise, and be immediately so careless and remiss in the pursuit of it, but that we find the root of the same treachery abiding and working in our own hearts, and do see the fruit of it brought forth every day, the most noble engagements unto obedience quickly ending in deplorable negligence (Rom. 7:18).

In this estate our Savior admonishes them of their condition, their weakness, their danger, and stirs them up to a prevention of that ruin which lay at the door. Says he, "Arise, watch and pray."

I shall not insist on the particular aimed at here by our Savior, in this caution to them that were then present with him; the great temptation that was coming on them, from the scandal of the cross, was doubtless in his eye—but I shall consider the words as containing a general direction to all the disciples of Christ, in their following of him throughout all generations.

There are three things in the words: (1) The *evil* cautioned against—*temptation;* (2) the *means* of its prevalency—by our *entering into* it; (3) the *way* of preventing it—*watch and pray.*

It is not in my thoughts to handle the common-place of temptations, but only the danger of them in general, with the means of preventing that danger; yet, that we may know what we affirm and whereof we speak, some concerns of the general nature of temptation may be premised.

The General Nature of Temptation

First, for the general nature of tempting and temptation, it lies among things indifferent; to try, to experiment, to prove, to pierce a vessel, that the liquor that is in it may be known, is as much as is signified by it. Hence God is said sometimes to tempt; and we are commanded as our duty to tempt, or try, or search ourselves, to know what is in us, and to pray that God would do so also. So temptation is like a knife, that may either cut the meat or the throat of a man; it may be his food or his poison, his exercise or his destruction.

The Special Nature of Temptation

Secondly, temptation in its special nature, as it denotes any evil, is considered either *actively,* as it leads to evil, or *passively,* as it has an evil and suffering in it: so temptation is taken for affliction (James 1:2); for in that sense, we are to "count it all joy when we fall into temptation"; in the other, that we "enter not into it."

Again, actively considered, it either denotes in the tempter a design for the bringing about of the special end of temptation, namely, *a leading into evil;* so it is said that "God tempts no man" (James 1:13), with a design for sin as such—or the general nature and end of temptation, which is *trial;* so "God tempted Abraham" (Gen. 22:1). And he proves or tempts by false prophets (Deut. 13:3).

Now, as to God's tempting of any, two things are to be considered: (1) The *end* why he does it; (2) The *way* whereby he does it.

The End for Which God Tempts

For the first, his general ends are two:

He does it to show unto man what is in him—that is, the man himself; and that either as to his *grace* or to his *corruption* (I speak not now of it as it may have a place and bear a part in judiciary obduration[2]). Grace and corruption lie deep in the heart; men oftentimes deceive themselves in the search after the one or the other of them. When we give vent to the soul, to try what grace is there, corruption comes out; and when we search for corruption, grace appears. So is the soul kept in uncertainty; we fail in our trials. God comes with a gauge that goes to the bottom.[3] He sends his instruments of trial into the bowels and the inmost parts of the soul, and lets man see what is in him, of what metal he is constituted. Thus he tempted Abraham to show him his *faith*. Abraham knew not what faith he had (I mean, what power and vigor was in his faith) until God drew it out by that great trial and temptation. When God says he knew it [Gen. 22:12], he made Abraham to know it. So he tried Hezekiah to discover his *pride* [cf. 2 Chron. 32:25-31ff.]. God left him that he might see what was in his heart, so apt to be lifted up, as he appeared to have, until God tried him, and so let out his filth and poured it out before his face. The issues[4] of such discoveries to the saints, in thankfulness, humiliation, and treasuring up of experiences, I shall not treat of.

God does it to show himself unto man, and that—

In a way of preventing grace.[5] A man shall see that it is God alone who keeps from all sin. Until we are tempted, we think we live on our own strength. Though all men do this or that, we will not [cf. Matt. 26:35]. When the trial comes, we quickly see whence is our preservation, by standing or falling. So was it in the case of Abimelech: "I withheld you" (Gen. 20:6).

In a way of renewing grace. He would have the temptation continue with

---

[2] hardening

[3] basis, foundation

[4] results, outcomes

[5] a special grace that, preceding human willing, protects against further sinning

St. Paul, that he might reveal himself to him in the sufficiency of his renewing grace (2 Cor. 12:9). We know not the power and strength that God puts forth in our behalf, nor what is the sufficiency of his grace, until, comparing the temptation with our own weakness, it appears unto us. The efficacy of an antidote is found when poison has been taken; and the preciousness of medicines is made known by diseases. We shall never know what strength there is in grace if we know not what strength there is in temptation. We must be tried, that we may be made sensible of being preserved. And many other good and gracious ends he has, which he accomplishes toward his saints by his trials and temptations, not now to be insisted on.

The Way God Tempts

For the ways whereby God accomplishes his search, trial, or temptation, these are some of them:

He puts men on great duties, such as they cannot apprehend that they have any strength for, nor indeed have. So he tempted Abraham by calling him to that duty of sacrificing his son—a thing absurd to reason, bitter to nature, and grievous to him on all accounts whatsoever. Many men know not what is in them, or rather what is ready for them, until they are put upon what seems utterly above their strength, indeed, upon what is really above their strength. The duties that God, in an ordinary way, requires at our hands are not proportioned to what strength we have in ourselves, but to what help and relief is laid up for us in Christ; and we are to address ourselves to the greatest performances with a settled persuasion that we have not ability for the least. This is the law of grace; but yet, when any duty is required that is extraordinary, that is a secret not often discovered. In the yoke of Christ it is a trial, a temptation.

By putting them upon great sufferings. How many have unexpectedly found strength to die at a stake, to endure tortures for Christ! Yet their call to it was a trial. This, Peter tells us, is one way whereby we are brought into trying temptations (1 Pet. 1:6-7). Our temptations arise from the "fiery trial," and yet the end is but a trial of our faith.

By his providential disposing of things so as that occasions unto sin will be administered unto men, which is the case mentioned (Deut. 13:3); and innumerable other instances may be adjoined.

Now, they are not properly the temptations of God, as coming from him, with his end upon them, that are here intended; and therefore I shall set these apart from our present consideration. It is, then, temptation in its special nature, as it denotes an *active efficiency toward sinning* (as it is managed with evil unto evil) that I intend.

The Way Satan Tempts

In this sense temptation may proceed either singly from Satan, or the world, or other men in the world, or from ourselves, or jointly from all or some of them, in their several combinations:

Satan tempts sometimes singly by himself, without taking advantage from the world, the things or persons of it, or ourselves. So he deals in his injection of evil and blasphemous thoughts of God into the hearts of the saints; which is his own work alone, without any advantage from the world or our own hearts: for nature will contribute nothing thereunto, nor anything that is in the world, nor any man of the world; for none can conceive a God and conceive evil of him. Herein Satan is alone in the *sin,* and shall be so in the *punishment.* These fiery darts are prepared in the forge of his own malice, and shall, with all their venom and poison, be turned into his own heart forever.

Sometimes he makes use of the world, and joins forces against us, without any helps from within. So he tempted our Savior, by "showing him all the kingdoms of the world, and the glory of them" [Matt. 4:8]. And the variety of the assistances he finds from the world, in persons and things which I must not insist on—the innumerable instruments and weapons he takes from thence of all sorts and at all seasons—are inexpressible.

Sometimes he takes in assistance from ourselves also. It is not with us as it was with Christ when Satan came to tempt him. He declares that he "had nothing in him" (John 14:30). It is otherwise with us: he has, for the compassing[6] of most of his ends, a sure party[7] within our own breasts (James 1:14-15). Thus he tempted Judas: he was at work himself; he put it into his heart to betray Christ (Luke 22:3), "he entered into him" for that purpose (Luke 22:3). And he sets the world at work, the things of it, providing for him "thirty pieces of silver" (v. 5: "They covenanted to give him money"); and the men of it, even the priests and the Pharisees; and calls in the assistance of his own corruption—he was covetous, "a thief, and had the bag" [John 12:6].

I might also show how the world and our own corruptions do act singly by themselves, and jointly in conjunction with Satan and one another, in this business of temptation. But the truth is, the principles, ways, and means

[6] attaining, achieving
[7] participant

of temptations, the kinds, degrees, efficacy, and causes of them, are so inexpressibly large and various—the circumstances of them, from providence, natures, conditions, spiritual and natural, with the particular cases thence arising, so innumerable and impossible to be comprised within any bound or order—that to attempt the giving an account of them would be to undertake that which would be endless. I shall content myself to give a description of the general nature of that which we are to watch against; which will make way for what I aim at.

The Definitions of Temptation

Temptation, then, in *general,* is any thing, state, way, or condition that, upon any account whatsoever, has a force or efficacy to seduce, to draw the mind and heart of a man from its obedience, which God requires of him, into any sin, in any degree of it whatsoever.

In *particular,* that is a temptation to any man which causes or occasions him to sin, or in anything to go off from his duty, either by bringing evil into his heart, or drawing out that evil that is in his heart, or any other way diverting him from communion with God and that constant, equal, universal obedience, in matter and manner, that is required of him.

For the clearing of this description I shall only observe, that though temptation seems to be of a more *active* importance, and so to denote only the power of seduction to sin itself, yet in the Scripture it is commonly taken in a *neuter* sense, and denotes the matter of the temptation or the thing whereby we are tempted. And this is a ground of the description I have given of it. Be it what it will, that from anything whatsoever, within us or without us, has advantage to hinder in duty, or to provoke unto or in any way to occasion sin—that is a temptation, and so to be looked on. Be it business, employment, course of life, company, affections, nature, or corrupt design, relations, delights, name, reputation, esteem, abilities, parts or excellencies of body or mind, place, dignity, art—so far as they further or occasion the promotion of the ends before mentioned, they are all of them no less truly temptations that the most violent solicitations of Satan or allurements of the world, and that soul lies at the brink of ruin who discerns it not. And this will be further discovered in our process.

PART 2:

THE DANGER OF ENTERING TEMPTATION

[Chapter 2]

What "Entering Temptation" Is and Is Not

Having showed what temptation is, I come, secondly, to manifest what it is to *enter* into temptation.

It Is Not Merely to Be Tempted

This [i.e., entering into temptation] is not merely to *be tempted.* It is impossible that we should be so freed from temptation as not to be at all tempted. While Satan continues in his power and malice, while the world and lust are in being, we shall be tempted. "Christ," says one, "was made like unto us, that he might be tempted; and we are tempted that we may be made like unto Christ." Temptation in general is comprehensive of our whole warfare; as our Savior calls the time of his ministry the time of his "temptations" (Luke 22:28). We have no promise that we shall not be tempted at all; nor are to pray for an absolute freedom from temptations, because we have no such promise of being heard therein. The direction we have for our prayers is, "Lead us not into temptation" (Matt. 6:13); it is "entering into temptation" that we are to pray against. We may be tempted, yet not enter into temptation. So that—

It Is More Than the Ordinary Work of Satan and Our Own Lusts

Something more is intended by this expression than the *ordinary work* of Satan and our own lusts, which will be sure to tempt us every day. There is something signal[1] in this entering into temptation, that is not the saints' every day's work. It is something that befalls them peculiarly[2] in reference to seduction unto sin, on one account or other, by the way of allurement or affrightment.

It Is Not Merely to Be Conquered by a Temptation or to Commit Sin

It is not to be conquered by a temptation, to fall down under it, to commit the sin or evil that we are tempted to, or to omit the duties that are opposed. A man may "enter into temptation" and yet not fall under temptation. God can make a way for a man to escape, when he is in; he can break the snare,

[1] significant, remarkable, out of the ordinary
[2] particularly, characteristically

tread down Satan, and make the soul more than a conqueror, though it have entered into temptation. Christ *entered* into it, but was not in the least *foiled* by it. But—

It Is to "Fall Into Temptation" and Be Entangled in It

It is, as the apostle expresses it, "to fall into temptation" (1 Tim. 6:9), as a man falls into a pit or deep place where [there] are gins[3] or snares, wherewith he is entangled; the man is not presently killed and destroyed, but he is entangled and detained—he knows not how to get free or be at liberty. So it is expressed again to the same purpose, "No temptation has taken you" (1 Cor. 10:13); that is, to be taken by a temptation and to be tangled with it, held in its cords, not finding at present a way to escape. Thence says Peter, "The Lord knows how to deliver the godly out of temptations" (2 Pet. 2:9). They are entangled with them; God knows how to deliver them out of them. When we suffer[4] a temptation to enter into us, then we "enter into temptation." While it knocks at the door we are at liberty; but when any temptation comes in and parleys[5] with the heart, reasons with the mind, entices and allures the affections, be it a long or a short time, do it thus insensibly and imperceptibly, or do the soul take notice of it, we "enter into temptation."

Conditions for Entering Temptation

So, then, unto our entering into temptation is required—

Satan Must Be More Earnest Than Usual in His Solicitations to Sin

That by some *advantage,* or on some occasion, Satan be more earnest than ordinary in his solicitations to sin, by affrightments or allurements, by persecutions or seductions, by himself or others; or that some lust or corruption, by his instigation and advantages of outward objects, provoking, as in prosperity, or terrifying, as in trouble, do tumultuate[6] more than ordinary within us. There is a special acting of the author and principles of temptation required thereunto.

[3] traps
[4] allow, permit
[5] discusses (especially with an enemy)
[6] agitate, disturb, stir up

The Hearer Can Argue His Defense But Not Expel the Sin

That the hearer be so far entangled with it as to be put to *dispute* and argue in its own defense, and yet not be wholly able to eject or cast out the poison and leaven that has been injected; but is surprised, if it be never so little off its watch, into an entanglement not easy to be avoided: so that the soul may cry, and pray, and cry again, and yet not be delivered; as Paul "besought the Lord" thrice for the departure of his temptation, and prevailed not [2 Cor. 12:7-9]. The entanglement continues. And this usually falls out in one of these two seasons:

When Satan, by the permission of God, for ends best known to himself, has got some *peculiar* advantage against the soul; as in the case of Peter—he sought to winnow[7] him [Luke 22:31-32], and prevailed.

When a man's lusts and corruptions meet with peculiarly provoking *objects* and occasions, through the condition of life that a man is in, with the circumstances of it; as it was with David: of both which afterward.

In this state of things, a man is entered into temptation; and this is called the "hour of temptation" (Rev. 3:10)—the season wherein it grows to a head[8]: the discovery whereof will give further light into the present inquiry, about what it is to "enter into temptation"; for when the hour of temptation is come upon us, we are entered into it. Every great and pressing temptation has its hour, a season wherein it grows to a head, wherein it is most vigorous, active, operative, and prevalent. It may be long in rising, it may be long urging, more or less; but it has a season wherein, from the conjunction of other occurrences, such as those mentioned, outward or inward, it has a dangerous hour; and then, for the most part, men enter into it. Hence that very temptation, which at one time has little or no power on a man—he can despise it, scorn the motions of it, easily resist it—at another, bears him away quite before it. It has, from other circumstances and occurrences, got new strength and efficacy, or the man is enervated[9] and weakened; the hour is come, he is entered into it, and it prevails. David probably had temptations before, in his younger days, to adultery or murder, as he had in the case of Nabal [1 Sam. 25:13]; but the hour of temptation was not come,[10] it had not got its advantages about it, and so he escaped until afterward. Let men look for it that are exposed unto temptations, as who is not? They will have

---

[7] separate as chaff from wheat
[8] ultimate outcome
[9] debilitated, deprived of strength
[10] had not yet come

a season wherein their solicitations will be more urgent, their reasonings more plausible, pretenses more glorious, hopes of recovery more appearing, opportunities more broad and open, the doors of evil made more beautiful than ever they have been. Blessed is he who is prepared for such a season; without which there is no escaping. This, as I said, is the first thing required to entering into temptation; if we stay here, we are safe.

How We Know When Temptation Is in Its Hour

Before I descend to other particulars, having now entered hereon, I shall show in general (1) How or by what means commonly any temptation attains its *hour;* (2) How we may know when any temptation is come to its high *noon,* and is in its hour.

How Temptation Generally Attains Its Hour

It does the first by several ways:

By long solicitations, causing the mind frequently to converse with the evil solicited unto, it begets extenuating[11] *thoughts of it.* If it makes this process, it is coming toward its hour. It may be when first it began to press upon the soul, the soul was amazed with the ugly appearance if what it aimed at, and cried, "Am I a dog?" If this indignation be not daily heightened, but the soul, by conversing with the evil, begins to grow, as it were, familiar with it, not to be startled as formerly, but rather inclines to cry, "Is it not a little one?" then the temptation is coming toward its high noon; lust has then enticed and entangled, and is ready to "conceive" (James 1:15): of which more at large afterward, in our inquiry how we may know whether we are entered into temptation or not.[12] Our present inquest[13] is after the hour and power of temptation itself.

When it has prevailed on others, and the soul is not filled with dislike and abhorrency of them and their ways, nor with pity and prayer for their deliverance. This proves an advantage unto it, and raises it toward its height. When that temptation sets upon any one which, at the same time, has possessed and prevailed with many, it has so great and so many advantages thereby, that it is surely growing toward its hour. Its prevailing with others is a means to give it its hour against us. The falling off of Hymeneus and Philetus is said to "overthrow the faith of some" (2 Tim. 2:17-18).

---

[11] making less serious
[12] see chapter 4.
[13] inquiry, investigation

By complicating itself with many considerations that, perhaps, are not absolutely evil. So did the temptation of the Galatians to fall from the purity of the gospel—freedom from persecution, union, and consent with the Jews. Things in themselves good were pleaded in it, and gave life to the temptation itself. But I shall not now insist on the several advantages that any temptation has to heighten and greaten itself, to make itself prevalent and effectual with the contribution that it receives to this purpose from various circumstances, opportunities, specious pleas and pretenses, necessities for the doing that which cannot be done without answering the temptation, and the like; because I must speak unto some of them afterward.

How We May Know When Temptation Has Attained Its High Noon

For the second, it may be known—

By its restless urgency and arguing. When a temptation is in its hour it is restless; it is the time of battle, and it gives the soul no rest. Satan sees his advantage, considers his conjunction of forces, and knows that he must now prevail, or be hopeless forever. Here are opportunities, here are advantages, here are specious pleas and pretenses; some ground is already got by former arguings; here are extenuations of the evil, hopes of pardon by after endeavors, all in a readiness: if he can do nothing now, he must sit down lost in his undertakings. So when he had got all things in a readiness against Christ, he made it the "hour of darkness." When a temptation discovers "*mille nocendi artes,*"[14] presses within doors by imaginations and reasonings, without by solicitations, advantages, and opportunities, let the soul know that the hour of it is come, and the glory of God, with its own welfare, depends on its behavior in this trial; as we shall see in the particular cases following.

When it makes a conjunction of affrightments and allurements, these two comprise the whole forces of temptation. When both are brought together, temptation is in its hour. They were both [present] in David's case as to the murder of Uriah [2 Samuel 11]. There was the *fear* of his revenge on his wife, and possibly on himself, and *fear* of the publication of his sin at least; and there was the *allurement* of his present enjoyment of her whom he lusted after. Men sometimes are carried into sin by love to it, and are continued in it by fear of what will ensue upon it. But in any case, where these two

[14] "a thousand arts of harming" (Virgil, *Aeneid* book 7)

meet, something allures us, something affrights us, and the reasonings that run between them are ready to entangle us—then is the hour of temptation.

This, then, it is to "enter into temptation," this is the "hour" of it; of which more in the process of our discourse.

Means of Preventing Temptation Prescribed by Our Savior

There is [a] means of prevention prescribed by our Savior; they are two: (1) "watch"; (2) "pray."

Watch

The first is a general expression by no means to be limited to its native signification of waking from sleep; to watch is as much as to be on our guard, to take heed, to consider all ways and means as to be on our guard, to take heed, to consider all ways and means whereby an enemy may approach to us: so the apostle (1 Cor. 16:13). This it is to "watch" in this business, to "stand fast in the faith" [1 Cor. 16:3] as good soldiers, to "quit[15] ourselves like men" [1 Sam. 4:9]. It is as much as to "take heed," or look to ourselves, as the same thing is by our Savior often expressed (so Rev. 3:2). A universal carefulness and diligence, exercising itself in and by all ways and means prescribed by God, over our hearts and ways, the baits and methods of Satan, the occasions and advantages of sin in the world, that we be not entangled, is that which in this word is pressed on us.

Pray

For the second direction, of prayer, I need not speak to it. The duty and its concerns are known to all. I shall only add that these two comprise the whole endeavor of faith for the soul's preservation from temptation.

[15] conduct

PART 3:

The Great Duty of All Believers

[Chapter 3]

The Great Duty of All Believers Is to Be Diligent Not to Fall into Temptation

Having thus opened the words in the foregoing chapters so far as is necessary to discover the foundation of the truth to be insisted on and improved, I shall lay it down in the ensuing observation:

It is the great duty of all believers
to use all diligence in the ways of Christ's appointment,
that they fall not into temptation.

I know God is "able to deliver the godly out of temptations" [2 Pet. 2:9]; I know he is "faithful not to suffer us to be tempted above what we are able, but will make a way for our escape" [1 Cor. 10:13]: yet I dare say I shall convince all those who will attend unto what is delivered and written, that *it is our great duty and concern to use all diligence, watchfulness, and care, that we enter not into temptation;* and I shall evince[1] it by the ensuing considerations.

Our Savior Instructs Us to Pray That We Not Enter into Temptation

In that compendious instruction given us by our Savior concerning what we ought to pray for, this of not entering into temptation is expressly one head. Our Savior knew of what concern it was to us not to "enter into temptation" when he gave us this as one special subject of our daily dealing with God (Matt. 6:13). And the order of the words shows us of what importance it is: "Lead us not into temptation, but deliver us from evil." If we are led into temptation, evil will befall us, more or less. How God may be said to tempt us, or to "lead us into temptation," I showed before. In this direction, it is not so much the *not giving us up to it* as the powerful *keeping us from it* that is intended. The last words are, as it were, exegetical or expository of the former: "Lead us not into temptation, but deliver us from evil"—"So deal with us that we may be powerfully delivered from that evil which attends our entering into temptation." Our blessed Savior knows full well our state and condition; he knows the power of temptations, having had experience of it (Heb. 2:18); he knows our vain confidence, and the reserves we have

[1] prove, provide evidence, make manifest

concerning our ability to deal with temptations, as he found it in Peter; but he knows our weakness and folly, and how soon we are cast to the ground, and therefore does he lay in this provision for instruction at the entrance of his ministry, to make us heedful, if possible, in that which is of so great concern to us. If, then, we will repose[2] any confidence in the wisdom, love, and care of Jesus Christ toward us, we must grant the truth pleaded for.

Christ Promises Freedom and Deliverance as a Reward for Obedience

Christ promises this freedom and deliverance as a great reward of most acceptable obedience (Rev. 3:10). This is the great promise made to the church of Philadelphia, wherein Christ found nothing that he would blame, "You shall be kept from the hour of temptation." Not, "You shall be preserved *in* it"; but he goes higher, "You shall be kept *from* it." "There is," says our Savior, "an hour of temptation coming; a season that will make havoc in the world: multitudes shall then fall from the faith, deny and blaspheme me. Oh, how few will be able to stand and hold out! Some will be utterly destroyed, and perish forever. Some will get wounds to their souls that shall never be well healed while they live in this world, and have their bones broken, so as to go halting all their days. But," says he, "'because you have kept the word of my patience,' I will be tender toward you, and 'keep you from this hour of temptation.'" Certainly that which Christ thus promises to his beloved church, as a reward of her service, love, and obedience, is not [a] light thing. Whatsoever Christ promises to his spouse is a fruit of unspeakable love; that is so in a special manner which is promised as a reward of special obedience.

The General Issues of Entering into Temptation

Let us to this purpose consider the general issues of men's entering into temptation, and that of bad and good men, of ungrounded professors,[3] and of the choicest saints.

For the first I shall offer but one or two texts of Scripture. "They on the rock are they, which, when they hear, receive the word with joy, and have no root, but for a while believe" (Luke 8:13). Well! How long do they believe? They are affected with the preaching of the word, and believe thereon, make profession,[4] bring forth some fruits; but until when do they abide? Says he,

[2] place, entrust
[3] those who make a religious confession; professing Christians
[4] confession

"In the time of temptation they fall away" [Luke 8:13]. When once they enter into temptation they are gone forever. Temptation withers all their profession and slays their souls. We see this accomplished every day. Men who have attended on the preaching of the gospel, been affected and delighted with it, that have made profession of it, and have been looked on, it may be, as believers, and thus have continued for some years—no sooner does temptation befall them that has vigor and permanency in it, but they are turned out of the way and are gone forever. They fall to hate the word they have delighted in, despise the professors of it, and are hardened by sin. So Matthew 7:26: "He that hears these sayings of mine, and does that not, is like unto a foolish man, who built his house upon the sand." But what does this house of profession do? It shelters him, keeps him warm, and stands for a while. But says he, "When the rain descends, when temptation comes, it falls utterly, and its fall is great" (v. 27). Judas follows our Savior three years, and all goes well with him: he no sooner enters into temptation, Satan has got him and winnowed him, but he is gone [John 13:27]. Demas will preach the gospel until the love of the world befall him, and he is utterly turned aside [2 Tim. 4:10]. It were[5] endless to give instances of this. Entrance into temptation is, with this sort of men, an entrance into apostasy, more or less, in part or in whole; it fails not.

For the *saints* of God themselves, let us see, by some instances, what issue they have had of their entering into temptation. I shall name a few:

Adam was the "son of God" (Luke 3:38), created in the image of God, full of that integrity, righteousness, and holiness, which might be and was an eminent resemblance of the holiness of God. He had a far greater inherent stock of ability than we, and had nothing in him to entice or seduce him; yet this Adam no sooner enters into temptation but he is gone, lost, and ruined, he and all his posterity with him. What can we expect in the like condition, that have not only in our temptations, as he had, a *cunning devil* to deal with, but a *cursed world* and a *corrupt heart* also?

Abraham was the father of the faithful, whose faith is proposed as a pattern to all them that shall believe; yet he, entering twice into the same temptation, namely, that of fear about his wife, was twice overpowered by it, to the dishonor of God and no doubt the disquietment of his own soul (Gen. 12:13; 20:2).

David is called a "man after God's own heart" by God himself [1 Sam. 13:14]; yet what a dreadful thing is the story of his entering into tempta-

[5] i.e., it would be

tion! He is no sooner entangled, but he is plunged into adultery; then seeking deliverance by his own invention, like a poor creature in a toil, he is entangled more and more, until he lies as one dead, under the power of sin and folly.

I might mention Noah, Lot, Hezekiah, Peter, and the rest, whose temptations and falls therein are on record for our instruction. Certainly he that has any heart in these things cannot but say, as the inhabitants of Samaria upon the letter of Jehu, "'Behold, two kings stood not before him, how shall we stand?' [2 Kings 10:4]. O Lord, if such mighty pillars have been cast to the ground, such cedars blown down, how shall I stand before temptations? Oh, keep me that I enter not in!" "*Vestigia terrent.*"[6] Behold the footsteps of them that have gone in. Whom do you see retiring without a wound? A blemish at least? On this account would the apostle have us to exercise tenderness toward them that are fallen into sin: "Considering yourself, lest you also be tempted" (Gal. 6:1). He does not say, "Lest you also sin, or fall, or see the power of temptation in others, and know not how soon you may be tempted, nor what will be the state and condition of your soul thereupon." Assuredly, he that has seen so many better, stronger men than himself fail, and cast down in the trial, will think it incumbent[7] on him to remember the battle, and, if it be possible, to come there no more. Is it not a madness for a man that can scarce crawl up and down, he is so weak (which is the case of most of us), if he avoid not what he has seen giants foiled in the undertaking of? You are yet whole and sound; take heed of temptation, lest it be with you as it was with Abraham, David, Lot, Peter, Hezekiah, [and] the Galatians, who fell in the time of trial.

In nothing does the folly of the hearts of men show itself more openly, in the days wherein we live, than in this cursed boldness, after so many warnings from God, and so many sad experiences every day under their eyes, of running into and putting themselves upon temptations. Any society, any company, any conditions of outward advantages, without once weighing what their strength, or what the concern of their poor souls is, they are ready for. Though they go over the dead and the slain that in those ways and paths but even now fell down before them, yet they will go on without regard or trembling. At this door are gone out hundreds, thousands of professors, within a few years. But—

---

[6] "the footprints frighten me" (Horace, *Epistles* I.i.74)
[7] obligatory

Let Us Consider Ourselves

Let us consider ourselves—what our weakness is; and what temptation is—its power and efficacy, with what it leads unto.

For ourselves, we are weakness itself. We have no strength, no power to withstand. Confidence of any strength in us is one great part of our weakness; it was so in Peter. He that says he can do anything, can do nothing as he should. And, which is worse, it is the worst kind of weakness that is in us—a weakness from treachery—a weakness arising from that party which every temptation has in us. If a castle or fort be never so strong and well fortified, yet if there be a treacherous party within, that is ready to betray it on every opportunity, there is no preserving it from the enemy. There are traitors in our hearts, ready to take part, to close[8] and side with every temptation, and to give up all to them; yea, to solicit and bribe temptations to do the work, as traitors incite an enemy. Do not flatter yourselves that you should hold out; there are secret lusts that lie lurking in your hearts, which perhaps now stir not, which, as soon as any temptation befalls you, will rise, tumultuate, cry, disquiet, seduce, and never give over until they are either killed or satisfied. He that promises himself that the frame of his heart will be the same under a temptation as it is before will be woefully mistaken. "Am I a dog, that I should do this thing?" says Hazael [2 Kings 8:13]. Yea, you will be such a dog if ever you be king of Syria; temptation from your interest will unman you. He that now abhors the thoughts of such and such a thing, if he once enters into temptation will find his heart inflamed toward it, and all contrary reasonings overborne and silenced. He will deride his former fears, cast out his scruples, and contemn the consideration that he lived upon. Little did Peter think he should deny and forswear his Master so soon as ever he was questioned whether he knew him or no. It was no better when the hour of temptation came; all resolutions were forgotten, all love to Christ buried; the present temptation closing with his carnal fear carried all before it.

To handle this a little more distinctly, I shall consider the means of safety from the power of temptation, if we enter therein, that may be expected from ourselves; and that in general as to the spring and rise of them, and in particular as to the ways of exerting that strength we have, or seem to have:

In general, all we can look for is from our *hearts*. What a man's heart is, that is he; but now what is the heart of a man in such a season?

Suppose a man is not a believer, but only a *professor* of the gospel, what

[8] consummate, bring to a conclusion

can the heart of such a one do? "The heart of the wicked is little worth" (Prov. 10:20), and surely that which is little worth in anything is not much worth in this. A wicked man may in outward things be of great use; but come to his heart, that is false and a thing of naught. Now, withstanding of temptation is heartwork; and when it comes like a flood, can such a rotten trifle as a wicked man's heart stand before it? But of these [we have discussed] before. Entering into temptation and apostasy is the same with them.

Let it be whose heart it will, "He that trusts in his own heart is a fool" (Prov. 28:26), he that does so, be he what he will, in that he is foolish. Peter did so in his temptation; he trusted in his own heart: "Though all men forsake you, I will not" [Matt. 26:33]. It was his folly; but why was it his folly? He shall not be delivered; it will not preserve him in snares; it will not deliver him in temptations. The heart of a man will promise him very fair before a temptation comes. "Am I a dog," says Hazael, "that I should do this thing?" "Though all men should deny you," says Peter, "I will not. Shall I do this evil? It cannot be." All the arguments that are suited to give check to the heart in such a condition are mustered up. Did not Peter, think you, do so? "What! Deny my Master, the Son of God, my Redeemer, who loves me? Can such ingratitude, unbelief, rebellion, befall me? I will not do it." Shall, then, a man rest in it that his heart will be steadfast? Let the wise man answer: "He that trusts in his own heart is a fool." "The heart is deceitful" (Jer. 17:9). We would not willingly trust anything wherein there is any deceit or guile; here is that which is "deceitful above all things." It has a thousand shifts and treacheries that it will deal with; when it comes to the trial, every temptation will steal it away (Hos. 4:11). Generally men's hearts deceive them no oftener than they do trust in them, and then they never fail so to do.

Consider the particular ways and means that such a heart has or can use to safeguard itself in the hour of temptation, and their insufficiency to that purpose will quickly appear. I shall instance in some few only:

Love of honor in the world. Reputation and esteem in the church, obtained by former profession and walking, is one of the heart's own weapons to defend itself in the hour of temptation. "Shall such a one as I fly? I who have had such a reputation in the church of God, shall I now lose it by giving way to this lust, to this temptation? by closing with this or that public evil?" This consideration has such an influence on the spirits of some that they think it will be a shield and buckler[9] against any assaults that may befall them. They will die a thousand times before they will forfeit that repute they

[9] a small, handheld shield

have in the church of God! But, alas! this is but a withe,[10] or a new cord, to bind a giant temptation with. What think you of the "third part of the stars of heaven?" (Rev. 12:4). Had they not shone in the firmament of the church? Were they not sensible, more than enough, of their own honor, height, usefulness, and reputation? But when the dragon comes with his temptations, he casts them down to the earth. Yea, great temptations will make men, who have not a better defense, insensibly fortify themselves against that dishonor and disreputation that their ways are attended with. *"Populus [me] sibilat, at mihi plaudo."*[11] Do we not know instances yet living of some who have ventured on compliance with wicked men after the glory of a long and useful profession, and within a while, finding themselves cast down thereby from their reputation with the saints, have hardened themselves against it and ended in apostasy (as John 15:6)? This kept not Judas; it kept not Hymeneus nor Philetus; it kept not the stars of heaven; nor will it keep you.

There is, on the other side, *the consideration of shame, reproach, loss, and the like.* This also men may put their trust in as a defense against temptations, and do not fear but to be safeguarded and preserved by it. They would not for the world bring that shame and reproach upon themselves that such and such miscarriages are attended with! Now, besides that this consideration extends itself only to *open sins,* such as the world takes notice of and abhors, and so is of no use at all in such cases as wherein pretenses and colors[12] may be invented and used, nor in public temptations to loose and careless walking, like those of our days, nor in cases that may be disputable in themselves, though expressly sinful to the consciences of persons under temptations, nor in heart sins—in all which and most other cases of temptation there are innumerable reliefs ready to be tendered[13] unto the heart against this consideration; besides all this, I say, we see by experience how easily this cord is broken when once the heart begins to be entangled. Each corner of the land is full of examples to this purpose.

They have yet that which outweighs these lesser considerations—namely, that they will not wound their own consciences, and disturb their peace, and bring themselves in danger of hell-fire. This, surely, if anything, will preserve men in the hour of temptation. They will not lavish away their peace, nor

[10] shackle made of green twigs [see Judg. 16:7, KJV]

[11] "The people hiss [at me], but I applaud"—truncated version of a quote from Horatius, *Satires,* I.i.66. The original manuscript mistakenly has "sibilet" rather than "sibilat." The same quote is found in John Calvin's *Commentary on a Harmony of the Evangelists, Matthew, Mark, and Luke* (Grand Rapids, Mich.: Eerdmans, 1965), 2:182.

[12] embellishments concealing the truth

[13] offered

venture their souls by running on God and the thick bosses[14] of his buckler [Job 15:26]! What can be of more efficacy and prevalency? I confess this is of great importance; and oh that it were more pondered than it is! That we laid more weight upon the preservation of our peace with God than we do! Yet I say that even this consideration in him who is otherwhere off from his watch, and does not make it his work to follow the other rules insisted on, will not preserve him; for—

The peace of such a one may be *false peace* or security, made up of presumption and false hopes; yea, though he be a believer, it may be so. Such was David's peace after his sin, before Nathan came to him; such was Laodicea's peace when ready to perish; and Sardis her peace when dying. What should secure a soul that it is otherwise, seeing it is supposed that it does not universally labor to keep the word of Christ's patience and to be watchful in all things? Think you that the peace of many in these days will be found to be true peace at last? Nothing less. They go alive down to hell, and death will have dominion over them in the morning. Now, if a man's peace be such, do you think that can preserve him which cannot preserve itself? It will give way at the first vigorous assault of a temptation in its height and hour. Like a broken reed, it will run into the hand of him that leans on it. But—

Suppose the *peace* cared for, and proposed to safeguard the soul, be true and good, yet when all is laid up in this one bottom, when the hour of temptation comes, so many reliefs will be tendered against this consideration as will make it useless. "This evil is *small;* it is *questionable;* it falls not openly and downright upon *conscience.* I do but fear *consequences;* it may be [the case that] I may keep my peace notwithstanding. Others of the people of God have fallen, and yet kept or recovered their peace. If it be lost for a season, it may be obtained again. I will not solicit its station[15] anymore; or though peace be lost, safety may remain." And a thousand such pleas there are, which are all planted as batteries against this fort, so that it cannot long hold out.

The fixing on this particular only is to make good one *passage* or entrance, while the enemy assaults us round about. It is true, a little armor would serve to defend a man if he might choose there his enemy should strike him; but we are commanded to take the "whole armor of God" if we intend to resist and stand (Ephesians 6). This we speak of is but one piece; and when our eye is only to that, temptation may enter and prevail twenty other ways. For instance, a man may be tempted to worldliness, unjust gain, revenge,

[14] the projecting parts of a small, handheld shield; i.e., a strong, imposing defense
[15] position

vainglory, or the like. If he fortify himself alone with this consideration, he will not do this thing, and wound his conscience and lose his peace; fixing his eye on this particular, and counting himself safe while he is not overcome on that hand, it may be neglect of private communion with God, sensuality, and the like, do creep in, and he is not one jot in a better condition than if he had fallen under the power of that part of the temptation which was most visibly pressing on him. Experience gives to see that this does and will *fail* also. There is no saint of God but puts a valuation on the peace he has; yet how many of them fail in the day of temptation!

But yet they have another consideration also, and that is, the vileness of sinning against God. How shall they do this thing, and sin against God, the God of their mercies, of their salvation? How shall they wound Jesus Christ, who dies for them? This surely cannot but preserve them. I answer—

First, we see every day this consideration failing also. There is no child of God that is overcome of temptation but overcomes this consideration. It is not, then, a sure and infallible defensative.[16]

Secondly, this consideration is twofold: either it expresses the thoughts of the soul with particular reference to the temptation contended with and then it will not preserve it; or it expresses the universal, habitual frame of heart that is in us, upon all accounts, and then it falls in with what I shall tender as the universal medicine and remedy in this case in the process of this discourse; whereof afterward.

Consider the power of temptation, partly from what was showed before, from the effects and fruits of it in the saints of old, partly from such other effects in general as we find ascribed to it; as—

It will darken the mind, that a man shall not be able to make a right judgment of things, so as he did before he entered into it. As in the men of the world, the god of this world blinds their minds that they should not see the glory of Christ in the gospel (2 Cor. 4:4), and "whoredom, and wine, and new wine, take away their hearts" (Hos. 4:11); so it is in the nature of every temptation, more or less, to take away the heart, or to darken the understanding of the person tempted.

And this it does [in] diverse ways:

By fixing the imagination and the thoughts upon the object whereunto it tends, so that the mind shall be diverted from the consideration of the things that would relieve and succor[17] it in the state wherein it is. A man is tempted

[16] that which defends or protects
[17] assist, relieve

to apprehend that he is forsaken of God, that he is an object of his hatred, that he has no interest[18] in Christ. By the craft of Satan the mind shall be so *fixed* to the consideration of this state and condition, with the distress of it, that he shall not be able to manage any of the reliefs suggested and tendered to him against it; but, following the fullness of his own thoughts, shall walk on in darkness and have no light. I say, a temptation will so possess and fill the mind with thoughtfulness of itself and the matter of it, that it will take off from that clear consideration of things which otherwise it might and would have. And those things whereof the mind was wont[19] to have a vigorous sense, to keep it from sin, will by this means come to have no force or efficacy with it; nay, it will commonly bring men to that state and condition, that when others, to whom their estate is known, are speaking to them the things that concern their deliverance and peace, their minds will be so possessed with the matter of their temptation as not at all to understand, scarce to hear one word, that is spoken to them.

By *woeful entangling of the affections;* which, when they are engaged, what influence they have in blinding the mind and darkening the understanding is known. If any know it not, let him but open his eyes in these days, and he will quickly learn it. By what ways and means it is that engaged affections will becloud the mind and darken it I shall not now declare; only, I say, give me a man engaged in hope, love, fear, in reference to any particulars wherein he ought not, and I shall quickly show you wherein he is darkened and blinded. This, then, you will fail in if you enter into temptation: The present judgment you have of things will not be utterly altered, but darkened and rendered infirm[20] to influence the will and master the affections. These, being set at liberty by temptation, will run on in madness. Forthwith detestation of sin, abhorring of it, terror of the Lord, sense of love, presence of Christ crucified, all depart and leave the heart a prey to its enemy.

Temptation will give *oil and fuel* to our lusts—incite, provoke, and make them tumultuate and rage beyond measure. Tendering a lust, a corruption, a suitable object, advantage, occasion, it heightens and exasperates it, makes it for a season wholly predominant: so dealt it with carnal fear in Peter [Luke 22:56-60], with pride in Hezekiah [2 Chron. 32:25], with covetousness in Achan [Josh. 7:1], with uncleanness in David [2 Sam. 11:4], with worldliness in Demas [2 Tim. 4:10], with ambition in Diotrephes [3 John 9]. It will lay

[18] share or stake
[19] accustomed
[20] feeble

the reins on the neck of a lust and put to the sides of it, that it may rush forward like a horse into the battle. A man knows not the pride, fury, madness of a corruption until it meet with a suitable temptation. And what now will a poor soul think to do? His mind is darkened, his affections entangled, his lusts inflamed and provoked, his relief is defeated; and what will be the issue of such a condition?

Consider that temptations are either public or private; and let us a little view the efficacy and power of them apart.

There are *public temptations* (such as that mentioned [in] Rev. 3:10), that was to come upon the world, "to try them that dwell upon the earth," or a combination of persecution and seduction for the trial of a careless generation of professors. Now, concerning such a temptation, consider that—

It has an *efficacy* in respect of God, who sends it to revenge the neglect and contempt of the gospel on the one hand, and treachery of false professors on the other. Hence it will certainly accomplish what it receives commission[21] from him to do. When Satan offered his service to go forth and seduce Ahab that he might fall, God says to him, "You shall persuade him, and prevail also: go forth, and do so" (1 Kings 22:22). He is permitted as to his wickedness, and commissionated[22] as to the event and punishment intended. When the Christian world was to be given up to folly and false worship for their neglect of the truth, and their naked, barren, fruitless, Christ-dishonoring profession, it is said of the temptation that fell upon them, that "God sent them strong delusion, that they should believe a lie" (2 Thess. 2:11). That that comes so from God in a *judiciary* manner, has a power with it and shall prevail. That selfish, spiritually-slothful, careless, and worldly frame of spirit, which in these days has infected almost the body of professors, if it have a commission from God to kill hypocrites, to wound negligent saints, to break their bones, and make them scandalous, that they may be ashamed, shall it not have a power and efficacy so to do? What work has the spirit of error made among us! Is it not from hence, that as some men delighted not to retain God in their hearts, so he has "given them up to a reprobate mind" (Rom. 1:28). A man would think it strange, yea, it is [a] matter of amazement, to see persons of a sober spirit, pretending to great things in the ways of God, overcome, captivated, ensnared, destroyed by weak means, sottish[23] opinions, foolish imaginations, such as a man would

[21] authority
[22] commissioned, appointed
[23] foolish, especially as it relates to drunkenness

think it impossible that they should ever lay hold on sensible or rational men, much less on professors of the gospel. But that which God will have to be strong, let us not think weak. No strength but the strength of God can stand in the way of the weakest things of the world that are commissionated from God for any end or purpose whatsoever.

There is in such temptations the secret insinuation of *examples* in those that are accounted *godly* and are professors: "Because iniquity shall abound, the love of many shall wax cold," etc. (Matt. 24:12). The abounding of iniquity in some will insensibly cast water on the zeal and love of others, that by little and little it shall wax cold. Some begin to grow negligent, careless, worldly, wanton.[24] They break the ice toward the pleasing of the flesh. At first their love also waxes[25] cold; and the brunt being over, they also conform to them and are cast into the same mold with them. "A little leaven leavens the whole lump." Paul repeats this saying twice (1 Cor. 5:6 and Gal. 5:9). He would have us take notice of it; and it is of the danger of the infection of the whole body, from the ill examples of some, whereof he speaks. We know how insensibly leaven proceeds to give savor to the whole; so it is termed a "root of bitterness" that "springs up and defiles many" (Heb. 12:15). If one little piece of leaven, if one bitter root, may endanger the whole, how much more when there are many roots of that nature, and much leaven is scattered abroad! It is easy following a multitude to do evil, and saying "a conspiracy" to them to whom the people say "a conspiracy" [Isa. 8:12]. Would anyone have thought it possible that such and such professors, in our days, should have fallen into ways of self, of flesh, of the world? To play at cards, dice, revel, dance? To neglect family, closet[26] duties? To be proud, haughty, ambitious, worldly, covetous, oppressive? Or that they should be turned away after foolish, vain, ridiculous opinions, deserting the gospel of Christ? In which two lies the great temptation that is come on us, the inhabitants of this world, to try us. But does not every man see that this is come to pass? And may we not see how it is come to pass? Some loose, empty professors, who had never more than a form of godliness, when they had served their turn of that, began the way to them; then others began a little to comply, and to please the flesh in so doing. This, by little and little, has reached even the top boughs and branches of our profession, until almost all flesh has corrupted

[24] lacking discipline
[25] grows, becomes
[26] i.e., private, spiritual

its way. And he that departs from these iniquities makes his *name* a prey, if not his *person.*

Public temptations are usually accompanied with *strong reasons and pretenses* that are too hard for men, or at least insensibly prevail upon them to an undervaluation of the evil whereunto the temptation leads, to give strength to that complicated temptation which in these days has even cast down the people of God from their excellency—has cut their locks, and made them become like other men [cf. Judges 16]. How full is the world of specious pretenses and pleadings! As there is the liberty and freedom of Christians, delivered from a bondage frame, this is a door that, in my own observation, I have seen sundry[27] going out at, into sensuality and apostasy; beginning at a light conversation, proceeding to a neglect of the Sabbath, public and private duties, ending in dissoluteness and profaneness. And then there is leaving of public things to Providence, being content with what is—things good in themselves, but disputed into wretched, carnal compliances, and the utter ruin of all zeal for God, the interest of Christ or his people in the world. These and the like considerations, joined with the ease and plenty, the greatness and promotion of professors, have so brought things about, that whereas we have by Providence shifted places with the men of the world, we have by sin shifted spirits with them also. We are like a plantation of men carried into a foreign country. In a short space they degenerate from the manners of the people from whence they came, and fall into that thing in the soil and the air that transformed them. Give me leave a little to follow my similitude: He that should see the prevailing party of these nations, many of those in rule, power, favor, with all their adherents, and remember that they were a colony of Puritans—whose habitation was "in a low place," as the prophet speaks of the city of God [Isa. 32:19]—translated by a high hand to the mountains they now possess, cannot but wonder how soon they have forgot the customs, manners, ways, of their own old people, and are cast into the mold of them that went before them in the places whereunto they are translated. I speak of us all, especially of us who are among the lowest of the people, where perhaps this iniquity does most abound. What were those before us that we are not? What did they that we do not? Prosperity has slain the foolish and wounded the wise.

Suppose the *temptation is private.* This has been spoken to before; I shall add two things:

Its *union and incorporation* with lust, whereby it gets within the soul, and lies at the bottom of its actings. John tells us that the things that are "in

[27] various (people)

the world" are "the lust of the flesh, the lust of the eyes, the pride of life" (1 John 2:16). Now, it is evident that all these things are principally in the *subject*, not in the *object*—in the *heart*, not in the *world*. But they are said to be "in the world" because the world gets into them, mixes itself with them, unites, incorporates. As faith and the promises are said to be "mixed" (Heb. 4:2), so are lust and temptation mixed: they twine together; receive mutual improvement[28] from one another; grow each of them higher and higher by the mutual strength they administer to one another. Now, by this means temptation gets so deep in the heart that no contrary reasonings can reach unto it; nothing but what can kill the lust can conquer the temptation. Like leprosy that has mingled itself with the wall [Lev. 14:33-53], the wall itself must be pulled down or the leprosy will not be cured. Like a gangrene that mixes poison with the blood and spirits, and cannot be separated from the place where it is, but both must be cut off together. For instance, in David's temptation to uncleanness, ten thousand considerations might have been taken in to stop the mouth of the temptation; but it had united itself with his lust, and nothing but the killing of that could destroy it, or get him the conquest. This deceives many a one. They have some pressing temptation, that, having got some advantages, is urgent upon them. They pray against it, oppose it with all powerful considerations, such as whereof every one seems sufficient to conquer and destroy it, at least to overpower it, that it should never be troublesome any more; but no good is done, no ground is got or obtained, yea, it grows upon them more and more. What is the reason of it? It has incorporated and united itself with the lust and is safe from all the opposition they make. If they would make work indeed, they are to set upon the whole of the lust itself; their ambition, pride, worldliness, sensuality, or whatever it be, that the temptation is united with. All other dealings with it are like tamperings with a prevailing gangrene: the part or whole may be preserved a little while, in great torment; excision[29] or death must come at last. The soul may cruciate[30] itself for a season with such a procedure; but it must come to this—its lust must die, or the soul must die.

In whatsoever part of the soul the lust be seated wherewith the temptation is united, it draws after it *the whole soul* by one means or other, and so prevents or anticipates any opposition. Suppose it be a lust of the mind—as there are lusts of the mind and uncleanness of the spirit, such as ambition,

---

[28] enhancement
[29] surgical removal by cutting
[30] torment, torture

vain-glory, and the like—what a world of ways has the understanding to bridle the affections that they should not so tenaciously cleave to God, seeing in what it aims at there is so much to give them contentment and satisfaction! It will not only prevent all the reasonings of the mind, which it does necessarily—being like a bloody infirmity in the eyes, presenting all things to draw the whole soul, on other accounts and collateral considerations, into the same frame. It promises the whole a share in the spoil aimed at; as Judas's money, that he first desired from covetousness, was to be shared among all his lusts. Or be it in the more sensual[31] part, and first possesses the affections—what prejudices they will bring upon the understanding, how they will bribe it to an acquiescence, what arguments, what hopes they will supply it with, cannot easily be expressed, as was before showed. In brief, there is no particular temptation, but, when it is in its hour, it has such a contribution of assistance from things good, evil, indifferent, is fed by so many considerations that seem to be most alien and foreign to it, in some cases has such specious pleas and pretenses, that its strength will easily be acknowledged.

Consider the end of any temptation; this is Satan's end and sin's end—that is, the dishonor of God and the ruin of our souls.

Consider what has been the issue of your former temptations that you have had. Have they not defiled your conscience, disquieted your peace, weakened you in your obedience, [and] clouded the face of God? Though you were not prevailed on to the outward evil or utmost issue of your temptation, yet have you not been foiled? Has not your soul been sullied[32] and grievously perplexed with it? Yea, did you ever in your life come fairly off, without sensible loss, from any temptation almost that you had to deal with; and would you willingly be entangled again? If you are at liberty, take heed; enter no more, if it be possible, lest a worse thing happen to you.

These, I say, are some of those many considerations that might be insisted on, to manifest the importance of the truth proposed and the fullness of our concern in taking care that we "enter not into temptation."

Objections and Answers

Against what has been spoken, some objections that secretly insinuate themselves into the souls of men, and have an efficacy to make them negligent and careless in this thing, which is of such importance to them—a duty of such indispensable necessity to them who intend to walk with God in any peace,

[31] perceived by the senses (not necessarily sexual)

[32] polluted, soiled

or with any faithfulness—are to be considered and removed. And they are these that follow.

Objection #1

Why should we so fear and labor to avoid temptation? We are commanded to "count it all joy when we fall into divers temptations" (James 1:2). Now, certainly I need not solicitously avoid the falling into that which, when I am fallen into, I am to count it all joy.

Answer

To which I answer—

You will not hold by this rule in all things—namely, that a man need not seek to avoid that which, when he cannot but fall into, it is his duty to rejoice therein. The same apostle bids the rich "rejoice that they are made low" (James 1:10). And, without doubt, to him who is acquainted with the goodness and wisdom and love of God in his dispensations,[33] in every condition that is needful for him, it will be a matter of rejoicing to him: but yet, how few rich, godly men can you persuade not to take heed and use all lawful means that they be not made poor and low! And, in most cases, the truth is, it were their sin not to do so. It is our business to make good our stations and to secure ourselves as we can; if God alter our condition we are to rejoice in it. If the temptations here mentioned befall us, we may have cause to rejoice; but not if, by a neglect of duty, we fall into them.

Temptations are taken two ways: (1) *passively and merely materially,* for such things as are, or in some cases may be, temptations; or (2) *actively,* for such as do entice to sin. James speaks of temptations in the first sense only; for having said, "Count it all joy when you fall into divers temptations" (v. 2); he adds, "Blessed is the man that endures temptation: for when he is tried, he shall receive the crown of life" (v. 12). But now whereas a man might say, "If this be so, then temptations are good, and from God"—"No," says James; "take temptation in such a sense as that it is a thing enticing and leading to sin, so God tempts none; but every man is tempted of his own lust" (vv. 13-14). "To have such temptations, to be tempted to sin, that is not the blessed thing I intend; but the enduring of afflictions that God sends for the trial of our faith, that is a blessed thing. So that, though I must count it all joy when, through the will of God, I fall into diverse afflictions for my trial, which

[33] provisions, orderings

yet have the matter of temptation in them, yet I am to use all care and diligence that my lust have no occasions or advantages given unto it to tempt me to sin."

Objection #2

But was not our Savior Christ himself tempted; and is it evil to be brought into the same state and condition with him? Yea, it is not only said that he was tempted, but his being so is expressed as a thing advantageous, and conducing to his mercifulness as our priest: "In that he himself has suffered, being tempted, he is able to succor them that are tempted" (Heb. 2:17-18). And he makes it a ground of a great promise to his disciples, that they had "abode with him in his temptations" (Luke 22:28).

Answer

It is true, our Savior was tempted; but yet his temptations are reckoned among the *evils* that befell him in the days of his flesh—things that came on him through the malice of the world and the prince thereof. He did not willfully cast himself into temptation, which he said was "to tempt the Lord our God" (Matt. 4:7); as, indeed, willingly to enter into any temptation is highly to tempt God. Now, our condition is so, that, [even if we] use the greatest diligence and watchfulness that we can, yet we shall be sure to be tempted and be made like to Christ therein. This hinders not but that it is our duty to the utmost to prevent our falling into them; and that namely on this account: Christ had only the *suffering* part of temptation when he entered into it; we have also the *sinning* part of it. When the prince of this world came to Christ, he had "no part in him" [John 14:30]; but when he comes to us, he has so in us. So that though in one effect of temptations, namely trials and disquietness, we are made like to Christ, and so are to rejoice as far as by any means that is produced; yet by another we are made unlike to him—which is our being defiled and entangled: and are therefore to seek by all means to avoid them. We never come off like Christ. Who of us "enter into temptation" and is not defiled?

Objection #3

But what [is the] need [for] this great endeavor and carefulness? Is it not said that "God is faithful, who will not suffer us to be tempted above what we are able, but will with the temptation also make a way to escape?" (1 Cor. 10:13); and "He knows how to deliver the godly out of temptations" (2 Pet. 2:9)? What need we, then, be solicitous that we enter not into them?

Answer

I much question what assistance he will have from God in his temptation who willingly enters into it because he supposes God has promised to deliver him out of it. The Lord knows that, through the craft of Satan, the subtlety and malice of the world, the deceitfulness of sin, that does so easily beset us, when we have done our utmost, yet we shall enter into diverse temptations. In his love, care, tenderness, and faithfulness, he has provided such a sufficiency of grace for us that they shall not utterly prevail to make an everlasting separation between him and our souls. Yet I have three things to say to this objection:

First, he that *willfully* or negligently enters into temptation has no reason in the world to promise himself any assistance from God, or any deliverance from the temptation whereunto he is entered. The promise is made to them whom temptations do befall in their way, whether they will or not; not them that willfully fall into them—that run out of their way to meet with them. And therefore the devil (as is usually observed), when he tempted our Savior, left out that expression of the text of Scripture, which he wrested to his purpose, "All your ways" [cf. Matt. 4:6 with Ps. 91:11]. The promise of deliverance is to them who are in their ways, whereof this is one principal [way] to beware of temptation.

Second, though there be a sufficiency of grace provided for all the *elect,* that they shall by no temptation fall utterly from God, yet it would make any gracious heart to tremble to think what dishonor to God, what scandal to the gospel, what woeful darkness and disquietness they may bring upon their own souls, though they perish not. And they who are scared by nothing but fear of hell, on whom other considerations short thereof have no influence, in my apprehension[34] have more reason to fear it than perhaps they are aware of.

Third, to enter on temptation on this account is to venture on sin (which is the same with "continuing with sin") "that grace may abound" (Rom. 6:1-2); which the apostle rejects the thoughts of with greatest detestation. Is it not a madness for a man willingly to suffer the ship wherein he is to split itself on a rock, to the irrecoverable loss of his merchandise, because he supposes he shall in his own person swim safely to shore on a plank? Is it less in him who will hazard the shipwreck of all his comfort, peace, joy, and so much of the glory of God and honor of the gospel as he is entrusted with, merely on supposition that his soul shall yet escape? These things a man would think did not deserve to be mentioned, and yet with such as these do poor souls sometimes delude themselves.

[34] perception, conception

PART 4:

Particular Cases and General Directions

[Chapter 4]

These things being premised in general, I proceed to the consideration of *three particular cases arising* from the truth proposed: the first whereof relates unto the *thing* itself; the second unto the *time* or season thereof; and the last unto *deportment*[1] in reference unto the prevention of the evil treated of.

It may be inquired: (1) How a man may know when he is entered into temptation; (2) What directions are to be given for the preventing of our entering into temptation; (3) What seasons there are wherein a man may and ought to fear that an hour of temptation is at hand.

How One Knows He Has Entered into Temptation

I say, then—

When a man is drawn into any sin, he may be sure that he has entered into temptation. All sin is from temptation (James 1:14). Sin is a fruit that comes only from that root. Though a man be never so suddenly or violently surprised in or with any sin, yet it is from some temptation or other that he has been so surprised (so the apostle, Gal. 6:1). If a man be surprised, overtaken with a fault, yet he was tempted to it; for says he, "Consider yourself, lest you also be tempted"—that is, as he was when he was so surprised, as it were, at unawares. This men sometimes take no notice of, to their great disadvantage. When they are overtaken with a sin they set themselves to repent of that sin, but do not consider the temptation that was the cause of it, to set themselves against that also to take care that they enter no more into it. Hence are they quickly again entangled by it, though they have the greatest detestation of the sin itself that can be expressed. He that would indeed get the conquest over any sin must consider his temptations to it, and strike at that root; without deliverance from thence, he will not be healed.

This is a folly that possesses many who have yet a quick and living sense of sin. They are sensible of their *sins,* not of their *temptations*—are displeased with the bitter fruit, but cherish the poisonous root. Hence, in the midst of their humiliations for sin, they will continue in those ways, those societies, in the pursuit of those ends, which have occasioned that sin; of which more afterward.

Temptations have several degrees. Some arise to such a height, do so press on the soul, so cruciate and disquiet it, so fight against all opposition that is

[1] behavior

made to it, that it is a peculiar power of temptation that he is to wrestle with. When a fever rages, a man knows he is sick, unless his distemper has made him mad. The lusts of men, as James tells us, "entice, draw away," and seduce them to sin [1:14]; but this they do of themselves, without peculiar instigation, in a more quiet, even, and sedate manner. If they grow violent, if they hurry the soul up and down, give it no rest, the soul may know that they have got the help of temptation to their assistance.

Take an empty vessel and put it into some stream that is in its course to the sea, it will infallibly be carried thither, according to the course and speed of the stream; but let strong winds arise upon it, it will be driven with violence on every bank and rock, until, being broken in pieces, it is swallowed up of the ocean. Men's lusts will infallibly (if not mortified in the death of Christ) carry them into eternal ruin, but oftentimes without much noise, according to the course of the stream of their corruptions; but let the wind of strong temptations befall them, they are hurried into innumerable scandalous sins, and so, broken upon all accounts, are swallowed up in eternity. So is it in general with men; so in particular. Hezekiah had the root of *pride* in him always; yet it did not make him run up and down to show his treasure and his riches until he fell into temptation by the ambassadors of the king of Babylon [2 Chron. 32:31]. So had David; yet could he keep off from numbering the people until Satan stood up and provoked him and solicited him to do it [1 Chron. 21:1]. Judas was covetous from the beginning; yet he did not contrive to satisfy it by selling of his Master until the devil entered into him, and he thereby into temptation [Luke 22:3]. The like may be said of Abraham, Jonah, Peter, and the rest. So that when any lust or corruption whatsoever tumultuates and disquiets the soul, puts it with violence on sin, let the soul know that it has got the advantage of some outward temptation, though as yet it perceives not wherein, or at least is become itself a peculiar temptation by some incitation or provocation that has befallen it, and is to be looked to more than ordinarily.

Entering into temptation may be seen in the lesser degrees of it; as, for instance, when the heart begins secretly to like the matter of the temptation, and is content to feed it and increase it by any ways that it may without downright sin. In particular, a man begins to be in repute for piety, wisdom, learning, or the like—he is spoken of much to that purpose; his heart is tickled to hear of it, and his pride and ambition affected with it. If this man now, with all his strength, ply the things from whence his repute, and esteem, and glory among men do spring, with a secret eye to have it increased, he is entering into temptation; which, if he take not heed, will quickly render him a slave of lust. So was it with Jehu. He perceived that his repute for zeal began to grow abroad, and he got honor by it. Jonadab[2] comes in his way, a good and holy man. "Now," thinks Jehu, "I have an opportunity to grow in honor of my zeal." So he calls Jonadab to him, and to work he goes most seriously [2 Kings 10:16ff.]. The things he did were good in themselves, but he was entered into temptation, and served his lust in that he did. So is it with many scholars. They find themselves esteemed and favored for their learning. This takes hold of the pride and ambition of their hearts. Hence they set themselves to study with all diligence day and night—a thing good in itself; but they do it that they might satisfy the thoughts and words of men, wherein they delight: and so in all they do they make provision for the flesh to fulfill the lusts thereof [Rom. 13:14].

It is true, God oftentimes brings light out of this darkness and turns things to a better issue. After, it may be, a man has studied sundry years, with an eye upon his lusts—his ambition, pride, and vain-glory—rising early and going to bed late, to give them satisfaction, God comes in with his grace, turns the soul to himself, robs those Egyptian lusts [cf. Num. 11:5], and so consecrates that to the use of the tabernacle which was provided for idols.

Men may be thus entangled in better things than learning, even in the *profession* of piety, in their labor in the ministry, and the like. Some men's profession is a snare to them. They are in reputation, and are much honored on the account of their profession and strict walking. This often falls out in the days wherein we live, wherein all things are carried by parties. Some find themselves on the accounts mentioned, perhaps, to be the darlings and "ingentia decora,"[3] or glory of their party. If thoughts hereof secretly insinuate themselves into their hearts and influence them into more than ordinary diligence and activity in their way and profession, they are entangled, and instead of aiming at more glory, had need lie in the dust, in a sense of their own vileness. And so close is this temptation that oftentimes it requires no food to feed upon but that he who is entangled with it do avoid all means and ways of honor and reputation; so that it can but whisper in the heart that that avoidance is honorable. The same may be the condition with men, as was said, in *preaching the gospel,* in the work of the ministry. Many things in that work may yield them esteem—their ability, their plainness, their frequency, their success; and all in this sense may be fuel unto temptations. Let, then, a man know that when he likes that which feeds his lust, and keeps it

[2] Jehonadab
[3] "grand ornaments"

up by ways either good in themselves or not downright sinful, he is entered into temptation.

When by a man's state or condition of life, or any means whatsoever, it comes to pass that his lust and any temptation meet with occasions and opportunities for its provocation and stirring up, let that man know, whether he perceive it or not, that he is certainly entered into temptation. I told you before that to enter into temptation is not merely to be tempted, but so to be under the *power* of it as to be entangled by it. Now, it is impossible almost for a man to have opportunities, occasions, advantages, suited to his lust and corruption, but he will be entangled. If ambassadors come from the king of Babylon, Hezekiah's pride will cast him into temptation. If Hazael be king of Syria, his cruelty and ambition will make him to rage savagely against Israel. If the priests come with their pieces of silver, Judas's covetousness will instantly be at work to sell his Master. And many instances of the like kind may, in the days wherein we live, be given. Some men think not to play on the hole of the asp[4] and not be stung [Isa. 11:8], to touch pitch and not be defiled,[5] to take fire in their clothes and not be burnt [Prov. 6:27]; but they will be mistaken. If your business, course of life, societies, or whatever else it be of the like kind, do cast you on such things, ways, persons, as suit your lust or corruption, know that you are entered into temptation; how you will come out God only knows. Let us suppose a man that has any seeds of filth in his heart engaged, in the course of his life, in society, light, vain, and foolish, whatsoever notice, little, great, or none at all, it be that he takes of it, he is undoubtedly entered into temptation. So is it with ambition in high places; passion in a multitude of perplexing affairs; polluted corrupt fancy in vain societies; and the perusal of idle books or treatises of vanity and folly. Fire and things combustible may more easily be induced to lie together without affecting each other than *peculiar* lusts and *suitable* objects or occasions for their exercise.

When a man is weakened, made negligent or formal in duty, when he can omit duties or content himself with a careless, lifeless performance of them, without delight, joy, or satisfaction to his soul, who had another frame formerly; let him know, that though he may not be acquainted with the particular distemper wherein it consists, yet in something or other he is entered into temptation, which at the length he will find evident, to his trouble and peril. How many have we seen and known in our days, who, from a warm profession have fallen to be negligent, careless, indifferent in praying, reading, hear-

---

[4] cobra

[5] William Shakespeare, *Much Ado About Nothing*, III.iii.

ing, and the like! Give an instance of one who has come off without a wound, and I dare say you may find out a hundred for him that have manifested themselves to have been asleep on the top of the mast; that they were in the jaws of some vile temptation or other, that afterward brought forth bitter fruit in their lives and ways. From some few returners from folly we have every day these doleful complaints made: "Oh! I neglected private prayer; I did not meditate on the word, nor attend to hearing, but rather despised these things: and yet said I was rich and wanted nothing. Little did I consider that this unclean lust was ripening in my heart; this atheism, these abominations were fomenting[6] there." This is a certain rule: If his heart grow cold, negligent, or formal in duties of the worship of God, and that either as to the matter or manner of them, who has had another frame, one temptation or other has laid hold upon him. World, or pride, or uncleanness, or self-seeking, or malice and envy, or one thing or other, has possessed his spirit; gray hairs are here and there upon him, though he perceive it not. And this is to be observed as to the manner of duties, as well as to the matter. Men may, upon many sinister accounts, especially for the satisfaction of their consciences, keep up and frequent duties of religion, as to the substance and matter of them, when they have no heart to them, no life in them, as to the spirituality required in their performance. Sardis kept up the performance of duties, and had therefore a name to live, but wanted spiritual life in their performances, and, was therefore "dead" (Rev. 3:1). As it is in distempers of the body, if a man find his spirits faint, his heart oppressed, his head heavy, the whole person indisposed, though he do not yet actually burn nor rave, yet he will cry, "I fear I am entering into a fever, I am so out of order and indisposed"—a man may do so in this sickness of the soul. If he find his pulse not beating aright and evenly toward duties of worship and communion with God—if his spirit be low and his heart faint in them—let him conclude, though his lust does not yet burn nor rage, that he is entered into temptation, and it is high time for him to consider the particular causes of his distemper. If the head be heavy and slumber in the things of grace, if the heart be cold in duties, evil lies at the door. And if such a soul does escape a great temptation unto sin, yet it shall not escape a great temptation by desertion. The spouse cries, "I sleep" (Song 5:2) and that she had "put off her coat, and could not put it on" [v. 3]—had an indisposition[7] to duties and communion with Christ.[8] What is the next news you have of her? Her "Beloved had with-

[6] inciting, agitating

[7] disinclination, unwillingness

[8] Owen—along with most interpreters in the seventeenth century—interpreted the Song of Solomon (or Canticles, as they referred to it) as a "description of the communion that is between the Lord Christ and his saints" (*Works,* 2:46).

drawn himself" (v. 6)—Christ was gone; and she seeks him long and finds him not. There is such a suitableness between the new nature that is wrought[9] and created in believers and the duties of the worship of God, that they will not be parted nor kept asunder, unless it be by the interposition[10] of some disturbing distemper. The new creature feeds upon them, is strengthened and increased by them, finds sweetness in them, yea, meets in them with its God and Father; so that it cannot but of itself, unless made sick by some temptation, delight in them, and desire to be in the exercise of them. This frame is described in the 119th Psalm throughout. It is not, I say, cast out of this frame and temper[11] or other. Sundry other evidences there are of a soul's entering into temptation, which upon inquiry it may discover.

I propose this to take off the *security* that we are apt to fall into, and to manifest what is the peculiar duty that we are to apply ourselves unto in the special seasons of temptation; for he that is already entered into temptation is to apply himself unto means for disentanglement, not to labor to prevent his entering in. How this may be done I shall afterward declare.

[Chapter 5]

General Directions to Preserve a Soul from Entering into Temptation: Watch and Pray

Having seen the danger of entering into temptation, and [having] also discovered the ways and seasons whereby and wherein men usually [do] so, our second inquiry is: What general directions may be given to preserve a soul from that condition that has been spoken of? And we see our Savior's direction in the place spoken of before (Matt. 26:41). He sums up all in these two words: "watch and pray." I shall a little labor to unfold them and show what is enwrapped and contained in them; and that both jointly and severally.

There is included in them a clear, abiding apprehension of great evil that there is in entering into temptation. That which a man watches and prays against, he looks upon as evil to him, and by all means to be avoided. This, then, is the first direction: *Always bear in mind the great danger that it is for any soul to enter into temptation.*

It is a woeful thing to consider what slight thoughts that most have of

[9] shaped, molded, fashioned
[10] interjection, intervention
[11] character, disposition

this thing. [If it] so [be that] men can keep themselves from sin itself in open action, they are content, they scarce aim at more; on any temptation in the world, all sorts of men will venture at any time. How will young men put themselves on company, any society; at first, being delighted with *evil company,* then with the *evil of the company!* How vain are all admonitions and exhortations to them to take heed of such persons, debauched in themselves, corrupters of others, destroyers of souls! At first they will venture on the company, abhorring the thoughts of practicing their lewdness; but what is the issue? Unless it be here or there one, whom God snatches with a mighty hand from the jaws of destruction, they are all lost, and become after a while in love with the evil which at first they abhorred. This open door to the ruin of souls is too evident; and woeful experience makes it no less evident that it is almost impossible to fasten upon many poor creatures any fear or dread of temptation, who yet will profess a fear and abhorrency of sin. Would it were only thus with young men, such as are unaccustomed to the yoke of their Lord! What sort of men is free from this folly in one thing or other? How many professors have I known that would plead for their *liberty,* as they called it! They could hear anything, all things—all sorts of men, all men; they would try all things whether they came to them in the way of God or no; and on that account would run to hear and to attend to every broacher of false and abominable opinions, every seducer, though stigmatized by the generality of the saints: for such a one they had their liberty—they could do it; but the opinions they hated as much as any. What has been the issue? I scarce ever knew any come off without a wound; the most have had their faith overthrown. Let no man, then, pretend to fear sin that does not fear temptation to it. They are too nearly allied to be separated. Satan has put them so together that it is very hard for any man to put them asunder. He hates not the fruit who delights in the root.

When men see that such ways, such companies, such *courses,* such businesses, such studies and *aims,* do entangle them, make them cold, careless, are quench-coals to them, indispose them to even, universal, and constant obedience, if they adventure on them, sin lies at the door. It is a tender frame of spirit, sensible of its own weakness and corruption, of the craft of Satan, of the evil of sin, of the efficacy of temptation, that can perform his duty. And yet until we bring our hearts to this frame, upon the considerations beforementioned, or the like that may be proposed, we shall never free ourselves from sinful entanglements. Boldness upon temptation, springing from several pretenses, has, as is known, ruined innumerable professors in these days, and still continues to cast many down from their excellency; nor have I the least hope of a more fruitful profession among us until I see more fear of temptation. Sin will not long seem great or heavy unto any to whom temptations seem light or small.

This is the first thing enwrapped in this general direction: *The daily exercise of our thoughts with an apprehension of the great danger that lies in entering into temptation, is required of us.* Grief of the Spirit of God, disquietment of our own souls, loss of peace, hazard of eternal welfare, lies at the door. If the soul be not prevailed with to the observation of this direction, all that ensues will be of no value. Temptation despised will conquer; and if the heart be made tender and watchful here, half the work of securing a good conversation is over. And let not him go any further who resolved not to improve this direction in a daily conscientious observation of it.

There is this in it also, that *it is not a thing in our own power, to keep and preserve ourselves from entering into temptation.* Therefore are we to pray that we may be preserved from it, because we cannot save ourselves.

This is another means of preservation. As we have no strength to resist a temptation when it does come, when we are entered into it, but shall fall under it, without a supply of sufficiency of grace from God; so to reckon that we have no power or wisdom to keep ourselves from entering into temptation, but must be kept by the power and wisdom of God, is a preserving principle (1 Pet. 1:5). We are in all things "kept by the power of God." This our Savior instructs us in, not only by directing us to pray that we be not led into temptation, but also by his own praying for us that we may be kept from it: "I pray not that you should take them out of the world, but that you should keep them from the evil" (John 17:15)—that is, the temptations of the world unto evil, unto sin—*ek tou ponērou,* "out of evil" that is in the world, that is temptation, which is all that is evil in the world; or from the evil one, who in the world makes use of the world unto temptation. Christ prays [to] his Father to keep us, and instructs us to pray that we be so kept. It is not, then, a thing in our own power. The ways of our entering into temptation are so many, various, and imperceptible—the means of it so efficacious and powerful—our weakness, our unwatchfulness, so unspeakable—that we cannot in the least keep or preserve ourselves from it. We fail both in wisdom and power for this work.

Let the heart, then, commune with itself and say, "*I* am poor and weak; *Satan* is subtle, cunning, powerful, watching constantly for advantages against my soul; the *world* earnest, pressing, and full of specious pleas, innumerable pretenses, and ways of deceit; my *own corruption* violent and tumultuating, enticing, entangling, conceiving sin, and warring in me, against me; *occasions* and advantages of temptation innumerable in all things I have done or suffer, in all businesses and persons with whom I converse.

The *first beginnings* of temptation [are] insensible[12] and plausible, so that, left unto myself, I shall not know I am ensnared, until my bonds be made strong, and sin has got ground in my heart: therefore on God alone will I rely for preservation, and continually will I look up to him on that account." This will make the soul be always committing itself to the care of God, resting itself on him, and to do nothing, undertake nothing, etc, without asking counsel of him. So that a double advantage will arise from the observation of this direction, both of singular use for the soul's preservation from the evil feared:

The engagement of the grace and compassion of God, who has called the *fatherless* and *helpless* to rest upon him; nor did ever soul fail of supplies, who, in a sense of want, rolled itself on him, on the account of his gracious invitation.

The *keeping* of it in such a frame as, on various accounts, is useful for its preservation. He that looks to God for assistance in a due manner is both sensible of his danger and conscientiously careful in the use of means to preserve himself: which two, of what importance they are in this case, may easily be apprehended by them who have their hearts exercised in these things.

This also is in it—act *faith* on the *promise* of God for preservation. To believe that he will preserve us is a means of preservation; for this God will certainly do, or make a way for us to escape out of temptation, if we fall into it under such a believing frame. We are to pray for what God has promised. Our requests are to be regulated by his promises and commands, which are of the same extent. Faith closes with the promises and so finds relief in this case. This James instructs us in James 1:5-7. What we want we must "ask of God," but we must "ask in faith," for otherwise we must not "think that we shall receive anything of the Lord." This then, also, is in this direction of our Savior, that we act faith on the promises of God for our preservation out of temptation. He has promised that he will keep us in all our ways; that we shall be directed in a way that, though we are fools, "we shall not err therein" (Isa. 35:8); that he will lead us, guide us, and deliver us from the evil one. Set faith on work on these promises of God, and expect a good and comfortable issue. It is not easily conceived what a train of graces

[12] imperceptible

faith is attended with when it goes forth to meet Christ in the promises, nor what a power for the preservation of the soul lies in this thing; but I have spoken to this elsewhere.

Weigh these things severally and, first, take prayer into consideration. To pray that we enter not into temptation is a means to preserve us from it. Glorious things are, by all men that know aught[13] of those things, spoken of this *duty* [Ps. 87:3]; and yet the truth is, not one half of its excellency, power, and efficacy is known. It is not my business to speak of it in general; but this I say as to my present purpose—he that would be little in temptation, let him be much in prayer. This calls in the suitable help and succor that is laid up in Christ for us (Heb. 4:16). This casts our souls into a frame of opposition to every temptation. When Paul had given instruction for the taking to ourselves "the whole armor of God" that we may resist and stand in the time of temptation [Eph. 6:11, 13], he adds this general close of the whole: "praying always with all prayer and supplication in the Spirit, and watching thereunto with all perseverance and supplication" (Eph. 6:18).

Without this, all the rest will be of no efficacy for the end proposed. And therefore consider what weight he lays on it: "praying always"—that is, at all times and seasons, or be always ready and prepared for the discharge of that duty (Luke 18:1; Eph. 6:18); "with all prayer and supplication in the Spirit"—putting forth all kinds of desires unto God that are suited to our condition, according to his will, lest we [be] diverted by anything whatsoever; and that not for a little while, but "with all perseverance"—continuance lengthened out to the utmost: so shall we stand. The soul so framed is in a sure posture; and this is one of the means without which this work will not be done. If we do not abide in prayer, we shall abide in cursed temptations. Let this, then, be another direction: *abide in prayer, and that expressly to this purpose, that we "enter not into temptation."* Let this be one part of our daily contending with God—that he would preserve our souls, and keep our hearts and our ways, that we be not entangled; that his good and wise providence will order our ways and affairs, that no pressing temptation befall us; that he would give us diligence, carefulness, and watchfulness over our own ways. So shall we be delivered when others are held with the cords of their own folly.

[13] anything, i.e., anything worthwhile

[Chapter 6]

Watch

The other part of our Savior's direction—namely, to "watch"—is more general, and extends itself to many particulars. I shall fix on some things that are contained therein.

Watch the Seasons

Watch the *seasons* wherein men usually do "enter into temptations." There are sundry seasons wherein an hour of temptation is commonly at hand, and will unavoidably seize upon the soul unless it be delivered by mercy in the use of watchfulness. When we are under such a season, then are we peculiarly to be upon our guard that we enter not into, that we fall not under, the power of temptation. Some of those seasons may be named.

A season of unusual outward prosperity is usually accompanied with an hour of temptation. Prosperity and temptation go together; yea, prosperity is a temptation, many temptations, and that because without eminent supplies of grace it is apt to cast a soul into a frame and temper exposed to any temptation, and provides it with fuel and food for all. It has provision for lust and darts for Satan.

The wise man tells us that the "prosperity of fools destroys them" (Prov. 1:32). It *hardens* them in their way, makes them despise instruction, and puts the evil day (whose terror should influence them into amendment[14]) far from them. Without a special assistance, it has an inconceivably malignant influence on believers themselves. Hence Agur prays against riches because of the temptation that attends them: "Lest," says he, "I be full and deny you, and say, Who is the Lord?" (Prov. 30:8-9)—lest, being filled with them, he should forget the Lord; as God complains that his people did (Hos. 13:6). We know how David was mistaken in this case: "I said in my prosperity, I shall never be moved" (Ps. 30:6). All is well, and will be well. But what was at hand, what lay at the door, that David thought not of? "You did hide your face, and I was troubled" (v. 7). God was ready to hide his face, and David to enter into a temptation of desertion, and he knew it not.

As, then, unto a *prosperous* condition. I shall not run cross to[15] Solomon's counsel, "In the day of prosperity rejoice" (Eccles. 7:14). Rejoice in the God

[14] moral improvement, reformation
[15] contradict, go against

of your mercies, who does you good in his patience and forbearance, notwithstanding all your unworthiness. Yet I may add to it, from the same fountain of wisdom, "Consider," also, lest evil lie at the door. A man in that state is in the midst of snares. Satan has many advantages against him; he forges darts out of all his enjoyments; and, if he watch not, he will be entangled before he is aware.

You want that which should poise and ballast your heart. Formality in religion will be apt to creep upon you; and that lays the soul open to all temptations in their full power and strength. Satisfaction and delight in creature-comforts, the poison of the soul, will be apt to grow upon you. In such a time be vigilant, be circumspect,[16] or you will be surprised. Job says that in his affliction "God made his heart soft" (Job 23:16). There is a hardness, an insensible[17] want[18] of spiritual sense, gathered in prosperity, that, if not watched against, will expose the heart to the deceits of sin and baits of Satan. "Watch and pray" in this season. Many men's negligence in it has cost them dear; their woeful experience cries out to take heed. Blessed is he that fears always, but especially in a time of prosperity.

As in part was manifested before, *a time of the slumber of grace, of neglect in communion with God, of formality in duty,* is a season to be watched in, as that which certainly [has] some other temptation attending it.

Let a soul in such an estate awake and look about him. His enemy is at hand, and he is ready to fall into such a condition as may cost him dear all the days of his life. His present estate is bad enough in itself; but it is an indication of that which is worse that lies at the door. The disciples that were with Christ in the mount had not only a bodily, but a spiritual drowsiness upon them. What says our Savior to them? "Arise; watch and pray, that you enter not into temptation." We know how near one of them [Peter] was to a bitter hour of temptation, and not watching as he ought, he immediately entered into it.

I mentioned before the case of the spouse (Song 5:2-8). She slept, and was drowsy and unwilling to gird up herself to a vigorous performance of duties in a way of quick, active communion with Christ. Before she is aware, she has lost her Beloved; then she moans, inquires, cries, endures woundings, reproaches, and all before she obtains him again. Consider, then, O poor soul, your state and condition! Does your light burn dim? Or though it give to others as great a blaze as formerly, yet you see not so clearly the face of

---

[16] watchful, attentive, cautious
[17] apathetic, callous, uncomprehending
[18] lack

God in Christ by it as you have done (2 Cor. 4:6)? Is your zeal cold? Or if it do the same works as formerly, yet your heart is not warmed with the love of God and to God in them as formerly, but only you proceed in the course you have been in? Are you negligent in the duties of praying or hearing? Or if you do observe them, you do it not with that life and vigor as formerly? Do you flag[19] in your profession? Or if you keep it up, yet your wheels are oiled by some sinister respects from within or without? Does your delight in the people of God faint and grow cold? Or is your love to them changing from that which is purely spiritual into that which is very carnal, upon the account of suitableness of principles and natural spirits, if not worse foundations? If you are drowsing in such a condition as this, take heed; you are falling into some woeful temptation that will break all your bones, and give you wounds that shall stick by you all the days of your life. Yea, when you awake, you will find that it has indeed laid hold of you already, though you perceive it not; it has smitten and wounded you, though you have not complained nor sought for relief or healing.

Such was the state of the church of Sardis. "The things that remained were ready to die" (Rev. 3:2). "Be watchful," says our Savior, "and strengthen them, or a worse thing will befall you." If any that reads the word of this direction be in this condition, if he has any regard of his poor soul, let him now awake, before he be entangled beyond recovery. Take this warning from God; despise it not.

A season of great spiritual enjoyments is often, by the malice of Satan and the weakness of our hearts, turned into a season of danger as to this business of temptation.

We know how the case stood with Paul (2 Cor. 12:7). He had glorious spiritual revelations of God and Jesus Christ. Instantly Satan falls upon him, a messenger from him buffets[20] him, so that he earnestly begs its departure, but yet is left to struggle with it. God is pleased sometimes to give us special discoveries of himself and his love, to fill the heart with his kindness; Christ takes us into the banqueting-house, and gives our hearts their fill of love; and this by some signal work of his Spirit, overpowering us with a sense of love in the unspeakable privilege of adoption, and so fills our souls with joy unspeakable and glorious. A man would think this was the securest condition in the world. What soul does not cry with Peter in the mount, "It is good for me to be here; to abide here forever" [Matt. 17:4]? But yet very frequently

[19] decline in vigor or strength
[20] strikes repeatedly

some bitter temptation is now at hand. Satan sees that, being possessed by the joy before us, we quickly neglect many ways of approach to our souls, wherein he seeks and finds advantages against us. Is this, then, our state and condition? Does God at any time give us to drink of the rivers of pleasure that are at his right hand [Ps. 36:8], and satisfy our souls with his kindness as with marrow and fatness[21] [Ps. 63:5]? Let us not say, "We shall never be moved"—we know not how soon God may hide his face, or a messenger from Satan may buffet us.

Besides, there lies oftentimes a greater and worse deceit in this business. Men cheat their souls with their own fancies, instead of a sense of God's love by the Holy Ghost; and when they are lifted up with their imaginations, it is not expressible how fearfully they are exposed to all manner of temptations—and how, then, are they able to find relief against their consciences from their own foolish fancies and deceivings, wherewith they sport themselves? May we not see such every day—persons walking in the vanities and ways of this world, yet boasting of their sense of the love of God? Shall we believe them? We must not, then, believe truth itself; and how woeful, then, must their condition needs be!

A fourth season is *a season of self-confidence;* then usually temptation is at hand.

The case of Peter is clear unto this: "I will not deny you; though all men should deny you I will not; though I were to die for it, I would not do it" [Matt. 26:33, 35]. This said the poor man when he stood on the very brink of that temptation that cost him in the issue such bitter tears. And this taught him so far to know himself all his days, and gave him such acquaintance with the state of all believers, that when he had received more of the Spirit and of power, yet he had less of confidence, and saw it was fit that others should have so also, and therefore persuades all men to "pass the time of their sojourning here in fear" (1 Pet. 1:17), not to be confident and high as he was, lest, as he did, they fall. At the first trial he compares himself with others, and vaunts himself above them: "Though all men should forsake you, yet I will not." He fears every man more than himself. But when our Savior afterward comes to him, and puts him directly upon the comparison, "Simon, son of Jonas, do you love me more than these?" (John 21:15), he is done comparing himself with others, and only cries, "Lord, you know that I love you" [John 21:15, 16, 17]. He will lift up himself above others no more. Such a season oftentimes falls out. Temptations are abroad in the world, false doctrines,

[21] richness, fertility

with innumerable other allurements and provocations: we are ready every one to be very confident that we shall not be surprised with them: though all men should fall into these follies yet we would not: surely we shall never go off from our walking with God; it is impossible [that] our hearts should be so sottish. But says the apostle, "Be not high-minded, but fear; let him that thinks he stands take heed lest he fall" [1 Cor. 10:12]. Would you think that Peter, who had walked on the sea with Christ, confessed him to be the Son of God, been with him on the mount when he heard the voice from the excellent glory, should, at the word of a servant-girl, when there was no legal inquisition after him, no process against him, nor anyone in his condition, instantly fall a-cursing and swearing that he knew him not? Let them take heed of self-confidence who have any mind to take heed of sin. And this is the first thing in our watching, to consider well the seasons wherein temptation usually makes its approaches to the soul, and be armed against them. And these are some of the seasons wherein temptations are nigh[22] at hand.

[Chapter 7]

Watch the Heart

That part of watchfulness against temptation which we have considered regards the outward means, occasions, and advantages of temptation; we now proceed to that which respects the *heart itself,* which is wrought upon and entangled by temptation. Watching or keeping of the heart, which above all keepings we are obliged unto, comes within the compass of this duty also; for the right performance whereof take these ensuing directions:

Let him that would not enter into temptations labor to know his own heart, to be acquainted with his own spirit, his natural frame and temper, his lusts and corruptions, his natural, sinful, or spiritual weaknesses, that, finding where his weakness lies, he may be careful to keep at a distance from all occasions of sin.

Our Savior tells the disciples that "they knew not what spirit they were of" [Luke 9:55], which, under a pretense of zeal, betrayed them into ambition and desire of revenge. Had they known it they would have watched over themselves. David tells us that he considered his ways, and "kept himself from his iniquity," which he was particularly prone unto (Ps. 18:23).

---

[22] near

There are advantages for temptations lying oftentimes in men's *natural tempers and constitutions.* Some are naturally gentle, facile,[23] easy to be entreated, pliable; which, though it be the noblest temper of nature, and the best and choicest ground, when well broken up and fallowed[24] for grace to grow in, yet, if not watched over, will be a means of innumerable surprises and entanglements in temptation. Others are earthy, froward,[25] morose,[26] so that envy, malice, selfishness, peevishness,[27] harsh thoughts of others, repinings[28] lie at the very door of their natures, and they can scarce step out but they are in the snare of one or other of them. Others are passionate and the like. Now, he that would watch that he enter not into temptation had need be acquainted with his own natural temper that he may watch over the treacheries that lie in it continually. Take heed lest you have a Jehu in you, that shall make you drive furiously; or a Jonah in you, that will make you ready to repine; or a David, that will make you hasty in your determinations, as he was often, in the warmth and goodness of his natural temper. He who watches not this thoroughly, who is not exactly skilled in the knowledge of himself, will never be disentangled from one temptation or another all his days.

Again: as men have peculiar natural tempers, which, according as they are attended or managed, prove a great *fomes*[29] of sin, or advantage to the exercise of grace, so men may have *peculiar lusts* or corruptions, which, either by their natural constitution or education, and other prejudices, have got deep rooting and strength in them. This, also, is to be found out by him who would not enter into temptation. Unless he know it, unless his eyes be always on it, unless he observes its actings, motions, advantages, it will continually be entangling and ensnaring of him. This, then, is our sixth direction in this kind:

Labor to know your own frame and temper;
what spirit you are of;
what associates in your heart Satan has;
where corruption is strong,
where grace is weak;
what stronghold lust has in your natural constitution,
and the like.

---

[23] mild-mannered
[24] plowed but unseeded
[25] stubbornly contrary, obstinate
[26] sullenly melancholy, gloomy
[27] irritability, discontentment
[28] discontentment, grumblings
[29] diseased material

How many have all their comforts blasted and peace disturbed by their natural passion and peevishness! How many are rendered useless in the world by their frowardness and discontent! How many are disquieted even by their own gentleness and facility![30] Be acquainted, then, with your own heart: though it be deep, search it; though it be dark, inquire into it; though it give all its distempers other names than what are their due, believe it not. Were not men utter strangers to themselves—did they not give flattering titles to their natural distempers—did they not strive rather to justify, palliate,[31] or excuse the evils of their hearts that are suited to their natural tempers and constitutions, than to destroy them, and by these means keep themselves off from taking a clear and distinct view of them—it were impossible that they should all their days hang in the same briers without attempt for deliverance. Uselessness and scandal in professors are branches growing constantly on this root of unacquaintedness with their own frame and temper; and how few are there who will either study them themselves or bear with those who would acquaint them with them!

When you know the state and condition of your heart as to the particulars mentioned, *watch against all such occasions and opportunities, employments, societies, retirements,*[32] *businesses, as are apt to entangle your natural temper or provoke your corruption.* It may be there are some ways, some societies, some businesses, that you never in your life escaped them, but suffered by them, more or less, through their suitableness to entice or provoke your corruption. It may be you are in a state and condition of life that weary you day by day, on the account of your ambition, passion, discontent, or the like: if you have any love to your soul, it is time for you to awake and to deliver yourself as a bird from the evil snare. Peter will not come again in haste to the high priest's hall; nor would David walk again on the top of his house, when he should have been on the high places of the field. But the particulars of this instance are so various, and of such several natures in respect of several persons, that it is impossible to enumerate them (Prov. 4:14-15). Herein lies no small part of that wisdom which consists in our ordering our conversation aright. Seeing we have so little power over our hearts when once they meet with suitable provocations, we are to keep them asunder, as a man would do fire and the combustible parts of the house wherein he dwells.

Be sure to *lay in provision in store against the approaching of any temptation.* This also belongs to our watchfulness over our hearts. You will say,

---

[30] aptitude, ease
[31] moderate the seriousness or intensity of
[32] privacy, seclusion, leisure

"What provision is intended, and where is it to be laid up?" Our hearts, as our Savior speaks, are our treasury. There we lay up whatsoever we have, good or bad; and thence do we draw it for our use (Matt. 12:35). It is the heart, then, wherein provision is to be laid up against temptation. When an enemy draws nigh to a fort or castle to besiege and take it, oftentimes, if he find it well manned and furnished with provision for a siege, and so able to hold out, he withdraws and assaults it not. If Satan, the prince of this world, come and find our hearts fortified against his batteries, and provided to hold out, he not only departs, but, as James says, he flees: "He will flee from us" (4:7). For the provision to be laid up it is that which is provided in the gospel for us. Gospel provisions will do this work; that is, keep the heart full of a sense of the love of God in Christ. This is the greatest preservative against the power of temptation in the world. Joseph had this; and therefore, on the first appearance of temptation, he cries out, "How can I do this great evil, and sin against God?"—and there is an end of the temptation as to him; it lays no hold on him, but departs. He was furnished with such a ready sense of the love of God as temptation could not stand before (Gen. 39:9). "The love of Christ constrains us," says the apostle, "to live to him" (2 Cor. 5:14); and so, consequently, to withstand temptation. A man may, nay, he ought to lay in provisions of the law also—fear of death, hell, punishment, with the terror of the Lord in them. But these are far more easily conquered than the other; nay, they will never stand alone against a vigorous assault. They are conquered in convinced persons every day; hearts stored with them will struggle for a while, but quickly give over. But store the heart with a sense of the love of God in Christ, and his love in the shedding[33] of it; get a relish of the privileges we have thereby—our adoption, justification, acceptance with God; fill the heart with thoughts of the beauty of his death—and you will, in an ordinary course of walking with God, have great peace and security as to the disturbance of temptations. When men can live and plod on in their profession, and not be able to say when they had any living sense of the love of God or of the privileges which we have in the blood of Christ, I know not what they can have to keep them from falling into snares. The apostle tells us that the "peace of God shall keep our hearts" (Phil. 4:7). The Greek [*phroureō*] denotes a military word—a garrison; and so is, "shall keep as in a garrison." Now, a garrison has two things attending it—first, that it is exposed to the assaults of its enemies; second, that safety lies in it from their attempts. It is so with our souls; they are exposed to temptations, assaulted

[33] diffusing, spreading abroad

continually; but if there be a garrison in them, or if they be kept as in a garrison, temptation shall not enter, and consequently we shall not enter into temptation. Now, how is this done? Says he, "The peace of God shall do it." What is this "peace of God"? A sense of his love and favor in Jesus Christ. Let this abide in you, and it shall garrison you against all assaults whatsoever. Besides, there is that, in a special manner, which is also in all the rest of the directions—and means that temptation can make use of to approach unto our souls. Contending to obtain and keep a sense of the love of God in Christ, in the nature of it, obviates[34] all the workings and insinuations of temptation. Let this be a third direction, then, in our watching against temptation: *Lay in store of gospel provisions that may make the soul a defensed place against all the assaults thereof.*

In the first approach of any temptation, as we are all tempted, these directions following are also suited to carry on the work of watching, which we are in the pursuit of:

Be always awake, that you may have an early discovery of your temptation, that you may know it so to be. Most men perceive not their enemy until they are wounded by him. Yea, others may sometimes see them deeply engaged, while themselves are utterly insensible; they sleep without any sense of danger, until others come and awake them by telling them that their house is on fire. Temptation in a neuter sense is not easily discoverable—namely, as it denotes such a way, or thing, or matter, as is or may be made use of for the ends of temptation. Few take notice of it until it is too late, and they find themselves entangled, if not wounded. Watch, then, to understand betimes[35] the snares that are laid for you—to understand the advantages your enemies have against you, before they get strength and power, before they are incorporated with your lusts, and have distilled poison into your soul.

Consider the aim and tendency of the temptation, whatsoever it be, and of all that are concerned in it. Those who have an active concurrence into[36] your temptation are Satan and your own lusts. For your own lust, I have manifested elsewhere what it aims at in all its actings and enticings. It never rises up but its intent is the worst of evils. Every acting of it would be a formed enmity against God. Hence look upon it in its first attempts, whatsoever pretenses may be made, as your mortal enemy. "I hate it," says the apostle (Rom. 7:15)—that is, the working of lust in me. "I hate it; it is the greatest

[34] anticipates and prevents
[35] early, in due time
[36] cooperation with

enemy I have. Oh, that it were killed and destroyed! Oh, that I were delivered out of the power of it!" Know, then, that in the first attempt or assault in any temptation, the most cursed, sworn enemy is at hand, is setting on you, and that for your utter ruin; so that it were the greatest madness in the world to throw yourself into his arms to be destroyed. But of this I have spoken in my discourse of Mortification.

Has Satan any more friendly aim and intention toward you who is a sharer in every temptation? To beguile you as a serpent, to devour you as a lion, is the friendship that he owes you. I shall only add that the sin he tempts you to against the law, it is not the thing he aims at; his design lies against your interest in the gospel. He would make sin but a bridge to get over to a better ground, to assault you as to your interest in Christ. He who perhaps will say today, "You may venture on sin, because you have an interest in Christ," will tomorrow tell you to the purpose that you have none because you have done so.

Meet your temptation in its entrance with thoughts of faith concerning Christ on the cross; this will make it sink before you. Entertain no parley, no dispute with it, if you would not enter into it. Say, "'It is Christ that died'—that died for such sins as these." This is called "taking the shield of faith to quench the fiery darts of Satan" (Eph. 6:16). Faith does it by laying hold on Christ crucified, his love therein, and what from thence he suffered for sin. Let your temptation be what it will—be it unto sin, to fear or doubting for sin, or about your state and condition—it is not able to stand before faith lifting up the standard of the cross. We know what means the papists,[37] who have lost the power of faith, use to keep up the form. They will sign themselves with the sign of the cross, or make aerial crosses; and by virtue of that work done, think to scare away the devil. To act faith on Christ crucified is really to sign ourselves with the sign of the cross, and thereby shall we overcome that wicked one (1 Pet. 5:9).

Suppose the soul has been surprised by temptation, and entangled at unawares, so that now it is too late to resist the first entrances of it. What shall such a soul do that it be not plunged into it, and carried away with the power thereof?

First, do as Paul did: *beseech God again and again that it may "depart from you"* (2 Cor. 12:8). And if you abide therein, you shall certainly either be speedily delivered out of it, or receive a sufficiency of grace [so as] not to be foiled utterly by it. Only, as I said in part before, do not so much employ

[37] negative label for Roman Catholics, relating to belief in papal supremacy; from the Latin *papa* ("pope")

your thoughts about the things whereunto you are tempted, which oftentimes raises further entanglements, but set yourself against the temptation itself. Pray against the temptation that it may depart; and when that is taken away, the things themselves may be more calmly considered.

Second, *fly to Christ, in a peculiar manner, as he was tempted, and beg of him to give you succor in this "needful time of trouble."* The apostle instructs us herein: "In that he has been tempted, he is able to succor them that are tempted" (Heb. 4:16). This is the meaning of it: "When you are tempted and are ready to faint, when you want succor—you must have it or you die—act faith peculiarly on Christ as he was tempted; that is, consider that he was tempted himself—that he suffered thereby—that he conquered all temptations, and that not merely on his own account, seeing for our sakes he submitted to be tempted, but for us." (He conquered in and by himself, but for us.) And draw, yea, expect succor from him (Heb. 4:15-16). Lie down at his feet, make your complaint known to him, beg his assistance, and it will not be in vain.

Third, *look to him who has promised deliverance.* Consider that he is faithful and will not suffer you to be tempted above what you are able. Consider that he has promised a comfortable issue of these trials and temptations. Call all the promises to mind of assistance and deliverance that he has made; ponder them in your heart. And rest upon it, that God has innumerable ways that you know not of to give you in deliverance; as—

He can send an *affliction* that shall mortify your heart unto the matter of the temptation, whatever it be, that that which was before a sweet morsel under the tongue shall neither have taste or relish in it unto you—your desire to it shall be killed; as was the case with David; or,

He can, by *some providence,* alter that whole state of things from whence your temptation does arise, so taking fuel from the fire, causing it to go out of itself; as it was with the same David in the day of battle; or,

He can *tread down Satan under your feet,* that he shall not dare to suggest anything any more to your disadvantage (the God of peace shall do it), that you shall hear of him no more; or,

He can give you such *supply of grace* as that you may be freed, though not from the temptation itself, yet from the tendency and danger of it; as was the case with Paul [2 Cor. 12:8-9]; or,

He can give you such a comfortable persuasion of *good success* in the issue as that you shall have refreshment in your trials, and be kept from the trouble of the temptation; as was the case with the same Paul; or,

He can *utterly remove* it, and make you a complete conqueror. And innumerable other ways he has of keeping you from entering into temptation, so as to be foiled by it.

Fourth, *consider where the temptation, wherewith you are surprised, has made its entrance, and by what means and with all speed make up the breach.*[38] Stop that passage which the waters have made to enter in at. Deal with your soul like a wise physician. Inquire when, how, by what means, you fell into this distemper; and if you find negligence, carelessness, want of keeping watch over yourself, to have lain at the bottom of it, fix your soul there—bewail that before the Lord—make up that breach—and then proceed to the work that lies before you.

[Chapter 8]

Keep the Word of Christ's Patience

The directions insisted on in the former chapters are such as are partly given us, in their several particulars, up and down the Scripture, [and they] partly arise from the nature of the thing itself. There is one general direction [that] remains, which is comprehensive of all that went before and also adds many more particulars unto them. This contains an approved antidote against the poison of temptation—a remedy that Christ himself has marked with a note of efficacy and success; that is given us in the words of our Savior himself to the church of Philadelphia. "Because," says he, "you have kept the word of my patience, I will also keep you from the hour of temptation, which shall come upon all the world, to try them that dwell in the earth" (Rev. 3:10). Christ is "the same yesterday, today, and forever" [Heb. 13:8]. As he dealt with the church of Philadelphia, so will he deal with us. If we "keep the word of his patience," he will "keep us from the hour of temptation." This, then, being a way of rolling the whole care of this weighty affair on him who is able to bear it, it requires our peculiar attention.

And, therefore, I shall show: (1) What it is to "keep the word of Christ's patience," that we may know how to perform our duty; and (2) How this will be a means of our preservation, which will establish us in the faith of Christ's promise.

[38] gap, broken area

What It Means to "Keep the Word of Christ's Patience"

The word of Christ is the word of the gospel; the word by him revealed from the bosom of the Father; the word of the Word; the word spoken in time of the eternal Word. So it is called "the word of Christ" (Col. 3:16), or "the gospel of Christ" (Rom. 1:16; 1 Cor. 9:12), and "the doctrine of Christ" (Heb. 6:1). "Of Christ," that is, as its author (Heb. 1:1-2); and of him, as the chief subject or matter of it (2 Cor. 1:20). Now this word is called "the word of Christ's patience," or tolerance and forbearance, upon the account of that patience and longsuffering which, in the dispensation of it, the Lord Christ exercises toward the whole, and to all persons in it; and that both actively and passively, in his bearing with men and enduring from them.

He is patient toward his *saints*—he bears with them, suffers from them. He is "patient toward us" (2 Pet. 3:9)—that is, that believe. The gospel is the word of Christ's patience even to believers. A soul acquainted with the gospel knows that there is no property[39] of Christ rendered more glorious therein than that of his patience. That he should bear with so many unkindnesses, so many causeless breaches, so many neglects of his love, so many affronts done to his grace, so many violations of engagements as he does, it manifests his gospel to be not only the word of his grace, but also of his patience. He suffers also *from* them in all the reproaches they bring upon his name and ways; and he suffers *in* them, for "in all their afflictions he is afflicted."

[He is patient] toward the *elect* not yet effectually called. He stands waiting at the door of their hearts and knocks for an entrance (Rev. 3:20). He deals with them by all means, and yet stands and waits until "his head is filled with the dew, and his locks with the drops of the night" (Song 5:2), as enduring the cold and inconveniences of the night, that when his morning is come he may have entrance. Oftentimes for a long season he is by them scorned in his person, persecuted in his saints and ways, reviled in his word, while he stands at the door in the word of his patience, with his heart full of love toward their poor rebellious souls.

[He is patient] to the *perishing world.* Hence the time of his kingdom in this world is called the time of his "patience" (Rev. 1:9). He "endures the vessels of wrath with much longsuffering" (Rom. 9:22). While the gospel is administered in the world he is patient toward the men thereof, until the saints in heaven and earth are astonished and cry out, "How long?" (Ps. 13:1-2; Rev. 6:10). And themselves do mock at him as if he were an idol (2 Pet. 3:4). He endures from them bitter things, in his name, ways, worship,

[39] characteristic, quality

saints, promises, threats, all his interest of honor and love; and yet passes by them, lets them alone, does them good. Nor will he cut this way of proceeding short until the gospel shall be preached no more. Patience must accompany the gospel.

Now, this is the word that is to be kept, that we may be kept from "the hour of temptation." Three things are implied in the keeping of this word: (1) knowledge; (2) valuation; (3) obedience:

Knowledge. He that will keep this word must know it, be acquainted with it, under a fourfold notion: first, as a word of *grace* and *mercy* to save him; second, as a word of *holiness* and *purity* to sanctify him; third, as a word of *liberty* and *power* to ennoble him and set him free; and fourth, as a word of *consolation* to support him in every condition.

First, as a word of *grace* and *mercy* able to save us: "It is the power of God unto salvation" (Rom. 1:16); "the grace of God that brings forth salvation" (Titus 2:11); "the word of grace that is able to build us up, and to give us an inheritance among all them that are sanctified" (Acts 20:32); "The word that is able to save our souls" (James 1:21). When the word of the gospel is known as a word of mercy, grace, and pardon, as the sole evidence for, as the conveyance of an eternal inheritance; when the soul finds it such to itself, it will strive to keep it.

Second, as a word of *holiness* and *purity* able to sanctify him: "You are clean through the word I have spoken unto you," says our Savior (John 15:3). To that purpose is his prayer (John 17:17). He that knows not the word of Christ's patience as a sanctifying, cleansing word, in the power of it upon his own soul, neither knows it nor keeps it. The empty profession of our days knows not one step toward this duty; and thence it is that the most are so overborne under the power of temptations. Men full of self, of the world, of fury, ambition, and almost all unclean lusts, do yet talk of keeping the word of Christ! (See 1 Peter 1:2; 2 Timothy 2:19.)

Third, as a word of *liberty* and *power* to ennoble him and set him free—and this not only from the guilt of sin and from wrath, for that it does as it is a word of grace and mercy; not only from the power of sin, for that it does as it is a word of holiness; but also from all outward respects of men or the world that might entangle him or enslave him. It declares us to be "Christ's freemen" and in bondage unto none (John 8:32; 1 Cor. 7:23). We are not by it freed from due subjection unto superiors, nor from any duty, nor unto any sin (1 Pet. 2:16); but in two respects it is a word of freedom, liberty, largeness of mind, power and deliverance from bondage: first, in respect of *conscience* as to the worship of God (Gal. 5:1); second, in respect of *ignoble,* slavish respects unto the men or things of the world, in the course of our pilgrimage. The gospel gives a free, large, and noble spirit, in subjection to God and none else. There is administered in it a spirit "not of fear, but of power, and of love, and of a sound mind" (2 Tim. 1:7); a mind "in nothing terrified" (Phil. 1:28)—not swayed with any by-respect[40] whatsoever. There is nothing more unworthy of the gospel than a mind in bondage to persons or things, prostituting itself to the lusts of men or affrightments of the world. And he that thus knows the word of Christ's patience, really and in power, is even thereby freed from innumerable, from unspeakable temptations.

Fourth, as a word of *consolation* to support him in every condition and to be a full portion in the want of all. It is a word attended with "joy unspeakable and full of glory" [1 Pet. 1:8]. It gives support, relief, refreshment, satisfaction, peace, consolation, joy, boasting, glory, in every condition whatsoever. Thus to know the word of Christ's patience, thus to know the gospel, is the first part, and it is a great part of this condition of our preservation from the hour and power of temptation.

Valuation of what is thus known belongs to the keeping of this word. It is to be kept as a treasure. That excellent *depositum*[41] (that is, the word of the gospel)—"keep it," says the apostle, "by the Holy Ghost" (2 Tim. 1:14); and "Hold fast the faithful word" (Titus 1:9). It is a good treasure, a faithful word; hold it fast. It is a word that comprises the whole interest of Christ in the world. To value that as our chief treasure is to keep the word of Christ's patience. They that will have a regard from Christ in the time of temptation are not to be regardless of his concerns.

Personal obedience, in the universal observation of all the commands of Christ, is the keeping of his word (John 14:15). Close adherence unto Christ in holiness and universal obedience, then when the opposition that the gospel of Christ does meet with in the world does render it signally the word of his patience, is the life and soul of the duty required.

Now, all these are to be so managed with that intension[42] of mind and spirit, that care of heart and diligence of the whole person, as to make up a keeping of this word; which evidently includes all these considerations.

We have arrived, then, to the sum of this safeguarding duty, of this condition of freedom from the power of temptation: He that, having a due acquaintance with the gospel in its excellencies, as to him a word of mercy,

---

40 private advantage
41 deposit
42 intention

holiness, liberty, and consolation, values it, in all its concerns, as his choicest and only treasure—makes it his business and the work of his life to give himself up unto it in universal obedience, then especially when opposition and apostasy put the patience of Christ to the utmost—he shall be preserved from the hour of temptation.

How Keeping the Word of Christ's Patience Will Be a Means of Preservation

This is that which is comprehensive of all that went before and is exclusive of all other ways for the obtaining of the end purposed. Nor let any man think without this to be kept one hour from entering into temptation; wherever he fails, there temptation enters. That this will be a sure preservative may appear from the ensuing considerations:

It has the promise of preservation, and this alone has so. It is solemnly promised, in the place mentioned, to the church of Philadelphia on this account. When a great trial and temptation was to come on the world, at the opening of the seventh seal (Rev. 7:3), a caution is given for the preservation of God's sealed ones, which are described to be those who keep the word of Christ; for the promise is that it should be so.

Now, in every promise there are three things to be considered: (1) The *faithfulness* of the Father, who gives it; (2) The *grace* of the Son, which is the matter of it; (3) The *power* and *efficacy* of the Holy Ghost, which puts the promise in execution. And all these are engaged for the preservation of such persons from the hour of temptation.

The *faithfulness of God* accompanies the promise. On this account is our deliverance laid (1 Cor. 10:13). Though we be tempted, yet we shall be kept from the hour of temptation; it shall not grow too strong for us. What comes on us we shall be able to bear; and what would be too hard for us we shall escape. But what security have we hereof? Even the faithfulness of God: "God is faithful, who will not suffer you," etc. And wherein is God's faithfulness seen and exercised? "He is faithful that promised" (Heb. 10:23); his faithfulness consists in his discharge of his promises. "He abides faithful: he cannot deny himself" (2 Tim. 2:13). So that by being under the promise, we have the faithfulness of God engaged for our preservation.

There is in every promise of the covenant *the grace of the Son;* that is the subject matter of all promises: "I will keep you." How? "By my grace with you." So that what assistance the grace of Christ can give a soul that has a right in this promise, in the hour of temptation it shall enjoy it. Paul's temptation grew very high; it was likely to have come to its prevalent hour. He besought the Lord, that is, the Lord Jesus Christ, for help (2 Cor. 12:8), and received that answer from him, "My grace is sufficient for you" (v. 9). That it was the Lord Christ and his grace with whom he had peculiarly to do is evident from the close of that verse: "I will glory in my infirmity, that the power of Christ may rest upon me," or "the efficacy of the grace of Christ in my preservation be made evident" (so Heb. 2:18).

The *efficacy of the Spirit* accompanies the promises. He is called "the Holy Spirit of promise" [Eph. 1:13], not only because he is promised by Christ, but also because he effectually makes good the promise and gives it accomplishment in our souls. He also, then, is engaged to preserve the soul walking according to the rule laid down (see Isa. 59:21). Thus, where the promise is, there is all this assistance. The faithfulness of the Father, the grace of the Son, the power of the Spirit, all are engaged in our preservation.

This constant, universal keeping of Christ's word of patience will keep the heart and soul in such a frame, as wherein no prevalent temptation, by virtue of any advantages whatsoever, can seize upon it, so as totally to prevail against it. So David prays, "Let integrity and uprightness preserve me" (Ps. 25:21). This integrity and uprightness is the Old Testament keeping the word of Christ—universal close walking with God. Now how can they preserve a man? Why, by keeping his heart in such a frame, so defended on every side, that no evil can approach or take hold on him. Fail a man in his integrity, he has an open place for temptation to enter (Isa. 57:21). To keep the word of Christ is to do this universally, as has been showed. This exercises grace in all the faculties of the soul,[43] and compasses it with the whole armor of God. The understanding is full of light; the affections, of love and holiness. Let the wind blow from what quarter it will, the soul is fenced and fortified; let the enemy assault when or by what means he pleases, all things in the soul of such a one are upon the guard; "How can I do this thing, and sin against God?" [Gen. 39:9] is at hand. Especially, upon a twofold account does deliverance and security arise from his hand:

By *the mortification of the heart* unto the matter of temptations. The prevalency of any temptation arises from hence, that the heart is ready to close with the matter of it. There are lusts within, suited to the proposals of the world or Satan without. Hence James resolves all temptations into our "own lusts" (1:14); because either they proceed from or are made effectual by them, as has been declared. Why do terror or threats turn us aside from

[43] The traditional "faculties of the soul" are understanding (intellect), will (volition), and affection (emotion).

a due constancy in the performance of our duty? Is it not because there is unmortified, carnal fear abiding in us, that tumultuates in such a season? Why is it that the allurements of the world and compliances with men entangle us? Is it not because our affections are entangled with the things and considerations proposed unto us? Now, keeping the word of Christ's patience, in the manner declared, keeps the heart mortified to these things, and so it is not easily entangled by them. Says the apostle, "I am crucified with Christ" (Gal. 2:20). He that keeps close to Christ is crucified with him and is dead to all the desires of the flesh and the world (as more fully: Gal. 6:14). Here the match is broken, and all love, entangling love, dissolved. The heart is crucified to the world and all things in it. Now the matter of all temptations almost is taken out of the world; the men of it, or the things of it, make them up. "As to these things," says the apostle, "I am crucified to them" (and it is so with everyone that keeps the word of Christ). "My heart is mortified unto them. I have no desire after them, nor affection to them, nor delight in them, and they are crucified unto me. The crowns, glories, thrones, pleasures, profits of the world, I see nothing desirable in them. The reputation among them, they are all as a thing of nought.[44] I have no value nor estimation of them." When Achan saw the "goodly Babylonian garment, and two hundred shekels of silver, and a wedge of gold," first he "coveted them," then he "took them" (Josh. 7:21). Temptation subtly spreads the Babylonish garment of favor, praise, peace, the silver of pleasure or profit, with the golden contentments of the flesh, before the eyes of men. If now there be that in them alive, unmortified, that will presently fall a-coveting; let what fear of punishment will ensue, the heart of hand will be put forth into iniquity.

Herein, then, lies the security of such a frame as that described: It is always accompanied with a mortified heart, crucified unto the things that are the matter of our temptations; without which it is utterly impossible that we should be preserved one moment when any temptation does befall us. If liking and love of the things proposed, insinuated, commended in the temptation be living and active in us, we shall not be able to resist and stand.

In this frame *the heart is filled with better things and their excellency,* so far as to be fortified against the matter of any temptation. See what resolution this puts Paul upon; all is "loss and dung" to him (Phil. 3:8). Who would go out of his way to have his arms full of loss and dung? And whence is it that he has this estimation of the most desirable things in the world? It is from that dear estimation he had of the excellency of Christ. So (v. 10), when the soul

[44] they are all as nothing

is exercised to communion with Christ, and to walking with him, he drinks new wine, and cannot desire the old things of the world, for he says "the new is better." He tastes every day how gracious the Lord is; and therefore longs not after the sweetness of forbidden things—which indeed have none. He that makes it his business to eat daily of the tree of life will have no appetite unto other fruit, though the tree that bear them seem to stand in the midst of paradise. This the spouse makes the means of her preservation: even the excellency which, by daily communion, she found in Christ and his graces above all other desirable things. Let a soul exercise itself to a communion with Christ in the good things of the gospel—pardon of sin, fruits of holiness, hope of glory, peace with God, joy in the Holy Ghost, dominion over sin—and he shall have a mighty preservative against all temptations. As the full soul loathes the honeycomb—as a soul filled with carnal, earthly, sensual contentments finds no relish nor savor in the sweetest spiritual things; so he that is satisfied with the kindness of God, as with marrow and fatness—that is, every day entertained at the banquet of wine, wine upon the lees,[45] and well refined [Isa. 25:6]—has a holy contempt of the baits and allurements that lie in prevailing temptations, and is safe.

He that so keeps the word of Christ's patience is always furnished with *preserving considerations* and *preserving principles*—moral and real advantages of preservation.

He is furnished with preserving *considerations* that powerfully influence his soul in his walking diligently with Christ. Besides the sense of duty which is always upon him, he considers—

The concern of Christ, whom his soul loves, in him and his careful walking. He considers that the presence of Christ is with him, his eye upon him; that he ponders his heart and ways, as one greatly concerned in his deportment of himself, in a time of trial. So Christ manifests himself to do (Rev. 2:19-23). He considers all—what is acceptable, what is to be rejected. He knows that Christ is concerned in his honor, that his name be not evil spoken of by reason of him; that he is concerned in love to his soul, having that design upon him to "present him holy, and unblamable, and unreprovable in his sight" (Col. 1:22)—and his Spirit is grieved where he is interrupted in this work; concerned on the account of his gospel, the progress and acceptation of it in the world—its beauty would be slurred, its good things reviled, its progress stopped, if such a one be prevailed against; concerned in his love to others, who are grievously scandalized, and perhaps ruined, by the

[45] wine that has been aged properly

miscarriages of such. When Hymeneus and Philetus fell, they overthrew the faith of some [2 Tim. 2:17-18]. And says such a soul, then, who is exercised to keep the word of Christ's patience, when intricate, perplexed, entangling temptations, public, private, personal, do arise, "Shall I now be careless? Shall I be negligent? Shall I comply with the world and the ways of it? Oh what thoughts of heart has he concerning me, whose eye is upon me! Shall I contemn his honor, despise his love, trample his gospel in the mire under the feet of men, turn aside others from his ways? Shall such a man as I fly, give over resistings? It cannot be." There is no man who keeps the word of the patience of Christ but is full of this soul-pressing consideration. It dwells on his heart and spirit; and the love of Christ constrains him so to keep his heart and ways (2 Cor. 5:14).

The great consideration of the temptations of Christ in his behalf, and the conquest he made in all assaults for his sake and his God, dwell also on his spirit. The prince of this world came upon him, every thing in earth or hell that has either allurement or affrightment in it was proposed to him, to divert him from the work of mediation which for us he had undertaken. This whole life he calls the time of his "temptations," but he resisted all, conquered all, and became a Captain of salvation to them that obey him [Heb. 2:10]. "And," says the soul, "shall this temptation, these arguings, this plausible pretense, this sloth, this self-love, this sensuality, this bait of the world, turn me aside, prevail over me, to desert him who went before me in the ways of all temptations that his holy nature was obnoxious[46] unto, for my good?"

Dismal thoughts of the loss of love, of the smiles of the countenance[47] *of Christ, do also frequently exercise such a soul.* He knows what it is to enjoy the favor of Christ, to have a sense of his love, to be accepted in his approaches to him, to converse with him, and perhaps has been sometimes at some loss in this thing; and so knows also what it is to be in the dark, distanced from him. See the deportment of the spouse in such a case (Song 3:4). When she had once found him again, she holds him; she will not let him go; she will lose him no more.

He that keeps the word of Christ's patience has preserving *principles* whereby he is acted.[48] Some of them may be mentioned:

In all things he lives by faith, and is acted by it in all his ways (Gal. 2:20).

---

46 harmfully exposed
47 approval
48 activated

Now, upon a twofold account has faith, when improved, the power of preservation from temptation annexed unto it:

Because it empties the soul of its own wisdom, understanding, and fullness, that it may act in the wisdom and fullness of Christ. The only advice for the preservation in trials and temptations lies in that of the wise man, "Trust in the LORD with all your heart; and lean not unto your own understanding" (Prov. 3:5). This is the work of faith; it is faith; it is to live by faith. The great falling of men in trials is [due to] their leaning to, or leaning upon, their own understanding and counsel. What is the issue of it? "The steps of his strength shall be straitened,[49] and his own counsel shall cast him down" (Job 18:7). First, he shall be entangled, and then cast down; and all by his own counsel, until he come to be ashamed of it, as Ephraim was (Hos. 10:6). Whenever in our trials we consult our own understandings, hearken to self-reasonings, though they seem to be good, and tending to our preservation, yet the principle of living by faith is stifled, and we shall in the issue be cast down by our own counsels. Now, nothing can empty the heart of this self-fullness but faith, but living by it, but not living to ourselves, but having Christ live in us by our living by faith on him.

Faith, making the soul poor, empty, helpless, destitute in itself, engages the heart, will, and power of Jesus Christ for assistance; of which I have spoken more at large elsewhere.

Love to the saints, with care that they suffer not upon our account, is a great preserving principle in a time of temptations and trials. How powerful this was in David he declares in that earnest prayer, "Let not them that wait on you, O Lord GOD of hosts, be ashamed for my sake: let not those that seek you be confounded for my sake, O God of Israel" (Ps. 69:6)—"Oh, let not me so miscarry, that those for whom I would lay down my life should be put to shame, be evil spoken of, dishonored, reviled, contemned on my account, for my failings." A selfish soul, whose love is turned wholly inwards, will never abide in a time of trial.

Many other considerations and principles that those who keep the word of Christ's patience, in the way and manner before described, are attended with, might be enumerated; but I shall content myself to have pointed at these mentioned.

And will it now be easy to determine whence it is that so many in our days are prevailed on in the time of trial—that the hour of temptation comes upon them, and bears them down more or less before it? Is it not because,

[49] shortened

among the great multitude of professors that we have, there are few that keep the word of the patience of Christ? If we willfully neglect or cast away our interest in the promise of preservation, is it any wonder if we be not preserved? There is an hour of temptation come upon the world, to try them that dwell therein. It variously exerts its power and efficacy. There is not any way or thing wherein it may not be seen acting and putting forth itself. In worldliness; in sensuality; in looseness of conversation; in neglect of spiritual duties, private, public; in foolish, loose, diabolical opinions; in haughtiness and ambition; in envy and wrath; in strife and debate, revenge, selfishness; in atheism and contempt of God, does it appear. They are but branches of the same root, bitter streams of the same fountain, cherished by peace, prosperity, security, apostasies of professors, and the like. And, alas! How many do daily fall under the power of this temptation in general! How few keep their garments girded about them, and undefiled! And if any urging, particular temptation befall any, what instances almost have we of any that escape? May we not describe our condition as the apostle [described] that of the Corinthians, in respect of an outward visitation: "Some are sick, and some are weak, and many sleep" [1 Cor. 11:3]? Some are wounded, some defiled, many utterly lost. What is the spring and fountain of this sad condition of things? Is it not—as has been said—that we do not keep the word of Christ's patience in universal close walking with him, and so lose the benefit of the promise given and annexed[50] thereunto?

Examples of Professors Coming Short of Keeping the Word of Christ's Patience

Should I go about to give instances of this thing, of professors coming short of keeping the word of Christ, it would be a long work. These four heads would comprise the most of them: (1) *conformity to the world,* which Christ has redeemed us from, almost in all things, with joy and delight in promiscuous compliances with the men of the world; (2) *neglect of duties* which Christ has enjoined, from close meditation to public ordinances; (3) *strife, variance,*[51] and *debate* among ourselves, woeful *judging* and *despising* one another, upon account of things foreign to the bond of communion that is between the saints; (4) *self-fullness* as to principles, and *selfishness* as to ends. Now, where these things are, are not men carnal? Is the word of Christ's patience effectual in them? Shall they be preserved? They shall not.

[50] attached
[51] dissent, discord

Cautions to Take in Order to Be Preserved from Temptation

Would you, then, be preserved and kept from the hour of temptation? Would you watch against entering into it? As deductions from what has been delivered in this chapter, take the ensuing cautions:

First, *take heed of leaning on deceitful assistances;* as—

On your own counsels, understandings, reasonings. Though you argue in them never so plausibly in your own defense, they will leave you, betray you. When the temptation comes to any height, they will all turn about, and take part with your enemy, and plead as much for the matter of the temptation, whatever it be, as they pleaded against the end and issue of it before.

The most vigorous actings, by prayer, fasting, and other such means, against that particular lust, corruption, temptation, wherewith you are exercised and have to do. This will not avail you if, in the meantime, there be neglects on other accounts. To hear a man wrestle, cry, contend as to any particular of temptation, and immediately fall into worldly ways, worldly compliances, looseness, and negligence in other things—it is righteous with Jesus Christ to leave such a one to the hour of temptation.

The general security of saints' perseverance and preservation from total apostasy. Every security that God gives us is good in its kind, and for the purpose for which it is given to us; but when it is given for one end, to use it for another, that is not good or profitable. To make use of the general assurance of preservation from total apostasy, to support the spirit in respect of a particular temptation, will not in the issue advantage the soul; because notwithstanding that, this or that temptation may prevail. Many relieve themselves with this, until they find themselves to be in the depth of perplexities.

Second, *apply yourselves to this great preservation of faithful keeping the word of Christ's patience, in the midst of all trials and temptations:*

In particular, wisely consider wherein the word of Christ's patience is most likely to suffer in the days wherein we live and the seasons that pass over us, and so vigorously set yourselves to keep it in that particular peculiarly. You will say, "How will we know wherein the word of Christ's patience in any season is likely to suffer?" I answer: Consider what works he peculiarly performs in any season; and neglect of his word in reference to them is that wherein his word is likely to suffer. The works of Christ wherein he has been peculiarly engaged in our days and seasons seem to be these:

The *pouring of contempt* upon the great men and great things of the world, with all the enjoyments of it. He has discovered the nakedness of all earthly things, in overturning, overturning, overturning, both men and things, to make way for the things that cannot be shaken.

The *owning of the lot* of his own inheritance in a distinguishing manner, putting a difference between the precious and the vile, and causing his people to dwell alone, as not reckoned with the nations.

In being *nigh* to faith and prayer, honoring them above all the strength and counsels of the sons of men.

In recovering his *ordinances* and institutions from the carnal administrations that they were in bondage under by the lusts of men, bringing them forth in the beauty and the power of the Spirit.

Wherein, then, in such a season, must lie the peculiar neglect of the word of Christ's patience? Is it not in setting a value on the world and the things of it, which he has stained and trampled under foot? Is it not in the slighting of his peculiar lot, his people, and casting them into the same considerations with the men of the world? Is it not in leaning to our own counsels and understandings? Is it not in the defilement of his ordinances, by giving the outward court of the temple to be trod upon by unsanctified persons? Let us, then, be watchful, and in these things keep the word of the patience of Christ, if we love our own preservation.

In this frame urge the Lord Jesus Christ with his blessed promises, with all the considerations that may be apt to take and hold the King in his galleries, that may work on the heart of our blessed and merciful High Priest, to give suitable succor at time of need [Heb. 4:16].

[Chapter 9]

General Exhortations Related to the Duty of Watching

Having thus passed through the considerations of the duty of watching that we enter not into temptation, I suppose I need not add motives to the observance of it. Those who are not moved by their own sad experiences, nor the importance of the duty as laid down in the entrance of this discourse, must be left by me to the further patience of God. I shall only shut up[52] the whole with a general exhortation to them who are in any measure prepared for it by the consideration of what has been spoken. Should you go into a hospital

[52] summarize, sum up

and see many persons lying sick and weak, sore and wounded, with many filthy diseases and distempers, and should inquire of them how they fell into this condition, and they shall all agree to tell you such or such a thing was the occasion of it—"By that I got my wound," says one, "And my disease," says another—would it not make you a little careful how or what you had to do with that thing or place? Surely it would. Should you go to a dungeon, and see many miserable creatures bound in chains for an approaching day of execution, and inquire the way and means whereby they were brought into that condition, and they should all fix on one and the same thing, would you not take care to avoid it? The case is so with entering into temptation. Ah! How many poor, miserable, spiritually wounded souls have we everywhere!—one wounded by one sin, another by another; one falling into filthiness of the flesh, another of the spirit. Ask them, now, how they came into this estate and condition? They must all answer, "Alas! We entered into temptation, we fell into cursed snares and entanglements; and that has brought us into the woeful condition you see!" Nay, if a man could look into the dungeons of hell, and see the poor damned souls that lie bound in chains of darkness, and hear their cries, what would he be taught? What do they say? Are they not cursing their tempters and the temptations that they entered in? And shall we be negligent in this thing? Solomon tells us that the "simple one that follows the strange woman knows not that the dead are there, that her house inclines to death, and her paths to the dead" [Prov. 2:16-18] (which he repeats three times); and that is the reason that he ventures on her snares. If you knew what has been done by entering into temptation, perhaps you would be more watchful and careful. Men may think that they shall do well enough notwithstanding; but, "Can a man take fire in his bosom, and his clothes not be burnt? Can one go upon hot coals, and his feet not be burnt?" (Prov. 6:27-28). No such thing; men come not out of their temptation without wounds, burnings, and scars. I know not any place in the world where there is more need of pressing this exhortation than in this place. Go to our several colleges, inquire for such and such young men; what is the answer in respect of many? "Ah! Such a one was very hopeful for a season; but he fell into ill company, and he is quite lost. Such a one had some good beginning of religion, we were in great expectation of him; but he is fallen into temptation." And so in other places. "Such a one was useful and humble, adorned the gospel; but now he is so woefully entangled with the world that he is grown all self, has no sap nor savor. Such a one was humble and zealous; but he is advanced, and has lost his first love and ways." Oh, how full is the world, how full is this place, of these woeful examples; to say nothing of those innumerable poor creatures who are fallen into temptation by delusions in religion. And is it not time for us to awake before it be too late—to watch against the first rising of sin, the first attempts of Satan, and all ways whereby he has made his approaches to us, be they never so harmless in themselves?

Have we not experience of our weakness, our folly, *the invincible power* of temptation, when once it is gotten within us? As for this duty that I have insisted on, take these considerations:

If you neglect it, it being the only means prescribed by our Savior, you will certainly enter into temptation, and as certainly fall into sin. Flatter yourselves. Some of you are "old disciples," having a great abhorrency of sin; you think it impossible you should ever be seduced so and so; but "let him (whoever he be) that think he stands take heed lest he fall" [1 Cor. 10:12]. It is not any grace received, it is not any experience obtained, it is not any resolution improved, that will preserve you from any evil, unless you stand upon your watch: "What I say unto you," says Christ, "I say unto all, Watch." Perhaps you may have had some good success for a time in your careless frame; but awake, admire God's tenderness and patience, or evil lies at the door. If you will not perform this duty, whoever you are, one way or other, in one thing or other, spiritual or carnal wickedness, you will be tempted, you will be defiled; and what will be the end thereof? Remember Peter!

Consider that you are always under the eye of Christ, the great captain of our salvation, who has enjoined us to watch thus, and pray that we enter not into temptation. What do you think are the thoughts and the heart of Christ when he sees a temptation hastening toward us, a storm rising about us, and we are fast asleep? Does it not grieve him to see us expose ourselves so to danger, after he has given us warning upon warning? While he was in the days of his flesh he considered his temptation while it was yet coming, and armed himself against it. "The prince of this world comes," says he, "but has no part in me" [John 14:30]. And shall we be negligent under his eye? Do not think that you see him coming to you as he did to Peter, when he was asleep in the garden, with the same reproof: "What! Can you not watch one hour?" Would it not be a grief to you to be so reproved, or to hear him thundering against your neglect from heaven, as against the church of Sardis (Rev. 3:2)?

Consider that if you neglect this duty, and so fall into temptation— which assuredly you will do—*that when you are entangled God may with [it] bring some heavy affliction or judgment upon you,* which, by reason of your entanglement, you shall not be able to look on any otherwise than as an evidence of his anger and hatred; and then what will you do with your temptation and affliction together? All your bones will be broken, and your peace and strength will be gone in a moment. This may seem but as a noise of words for the present; but if ever it be your condition, you will find it to be full of woe and bitterness. Oh, then, let us strive to keep our spirits unentangled, avoiding all appearance of evil and all ways leading thereunto; especially all ways, businesses, societies, and employments that we have already found disadvantageous to us.

Overview of John Owen's

The Nature, Power, Deceit, and Prevalency of Indwelling Sin

Justin Taylor

JOHN OWEN begins Part 1 of *The Nature, Power, Deceit, and Prevalency of Indwelling Sin* with an examination of the nature of indwelling sin by looking at Romans 7:21: "I find then a law, that, when I would do good, evil is present with me." Owen observes that indwelling sin is a law found in believers despite their habitual inclination to good (chapter 1). Owen defines indwelling sin as a powerful and effectual principle that constantly inclines, presses, and works toward evil.

Part 2 is a lengthy look at the power and efficacy of this law of indwelling sin. As usual, Owen starts with the general and moves to the particular, explaining the common characteristics of every law, then showing what kind of law indwelling sin is (chapter 2), stressing its abiding nature. Chapter 3 examines the heart as the seat and subject of this law, while chapter 4 looks at the natural properties of the law, such as enmity and constancy.

Owen then begins to treat the actions and operations of indwelling sin, which will occupy his attention over the next eight chapters. He focuses on indwelling sin's "aversation" (chapter 5) and opposition, both by force (chapters 6–7) and by deceit (chapters 8–13). A major subset of this exposition concerns the degrees whereby sin works from temptation to sin: (1) it draws away the mind from its duty (chapters 8–10); (2) it entices the affections (chapter 11); (3) actual sin is conceived in the will (chapter 12); then (4) it is brought forth in its actual accomplishment (chapter 13).[1]

Part 3 concerns the effect of indwelling sin, in the lives of both believers (chapters 14–15) and unbelievers (chapter 16). Finally Owen demonstrates the strength of sin as evidenced by its resistance to the power of the law.

[1] Of the three books reprinted in this edition, *Indwelling Sin* is undoubtedly the most challenging from a structural standpoint. Consulting the extensive outline included at the end of this volume should be of assistance for readers wanting to follow the intricacies of Owen's arrangement.

THE

Nature, Power, Deceit, and Prevalency of the remainders of

Indwelling-Sin

IN

BELIEVERS.

Together with the wayes of its Working, And Means of Prevention.

Opened, evinced and applyed, with a Resolution of sundry Cases of Conscience thereunto appertaining.

O wretched man that I am, who shall deliver me from this Body of Death! I thank God through Jesus Christ our Lord, Rom.7.24,25.

LONDON,

Printed for *Thomas Cockerill*, at the Sign of the *Atlas* in *Cornhil* near the Royal Exchange. 1675.

Preface

THAT THE DOCTRINE OF original sin is one of the fundamental truths of our Christian profession has been always owned[1] in the church of God; and a special part it is of that peculiar[2] possession of truth which they enjoy whose religion toward God is built upon and resolved into divine revelation. As the world by its wisdom never knew God aright, so the wise men of it were always utterly ignorant of this inbred evil in themselves and others. With us the doctrine and conviction of it lie in the very foundation of all wherein we have to do with God, in reference unto our pleasing of him here, or obtaining the enjoyment of him hereafter. It is also known what influence it has into the great truths concerning the person of Christ, his mediation, the fruits and effects of it, with all the benefits that we are made partakers of thereby. Without a supposition of it, not any of them can be truly known or savingly believed. For this cause has it been largely treated of by many holy and learned men, both of old and of latter days. Some have labored in the discovery of its *nature,* some of its *guilt* and demerit; by whom also the truth concerning it has been vindicated from the opposition made unto it in the past and present ages. By most these things have been considered in their full extent and latitude, with respect unto all men by nature, with the estate and condition of them who are wholly under the power and guilt of it. How thereby men are disenabled and incapacitated in themselves to answer the obedience required either in the law or the gospel, so as to free themselves from the curse of the one or to make themselves partakers of the *blessing* of the other, has been by many also fully evinced.[3] Moreover, that there are remainders of it abiding in believers after their regeneration and conversion to God, as the Scripture abundantly testifies, so it has been fully taught and confirmed; as also how the guilt of it is pardoned unto them, and by what means the power of it is weakened in them. All these things, I say, have been largely treated on, to the great benefit and edification of the church. In what we have now in design we therefore take them all for granted, and endeavor

---

[1] admitted, acknowledged, confessed to be true
[2] particular, characteristic
[3] proven, evidenced, made manifest

only further to carry on the discovery of it in its actings and oppositions to the law and grace of God in believers. Neither do I intend the discussing of anything that has been controverted[4] about it. What the Scripture plainly reveals and teaches concerning it—what believers evidently find by experience in themselves—what they may learn from the examples and acknowledgments of others, shall be represented in a way suited unto the capacity of the meanest[5] and weakest who is concerned therein. And many things seem to render the handling of it at this season not unnecessary. The effects and fruits of it, which we see in the apostasies and backslidings of many, the scandalous sins and miscarriages of some, and the course and lives of the most, seem to call for a due consideration of it. Besides, of how great concern a full and clear acquaintance with the power of this indwelling sin (the matter designed to be opened) is unto believers, to stir them up to watchfulness and diligence, to faith and prayer, to call them to repentance, humility, and self-abasement, will appear in our progress.

These, in general, were the ends aimed at in the ensuing discourse, which, being at first composed and delivered for the use and benefit of a few, is now by the providence of God made public. And if the reader receive any advantage by these weak endeavors, let him know that it is his duty, as to give glory unto God, so to help them by his prayers who in many temptations and afflictions are willing to labor in the vineyard of the Lord, unto which work they are called.

[4] made an object of dispute

[5] most lowly, insignificant

PART 1:

The Nature of Indwelling Sin

[Chapter 1]

Foundational Text on Indwelling Sin: Romans 7:21

It is of *indwelling sin,* and that in the remainders of it in persons after their conversion to God, with its power, efficacy, and effects that we intend to treat. This also is the great design of the apostle to manifest and evince[1] in chapter 7 of the Epistle to the Romans. Many, indeed, are the contests about the principal scope of the apostle in that chapter, and in what state the person is, under the law or under grace, whose condition he expresses therein. I shall not at present enter into that dispute, but take that for granted which may be undeniably proved and evinced—namely, that it is the condition of a regenerate person, with respect unto the remaining power of indwelling sin which is there proposed and exemplified, by and in the person of the apostle himself. In that discourse, therefore, of his, shall the foundation be laid of what we have to offer upon this subject. Not that I shall proceed in an exposition of his revelation of this truth as it lies in its own contexture,[2] but only make use of what is delivered by him as occasion shall offer itself. And here first occurs that which he affirms: "I find then a law, that, when I would do good, evil is present with me" (v. 21).

There are four things observable in these words: (1) The appellation[3] he gives unto indwelling sin, whereby he expresses its power and efficacy: it is "a law"; for that which he terms "a law" in this verse, he calls in the foregoing, "sin that dwells in" him. (2) The way whereby he came to the discovery of this law; not absolutely and in its own nature, but in himself he found it: "I find a law." (3) The frame of his soul and inward man with this law of sin, and under its discovery: he "would do good." (4) The state and activity of this law when the soul is in that frame when it would do good: it "is present with" him. For what ends and purposes we shall show afterward.

Indwelling Sin Is a Law

The first thing observable is the compellation[4] here used by the apostle; he calls indwelling sin "a law." It is a law.

A law is taken either properly for a *directive rule* or improperly for an

[1] proven, evidenced, made manifest
[2] context
[3] name, designation
[4] address, naming

operative effective principle, which seems to have the force of a law. In its first sense, it is a moral rule which directs and commands, and sundry[5] ways moves and regulates, the mind and the will as to the things which it requires or forbids. This is evidently the general nature and work of a law. Some things it commands, some things it forbids, with rewards and penalties which move and impel men to do the one and avoid the other. Hence, in a secondary sense, *an inward principle* that moves and inclines constantly unto any actions is called a law. The principle that is in the nature of everything, moving and carrying it toward its own end and rest, is called *the law of nature.* In this respect, every inward principle that inclines and urges unto operations or actings suitable to itself is a law. So the powerful and effectual working of the Spirit and grace of Christ in the hearts of believers is called "the law of the Spirit of life" (Rom. 8:2). And for this reason does the apostle here call indwelling sin a law. It is *a powerful and effectual indwelling principle, inclining and pressing unto actions agreeable and suitable unto its own nature.* This, and no other, is the intention of the apostle in this expression: for although that term, "a law," may sometimes intend a state and condition—and if here so used, the meaning of the words should be, "I find that this is my condition, this is the state of things with me, that when I would do good evil is present with me," which makes no great alteration in the principal intention of the place—yet properly it can denote nothing here but the chief subject treated of; for although the name of a law be variously used by the apostle in this chapter, yet when it relates unto sin it is nowhere applied by him to the condition of the person, but only to express either the nature or the power of sin itself. So, "I see another law in my members, warring against the law of my mind, and bringing me into captivity to the law of sin which is in my members" (7:23). That which he here calls the "*law* of his mind," from the principal subject and seat of it, is in itself no other but the "law of the Spirit of life which is in Christ Jesus" (8:2); or the effectual power of the Spirit of grace, as was said. But "the law," as applied unto sin, has a double sense: for as, in the first place, "I see a law in my members," it denotes the being and nature of sin; so, in the latter, "Leading into captivity to the law of sin which is in my members," it signifies its power and efficacy. And both [of] these are comprised in the same name, singly used (7:21). Now, that which we observe from this name or term of a "law" attributed unto sin is that *there is an exceeding efficacy and power in the remainders of indwelling sin in believers, with a constant working toward evil.*

---

[5] various

Thus it is in believers; it is a law even *in* them, though not *to* them. Though its rule be broken, its strength weakened and impaired, its root mortified, yet it is a law still of great force and efficacy. There, where it is least felt, it is most powerful. Carnal men, in reference unto spiritual and moral duties, are nothing but this law; they do nothing but from it and by it. It is in them a ruling and prevailing principle of all moral actions, with reference unto a supernatural and eternal end. I shall not consider it in them in whom it has most power, but in them in whom its power is chiefly discovered and discerned—that is, in believers; in the others only in order to the further conviction and manifestation thereof.

The Law of Indwelling Sin Is Found in Believers

Secondly, the apostle proposes the way whereby he discovered this law in himself: *euriskō ara ton nomon,* "I find then a law." He *found* it. It had been *told* him there was such a law; it had been *preached* unto him. This convinced him that there was a law of sin. But it is one thing for a man to know in general that there is a law of sin; [it is] another thing for a man to have an experience of the power of this law of sin in himself. It is preached to all; all men that own[6] the Scripture acknowledge it as being declared therein. But they are but few that know it in themselves; we should else have more complaints of it than we have, and more contendings against it, and less fruits of it in the world. But this is that which the apostle affirms—not that the doctrine of it had been preached unto him, but that he found it by experience in himself. "I find a law"—"I have experience of its power and efficacy." For a man to find his sickness, and danger thereon from its effects, is another thing than to hear a discourse about a disease from its causes. And this experience is the great preservative of all divine truth in the soul. This it is to know a thing indeed, in reality, to know it for ourselves, when, as we are taught it from the word, so we find it in ourselves. Hence we observe, secondly, *believers have experience of the power and efficacy of indwelling sin.* They find it in themselves; they find it as a law. It has a self-evidencing efficacy to them that are alive to discern it. They that find not its power are under its dominion. Whosoever [would] contend against it shall know and find that it is present with them, that it is powerful in them. He shall find the stream to be strong who swims against it, though he who rolls along with it be insensible[7] of it.

[6] fully confess, acknowledge as true

[7] apathetic, callous, uncomprehending

The Habitual Inclination of Believers' Wills Is unto Good

Thirdly, the general frame of believers, notwithstanding the inhabitation of this law of sin, is here also expressed. They "would do good." This law is "present": *thelonti emoi poiein to kalon.* The habitual inclination of their will is unto good. The law *in* them is not a law *unto* them, as it is to unbelievers. They are not wholly obnoxious[8] to its power, nor *morally* unto its commands. Grace has the sovereignty in their souls: this gives them a will unto good. They "would do good," that is, always and constantly. 1 John 3:9, *poiein hamartian,*[9] "to commit *sin,*" is to make a trade[10] of sin, to make it a man's business to sin. So it is said [that] a believer "does not commit sin"; and so *poiein to kalon,* "to do that which is good." To will to do so is to have the habitual bent and inclination of the will set on that which is good—that is, morally and spiritually good, which is the proper subject treated of: whence is our third observation: *there is, and there is through grace, kept up in believers a constant and ordinarily prevailing will of doing good, notwithstanding the power and efficacy of indwelling sin to the contrary.*

This, in their worst condition, distinguishes them from unbelievers in their best. The will in unbelievers is under the power of the law of sin. The opposition they make to sin, either in the root or branches of it, is from their light and their consciences; the will of sinning in them is never taken away. Take away all other considerations and hindrances, whereof we shall treat afterward, and they would sin willingly always. Their faint endeavors to answer their convictions are far from a will of doing that which is good. They will plead, indeed, that they would leave[11] their sins if they could, and they would fain[12] do better than they do. But it is the working of their light and convictions, not any spiritual inclination of their wills, which they intend by that expression: for where there is a will of doing good, there is a choice of that which is good for its own excellency's sake—because it is desirable and suitable to the soul, and therefore to be preferred before that which is contrary. Now this is not in any unbelievers. They do not, they cannot, so choose that which is spiritually good, nor is it so excellent or suitable unto any principle that is in them; only they have some desires to attain that end whereunto that which is good does lead, and to avoid that evil which the

[8] harmfully exposed
[9] This precise phrase is not actually found in 1 John 3:9, though the concept is.
[10] make a habit
[11] cease
[12] eagerly, gladly

neglect of it tends unto. And these also are for the most part so weak and languid[13] in many of them, that they put them not upon any considerable endeavors. Witness that luxury, sloth, worldliness, and security that the generality of men are even drowned in. But in believers there is a will of doing good, a habitual disposition and inclination in their wills unto that which is spiritually good; and where this is, it is accompanied with answerable effects. The will is the principle of our moral actions; and therefore unto the prevailing disposition thereof will the general course of our actings be suited. Good things will proceed from the good treasures of the heart [Luke 6:45]. Nor can this disposition be evidenced to be in any but by its fruits. A will of doing good, without doing good, is but pretended.

Evil Is Present Within Believers

Fourthly, there is yet another thing remaining in these words of the apostle, arising from that respect that the presence of sin has unto the time and season of duty: "When I would do good," says he, "evil is present with me."

There are two things to be considered in the will of doing good that is in believers: (1) There is its *habitual residence* in them. They have always a habitual inclination of will unto that which is good. And this habitual preparation for good is always present with them; as the apostle expresses it (Rom. 7:18). (2) There are *special times and seasons* for the exercise of that principle. There is a "*When* I would do good"—a season wherein this or that good, this or that duty, is to be performed and accomplished suitably unto the habitual preparation and inclination of the will.

Unto these two there are two things in indwelling sin opposed. To the gracious principle residing in the will, inclining unto that which is spiritually good, it is opposed as it is a law—that is, a *contrary principle,* inclining unto evil, with an aversation[14] from that which is good. Unto the second, or the actual willing of this or that good in particular, unto this "When I would do good," is opposed the presence of this law: "Evil is present with me"—*emoi to kakon parakeitai*—evil is at hand, and ready to oppose the actual accomplishment of the good aimed at. Whence, fourthly, *indwelling sin is effectually operative in rebelling and inclining to evil, when the will of doing good is in a particular manner active and inclining unto obedience.*

And this is the description of him who is a believer and a sinner, as everyone who is the former is the latter also. These are the contrary principles and

---

[13] lacking power

[14] a moral turning away, estrangement, repulsion

the contrary operations that are in him. The principles are a will of doing good, on the one hand, from grace, and a law of sin on the other. Their adverse actings and operations are insinuated in these expressions: "When I would do good, evil is present with me." And these both are more fully expressed by the apostle: "For the flesh lusts against the Spirit, and the Spirit against the flesh: and these are contrary the one to the other; so that I cannot do the things that I would" (Gal. 5:17).

And here lie the springs of the whole course of our obedience. An acquaintance with these several principles and their actings is the principal part of our wisdom. They are upon the matter, next to the free grace of God in or justification by the blood of Christ, the only things wherein the glory of God and our own souls are concerned. These are the springs of our holiness and our sins, of our joys and troubles, of our refreshments and sorrows. It is, then, all our concerns to be thoroughly acquainted with these things, who intend to walk with God and to glorify him in this world.

And hence we may see what wisdom is required in the guiding and management of our hearts and ways before God. Where the subjects of a ruler are in feuds and oppositions, one against another, unless great wisdom be used in the government of the whole, all things will quickly be ruinous in that state. There are these contrary principles in the hearts of believers. And if they labor not to be spiritually wise, how shall they be able to steer their course aright? Many men live in the dark to themselves all their days; whatever else they know, they know not themselves. They know their outward estates, how rich they are, and the condition of their bodies as to health and sickness they are careful to examine; but as to their inward man, and their principles as to God and eternity, they know little or nothing of themselves. Indeed, few labor to grow wise in this matter, few study themselves as they ought, are acquainted with the evils of their own hearts as they ought; on which yet the whole course of their obedience, and consequently of their eternal condition, does depend. This, therefore, is our wisdom; and it is a needful wisdom, if we have any design to please God, or to avoid that which is a provocation to the eyes of his glory.

We shall find, also, in our inquiry hereinto, what diligence and watchfulness is required unto a Christian conversation.[15] There is a constant enemy unto it in everyone's own heart; and what an enemy it is we shall afterward show, for this is our design: to discover him to the uttermost. In the meantime, we may well bewail the woeful sloth and negligence that is in the most,

[15] way of life

even in professors.[16] They live and walk as though they intended to go to heaven hood-winked and asleep, as though they had no enemy to deal with. Their mistake, therefore, and folly will be fully laid open in our progress.

That which I shall principally fix upon, in reference unto our present design, from this place of the apostle, is that which was first laid down—namely, that *there is an exceeding efficacy and power in the remainder of indwelling sin in believers, with a constant inclination and working toward evil.*

Awake, therefore, all of you in whose hearts is anything of the ways of God! Your enemy is not only *upon* you, as on Samson of old, but is *in* you also. He is at work, by all ways of force and craft, as we shall see. Would you not dishonor God and his gospel; would you not scandalize the saints and ways of God; would you not wound your consciences and endanger your souls; would you not grieve the good and holy Spirit of God, the author of all your comforts; would you keep your garments undefiled, and escape the woeful temptations and pollutions of the days wherein we live; would you be preserved from the number of the apostates in these latter days? Awake to the consideration of this cursed enemy, which is the spring of all these and innumerable other evils, as also of the ruin of all the souls that perish in this world!

[16] those who make a religious confession; professing Christians

PART 2

The Power and Efficacy of Indwelling Sin

[Chapter 2]

That which we have proposed unto consideration is the power and efficacy of indwelling sin. The ways whereby it may be evinced are many. I shall begin with the appellation of it in the place before mentioned. It is a law. "I find a law," says the apostle [Rom. 7:21]. It is because of its power and efficacy that it is so called. So is also the principle of grace in believers the "law of the Spirit of life" (Rom. 8:2), as we observed before, which is the "exceeding greatness of the power of God" in them (Eph. 1:19). Where there is a law there is power.

We shall, therefore, show both what belongs unto it as it is a law in general, and also what is peculiar[1] or proper in it as being such a law as we have described.

Characteristics of Every Law

There are in general two things attending every law, as such:

Dominion

First, dominion. "The law has dominion over a man while he lives" (Rom. 7:1)—*Kurieuei tou anthrōpou*—"It lords it over a man." Where any law takes place, *kurieuei,* it has dominion. It is properly the act of a superior, and it belongs to its nature to exact obedience by way of dominion. Now, there is a twofold dominion, as there is a twofold law. There is a *moral authoritative dominion over a man,* and there is a *real effective dominion in a man.* The first is an affection[2] of the law of God, the latter of the law of sin. The law of sin has not in itself a moral dominion—it has not a rightful dominion or authority over any man; but it has that which is equivalent unto it; whence it is said *basileuein,* "to reign as a king" (Rom. 6:12), and *kurieuein,* "to lord it" or have dominion (v. 14), as a law in general is said to have (7:1). But because it has lost its complete dominion in reference unto believers, of whom alone we speak, I shall not insist upon it in this utmost extent of its power. But even in them it is a law still—though not a law unto them, yet, as was said, it is a law in them. And though it has not a complete, and, as it were, a rightful dominion over them, yet it will have a domination as to some things in them. It is still a law, and that in them; so that all its actings are the actings

[1] particular, characteristic
[2] effect

of a law—that is, it acts with power, though it has lost its complete power of ruling in them. Though it be *weakened,* yet its nature is not *thawed.* It is a law still, and therefore powerful. And as its particular workings, which we shall afterward consider, are the ground of this appellation, so the term itself teaches us in general what we are to expect from it, and what endeavors it will use for dominion, to which it has been accustomed.

Efficacy to Provoke

Secondly, a law, as a law, has *an efficacy to provoke* those that are obnoxious unto it unto the things that it requires. A law has rewards and punishments accompanying it. These secretly prevail on them to whom they are proposed, though the things commanded be not much desirable. And generally all laws have their efficacy on the minds of men, from the rewards and punishments that are annexed unto them. Nor is this law without this spring of power: it has its rewards and punishments. The pleasures of sin are the rewards of sin; a reward that most men lose their souls to obtain. By this the law of sin contended in Moses against the law of grace. "He chose rather to suffer affliction with the people of God than to enjoy the pleasures of sin for a season; for he looked unto the recompense of reward" (Heb. 11:25-26). The contest was in his mind between the law of sin and the law of grace. The motive on the part of the law of sin, wherewith it sought to draw him over and wherewith it prevails on the most, was the reward that it proposed unto him—namely, that he should have the present enjoyment of the pleasures of sin. By this it contended against the reward annexed unto the law of grace, called "the recompense of reward."

By this *sorry reward* does this law keep the world in obedience to its commands; and experience shows us of what power it is to influence the minds of men. It has also punishments that it threatens men with who labor to cast off its yoke. Whatever evil, trouble, or danger in the world attends gospel obedience—whatever hardship or violence is to be offered to the sensual[3] part of our natures in a strict course of mortification—sin makes use of, as if they were punishments attending the neglect of its commands. By these it prevails on the "fearful," who shall have no share in life eternal (Rev. 21:8). And it is hard to say by whether of these, its pretended rewards or pretended punishments, it does most prevail, in whether of them its greatest strength does lie. By its rewards it entices men to sins of commission, as they are called, in ways and actions tending to the satisfaction of its lusts. By its punishments

[3] perceived by the senses (not necessarily sexual)

it induces men to the omitting of duties; a course tending to no less a pernicious[4] event than the former. By which of these the law of sin has its greatest success in and upon the souls of men is not evident; and that because they are seldom or never separated, but equally take place on the same persons. But this is certain, that by tenders[5] and promises of the pleasures of sin on the one hand, by threats of the deprivation of all sensual contentments and the infliction of temporal evils on the other, it has an exceeding efficacy on the minds of men, oftentimes on believers themselves. Unless a man be prepared to reject the reasonings that will offer themselves from the one and the other of these, there is no standing before the *power* of the law. The world falls before them every day. With what deceit and violence they are urged and imposed on the minds of men we shall afterward declare; as also what advantages they have to prevail upon them. Look on the generality of men, and you shall find them wholly by these means at sin's disposal. Do the profits and pleasures of sin lie before them?—nothing can withhold them from reaching after them. Do difficulties and inconveniences attend the duties of the gospel?—they will have nothing to do with them; and so are wholly given up to the rule and dominion of this law.

And this light in general we have into the power and efficacy of indwelling sin from the general nature of a law, whereof it is partaker.

What Kind of Law Indwelling Sin Is

We may consider, nextly, what kind of law in particular it is; which will further evidence that power of it which we are inquiring after. It is not an outward, written, commanding, directing law, but an inbred, working, impelling, urging law. A law *proposed* unto us is not to be compared, for efficacy, to a law *inbred* in us. Adam had a law of sin proposed to him in his temptation; but because he had no law of sin inbred and working in him, he might have withstood it. An inbred law must needs be[6] effectual. Let us take an example from that law which is contrary to this law of sin. The law of God was at first inbred and natural unto man; it was concreated with[7] his faculties, and was their rectitude, both in being and operation, in reference to his end of living unto God and glorifying of him. Hence it had a special power in the whole soul to enable it unto all obedience, yea, and to make all obedience easy and

[4] deadly
[5] offers
[6] is of necessity
[7] created at the same time as

pleasant. Such is the power of an inbred law. And though this law, as to the rule and dominion of it, be now by nature cast out of the soul, yet the remaining sparks of it, because they are inbred, are very powerful and effectual; as the apostle declares (Rom. 2:14-15). Afterward God renews this law and writes it in tables of stone. But what is the efficacy of this law? Will it now, as it is external and proposed unto men, enable them to perform the things that it exacts and requires? Not at all. God knew it would not, unless it were turned to an internal law again; that is, until, of a moral outward rule, it be turned into an inward real principle. Wherefore God makes his law internal again, and implants it on the heart as it was at first, when he intends to give it power to produce obedience in his people: "I will put my law in their inward parts, and write it in their hearts" (Jer. 31:31-33). This is that which God fixes on, as it were, upon a discovery of the insufficiency of an outward law leading men unto obedience. "The written law," says he, "will not do it; mercies and deliverances from distress will not effect it; trials and afflictions will not accomplish it." "Then," says the Lord, "will I take another course: I will turn the *written law* into an internal living principle in their hearts; and that will have such an efficacy as shall assuredly make them my people, and keep them so." Now, such is this law of sin. It is an indwelling law: "It is sin that dwells in me" (Rom. 7:17); "sin that dwells in me" (v. 20); "It is present with me" (v. 21); "It is in my members" (v. 23)—yea, it is so far in a man, as in some sense it is said to be the man himself; "I know that in me (that is, in my flesh) dwells no good thing" (v. 18). The flesh, which is the seat and throne of this law, yea, which indeed *is* this law, is in some sense the man himself, as grace also is the new man. Now, from this consideration of it, that it is an indwelling law inclining and moving to sin as an inward habit or principle, it has sundry advantages increasing its strength and furthering its power, as:

It always abides in the soul—it is never absent. The apostle twice uses that expression, "It dwells in me." There is its constant residence and habitation. If it came upon the soul only at certain seasons, much obedience might be perfectly accomplished in its absence; yea, and as they deal with usurping[8] tyrants, whom they intend to thrust out of a city, the gates might be sometimes shut against it, that it might not return—the soul might fortify itself against it. But the soul is its home; there it dwells, and is no wanderer. Wherever you are, whatever you are about, this law of sin is always in you; in the best that you do, and in the worst. Men little consider what a dangerous companion is always at home with them. When they are in company,

[8] seizing, taking control with power and force

when alone, by night or by day, all is one, sin is with them. There is a living coal continually in their houses; which, if it be not looked unto, will fire them, and it may be consume them. Oh, the woeful security of poor souls! How little do the most of men think of this inbred enemy that is never from home! How little, for the most part, does the watchfulness of any professors answer the danger of their state and condition!

It is always ready to apply itself to every end and purpose that it serves unto. "It does not only dwell in me," says the apostle, "but when I would do good, it is present with me." There is somewhat more in that expression than mere indwelling. An inmate may dwell in a house, and yet not be always meddling with what the good-man[9] of the house has to do (that so we may keep to the allusion of indwelling, used by the apostle): but it is so with this law, it does so dwell in us, as that it will be present with us in everything we do; yea, oftentimes when with most earnestness we desire to be quit of it,[10] with most violence it will put itself upon us: "When I would do good, it is present with me." Would you pray, would you hear, would you give alms, would you meditate, would you be in any duty acting faith on God and love toward him, would you work righteousness, would you resist temptations—this troublesome, perplexing indweller will still more or less put itself upon you and be present with you; so that you cannot perfectly and completely accomplish the thing that is good (as our apostle speaks, v. 18). Sometimes men, by hearkening to their temptations, do stir up, excite, and provoke their lusts; and no wonder if then they find them present and active. But it will be so when with all our endeavors we labor to be free from them. This law of sin *"dwells"* in us—that is, it adheres as a depraved principle, unto our minds in darkness and vanity, unto our affections in sensuality, unto our wills in a loathing of and aversion from that which is good; and by some, more, or all of these, is continually putting itself upon us, in inclinations, motions, or suggestions to evil, when we would be most gladly quit of it.

It being an indwelling law, *it applies itself to its work with great facility and easiness,* like "the sin that does so easily beset us" (Heb. 12:1). It has a great facility and easiness in the application of itself unto its work; it needs no doors to be opened unto it; it needs no engines to work by. The soul cannot apply itself to any duty of a man but it must be by the exercise of those faculties wherein this law has its residence. Is the understanding or the *mind* to be applied unto anything?—there it is, in ignorance, darkness, vanity,

[9] male head of household
[10] be freed or released from it

folly, madness. Is the *will* to be engaged?—there it is also, in spiritual deadness, stubbornness, and the roots of obstinacy. Is the heart and *affections* to be set on work?—there it is, in inclinations to the world and present things, and sensuality, with proneness to all manner of defilements. Hence it is easy for it to insinuate itself into all that we do, and to hinder all that is good, and to further all sin and wickedness. It has an intimacy, an inwardness with the soul, and therefore, in all that we do, does easily beset us. It possesses those very faculties of the soul whereby we must do what we do, whatever it be, good or evil. Now, all these advantages it has as it is a law, as an indwelling law, which manifests its power and *efficacy*. It is always resident in the soul, it puts itself upon all its actings, and that with easiness and facility.

This is that law which the apostle affirms that he found in himself; this is the title that he gives unto the powerful and effectual remainder of indwelling sin even in believers; and these general evidences of its power, from that appellation, have we. Many there are in the world who find not this law in them—who, whatever they have been taught in the word, have not a spiritual sense and experience of the power of indwelling sin; and that because they are wholly under the dominion of it. They find not that there is darkness and folly in their minds because they are darkness itself, and darkness will discover nothing. They find not deadness and an indisposition[11] in their hearts and wills to God because they are dead wholly in trespasses and sins. They are at peace with their lusts by being in bondage unto them. And this is the state of most men in the world; which makes them woefully despise all their eternal concerns. Whence is it that men follow and pursue the world with so much greediness, that they neglect heaven, and life, and immortality for it, every day? Whence is it that some pursue their sensuality with delight?—they will drink and revel, and have their sports, let others say what they please. Whence is it that so many live so unprofitably under the word, that they understand so little of what is spoken unto them, that they practice less of what they understand, and will by no means be stirred up to answer the mind of God in his calls unto them? It is all from this law of sin and the power of it that rules and bears sway in men, that all these things do proceed; but it is not such persons of whom at present we particularly treat.

From what has been spoken it will ensue that if there be such a law in believers, it is doubtless their duty to find it out, to find it so to be. The more they find its power, the less they will feel its effects. It will not at all

[11] disinclination, unwillingness

advantage a man to have a hectical[12] distemper and not to discover it—a fire lying secretly in his house and not to know it. So much as men find of this law in them, so much they will abhor it and themselves, and no more. Proportionably also to their discovery of it will be their earnestness for grace, nor will it rise higher. All watchfulness and diligence in obedience will be answerable also thereunto. Upon this one hinge, or finding out and experiencing the power and the efficacy of this law of sin, turns the whole course of our lives. Ignorance of it breeds senselessness, carelessness, sloth, security, and pride; all which the Lord's soul abhors. Eruptions into great, open, conscience-wasting, scandalous sins are from want of a due spiritual consideration of this law. Inquire, then, how it is with your souls. What do you find of this law? What experience have you of its power and efficacy? Do you find it dwelling in you, always present with you, exciting itself, or putting forth its poison with facility and easiness at all times, in all your duties, "when you would do good"? What humiliation, what self-abasement, what intenseness in prayer, what diligence, what watchfulness, does this call for at your hands! What spiritual wisdom do you stand in need of! What supplies of grace, what assistance of the Holy Ghost, will be hence also discovered! I fear we have few of us a diligence proportionable to our danger.

[Chapter 3]

Having manifested indwelling sin, whereof we treat in the remainders of it in believers, to be a law, and evinced in general the power of it from thence, we shall now proceed to give particular instances of its efficacy and advantages from some things that generally relate unto it as such. And these are three: (1) its *seat* and subject; (2) its *natural* properties; and (3) its *operations* and the manner thereof—which principally we aim at and shall attend unto.

The Heart Is the Seat and Subject of This Law of Sin

First, for the seat and subject of this law of sin, the Scripture everywhere assigns it to be the heart. There indwelling sin keeps its special residence. It has invaded and possessed the throne of God himself: "Madness is in the heart of men while they live" (Eccles. 9:3). This is their madness, or the root

[12] fluctuating but persistent

of all that madness which appears in their lives. "Out of the heart proceed evil thoughts, murders, adulteries, fornications, thefts, false witness, blasphemies," etc. (Matt. 15:19). There are many outward temptations and provocations that befall men, which excite and stir them up unto these evils; but they do but as it were open the vessel, and let out what is laid up and stored in it. The root, rise, and stirring of all these things is in the heart. Temptations and occasions put nothing into a man, but only draw out what was in him before, hence is that summary description to the whole work and effect of this law of sin, "Every imagination of the thoughts of man's heart is only evil continually" (Gen. 6:5; so also 8:21). The whole work of the law of sin, from its first rise, its first coining of actual sin, is here described. And its seat, its work-house, is said to be the heart; and so it is called by our Savior "the evil treasure of the heart": "An evil man, out of the evil treasure of his heart, brings forth evil things" (Luke 6:45). This treasure is the prevailing principle of moral actions that is in men. So, in the beginning of the verse, our Savior calls grace "the good treasure of the heart" of a good man, whence that which is good does proceed. It is a principle constantly and abundantly inciting and stirring up unto, and consequently bringing forth, actions conformable and like unto it, of the same kind and nature with itself. And it is also called a treasure for its abundance. It will never be exhausted; it is not wasted by men's spending on it; yea, the more lavish men are of this stock, the more they draw out of this treasure, the more it grows and abounds! As men do not spend their grace, but increase it, by its exercise, no more do they their indwelling sin. The more men exercise their grace in duties of obedience, the more it is strengthened and increased; and the more men exert and put forth the fruits of their lust, the more is that enraged and increased in them—it feeds upon itself, swallows up its own poison, and grows thereby. The more men sin, the more are they inclined unto sin. It is from the deceitfulness of this law of sin, whereof we shall speak afterward at large, that men persuade themselves that by this or that particular sin they shall so satisfy their lusts as that they shall need to sin no more. Every sin increases the *principle,* and fortifies the habit of sinning. It is an evil treasure that increases by doing evil. And where does this treasure lie? It is in the heart; there it is laid up, there it is kept in safety. All the men in the world, all the angels in heaven, cannot dispossess a man of this treasure, it is so safely stored in the heart.

The "heart" in the Scripture is variously used; sometimes for the mind and understanding, sometimes for the will, sometimes for the affections, sometimes for the conscience, sometimes for the whole soul. Generally, it denotes the whole soul of man and all the faculties of it, not absolutely, but as they are all one principle of moral operations, as they all concur in our doing good or evil. The *mind,* as it inquires, discerns, and judges what is to be done, what refused; the *will,* as it chooses or refuses and avoids; the *affections,* as they like or dislike, cleave to or have an aversation from, that which is proposed to them; the *conscience,* as it warns and determines—are all together called the *heart.* And in this sense it is that we say the seat and subject of this law of sin is the heart of man. Only, we may add that the Scripture, speaking of the heart as the principle of men's good or evil actions, does usually insinuate together with it two things belonging unto the manner of their performance:

A suitableness and pleasingness unto the soul in the things that are done. When men take delight and are pleased in and with what they do, they are said to do it heartily, with their whole hearts. Thus, when God himself blesses his people in love and delight, he says he does it "with his whole heart and with his whole soul" (Jer. 32:41).

Resolution and *constancy in such actions.* And this also is denoted in the metaphorical expression before used of a treasure, from whence men do constantly take out the things which either they stand in need of or do intend to use.

This is the subject, the seat, the dwelling place of this law of sin—the heart; as it is the entire principle of moral operations, of doing good or evil, as out of it proceed good or evil [Luke 6:45]. Here dwells our enemy; this is the fort, the citadel of this tyrant, where it maintains a rebellion against God all our days. Sometimes it has more strength, and consequently more success; sometimes less of the one and of the other; but it is always in rebellion while we live.

That we may in our passage take a little view of the strength and power of sin from this seat and subject of it, we may consider one or two *properties of the heart* that exceedingly contribute thereunto. It is like an enemy in war, whose strength and power lie not only in his numbers and force of men or arms, but also in the unconquerable forts that he does possess. And such is the heart to this enemy of God and our souls; as will appear from the properties of it, whereof one or two shall be mentioned.

The heart is unsearchable: "Who can know the heart? I the Lord search it" (Jer. 17:9-10). The heart of man is pervious[13] to God only; hence he takes the honor of searching the heart to be as peculiar to himself, and as fully declaring him to be God, as any other glorious attribute of his nature. We

[13] permeable, penetrable

know not the hearts of one another; we know not our own hearts as we ought. Many there are that know not their hearts as to their general bent and disposition, whether it be good or bad, sincere and sound, or corrupt and naught; but no one knows all the secret intrigues, the windings and turnings, the actings and aversations of his own heart. Has anyone the perfect measure of his own light and darkness? Can anyone know what actings of choosing or aversation his will shall bring forth, upon the proposal of that endless variety of objects that it is to be exercised with? Can anyone traverse the various mutability of his afflictions? Do the secret springs of acting and refusing in the soul lie before the eyes of any man? Does anyone know what will be the motions of the mind or will in such and such conjunctions of things, such a suiting of objects, such a pretension of reasonings, such an appearance of things desirable? All in heaven and earth, but the infinite, all-seeing God, are utterly ignorant of these things. In this unsearchable heart dwells the law of sin; and much of its security, and consequently of its strength, lies in this, that it is past our finding out. We fight with an enemy whose secret strength we cannot discover, whom we cannot follow into its retirements.[14] Hence, oftentimes, when we are ready to think sin quite ruined, after a while we find it was but out of sight. It has coverts and retreats in an unsearchable heart, whither we cannot pursue it. The soul may persuade itself all is well, when sin may be safe in the hidden darkness of the mind, which it is impossible that he should look into; for whatever makes manifest is light. It may suppose the will of sinning is utterly taken away, when yet there is an unsearchable reserve for a more suitable object, a more vigorous temptation, than at present it is tried with. Has a man had a contest with any lust, and a blessed victory over it by the Holy Ghost as to that present trial?—when he thinks it is utterly expelled, he ere[15] long finds that it was but retired out of sight. It can lie so close in the mind's darkness, in the will's indisposition, in the disorder and carnality of the affections, that no eye can discover it. The best of our wisdom is but to watch its first appearances, to catch its first under-earth heavings and workings, and to set ourselves in opposition to them; for to follow it into the secret corners of the heart, that we cannot do. It is true, there is yet a relief in this case—namely, that he to whom the work of destroying the law of sin and body of death in us is principally committed, namely, the Holy Ghost comes with his axe to the very root; neither is there anything in

[14] privacy, seclusion, leisure
[15] before

an unsearchable heart that is not "naked and open unto him" (Heb. 4:13); but we in a way of duty may hence see what an enemy we have to deal with.

As it is unsearchable, so *it is deceitful,* as in the place above mentioned: "It is deceitful above all things"—incomparably so. There is great deceit in the dealings of men in the world; great deceit in their counsels and contrivances in reference to their affairs, private and public; great deceit in their words and actings: the world is full of deceit and fraud. But all this is nothing [compared] to the deceit that is in man's heart toward himself; for that is the meaning of the expression in this place, and not toward others. Now, incomparable deceitfulness, added to unsearchableness, gives a great addition and increase of strength to the law of sin, upon the account of its seat and subject. I speak not yet of the deceitfulness of sin itself, but the deceitfulness of the heart where it is seated. "There are seven abominations in the heart" (Prov. 26:25); that is, not only many, but an absolute complete number, as seven denotes. And they are such abominations as consist in deceitfulness; so the caution foregoing insinuates, "Trust him not"—for it is only deceit that should make us not to trust in that degree and measure which the object is capable of.

Now, this deceitfulness of the heart, whereby it is exceedingly advantaged in its harboring of sin, lies chiefly in these two things:

That *it abounds in contradictions,* so that it is not to be found and dealt with according to any constant rule and way of procedure. There are some men that have much of this, from their natural constitution, or from other causes, in their conversation. They seem to be made up of contradictions; sometimes to be very wise in their affairs, sometimes very foolish; very open and very reserved; very facile[16] and very obstinate; very easy to be entreated and very revengeful—all in a remarkable height. This is generally accounted a bad character, and is seldom found but when it proceeds from some notable predominant lust. But, in general, in respect of moral good or evil, duty or sin, it is so with the heart of every man—flaming hot and key cold; weak and yet stubborn; obstinate and facile. The frame of the heart is ready to contradict itself every moment. Now you would think you had it all for such a frame, such a way; anon[17] it is quite otherwise: so that none know what to expect from it. The rise of this is the disorder that is brought upon all its faculties by sin. God created them all in a perfect harmony and union. The mind and reason were in perfect subjection and subordination to God and his will; the

[16] mild-mannered
[17] presently, soon

will answered, in its choice of good, the discovery made of it by the mind; the affections constantly and evenly followed the understanding and will. The mind's subjection to God was the spring of the orderly and harmonious motion of the soul and all the wheels in it. That being disturbed by sin, the rest of the faculties move cross[18] and contrary one to another. The will chooses not the good which the mind discovers; the affections delight not in that which the will chooses; but all jar and interfere, cross and rebel against each other. This we have got by our falling from God. Hence sometimes the will leads, the judgment follows. Yea, commonly the affections, that should attend upon all, get the sovereignty and draw the whole soul captive after them. And hence it is, as I said, that the heart is made up of so many contradictions in its actings. Sometimes the mind retains its sovereignty, and the affections are in subjection, and the will ready for its duty. This puts a good face upon things. Immediately the rebellion of the affections or the obstinacy of the will takes place and prevails, and the whole scene is changed. This, I say, makes the heart deceitful above all things: it agrees not at all in itself, is not constant to itself, has no order that it is constant unto, is under no certain conduct that is stable; but, if I may so say, has a rotation in itself, where oftentimes the feet lead and guide the whole.

Its deceit lies in its full promisings upon the first appearance of things; and this also proceeds from the same principle with the former. Sometimes the affections are touched and wrought[19] upon; the whole heart appears in a fair frame; all promises to be well. Within a while the whole frame is changed; the mind was not at all affected or turned; the affections a little acted their parts and are gone off, and all the fair promises of the heart are departed with them. Now, add this deceitfulness to the unsearchableness before mentioned, and we shall find that at least the difficulty of dealing effectually with sin in its seat and throne will be exceedingly increased. A deceiving and a deceived heart, who can deal with it?—especially considering that the heart employs all its deceits unto the service of sin, contributes them all to its furtherance. All the disorder that is in the heart, all its false promises and fair appearances, promote the interest and advantages of sin. Hence God cautions the people to look to it, lest their own hearts should entice and deceive them.

Who can mention the treacheries and deceits that lie in the heart of man? It is not for nothing that the Holy Ghost so expresses it, "It is deceitful above all things"—uncertain in what it does, and false in what it promises.

[18] contradictory
[19] shaped, molded, fashioned

And hence moreover it is, among other causes, that, in the pursuit of our war against sin, we have not only the old work to go over and over, but new work still while we live in this world, still new stratagems and wiles to deal with; as the manner will be where unsearchableness and deceitfulness are to be contended with.

There are many other properties of this seat and subject of the law of sin which might be insisted on to the same end and purpose, but that would too far divert us from our particular design, and therefore I shall pass these over with some few considerations.

First, *never let us reckon that our work in contending against sin, in crucifying, mortifying, and subduing of it, is at an end.* The place of its habitation is unsearchable; and when we may think that we have thoroughly won the field, there is still some reserve remaining that we saw not, that we knew not of. Many conquerors have been ruined by their carelessness after a victory, and many have been spiritually wounded after great successes against this enemy. David was so; his great surprise into sin was after a long profession, manifold experiences of God, and watchful keeping himself from his iniquity. And hence, in part, has it come to pass that the profession of many has declined in their old age or riper time; which must more distinctly be spoken to afterward. They have given over the work of mortifying of sin before their work was at an end. There is no way for us to pursue sin in its unsearchable habitation but by being endless in our pursuit. And that command of the apostle which we have in Colossians 3:5, on this account is as necessary for them to observe who are toward the end of their race, as those that are but at the beginning of it: "Mortify therefore your members which are upon the earth"—be always doing it while you live in this world. It is true: great ground is obtained when the work is vigorously and constantly carried on; sin is much weakened, so that the soul presses forward toward perfection: but yet the work must be endless; I mean, while we are in this world. If we give over, we shall quickly see this enemy exerting itself with new strength and vigor. It may be under some great affliction, it may be in some eminent enjoyment of God, in the sense of the sweetness of blessed communion with Christ, we have been ready to say that there was an end of sin, that it was dead and gone forever; but have we not found the contrary by experience? Has it not manifested that it was only retired into some unsearchable recesses of the heart, as to its in-being and nature, though it may be greatly weakened in its power? Let us, then, reckon on it, that there is no way to have our work done but by always doing of it; and he who dies fighting in this warfare dies assuredly a conqueror.

Secondly, *has it its residence in that which is various, inconstant, deceit-*

ful above all things? This calls for perpetual watchfulness against it. An open enemy, that deals by violence only, always gives some respite.[20] You know where to have him and what he is doing, so as that sometimes you may sleep quietly without fear. But against adversaries that deal by deceit and treachery (which are long swords and reach at the greatest distance) nothing will give security but perpetual watchfulness. It is impossible we should in this case be too jealous, doubtful, suspicious, or watchful. The heart has a thousand wiles and deceits; and if we are in the least off from our watch, we may be sure to be surprised. Hence are those reiterated commands and cautions given for watching, for being circumspect,[21] diligent, careful, and the like. There is no living for them who have to deal with an enemy deceitful above all things, unless they persist in such a frame. All cautions that are given in this case are necessary, especially that, "Remember not to believe." Does the heart promise fair?—rest not on it, but say to the Lord Christ, "Lord, you do undertake for me." Does the sun shine fair in the morning?—reckon not therefore on a fair day; the clouds may arise and fall. Though the morning gives a fair appearance of serenity and peace, turbulent affections may arise and cloud the soul with sin and darkness.

Thirdly, then, *commit the whole matter with all care and diligence unto him who can search the heart to the uttermost, and knows how to prevent all its treacheries and deceits.* In the things before mentioned lies our duty, but here lies our safety. There is no treacherous corner in our hearts but he can search it to the uttermost; there is no deceit in them but he can disappoint[22] it. This course David takes in Psalm 139. After he had set forth the omnipresence of God and his omniscience (vv. 1-10), he makes improvement of it[23]: "Search me, O God, and try me" (v. 23). As if he had said, "It is but a little that I know of my deceitful heart, only I would be sincere; I would not have reserves for sin retained therein. Wherefore do you, who are present with my heart, who knows my thoughts long before, undertake this work, perform it thoroughly, for you alone are able so to do."

There are yet other arguments for the evidencing of the power and strength of indwelling sin, from whence it is termed a "law," which we must pass through, according to the order wherein before we laid them down.

---

[20] relief
[21] watchful, attentive, cautious
[22] undo an intended end or use
[23] applies it

[Chapter 4]

The Natural Properties of Indwelling Sin

Secondly, we have seen the seat and subject of this law of sin. In the next place we might take a view of its nature in general, which also will manifest its power and efficacy; but this I shall not enlarge upon, it being not my business to declare the nature of indwelling sin: it has also been done by others. I shall therefore only, in reference unto our special design in hand, consider one property of it that belongs unto its nature, and this always, wherever it is. And this is that which is expressed by the apostle, "The carnal mind is *enmity* against God" (Rom. 8:7). That which is here called *phronēma tēs sarkos,* "the wisdom of the flesh," is the same with "the law of sin" which we insist on. And what says he hereof? Why, it is *exthra eis theon*—"enmity against God." It is not only an enemy—for so possibly some reconciliation of it unto God might be made—but it is enmity itself, and so not capable of accepting any terms of peace. Enemies may be reconciled, but enmity cannot; yea, the only way to reconcile enemies is to destroy the enmity. So the apostle in another case tells us, "We, who were enemies, are reconciled to God" (Rom. 5:10); that is, a work compassed[24] and brought about by the blood of Christ—the reconciling of the greatest enemies. But when he comes to speak of enmity, there is no way for it, but it must be abolished and destroyed: "Having abolished in his flesh the enmity" (Eph. 2:15). There is no way to deal with any enmity whatsoever but by its abolition or destruction. And this also lies in it as it is enmity, that every part and parcel of it, if we may so speak, the least degree of it that can possibly remain in anyone, while and where there is anything of its nature, is enmity still. It may not be so effectual and powerful in operation as where it has more life and vigor, but it is enmity still. As every drop of poison is poison, and will infect, and every spark of fire is fire, and will burn, so is every thing of the law of sin, the last, the least of it—it is enmity, it will poison, it will burn. That which is anything in the abstract is still so while it has any being at all. Our apostle, who may well be supposed to have made as great a progress in the subduing of it as anyone on the earth, yet after all cries out for deliverance, as from an irreconcilable enemy (Rom. 7:24). The meanest acting, the meanest and most imperceptible working of it, is the acting and working of enmity. Mortification abates of its force, but does not change its nature. Grace changes the nature of man, but nothing can

[24] attained, achieved

change the nature of sin. Whatsoever effect be wrought upon it, there is no effect wrought in it, but that it is enmity still, sin still. This then, by it, is our state and condition: "God is love" (1 John 4:8). He is so in himself, eternally excellent, and desirable above all. He is so to us, he is so in the blood of his Son and in all the inexpressible fruits of it, by which we are what we are, and wherein all our future hopes and expectations are wrapped up. Against this God we carry about us an enmity all our days; an enmity that has this from its nature, that it is incapable of cure or reconciliation. Destroyed it may be, it shall be, but cured it cannot be. If a man has an enemy to deal with that is too mighty for him, as David had with Saul, he may take the course that he did—consider what it is that provoked his enemy against him, and so address himself to remove the cause and make up his peace: "If the LORD have stirred you up against me, let him accept an offering: but if they be the children of men, cursed be they before the LORD" (1 Sam. 26:19).

Come it from God or man, there is yet hope of peace. But when a man has enmity itself to deal with, nothing is to be expected but continual fighting, to the destruction of the one party. If it be not overcome and destroyed, it will overcome and destroy the soul. And herein lies no small part of its power, which we are inquiring after—it can admit of no terms of peace, of no composition. There may be a composition where there is no reconciliation—there may be a truce where there is no peace, but with this enemy we can obtain neither the one nor the other. It is never quiet, conquering nor conquered; which was the only kind of enemy that the famous warrior complained of old. It is in vain for a man to have any expectation of rest from his lust but by its death; of absolute freedom but by his own. Some, in the tumultuating of their corruptions, seek for quietness by laboring to satisfy them, "making provision for the flesh, to fulfill the lusts thereof," as the apostle speaks (Rom. 13:14). This is to aslake[25] fire by wood and oil. As all the fuel in the world, all the fabric of the creation that is combustible, being cast into the fire, will not at all satisfy it, but increase it, so is it with satisfaction given to sin by sinning—it does but inflame and increase. If a man will part with some of his goods unto an enemy, it may satisfy him; but enmity will have all, and is not one whit the more satisfied than if he had received nothing at all—like the lean cattle that were never the less hungry for having devoured the fat. You cannot bargain with the fire to take but so much of your houses; you have no way but to quench it. It is in this case as it is in the contest between a wise man and a fool: "Whether he rage or laugh, there is

[25] slacken, diminish

no rest" (Prov. 29:9). Whatever frame or temper[26] he be in, his importunate[27] folly makes him troublesome. It is so with this indwelling sin: whether it violently tumultuate,[28] as it will do on provocations and temptations, it will be outrageous in the soul; or whether it seem to be pleased and contented, to be satisfied, all is one, there is no peace, no rest to be had with it or by it. Had it, then, been of any other nature, some other way might have been fixed on; but seeing it consists in enmity, all the relief the soul has must lie in its ruin.

Secondly, it is not only said to be "enmity," but it is said to be *"enmity against God."* It has chosen a great enemy indeed. It is in sundry places proposed as our enemy: "Abstain from fleshly lusts, which war against the soul" (1 Pet. 2:11); they are enemies to the soul, that is, to ourselves. Sometimes as an enemy to the Spirit that is in us: "The flesh lusts" or fights "against the Spirit" (Gal. 5:17). It fights against the Spirit, or the spiritual principle that is in us, to conquer it; it fights against our souls to destroy them. It has special ends and designs against our souls, and against the principle of grace that is in us; but its proper formal object is God: it is "enmity against God." It is its work to oppose grace; it is a consequent of its work to oppose our souls, which follows upon what it does more than what it intends; but its nature and formal design is to oppose God—God as the lawgiver, God as holy, God as the author of the gospel, a way of salvation by grace, and not by works—this is the direct object of the law of sin. Why does it oppose duty, so that the good we would do we do not [Rom. 7:19], either as to matter or manner? Why does it render the soul carnal, indisposed, unbelieving, unspiritual, weary, wandering? It is because of its enmity to God, whom the soul aims to have communion with in duty. It has, as it were, that command from Satan which the Assyrians had from their king: "Fight neither with small nor great, save only with the king of Israel" (1 Kings 22:31). It is neither great nor small, but God himself, the King of Israel, that sin sets itself against. There lies the secret formal reason of all its opposition to good—even because it relates unto God. May a road, a trade, a way of duties be set up, where communion with God is not aimed at, but only the duty itself, as is the manner of men in most of their superstitious worship, the opposition that will lie against it from the law of sin will be very weak, easy, and gentle. Or, as the Assyrians, because of his show of a king, assaulted Jehoshaphat, but when they found that it was not Ahab, they turned back from pursuing of him [1 Kings 22:31-33]; so because there

[26] character, disposition
[27] persistent, pressing
[28] agitate, disturb, stir up

is a show and appearance of the worship of God, sin may make head[way] against it at first, but when the duty cries out in the heart that indeed God is not there, sin turns away to seek out its proper enemy, even God himself, elsewhere. And hence do many poor creatures spend their days in dismal, tiring superstitions, without any great reluctancy from within, when others cannot be suffered[29] freely to watch with Christ in a spiritual manner one hour. And it is no wonder that men fight with carnal weapons for their superstitious worship without,[30] when they have no fighting against it within; for God is not in it, and the law of sin makes not opposition to any duty, but to God in every duty. This is our state and condition: All the opposition that arises in us unto anything that is spiritually good, whether it be from darkness in the mind, or aversation in the will, or sloth in the affections, all the secret arguings and reasonings that are in the soul in pursuit of them, the direct object of them is God himself. The enmity lies against him; which consideration surely should influence us to a perpetual, constant watchfulness over ourselves. It is thus also in respect of all propensity unto sin, as well as aversation from God. It is God himself that is aimed at. It is true, the pleasures, the wages of sin, do greatly influence the sensual, carnal affections of men: but it is the holiness and authority of God that sin itself rises up against; it hates the yoke of the Lord. "You have been weary of me," says God to sinners [Isa. 43:22]; and that during their performance of abundance of duties. Every act of sin is a fruit of being weary of God. Thus Job tells us what lies at the bottom in the heart of sinners: "They say to God, Depart from us" [Job 21:14; 22:17]—it is enmity against him and aversation from him. Here lies the formal nature of every sin—it is an opposition to God, a casting off his yoke, a breaking off the dependence which the creature ought to have on the Creator. And the apostle gives the reason why he affirms "the carnal mind to be enmity against God," namely, "because it is not subject to the will of God, nor indeed can be" (Rom. 8:7). It never is, nor will, nor can be subject to God, its whole nature consisting in an opposition to him. The soul wherein it is may be subject to the law of God; but this law of sin sets up in contrariety[31] unto it, and will not be in subjection. To manifest a little further the power of this law of sin from this property of its nature, that it is enmity against God, one or two inseparable adjuncts[32] of it may be considered, which will further evince it:—

It is *universal.* Some contentions are bounded unto some particular

[29] cannot be bothered
[30] outwardly
[31] state of being contrary or in opposition to
[32] dependent statements that amplify meaning

concerns; this is about one thing, that about another. It is not so here; the enmity is absolute and universal, as are all enmities that are grounded in the nature of the things themselves. Such enmity is against the whole kind of that which is its object. Such is this enmity: for it is universal to all of God; and it is universal in all of the soul.

It is *universal to all of God.* If there were anything of God, his nature, properties, his mind or will, his law or gospel, any duty of obedience to him, of communion with him, that sin had not an enmity against, the soul might have a constant shelter and retreat within itself, by applying itself to that of God, to that of duty toward him, to that of communion with him, that sin would make no opposition against. But the enmity lies against God, and all of God, and everything wherein or whereby we have to do with him. It is not subject to the law, nor any part or parcel, word or tittle[33] of the law. Whatever is opposite to anything as such, is opposite unto all of it. Sin is enmity to God as God, and therefore to all of God. Not his goodness, not his holiness, not his mercy, not his grace, not his promises: there is not anything of him which it does not make head against; nor any duty, private, public, in the heart, in external works, which it opposes not. And the nearer (if I may so say) anything is to God, the greater is its enmity unto it. The more of spirituality and holiness is in anything, the greater is its enmity. That which has most of God has most of its opposition. Concerning them in whom this law is most predominant, God says, "You have set at nought[34] all my counsel, and would [have] none of my reproof" (Prov. 1:25). Not this or that part of God's counsel, his mind, or will is opposed, but all his counsel; whatsoever he calls for or guides unto, in every particular of it, all is set at nought, and nothing of his reproof attended unto. A man would think it not very strange that sin should maintain an enmity against God in his law, which comes to judge it, to condemn it; but it raises a greater enmity against him in his gospel, wherein he tenders mercy and pardon as a deliverance from it; and that merely because more of the glorious properties of God's nature, more of his excellencies and condescension, is manifested therein than in the other.

It is *universal in all of the soul.* Would this law of sin have contented itself to have subdued any one faculty of the soul—would it have left any one at liberty, any one affection free from its yoke and bondage—it might possibly have been with more ease opposed or subdued. But when Christ comes with his spiritual power upon the soul to conquer it to himself, he has no quiet

---

[33] a kind of accent in the Hebrew alphabet (see Matt. 5:18, KJV)

[34] you have treated as nothing

landing place. He can set foot on no ground but what he must fight for and conquer. Not the mind, not an affection, not the will, but all is secured against him. And when grace has made its entrance, yet sin will dwell in all its coasts. Were anything in the soul at perfect freedom and liberty, there a stand might be made to drive it from all the rest of its holds; but it is universal and wars in the whole soul. The mind has its own darkness and vanity to wrestle with—the will its own stubborness, obstinacy, and perverseness; every affection its own frowardness[35] and aversation from God, and its sensuality, to deal with: so that one cannot yield relief unto another as they ought; they have, as it were, their hands full at home. Hence it is that our knowledge is imperfect, our obedience weak, love not unmixed, fear not pure, delight not free and noble. But I must not insist on these particulars, or I could abundantly show how diffused this principle of enmity against God is through the whole soul.

Hereunto might be added its *constancy*. It is constant unto itself, it wavers not, it has no thoughts of yielding or giving over, notwithstanding the powerful opposition that is made unto it both by the law and gospel; as afterward shall be showed.

This, then, is a third evidence of the power of sin, taken from its nature and properties, wherein I have fixed but on one instance for its illustration—namely, that it is "enmity against God," and that universal and constant. Should we enter upon a full description of it, it would require more space and time than we have allotted to this whole subject. What has been delivered might give us a little sense of it, if it be the will of God, and stir us up unto watchfulness. What can be of a more sad consideration than that we should carry about us constantly that which is enmity against God, and that not in this or that particular, but in all that he is and in all wherein he has revealed himself? I cannot say it is well with them who find it not. It is well with them, indeed, in whom it is weakened, and the power of it abated; but yet, for them who say it is not in them, they do but deceive themselves, and there is no truth in them.

[Chapter 5]

The Actings and Operations of Indwelling Sin

Thirdly, we have considered somewhat of the nature of indwelling sin, not absolutely, but in reference unto the discovery of its power; but this more

---

[35] stubbornly contrary behavior, obstinacy

clearly evidenced itself in its actings and operations. Power is an act of life, and operation is the only discoverer of life. We know not that anything lives but by the effects and works of life; and great and strong operations discover a powerful and vigorous life. Such are the operations of this law of sin, which are all demonstrations of its power.

That which we have declared concerning its nature is that it consists in enmity. Now, there are two general heads[36] of the working or operation of enmity: aversation and opposition.

First, *aversation.* Our Savior, describing the enmity that was between himself and the teachers of the Jews, by the effects of it, says in the prophet, "My soul loathed them, and their soul also abhorred me" (Zech. 11:8). Where there is mutual enmity, there is mutual aversation, loathing, and abomination. So it was between the Jews and the Samaritans—they were enemies and abhorred one another (as John 4:9).

Secondly, *opposition,* or contending against one another, is the next product of enmity. "He was turned to be their enemy, and he fought against them" (Isa. 63:10), speaking of God toward the people. Where there is enmity, there will be fighting; it is the proper and natural product of it. Now, both these effects are found in this law of sin.

First, for aversation. There is an aversation in it unto God and everything of God, as we have in part discovered in handling the enmity itself, and so shall not need much to insist upon it again. All indisposition unto duty, wherein communion with God is to be obtained; all weariness of duty; all carnality, or formality unto duty—it all springs from this root. The wise man cautions us against this evil: "Keep your foot when you go to the house of God" (Eccles. 5:1)—"Have you any spiritual duty to perform, and do you design the attaining of any communion with God? Look to yourself, take care of your affections; they will be gadding[37] and wandering, and that from their aversation to what you have in hand." There is not any good that we would do wherein we may not find this aversation exercising itself. "When I would do good, evil is present with me" [Rom. 7:21]—"At any time, at all times, when I would do anything that is spiritually good, it is present—that is, to hinder me, to obstruct me in my duty; because it abhors and loathes the thing which I have in hand, it will keep me off from it if it be possible." In them in whom it prevails, it comes at length unto that frame which is expressed (Ezek.

[36] categories

[37] straggling, roving

33:31). It will allow an outward, bodily presence unto the worship of God, wherein it is not concerned, but it keeps the heart quite away.

It may be [the case that] some will pretend they find it not so in themselves, but they have freedom and liberty in and unto all the duties of obedience that they attend unto. But I fear this pretended liberty will be found, upon examination, to arise from one or both of these causes: First, ignorance of the true state and condition of their own souls, of their inward man and its actings toward God. They know not how it is with them, and therefore are not to be believed in what they report. They are in the dark, and neither know what they do, nor whither they are going. It is like the Pharisee [who] knew little of this matter; which made him boast of his duties to God himself. Or, secondly, it may be [the case that] whatever duties of worship or obedience such persons perform, they may, through want of faith and an interest[38] in Christ, have no communion with them; and if so, sin will make but little opposition unto them therein. We speak of them whose hearts are exercised with these things. And if under their complaints of them, and groanings for deliverance from them, others cry out unto them, "Stand off, we are holier than you," they are willing to bear their condition, as knowing that their way may be safe, though it be troublesome; and being willing to see their own dangers, that they may avoid the ruin which others fall into.

Let us, then, a little consider this aversation in such acts of obedience as wherein there is no concern but that of God and the soul. In public duties there may be a mixture of other considerations; they may be so influenced by custom and necessity that a right judgment cannot from them be made of this matter. But let us take into consideration the duties of retirement, as private prayer and meditation, and the like; or else extraordinary duties, or duties to be performed in an extraordinary manner.

In these will this aversation and loathing oftentimes discover itself in the *affections*. A secret striving will be in them about close and cordial dealing with God, unless the hand of God in his Spirit be high and strong upon his soul. Even when convictions, sense of duty, dear and real esteem of God and communion with him have carried the soul into its closet, yet if there be not the vigor and power of a spiritual life constantly at work, there will be a secret loathness[39] in them unto duty; yea, sometimes there will be a violent inclination to the contrary, so that the soul had rather do anything, embrace any diversion, though it wound itself thereby, than vigorously apply itself unto

---

[38] share or stake

[39] unwillingness, reluctance

that which in the inward man it breathes after. It is weary before it begins, and says, "When will the work be over?" Here God and the soul are immediately concerned; and it is a great conquest to do what we would, though we come exceedingly short of what we should do.

It discovers itself in the *mind* also. When we address ourselves to God in Christ, we are, as Job speaks, to "fill our mouths with arguments" (Job 23:4), that we may be able to plead with him, as he calls upon us to do: "Put me in remembrance; let us plead together" (Isa. 43:26). Whence the church is called upon to take unto itself words or arguments in going to God (Hos. 14:2). The sum is that the mind should be furnished with the considerations that are prevailing with God, and be in readiness to plead them, and to manage them in the most spiritual manner, to the best advantage. Now, is there no difficulty to get the mind into such a frame as to lay out itself to the utmost in this work; to be clear, steady, and constant in its duty; to draw out and make use of its stores and furniture[40] of promises and experiences? It starts, wanders, flags[41]—all from this secret aversation unto communion with God, which proceeds from the law of indwelling sin. Some complain that they can make no work of meditation—they cannot bend their minds unto it. I confess there may be a great cause of this in their want of a right understanding of the duty itself, and of the ways of managing the soul in it; which therefore I shall a little speak to afterward: but yet this secret enmity has its hand in the loss they are at also, and that both in their minds and in their affections. Others are forced to live in family and public duties, they find such little benefit and success in private. And here has been the beginning of the apostasy of many professors, and the source of many foolish, sensual opinions. Finding this aversation in their minds and affections from closeness and constancy in private spiritual duties, not knowing how to conquer and prevail against these difficulties through him who enables us, they have at first been subdued to a neglect of them, first partial, then total, until, having lost all conscience of them, they have had a door opened unto all sin and licentiousness, and so to a full and utter apostasy. I am persuaded there are very few that apostatize from a profession of any continuance, such as our days abound with, but their door of entrance into the folly of backsliding was either some great and notorious sin that bloodied their consciences, tainted their affections, and intercepted all delight of having anything more to do with God; or else it was a course of neglect in private duties, arising from a weariness of contending

[40] equipment, weapons
[41] declines in vigor or strength

against that powerful aversation which they found in themselves unto them. And this also, through the craft of Satan, has been improved into many foolish and sensual opinions of living unto God without and above any duties of communion. And we find, that after men have for a while choked and blinded their consciences with this pretense, cursed wickedness or sensuality has been the end of their folly. And the reason of all this is that the giving way to the law of sin in the least is the giving strength unto it. To let it alone is to let it grow; not to conquer it is to be conquered by it.

As it is in respect of private, so it is also in respect of *public duties* that have anything extraordinary in them. What strivings, strugglings, and pleadings are there in the heart about them, especially against the spirituality of them! Yea, in and under them, will not the mind and affections sometimes be entangled with things uncouth, new, and strange unto them, such as, at the time of the least serious business, a man would not deign[42] to take into his thoughts? But if the least loose,[43] liberty, or advantage be given unto indwelling sin, if it be not perpetually watched over, it will work to a strange and unexpected issue.[44] In brief, let the soul unclothe any duty whatsoever, private or public, anything that is called good—let a man divest it of all outward respects which secretly insinuate themselves into the mind and give it some complacency in what it is about, but do not render it acceptable unto God—and he shall assuredly find somewhat of the power and some of the effects of this aversation. It begins in loathness and indisposition; goes on with entangling the mind and affections with other things; and will end, if not prevented, in weariness of God, which he complains of in his people (Isa. 43:22). They ceased from duty because they were "weary of God." But this instance being of great importance unto professors in their walking with God, we must not pass it over without some intimations of directions for them in their contending against it and opposition to it. Only this must be premised, that I am not giving directions for the mortifying of indwelling sin in general—which is to be done alone by the Spirit of Christ, by virtue of our union with him (Rom. 8:13)—but only of our particular duty with reference unto this special evil or effect of indwelling sin that we have a little insisted on, or what in this single case the wisdom of faith seems to direct unto and call for; which will be our way and course in our process upon the consideration of other effects of it.

[42] condescend
[43] lack of restraint
[44] result, outcome

The great means to prevent the fruits and effects of this aversation is the constant keeping of the soul in a universally holy frame. As this weakens the whole law of sin, so answerably all its properties, and particularly this aversation. It is this frame only that will enable us to say with the psalmist, "My heart is fixed, O God, my heart is fixed" (Ps. 57:7). It is utterly impossible to keep the heart in a prevailing holy frame in any one duty, unless it be so in and unto all and every one. If sin-entanglements get hold in any one thing, they will put themselves upon the soul in everything. A constant, even frame and temper in all duties, in all ways, is the only preservative for any one way. Let not him who is neglective in public persuade himself that all will be clear and easy in private, or on the contrary. There is a harmony in obedience: break but one part, and you interrupt the whole. Our wounds in particular arise generally from negligence as to the whole course; so David informs us, "Then shall I not be ashamed, when I have respect unto all thy commandments" (Ps. 119:6). A universal respect to all God's commandments is the only preservative from shame; and nothing have we more reason to be ashamed of than the shameful miscarriages of our hearts in point of duty, which are from the principle before mentioned.

Labor to prevent the very beginnings of the workings of this aversation; let grace be beforehand with it in every duty. We are directed to "watch unto prayer" (1 Pet. 4:7); and as it is unto prayer, so unto every duty—that is, to consider and take care that we be not hindered from within nor from without as to a due performance of it. Watch against temptations, to oppose them; watch against the aversation that is in sin, to prevent it. As we are not to give place to Satan, no more are we to sin. If it be not prevented in its first attempts, it will prevail. My meaning is: Whatever good, as the apostle speaks, we have to do, and find evil present with us (as we shall find it present), prevent its parleying[45] with the soul, its insinuating of poison into the mind and affections, by a vigorous, holy, violent stirring up of the grace or graces that are to be acted[46] and set at work peculiarly in that duty. Let Jacob come first into the world; or, if prevented by the violence of Esau, let him lay hold on his heel, to overthrow him and obtain the birthright [Gen. 25:26]. Upon the very first motion of Peter to our Savior, crying, "Master, spare yourself," he immediately replies, "Get you behind me, Satan" [Matt. 16:23]. So ought we to say, "Get you gone, you law of sin, you present evil,"

[45] discussing (especially with an enemy)

[46] activated

and it may be of the same use unto us. Get grace, then, up betimes[47] unto duty, and be early in the rebukes of sin.

Though it do its worst, yet be sure it never prevails to a conquest. Be sure you be not wearied out by its pertinacity,[48] nor driven from your hold by its importunity[49]—do not faint by its opposition. Take the apostle's advice, "We desire that every one of you do show the same diligence to the full assurance of hope unto the end: that you be not slothful" (Heb. 6:11-12). Still hold out in the same diligence. There are many ways whereby men are driven from a constant holy performance of duties, all of them dangerous, if not pernicious to the soul. Some are diverted by business, some by company, some by the power of temptations, some discouraged by their own darkness; but none so dangerous as this, when the soul gives over in part or in whole, as wearied by the aversation of sin unto it, or to communion with God in it. This argues the soul's giving up of itself unto the power of sin; which, unless the Lord break the snare of Satan therein, will assuredly prove ruinous. Our Savior's instruction is that "we ought always to pray, and not to faint" (Luke 18:1). Opposition will arise—none so bitter and keen as that from our own hearts; if we faint, we perish. "Take heed lest you be wearied," says the apostle, "and faint in your minds" (Heb. 12:3). Such a fainting as attended with a weariness, and that with a giving place to the aversation working in our hearts, is to be avoided, if we would not perish. The caution is the same with that of the same apostle, "Rejoicing in hope, patient in tribulation, continuing instant[50] in prayer" (Rom. 12:12); and in general, "Let not sin therefore reign in your mortal body, that you should obey it in the lusts thereof" (Rom. 6:12) To cease from duty, in part or in whole, upon the aversation of sin unto its spirituality, is to give sin the rule, and to obey it in the lusts thereof. Yield not, then, unto it, but hold out the conflict; wait on God, and you shall prevail: "They that wait upon the LORD shall renew their strength; they shall mount up with wings as eagles; they shall run, and not be weary; and they shall walk, and not faint" (Isa. 40:31). But that which is now so difficult will increase in difficulty if we give way unto it; but if we abide in our station,[51] we shall prevail. The mouth of the Lord has spoken it [Isa. 40:5; 58:14; Mic. 4:4].

Carry about a constant, humbling sense of this close aversation unto

---

[47] early, in due time
[48] obstinance, stubbornness
[49] persistence
[50] insistent, constant, faithful
[51] position

spiritualness that yet lies in our nature. If men find the efficacy of it, what should, what consideration can, be more powerful to bring them unto humble walking with God? That after all the discoveries that God has made of himself unto them, all the kindness they have received from him, his doing of them good and not evil in all things, there should yet be such a heart of unkindness and unbelief still abiding as to have an aversation lying in it to communion with him—how ought the thoughts of it to cast us into the dust! to fill us with shame and self-abhorrency all our days! What have we found in God, in any of our approaches or addresses unto him, that it should be thus with us? What iniquity have we found in him? Has he been a wilderness unto us, or a land of darkness? Did we ever lose anything by drawing nigh[52] unto him? Nay, has not therein lain all the rest and peace which we have obtained? Is not he the fountain and spring of all our mercies, of all our desirable things? Has he not bid us welcome at our coming? Have we not received from him more than heart can conceive or tongue express?

What ails, then, our foolish and wretched hearts, to harbor such a cursed secret dislike of him and his ways? Let us be ashamed and astonished at the consideration of it, and walk in a humbling sense of it all our days. Let us carry it about with us in the most secret of our thoughts. And as this is a duty in itself acceptable unto God, who delights to dwell with them that are of a humble and contrite spirit [Isa. 57:15], so it is of exceeding efficacy to the weakening of the evil we treat of.

Labor to possess the mind with the beauty and excellency of spiritual things, so that they may be presented lovely and desirable to the soul; and this cursed aversation of sin will be weakened thereby. It is an innate acknowledged principle that the soul of man will not keep up cheerfully unto the worship of God unless it has a discovery of a beauty and comeliness in it. Hence, when men had lost all spiritual sense and savor of the things of God, to supply the want that was in their own souls, they invented outwardly pompous and gorgeous ways of worship, in images, paintings, pictures, and I know not what carnal ornaments; which they have called "The beauties of holiness!" [Ps. 110:3]. Thus much, however, was discovered therein, that the mind of man must see a beauty, a desirableness in the things of God's worship, or it will not delight in it; aversation will prevail. Let, then, the soul labor to acquaint itself with the spiritual beauty of obedience, of communion with God, and of all duties of immediate approach to him, that it may be rifled[53]

[52] near
[53] disordered, ruffled

with delight in them. It is not my present work to discover the heads[54] and springs of that beauty and desirableness which is in spiritual duties, in their relation to *God,* the eternal spring of all beauty—to *Christ,* the love, desire, and hope of all nations—to the *Spirit,* the great beautifier of souls, rendering them by his grace all glorious within; in their suitableness to the souls of men, as to their actings toward their last end, in the rectitude and holiness of the rule in attendance whereunto they are to be performed. But I only say at present, in general, that to acquaint the soul thoroughly with these things is an eminent way of weakening the aversation spoken of.

[Chapter 6]

How this enmity works by way of *aversation* has been declared, as also the means that the soul is to use for the preventing of its effects and prevalency. The second way whereby it exerts itself is *opposition.* Enmity will oppose and contend with that wherewith it is at enmity; it is so in things natural and moral. As light and darkness, heat and cold, so virtue and vice oppose each other. So is it with sin and grace; says the apostle, "These are contrary one to the other" (Gal. 5:17)—*allēlois antikeitai.* They are placed and set in mutual opposition, and that continually and constantly, as we shall see. Now, there are two ways whereby enemies manage an opposition—first, by force; and, secondly, by fraud and deceit. So when the Egyptians became enemies to the children of Israel and managed an enmity against them, Pharaoh says, "Let us deal wisely," or, rather, cunningly and subtly, "with this people" (Ex. 1:10); for so Stephen, with respect to this word, expresses it by *katasophisamenon*—he used "all manner of fraudulent sophistry" (Acts 7:19). And unto this deceit they added force in their grievous oppressions. This is the way and manner of things where there is a prevailing enmity; and both these are made use of by the law of sin in its enmity against God and our souls. I shall begin with the first, or its actings, as it were, in a way of force, in an open downright opposition to God and his law, or the good that a believing soul would do in obedience unto God and his law. And in this whole matter we must be careful to steer our course aright, taking the Scripture for our guide, with spiritual reason and experience for our companions; for there are many shelves in our course which must diligently be avoided, that none who consider these things be troubled without cause, or comforted without a just foundation.

[54] sources

In this first way, whereby this sin exerts its enmity in opposition—namely, as it were by force or strength—there are four things, expressing so many distinct degrees in its progress and procedure in the pursuit of its enmity. First, its *general inclination:* It "lusts" (Gal. 5:17). Secondly, its *particular way of contending:* It "fights or wars" (Rom. 7:23; James 4:1; 1 Pet. 2:11). Thirdly, its *success* in this contest: It "brings the soul into captivity to the law of sin" (Rom. 7:23). Fourthly, its *growth and rage* upon success: It comes up to "madness," as an enraged enemy will do (Eccles. 9:3). All which we must speak to in order.

The flesh lusts. First, in general it is said to lust: "The flesh lusts against the Spirit" (Gal. 5:17). This word expresses the general nature of that opposition which the law of sin makes against God and the rule of his Spirit or grace in them that believe; and, therefore, the least degree of that opposition is expressed hereby. When it does anything, it lusts; as, because burning is the general acting of fire, whatsoever it does else, it does also burn. When fire does anything it burns, and when the law of sin does anything it lusts.

Hence, all the actings of this law of sin are called "the lusts of the flesh": "You shall not fulfill the lust of the flesh" (Gal. 5:16); "Make no provision for the flesh, to fulfill the lusts thereof" (Rom. 13:14). Nor are these lusts of the flesh those only whereby men act [out] their sensuality in riot, drunkenness, uncleanness, and the like; but they comprehend all the actings of the law of sin whatsoever, in all the faculties and affections of the soul. Thus we have mention of the desires, or wills, or "lusts of the mind," as well as of the "flesh" (Eph. 2:3). The mind, the most spiritual part of the soul, has its lusts, no less than the sensual appetite, which seems sometimes more properly to be called the "flesh." And in the products of these lusts there are "defilements of the spirit" as well as of the "flesh" (2 Cor. 7:1)—that is, of the mind and understanding, as well [as] of the appetite and affections, and the body that attends their service. And in the blamelessness of all these consists our holiness:

"The God of peace sanctify you wholly; and I pray God, your whole spirit, and soul, and body, be preserved blameless unto the coming of our Lord Jesus Christ" (1 Thess. 5:23). Yea, by the "flesh" in this matter the whole old man, or the law of sin, is intended: "That which is born of the flesh is flesh" (John 3:6)—that is, it is all so, and nothing else; and whatsoever remains of the old nature in the new man is flesh still. And this flesh lusts—this law of sin does so; which is the general bottom[55] and foundation of all its opposition unto God. And this it does two ways:

[55] basis

In a hidden, close propensity unto all evil. This lies in it habitually. While a man is in the state of nature, fully under the power and dominion of this law of sin, it is said that "every figment of his heart is evil, and that continually" (Gen. 6:5). It can frame, fashion, produce, or act [on] nothing but what is evil; because this habitual propensity unto evil that is in the law of sin is absolutely predominant in such a one. It is in the heart like poison that has nothing to allay[56] its venomous qualities, and so infects whatsoever it touches. And where the power and dominion of it is broken, yet in its own nature it has still a habitual propensity unto that which is evil, wherein its lusting does consist.

But here we must distinguish between the habitual frame of the heart and the natural propensity or habitual inclination of the law of sin in the heart. The habitual inclination of the heart is denominated[57] from the principle that bears chief or sovereign rule in it; and therefore in believers it is unto good, unto God, unto holiness, unto obedience. The heart is not habitually inclined unto evil by the remainders of indwelling sin; but this sin in the heart has a constant, habitual propensity unto evil in itself or its own nature. This the apostle intends by its being present with us: "It is present with me"; that is, always and for its own end, which is to lust unto sin. It is with indwelling sin as with a river. While the springs and fountains of it are open, and waters are continually supplied unto its streams, set a dam before it, and it causes it to rise and swell until it bear down all or overflow the banks about it. Let these waters be abated, dried up in some good measure in the springs of them, and the remainder may be coerced and restrained. But still, as long as there is any running water, it will constantly press upon what stands before it, according to its weight and strength, because it is its nature so to do; and if by any means it [would] make a passage, it will proceed. So is it with indwelling sin: while the springs and fountains of it are open, in vain is it for men to set a dam before it by their convictions, resolutions, vows, and promises. They may check it for a while, but it will increase, rise high, and rage, at one time or another, until it bears down all those convictions and resolutions, or makes itself an under-ground passage by some secret lust, that shall give a full vent unto it. But now, suppose that the springs of it are much dried up by regenerating grace, the streams or actings of it abated by holiness, yet while anything remains of it, it will be pressing constantly to have vent, to press forward into actual sin; and this is its lusting. And this habitual propensity in it is discovered two ways:

---

[56] relieve
[57] designated

In its unexpected surprises of the soul into foolish, sinful figments and imaginations, which it looked not for, nor was any occasion administered unto them. It is with indwelling sin as it is with the contrary principle of sanctifying grace. This gives the soul, if I may so say, many a blessed surprise. It oftentimes ingenerates[58] and brings forth a holy, spiritual frame in the heart and mind, when we have had no previous rational considerations to work them thereunto. And this manifests it to be a habitual principle prevailing in the mind: so Song of Solomon 6:12, "Or ever I was aware, my soul made me as the chariots of Amminadib"; that is, free, willing, and ready for communion with Christ.[59] *Lo' yada'ti*—"I knew not; it was done by the power of the Spirit of grace; so that I took no notice of it, as it were, until it was done." The frequent actings of grace in this manner, exciting acts of faith, love, and complacency in God, are evidences of much strength and prevalency of it in the soul. And thus, also, is it with indwelling sin; ere the soul is aware, without any provocation or temptation, when it knows not, it is cast into a vain and foolish frame. Sin produces its figments secretly in the heart, and prevents the mind's consideration of what it is about. I mean hereby those "*actus primo primi,*" first acts of the soul; which are thus far involuntary, as that they have not the actual consent of the will unto them, but are voluntary as far as sin has its residence in the will. And these surprises, if the soul be not awake to take speedy care for the prevention of their tendency, do oftentimes set all as it were on fire, and engage the mind and affections into actual sin: for as by grace we are oftentimes, ere[60] we are aware, "made as the chariots of a willing people," and are far engaged in heavenly-mindedness and communion with Christ, making speed in it as in a chariot; so by sin are we oftentimes, ere we are aware, carried into distempered affections, foolish imaginations, and pleasing delightfulness in things that are not good nor profitable. Hence is that caution of the apostle, Galatians 6:1, *ean prolēphthē*—"If a man be surprised at unawares with a fault, or in a transgression." I doubt not but the subtlety of Satan and the power of temptation are here taken into consideration by the apostle, which causes him to express a man's falling into sin by *prolephthe*—"if he be surprised." So this working of indwelling sin also has its consideration in it, and that in the chief place, without which nothing else could surprise us; for without the help thereof, whatsoever comes from with-

[58] begets, produces

[59] Owen—along with most interpreters in the seventeenth century—interpreted the Song of Solomon (or Canticles, as they referred to it) as a "description of the communion that is between the Lord Christ and his saints" (*Works*, 2:46).

[60] before

out, from Satan or the world, must admit of some parley in the mind before it be received, but it is from within, from ourselves, that we are surprised. Hereby are we disappointed and wrought over to do that which we would not, and hindered from the doing of that which we would.

Hence it is that when the soul is oftentimes doing as it were quite another thing, engaged quite upon another design, sin starts that in the heart or imaginations of it that carries it away into that which is evil and sinful. Yea, to manifest its power, sometimes, when the soul is seriously engaged in the mortification of any sin, it will, by one means or other, lead it away into a dalliance with that very sin whose ruin it is seeking, and whose mortification it is engaged in! But as there is in this operation of the law of sin a special enticing or entangling, we shall speak unto it fully afterward. Now, these surprises can be from nothing but a habitual propensity unto evil in the principle from whence they proceed; not a habitual inclination unto actual sin in the mind or heart, but a habitual propensity unto evil in the sin that is in the mind or heart. This prevents the soul with its figments. How much communion with God is hereby prevented, how many meditations are disturbed, how much the minds and consciences of men have been defiled by this acting of sin, some may have observed. I know no greater burden in the life of a believer than these involuntary surprises of soul; involuntary, I say, as to the actual consent of the will, but not so in respect of that corruption which is in the will, and is the principle of them. And it is in respect unto these that the apostle makes his complaint (Rom. 7:25).

This habitual inclination manifests itself in its readiness and promptness, without dispute or altercation, to join and close with every temptation whereby it may possibly be excited. As we know it is in the nature of fire to burn, because it immediately lays hold on whatsoever is combustible, let any temptation whatsoever be proposed unto a man, the suitableness of whose matter unto his corruptions, or manner of its proposal, makes it a temptation; immediately he has not only to do with the temptation as outwardly proposed, but also with his own heart about it. Without further consideration or debate, the temptation has got a friend in him. Not a moment's space is given between the proposal and the necessity there is incumbent[61] on the soul to look to its enemy within. And this also argues a constant, habitual propensity unto evil. Our Savior said of the assaults and temptations of Satan, "The prince of this world comes, and he has no part in me" (John 14:30). He had more temptations, intensively and extensively, in number, quality, and

[61] obligatory

fierceness, from Satan and the world, than ever had any of the sons of men; but yet in all of them he had to deal only with that which came from without. His holy heart had nothing like to them, suited to them, or ready to give them entertainment: "The prince of this world had nothing in him." So it was with Adam. When a temptation befell him, he had only the outward proposal to look unto; all was well within until the outward temptation took place and prevailed. With us it is not so. In a city that is at unity in itself, compact and entire, without divisions and parties, if an enemy approach about it, the rulers and inhabitants have no thoughts at all but only how they may oppose the enemy without, and resist him in his approaches. But if the city be divided in itself, if there be factions and traitors within, the very first thing they do is to look to the enemies at home, the traitors within, to cut off the head of Sheba [2 Sam. 20:22], if they will be safe. All was well with Adam within doors when Satan came, so that he had nothing to do but to look to his assaults and approaches. But now, on the access of any temptation, the soul is instantly to look in, where it shall find this traitor at work, closing with the baits of Satan, and stealing away the heart; and this it does always, which evinces an habitual inclination. [In] Psalm 38:17, David says, "I am ready to halt," or for halting: *ki-'ani l^e^tsela' nakon*—"I am prepared and disposed unto hallucination, to the slipping of my foot into sin" (v. 16), as he expounds the meaning of that phrase (Ps. 78:2-3). There was from indwelling sin a continual disposition in him to be slipping, stumbling, halting, on every occasion or temptation. There is nothing so vain, foolish, ridiculous, fond, nothing so vile and abominable, nothing so atheistical or execrable,[62] but, if it be proposed unto the soul in a way of temptation, there is that in this law of sin which is ready to answer it before it be decried by grace. And this is the first thing in this lusting of the law of sin—it consists in its habitual propensity unto evil, manifesting itself by the involuntary surprises of the soul unto sin, and its readiness, without dispute or consideration, to join in all temptations whatsoever.

Its lusting consists in its actual pressing after that which is evil, and actual opposition unto that which is good. The former instance showed its constant readiness to this work; this now treats of the work itself. It is not only ready, but for the most part always engaged. "It lusts," says the Holy Ghost. It does so continually. It stirs in the soul by one act or other constantly, almost as the spirits in the blood, or the blood in the veins. This the apostle calls its tempting: "Every man is tempted of his own lust" (James 1:14). Now, what is it

[62] extremely inferior or detestable

to be tempted? It is to have that proposed to a man's consideration which, if he close with, it is evil, it is sin unto him. This is sin's trade: *epithumei*—"it lusts." It is raising up in the heart, and proposing unto the mind and affections, that which is evil; trying, as it were, whether the soul will close with its suggestions, or how far it will carry them on, though it does not wholly prevail. Now, when such a temptation comes from without, it is unto the soul an indifferent thing, neither good nor evil, unless it be consented unto; but the very proposal from within, it being the soul's own act, is its sin. And this is the work of the law of sin—it is restlessly and continually raising up and proposing innumerable various forms and appearances of evil, in this or that kind, indeed in every kind that the nature of man is capable to exercise corruption in. Something or other, in matter, or manner, or circumstance, inordinate, unspiritual, unanswerable unto the rule, it hatches and proposes unto the soul. And this power of sin to beget figments and ideas of actual evil in the heart the apostle may have respect unto, *apo pantos eidous ponērou apexesthe*—"Keep yourselves from every figment or idea of sin in the heart" (1 Thess. 5:22); for the word there used does not anywhere signify an outward form or appearance: neither is it the appearance of evil, but an evil idea or figment that is intended. And this lusting of sin is that which the prophet expresses in wicked men, in whom the law of it is predominant: "The wicked are like the troubled sea, when it cannot rest, whose waters cast up mire and dirt" (Isa. 57:20); a similitude most lively, expressing the lustings of the law of sin, restlessly and continually bubbling up in the heart, with wicked, foolish, and filthy imaginations and desires. This, then, is the first thing in the opposition that this enmity makes to God—namely, in its general inclination, it "lusts."

Secondly, there is its particular way of contending—*it fights or wars;* that is, it acts with strength and violence, as men do in war. First, it lusts, stirring and moving inordinate figments in the mind, desires in the appetite and the affections, proposing them to the will. But it rests not there, it cannot rest; it urges, presses, and pursues its proposals with earnestness, strength, and vigor, fighting, and contending, and warring to obtain its end and purpose. Would it merely stir up and propose things to the soul, and immediately acquiesce in the sentence, and judgment of the mind, that the thing is evil, against God and his will, and not further to be insisted on, much sin might be prevented that is now produced; but it rests not here—it proceeds to carry on its design, and that with earnestness and contention. By this means wicked men "inflame themselves" (Isa. 57:5). They are self-inflamers, as the word signifies, unto sin; every spark of sin is cherished in them until it grows into a flame: and so it will do in others, where it is so cherished. Now, this fighting or warring of sin consists in two things: (1) in its *rebellion against grace,* or the law of the mind; (2) in its *assaulting the soul,* contending for rule and sovereignty over it.

The first is expressed by the apostle in Romans 7:23: "I find," says he, "another law," *antistrateuomenon tō nomō tou noos mou,* "rebelling against the law of my mind." There are, it seems, two laws in us—the "law of the flesh," or of sin; and the "law of the mind," or of grace. But contrary laws cannot both obtain sovereign power over the same person at the same time. The sovereign power in believers is in the hand of the law of grace; so the apostle declares, "I delight in the law of God in the inward man" (v. 22). Obedience unto this law is performed with delight and complacency in the inward man, because its authority is lawful and good. So more expressly, "For sin shall not have dominion over you, for you are not under the law, but under grace" (6:14). Now, to war against the law that has a just sovereignty is to rebel; and so *antistrateuomai* signifies, it is to rebel, and ought to have been so translated, "Rebelling against the law of my mind." And this rebellion consists in a stubborn, obstinate opposition unto the commands and directions of the law of grace. Does the "law of the mind" command anything as duty? Does it severely rise up against anything that is evil? When the lusting of the law of sin rises up to this degree, it contends against obedience with all its might; the effect whereof, as the apostle tells us, is "the doing of that which we would not, and the not doing of that which we would" (7:15, 16). And we may gather a notable instance of the power of sin in its rebellion from this place. The law of grace prevails upon the will, so that it would do that which is good: "To will is present with me" (v. 18); "When I would do good" (v. 21); and again, "And I would not do evil" (v. 19). And it prevails upon the understanding, so that it approves or disapproves, according to the dictates of the law of grace: Verse 16: "I consent unto the law that it is good"; and verse 15. The judgment always lies on the side of grace. It prevails also on the affections: "I delight in the law of God in the inward man" (v. 22). Now, if this be so, that grace has the sovereign power in the understanding, will, and affections, whence is it that it does not always prevail, that we do not always do that which we would, and abstain from that which we would not? Is it not strange that a man should not do that which he chooses, wills, likes, delights in? Is there anything more required to enable us unto that which is good? The law of grace does all, as much as can be expected from it, that which in itself is abundantly sufficient for the perfecting of all holiness in the fear of the Lord. But here lies the difficulty, in the entangling opposition that is made by the rebellion of this "law of sin." Neither is it expressible with what vigor and variety sin acts itself in this matter. Sometimes it proposes diversions, sometimes it causes weariness, sometimes it finds out difficulties, sometimes it stirs up contrary affections, sometimes it begets prejudices, and one way or other entangles the soul; so that it never suffers grace to have an absolute and complete success in any duty. Verse 18, *to katergazesthai to kalon ou*—"I find not the way perfectly to work out, or accomplish, that which is good," so the word signifies; and that from this opposition and resistance that is made by the law of sin. Now, this rebellion appears in two things: (1) In the opposition that it makes unto the general purpose and course of the soul; (2) In the opposition it makes unto particular duties.

In the opposition it makes to the general purpose and course of the soul. There is none in whom is the Spirit of Christ, that is his, but [who does not make] it is his general design and purpose to walk in a universal conformity unto him in all things. Even from the inward frame of the heart to the whole compass of his outward actions, so it is with him. This God requires in his covenant: "Walk before me, and be perfect" (Gen. 17:1). Accordingly, his design is to walk before God; and his frame is sincerity and uprightness therein. This is called "cleaving unto the Lord with purpose of heart" (Acts 11:23)—that is, in all things; and that not with a slothful, dead, ineffectual purpose, but such as is operative, and sets the whole soul at work in pursuit of it. This the apostle sets forth in Philippians 3:12-14: "Not as though I had already attained, either were already perfect: but I follow after, if that I may apprehend that for which also I am apprehended of Christ Jesus. Brethren, I count not myself to have apprehended: but this one thing I do, forgetting those things which are behind, and reaching forth unto those things which are before, I press toward the mark for the prize of the high calling of God in Christ Jesus." He uses three words excellently expressing the soul's universal pursuit of this purpose of heart in cleaving unto God: First, says he, *diōkō* (v. 12)—"I follow after," prosecute. The word signifies properly to persecute, which with what earnestness and diligence it is usually done we know. Secondly, *epekteinomai*—"I reach forward," reaching with great intension[63] of spirit and affections. It is a great and constant endeavor that is expressed in that word. Thirdly, *kata skopon diōko*—say we, "I press toward the mark," that is, even as men that are running for a prize. All set forth the vigor, earnestness, diligence, and constancy that is used in the pursuit of this purpose. And this the nature of the principle of grace requires in them in whom it is.

[63] intention

But yet we see with what failings, yea failings, their pursuit of this course is attended. The frame of the heart is changed, the heart is stolen away, the affections entangled, eruptions of unbelief and distempered passions discovered, carnal wisdom, with all its attendancies,[64] are set on work; all contrary to the general principle and purpose of the soul. And all this is from the rebellion of this law of sin, stirring up and provoking the heart unto disobedience. The prophet gives this character of hypocrites, "Their heart is divided; therefore shall they be found faulty" (Hos. 10:2). Now, though this be wholly so in respect of the mind and judgment in hypocrites only, yet it is partially so in the best [of believers], in the sense described. They have a division, not of the heart, but in the heart; and thence it is that they are so often found faulty. So says the apostle, "So that we cannot do the things that we would" (Gal. 5:17). We cannot accomplish the design of close walking according to the law of grace, because of the contrariety and rebellion of this law of sin.

It rebels also in respect unto particular duties. It raises a combustion in the soul against the particular commands and designings of the law of grace. "You cannot do the things that you would"; that is, "The duties which you judge incumbent on you, which you approve and delight is in the inward man, you cannot do them as you would." Take an instance in prayer. A man addresses himself unto that duty; he would not only perform it, but he would perform it in that manner that the nature of the duty and his own condition do require. He would "pray in the spirit," fervently, "with sighs and groans that cannot be uttered" [Rom. 8:26]; in faith, with love and delight, pouring forth his soul unto the Lord. This he aims at. Now, oftentimes he shall find a rebellion, a fighting of the law of sin in this matter. He shall find difficulty to get anything done who thought to do all things. I do not say that it is thus always, but it is so when sin "wars and rebels," which expresses a special acting of its power. Woeful entanglements do poor creatures oftentimes meet with upon this account. Instead of that free, enlarged communion with God that they aim at, the best that their souls arrive unto is but to go away mourning for their folly, deadness, and indisposition. In a word, there is no command of the law of grace that is known, liked of, and approved by the soul, but when it comes to be observed, this law of sin one way or other makes head[way] and rebels against it. And this is the first way of its fighting.

It does not only rebel and resist, but *it assaults the soul.* It sets upon the law of the mind and grace; which is the second part of its warring: *strateuontai kata tēs psuchēs*—"they fight," or war, "against the soul" (1 Pet.

[64] things that accompany

2:11); *strateuontai en tois melesin humōn*—"they fight," or war, "in your members" (James 4:1). Peter shows what they oppose and fight against—namely, the "soul" and the law of grace therein; James [shows] what they fight with or by—namely, the "members," or the corruption that is in our mortal bodies. *Antistrateuesthai* is to rebel against a superior; *strateuesthai* is to assault or war for a superiority. It takes the part of an assailant as well as of a resister. It makes attempts for rule and sovereignty, as well as opposes the rule of grace. Now, all war and fighting has somewhat of violence in it; and there is therefore some violence in that acting of sin which the Scripture calls "fighting and warring." And this assailing efficacy of sin, as distinguished from its rebelling, before treated of, consists in these things that ensue:

All its positive actings in stirring up unto sin belong to this head. Oftentimes, by the vanity of the mind, or the sensuality of the affections, the folly of the imaginations, it sets upon the soul then when the law of grace is not actually putting it on duty; so that therein it does not rebel but assault. Hence the apostle cries out, "Who shall deliver me from it?" (Rom. 7:24). "Who shall rescue me out of its hand?" as the word signifies. When we pursue an enemy, and he resists us, we do not cry out, "Who shall deliver us?" for we are the assailants; but "Who shall rescue me?" is the cry of one who is set upon by an enemy. So it is here; a man is assaulted by his "own lust," as James speaks. By the wayside, in his employment, under a duty, sin sets upon the soul with vain imaginations, foolish desires, and would willingly employ the soul to make provision for its satisfaction; which the apostle cautions us against: *tēs sarx pronoian me poiēisthe eis epithumias*—"do not accomplish the providence or projection of the flesh for its own satisfaction" (Rom. 13:14).

Its importunity[65] *and urgency seems to be noted in this expression, of its warring.* Enemies in war are restless, pressing, and importunate; so is the law of sin. Does it set upon the soul? Cast off its motions; it returns again. Rebuke them by the power of grace; they withdraw for a while, and return again. Set before them the cross of Christ; they do as those that came to take him—at sight of him they went backwards and fell unto the ground, but they arose again and laid hands on him—sin gives place for a season, but returns and presses on the soul again. Mind it of the love of God in Christ; though it be stricken, yet it gives not over. Present hell-fire unto it; it rushes into the midst of those flames. Reproach it with its folly and madness; it knows no

[65] persistence

shame, but presses on still. Let the thoughts of the mind strive to fly from it; it follows as on the wings of the wind. And by this importunity it wearies and wears out the soul; and if the great remedy (Rom. 8:3) comes not timely, it prevails to a conquest. There is nothing more marvelous nor dreadful in the working of sin than this of its importunity. The soul knows not what to make of it; it dislikes, abhors, abominates the evil it tends unto; it despises the thoughts of it, hates them as hell; and yet is by itself imposed on with them, as if it were another person, an express enemy got within him. All this the apostle discovers: "The things that I do I hate" (Rom. 7:15-17). It is not of outward actions, but the inward risings of the mind that he treats. "I hate them," says he; "I abominate them." But why, then, will he have anything more to do with them? If he hate them, and abhor himself for them, let them alone, have no more to do with them, and so end the matter. Alas! says he, "It is no more I that do it, but sin that dwells in me" (v. 17)—"I have one within me that is my enemy, that with endless, restless importunity puts these things upon me, even the things that I hate and abominate. I cannot be rid of them, I am weary of myself, I cannot fly from them. 'O wretched man that I am! who shall deliver me?'" I do not say that this is the ordinary condition of believers, but thus it is often when this law of sin rises up to war and fighting. It is not thus with them in respect of particular sins—this or that sin, outward sins, sins of life and conversation—but yet in respect of vanity of mind, inward and spiritual distempers, it is often so. Some, I know, pretend to great perfection; but I am resolved to believe the apostle before them all and every one.

It carries on its war by entangling of the affections, and drawing them into a combination against the mind. Let grace be enthroned in the mind and judgment, yet if the law of sin lays hold upon and entangles the affections, or any of them, it has gotten a fort from whence it continually assaults the soul. Hence the great duty of mortification is chiefly directed to take place upon the affections: "Mortify therefore your members which are upon the earth; fornication, uncleanness, inordinate affection, concupiscence, and covetousness, which is idolatry" (Col. 3:5). The "members that are upon the earth" are our affections: for in the outward part of the body sin is not seated; in particular, not "covetousness," which is there enumerated, to be mortified among our members that are on the earth. Yea, after grace has taken possession of the soul, the affections do become the principal seat of the remainders of sin—and therefore Paul says that this law is "in our members" (Rom. 7:23); and James, that it "wars in our members" (James 4:1)—that is, our affections. And there is no estimate to be taken of the work of mortification aright but by the affections. We may every day see persons of very eminent light, that yet visibly have unmortified hearts and conversations; their affections have not been crucified with Christ. Now, then, when this law of sin can possess any affection, whatsoever it be, love, delight, fear, it will make from it and by it fearful assaults upon the soul. For instance, has it got the love of anyone entangled with the world or the things of it, the lust of the flesh, the lust of the eyes, or the pride of life—how will it take advantage on every occasion to break in upon the soul! It shall do nothing, attempt nothing, be in no place or company, perform no duty, private or public, but sin will have one blow or other at it; it will be one way or other soliciting for itself.

This is the sum of what we shall offer unto this acting of the law of sin, in a way of fighting and warring against our souls, which is so often mentioned in the Scripture; and a due consideration of it is of no small advantage unto us, especially to bring us unto self-abasement, to teach us to walk humbly and mournfully before God. There are two things that are suited to humble the souls of men, and they are, first, a due consideration of God, and then of themselves—of *God,* in his greatness, glory, holiness, power, majesty, and authority; of *ourselves,* in our mean,[66] abject, and sinful condition. Now, of all things in our condition, there is nothing so suited unto this end and purpose as that which lies before us; namely, the vile remainders of enmity against God which are yet in our hearts and natures. And it is no small evidence of a gracious soul when it is willing to search itself in this matter, and to be helped therein from a word of truth; when it is willing that the word should dive into the secret parts of the heart and rip open whatsoever of evil and corruption lies therein. The prophet says of Ephraim, "He loved to tread out the corn" (Hos. 10:11); he loved to work when he might eat, to have always the corn before him: but God, says he, would "cause him to plough"—a labor no less needful, though at present not so delightful. Most men love to hear of the doctrine of grace, of the pardon of sin, of free love, and suppose they find food therein; however, it is evident that they grow and thrive in the life and notion of them. But to be breaking up the fallow[67] ground of their hearts, to be inquiring after the weeds and briars that grow in them, they delight not so much, though this be no less necessary than the other. This path is not so beaten as that of grace, nor so trod in, though it be the only way to come to a true knowledge of grace itself. It may be

[66] lowly, insignificant
[67] plowed but unseeded

some, who are wise and grown in other truths, may yet be so little skilled in searching their own hearts, that they may be slow in the perception and understanding of these things. But this sloth and neglect is to be shaken off, if we have any regard unto our own souls. It is more than probable that many a false hypocrite, who have deceived themselves as well as others, because they thought the doctrine of the gospel pleased them, and therefore supposed they believed it, might be delivered from their soul-ruining deceits if they would diligently apply themselves unto this search of their own hearts. Or, would other professors walk with so much boldness and security as some do if they considered aright what a deadly watchful enemy they continually carry about with them and in them? Would they so much indulge as they do carnal joys and pleasures, or pursue their perishing affairs with so much delight and greediness as they do? It were to be wished that we would all apply our hearts more to this work, even to come to a true understanding of the nature, power, and subtlety of this our adversary, that our souls may be humbled; and that—

In walking with God. His delight is with the humble and contrite ones [Isa. 57:15], those that tremble at his word [Isa. 66:2], the mourners in Zion [Isa. 61:3]; and such are we only when we have a due sense of our own vile condition. This will beget reverence of God, a sense of our distance from him, admiration of his grace and condescension, a due valuation of mercy, far above those light, verbal, airy attainments, that some have boasted of.

In walking with others. It lays in provision to prevent those great evils of judging, spiritual unmercifulness, harsh censuring, which I have observed to have been pretended by many, who, at the same time, as afterward has appeared, have been guilty of greater or worse crimes than those which they have raved against in others. This, I say, will lead us to meekness, compassion, readiness to forgive, to pass by offenses; even when we shall "consider" what is our state, as the apostle plainly declares (Gal. 6:1). The man that understands the evil of his own heart, how vile it is, is the only useful, fruitful, and solid believing and obedient person. Others are fit only to delude themselves, to disquiet families, churches, and all relations whatsoever. Let us, then, consider our hearts wisely, and then go and see if we can be proud of our gifts, our graces, our valuation and esteem among professors, our enjoyments. Let us go then and judge, condemn, reproach others that have been tempted; we shall find a great inconsistency in these things. And many things of the like nature might be here added upon the consideration of this woeful effect of indwelling sin. The way of opposing and defeating its design herein shall be afterward considered.

[Chapter 7]

The third thing assigned unto this law of sin in its opposition unto God and the law of his grace is that *it leads the soul captive:* "I find a law leading me captive" (captivating me) "unto the law of sin" (Rom. 7:23). And this is the utmost height which the apostle in that place carries the opposition and warring of the remainders of indwelling sin unto; closing the consideration of it with a complaint of the state and condition of believers thereby, and an earnest prayer for deliverance from it: "O wretched man that I am! who shall deliver me from this body of death?" (v. 24). What is contained in this expression and intended by it shall be declared in the ensuing observations.

It is not directly the power and actings of the law of sin that are here expressed, *but its success in and upon its actings.* But success is the greatest evidence of power, and leading captive in war is the height of success. None can aim at greater success than to lead their enemies captive; and it is a peculiar expression in the Scripture of great success. So the Lord Christ, on his victory over Satan, is said to "lead captivity captive" (Eph. 4:8)—that is, to conquer him who had conquered and prevailed upon others; and this he did when "by death he destroyed him that had the power of death, that is, the devil" (Heb. 2:14). Here, then, a great prevalency and power of sin in its warring against the soul is discovered. It so wars as to "lead captive," which, had it not great power, it could not do, especially against that resistance of the soul which is included in this expression.

It is said that *it leads the soul captive "unto the law of sin"*—not to this or that sin, particular sin, actual sin, but to the "law of sin." God, for the most part, orders things so, and gives out such supplies of grace unto believers, as that they shall not be made a prey unto this or that particular sin, that it should prevail in them and compel them to serve it in the lusts thereof, that it should have dominion over them, that they should be captives and slaves unto it. This is that which David prays so earnestly against: "Cleanse me from secret faults. Keep back your servant also from presumptuous sins; let them not have dominion over me: then shall I be upright" (Ps. 19:12-13). He supposes the continuance of the law of sin in him (v. 12), which will bring forth errors of life and secret sins; against which he finds relief in pardoning and cleansing mercy, which he prays for. "This," says he, "will be my condition. But for sins of pride and boldness, such as all sins are that get dominion in a man, that make a captive of a man, the Lord restrain your servant from them." For whatsoever sin gets such power in a man, be it in its own nature small or great, it becomes in him in whom it is a sin of boldness, pride, and presumption; for these things are not reckoned from the nature or kind of the sin, but from its prevalency and customariness, wherein its pride, boldness, and contempt of God does consist. To the same purpose, if I mistake not, prays Jabez: "Oh that you would bless me indeed, and enlarge my coast, and that your hand might be with me, and that you would keep me from evil, that it may not grieve me!" (1 Chron. 4:10). The holy man took occasion from his own name to pray against sin, that that might not be a grief and sorrow to him by its power and prevalency. I confess, sometimes it may come to this with a believer, that for a season he may be led captive by some particular sin; it may have so much prevalency in him as to have power over him. So it seems to have been with David, when he lay so long in his sin without repentance; and was plainly so with those in Isaiah 57:17-18: "For the iniquity of his covetousness was I wroth[68] and smote him: I hid me, and was wroth, and he went on frowardly in the way of his heart. I have seen his ways and will heal him." They continued under the power of their covetousness, so that no dealings of God with them, for so long a time, could reclaim them. But, for the most part, when any lust or sin does so prevail, it is from the advantage and furtherance that it has got by some powerful temptation of Satan. He has poisoned it, inflamed it, and entangled the soul. So the apostle, speaking of such as through sin were fallen off from their holiness, says, "They were in the snare of the devil, being taken captive by him at his will" (2 Tim. 2:26). Though it were their own lusts that they served, yet they were brought into bondage thereunto by being entangled in some snare of Satan; and thence they are said to be "taken alive," as a poor beast in a toil.

And here, by the way, we may a little inquire, whether the prevailing power of a particular sin in any be from itself, or from the influence of temptation upon it; concerning which at present take only these two observations:

Much of the prevalency of sin upon the soul is certainly from Satan, when the perplexing and captivating sin has no peculiar footing nor advantage in the nature, constitution, or condition of the sinner. When any lust grows high and prevailing more than others, upon its own account, it is from the peculiar advantage that it has in the natural constitution, or the station or condition of the person in the world; for otherwise the law of sin gives an equal propensity unto all evil, an equal vigor unto every lust. When, therefore, it cannot be discerned that the captivating sin is peculiarly fixed in the nature of the sinner, or is advantaged from his education or employment in the world, the prevalency of it is peculiarly from Satan. He has got to the

---

[68] filled with wrath

root of it, and has given it poison and strength. Yea, perhaps, sometimes that which may seem to the soul to be the corrupt lusting of the heart, is nothing but Satan's imposing his suggestions on the imagination. If, then, a man find an importunate rage from any corruption that is not evidently seated in his nature, let him, as the papists[69] say, cross himself, or fly by faith to the cross of Christ, for the devil is nigh at hand.

When a lust is prevalent unto captivity, where it brings in no advantage to the flesh, it is from Satan. All that the law of sin does of itself is to serve the providence of the flesh (Rom. 13:14); and it must bring in unto it somewhat of the profits and pleasures that are its object. Now, if the prevailing sin does not so act in itself, if it be more spiritual and inward, it is much from Satan by the imagination, more than the corruption of the heart itself. But [more on] this, by the way.

I say, then, that the apostle treats not here of our being captivated unto this or that sin, but unto the law of sin; that is, we are compelled to bear its presence and burden whether we will or no. Sometimes the soul thinks or hopes that it may through grace be utterly freed from this troublesome inmate. Upon some sweet enjoyment of God, some full supply of grace, some return from wandering, some deep affliction, some thorough humiliation, the poor soul begins to hope that it shall now be freed from the law of sin; but after a while it perceives that it is quite otherwise. Sin acts again, makes good its old station; and the soul finds that, whether it will or no, it must bear its yoke. This makes it sigh and cry out for deliverance.

This leading captive argues a prevalency against the renitency[70] *or contrary actings of the will.* This is intimated plainly in this expression—namely, that the will opposes and makes head[way], as it were, against the working of sin. This the apostle declares in those expressions which he uses (Rom. 7:15, 19, 20). And herein consists the "lusting of the Spirit against the flesh" (Gal. 5:17); that is, the contending of grace to expel and subdue it. The spiritual habits of grace that are in the will do so resist and act against it; and the excitation of those habits by the Spirit are directed to the same purpose. This leading captive is contrary, I say, to the inclinations and actings of the renewed will. No man is made a captive but against his will. Captivity is misery and trouble, and no man willingly puts himself into trouble. Men choose it in its causes, and in the ways and means leading unto it, but not in itself. So the prophet informs us in Hosea 5:11, "Ephraim was," not willingly,

[69] negative label for Roman Catholics, relating to belief in papal supremacy; from the Latin *papa* ("pope")
[70] resistance, reluctance

"oppressed and broken in judgment"—that was his misery and trouble; but he "willingly walked after the commandment" of the idolatrous kings, which brought him thereunto. Whatever consent, then, the soul may give unto sin, which is the means of this captivity, it gives none to the captivity itself; that is against the will wholly. Hence these things ensue:

That *the power of sin is great*—which is that which we are in demonstration of; and this appears in its prevalency unto captivity against the actings and contendings of the will for liberty from it. Had it no opposition made unto it, or were its adversary weak, negligent, slothful, it were no great evidence of its power that it made captives; but its prevailing against diligence, activity, watchfulness, the constant renitency of the will, this evinces its efficacy.

This leading captive intimates manifold particular successes. Had it not success in particular, it could not be said at all to lead captive. Rebel it might, assail it might; but it cannot be said to lead captive without some successes. And there are several degrees of the success of the law of sin in the soul. Sometimes it carries the person unto outward actual sin, which is its utmost aim; sometimes it obtains the consent of the will, but is cast out by grace, and proceeds no further; sometimes it wearies and entangles the soul, that it turns aside, as it were, and leaves contending—which is a success also. One or more, or all of these, must be where captivity takes place. Such a kind of course does the apostle ascribe unto covetousness (1 Tim. 6:9-10).

This leading captive manifests this condition to be miserable and wretched. To be thus yoked and dealt with, against the judgment of the mind, the choice and consent of the will, its utmost strivings and contendings—how sad is it! When the neck is sore and tender with former pressures, to be compelled to bear the yoke again—this pierces, this grieves, this even breaks the heart. When the soul is principled by grace unto a loathing of sin, of every evil way, to a hatred of the least discrepancy between itself and the holy will of God, then to be imposed on by this law of sin, with all that enmity and folly, that deadness and filth wherewith it is attended, what more dreadful condition? All captivity is dreadful in its own nature. The greatest aggravation of it is from the condition of the tyrant unto whom anyone is captivated. Now, what can be worse than this law of sin? Hence the apostle, having once mentioned this captivity, cries out, as one quite weary and ready to faint (Rom. 7:24).

This condition is peculiar to believers. Unregenerate men are not said to be led captive to the law of sin. They may, indeed, be led captive unto this or that particular sin or corruption—that is, they may be forced to serve it against the power of their convictions. They are convinced of the evil of it—

an adulterer of his uncleanness, a drunkard of his abomination—and make some resolutions, it may be, against it; but their lust is too hard for them, they cannot cease to sin, and so are made captives or slaves to this or that particular sin. But they cannot be said to be led captive to the law of sin, and that because they are willingly subject thereunto. It has, as it were, a rightful dominion over them, and they oppose it not, but only when it has eruptions to the disturbance of their consciences; and then the opposition they make unto it is not from their wills, but is the mere acting of an affrighted conscience and a convinced mind. They regard not the nature of sin, but its guilt and consequences. But to be brought into captivity is that which befalls a man against his will; which is all that shall be spoken unto this degree of the actings of the power of sin, manifesting itself in its success.

The fourth and last degree of the opposition made by the law of sin to God and the law of his will and grace is in *its rage and madness*. There is madness in its nature: "The heart of the sons of men is full of evil, and madness is in their heart" (Eccles. 9:3). The evil that the heart of man is full of by nature is that indwelling sin whereof we speak; and this is so in their heart, that it rises up unto madness. The Holy Ghost expresses this rage of sin by a fit similitude, which he uses in sundry places (as Jer. 2:24; Hos. 8:9). It makes men as "a wild ass"; "she traverses her ways," and "snuffs up the wind," and runs whither her mind or lust leads her. And he says of idolaters, enraged with their lusts, that they are "mad upon their idols" (Jer. 50:38). We may a little consider what lies in this madness and rage of sin, and how it rises up thereunto:

For the nature of it; it seems to consist in a violent, heady, pertinacious pressing unto evil or sin. Violence, importunity, and pertinacy are in it. It is the tearing and torturing of the soul by any sin to force its consent and to obtain satisfaction. It rises up in the heart, is denied by the law of grace, and rebuked—it returns and exerts its poison again; the soul is startled, casts it off—it returns again with new violence and importunity; the soul cries out for help and deliverance, looks round about to all springs of gospel grace and relief, trembles at the furious assaults of sin, and casts itself into the arms of Christ for deliverance. And if it be not able to take that course, it is foiled and hurried up and down through the mire and filth of foolish imaginations, corrupt and noisome[71] lusts, which rend and tear it, as if they would devour its whole spiritual life and power (see 1 Tim. 6:9-10; 2 Pet. 2:14). It was not much otherwise with them whom we instanced in before (Isa. 57:17). They had an inflamed, enraged lust working in them, even "covetousness," or the

[71] dangerous, offensive, foul

love of this world; by which, as the apostle speaks, men "pierce themselves through with many sorrows" [1 Tim. 6:10]. God is angry with them, and discovers his wrath by all the ways and means that it was possible for them to be made sensible thereof. He was "wroth and smote them"; but [even] though, it may be, this staggered them a little, yet they "went on." He is angry and "hides himself" from them—deserts them as to his gracious, assisting, comforting presence. Does this work the effect? No; they go on frowardly still, as men mad on their covetousness. Nothing can put a stop to their raging lusts. This is plain madness and fury. We need not seek far for instances. We see men mad on their lusts every day; and, which is the worst kind of madness, their lusts do not rage so much in them, as they rage in the pursuit of them. Are those greedy pursuits of things in the world, which we see some men engaged in, though they have other pretenses, indeed anything else but plain madness in the pursuit of their lusts? God, who searches the hearts of men, knows that the most of things that are done with other pretenses in the world are nothing but the actings of men mad and furious in the pursuit of their lusts.

That sin arises not unto this height ordinarily, but when it has got a double advantage—

That it be provoked, enraged, and heightened by some great temptation. Though it be a poison in itself, yet, being inbred in nature, it grows not violently outrageous without the contribution of some new poison of Satan unto it, in a suitable temptation. It was the advantage that Satan got against David, by a suitable temptation, that raised his lust to that rage and madness which it went forth unto in the business of Bathsheba and Uriah. Though sin be always a fire in the bones, yet it flames not unless Satan come with his bellows[72] to blow it up. And let anyone in whom the law of sin arises to this height of rage seriously consider, and he may find out where the devil stands and puts in in the business.

It must be advantaged by some former entertainment and prevalency. Sin grows not to this height at its first assault. Had it not been suffered to make its entrance, had there not been some yielding in the soul, this had not come about. The great wisdom and security of the soul in dealing with indwelling sin is to put a violent stop unto its beginnings, its first motions and actings. Venture all on the first attempt. Die rather than yield one step unto it. If, through the deceit of sin, or the negligence of the soul, or its carnal confidence to give bounds to lust's actings at other seasons, it makes any entrance into

[72] blacksmith's device for blowing air into fire

the soul, and finds any entertainment, it gets strength and power, and insensibly arises to the frame under consideration. You had never had the experience of the fury of sin, if you had not been content with some of its dalliances. Had you not brought up this servant, this slave, delicately, it would not have now presumed beyond a son. Now, when the law of sin in any particular has got this double advantage—the furtherance of a vigorous temptation, and some prevalency formerly obtained, whereby it is let into the strengths of the soul—it often rises up to this frame whereof we speak.

We may see what accompanies this rage and madness, what are the properties of it, and what effects it produces—

There is in it the casting off, for a time at least, of the yoke, rule, and government of the Spirit and law of grace. Where grace has the dominion, it will never utterly be expelled from its throne, it will still keep its right and sovereignty; but its influences may for a season be intercepted, and its government be suspended, by the power of sin. Can we think that the law of grace had any actual influence of rule on the heart of David, when, upon the provocation received from Nabal, he was so hurried with the desire of self-revenge that he cried, "Gird on your swords," to his companions, and resolved not to leave alive one man of his whole household? (1 Sam. 25:34); or that Asa was in any better frame when he smote the prophet and put him in prison that spoke unto him in the name of the Lord [2 Chron. 16:10]? Sin in this case is like an untamed horse, which, having first cast off his rider, runs away with fierceness and rage. It first casts off a present sense of the yoke of Christ and the law of his grace, and then hurries the soul at its pleasure.

Let us a little consider how this is done. The seat and residence of grace is in the whole soul. It is in the inner man; it is in the mind, the will, and the affections: for the whole soul is renewed by it into the image of God (Eph. 4:23-24), and the whole man is a "new creature" (2 Cor. 5:17). And in all these does it exert its power and efficacy. Its rule or dominion is the pursuit of its effectual working in all the faculties of the soul, as they are one united principle of moral and spiritual operations. So, then, the interrupting of its exercise, of its rule and power, by the law of sin, must consist in its contrary acting in and upon the faculties and affections of the soul, whereon and by which grace should exert its power and efficacy. And this it does. It darkens the *mind;* partly through innumerable vain prejudices and false reasonings, as we shall see when we come to consider its deceitfulness; and partly through the steaming of the affections, heated with the noisome lusts that have laid hold on them. Hence that saving light that is in the mind is clouded and stifled, that it cannot put forth its transforming power to change the soul into the likeness of Christ discovered unto it, which is its proper work (Rom. 12:2). The habitual inclination of the *will* to obedience, which is the next way of the working of the law of grace, is first weakened, then cast aside and rendered useless, by the continual solicitations of sin and temptation; so that the will first lets go its hold, and disputes whether it shall yield or no, and at last gives up itself to its adversary. And for the *affections*, commonly the beginning of this evil is in them. They cross one another, and torture the soul with their impetuous[73] violence. By this way is the rule of the law of grace intercepted by the law of sin, even by imposing upon it in the whole seat of its government.

When this is done, it is sad work that sin will make in the soul. The apostle warns believers to take heed hereof, "Let not sin therefore reign in your mortal body, that you should obey it in the lusts thereof" (Rom. 6:12). Look to it that it get not the dominion, that it usurp not rule, no, not for a moment. It will labor to intrude itself unto the throne; watch against it, or a woeful state and condition lies at the door. This, then, accompanies this rage and madness of the law of sin: It casts off, during its prevalency, the rule of the law of grace wholly; it speaks in the soul, but is not heard; it commands the contrary, but is not obeyed; it cries out, "Do not this abominable thing which the Lord hates," but is not regarded—that is, not so far as to be able to put a present stop to the rage of sin, and to recover its own rule, which God in his own time restores to it by the power of his Spirit dwelling in us.

Madness or rage is accompanied with fearlessness and contempt of danger. It takes away the power of consideration and all that influence that it ought to have upon the soul. Hence sinners that are wholly under the power of this rage are said to "run upon God and the thick bosses[74] of his buckler"[75] (Job 15:26)—that wherein he is armed for their utter ruin. They despise the utmost that he can do to them, being secretly resolved to accomplish their lusts, though it cost them their souls. Some few considerations will further clear this unto us—

Oftentimes, when the soul is broken loose from the power of renewing grace, God deals with it, to keep it within bounds, by preventing grace.[76] So the Lord declares that he will deal with Israel—"Seeing you have rejected me, I will take another course with you. I will lay obstacles before you that you shall not be able to pass on whither the fury of your lusts would drive you"

[73] vehement; impulsive
[74] the projecting parts of a small, handheld shield; i.e., a strong, imposing defense
[75] a small, handheld shield
[76] a special grace that, preceding human willing, protects against further sinning

(Hos. 2:6). He will propose that to them from without that shall obstruct them in their progress.

These hindrances that God lays in the way of sinners, as shall be afterward at large declared, are of two sorts—

Rational considerations, taken from the consequence of the sin and evil that the soul is solicited unto and perplexed with. Such are the fear of death, judgment, and hell—falling into the hands of the living God, who is a consuming fire. While a man is under the power of the law of the Spirit of life, the "love of Christ constrains him" (2 Cor. 5:14). The principle of his doing good and abstaining from evil is faith working by love, accompanied with a following of Christ because of the sweet savor of his name. But now, when this blessed, easy yoke is for a season cast off, so as was manifested before, God sets a hedge of terror before the soul, minds it of death and judgment to come, flashes the flames of hell-fire in the face, fills the soul with consideration of all the evil consequence of sin, to deter it from its purpose. To this end does he make use of all threatenings recorded in the law and gospel. To this head also may be referred all the considerations that may be taken from things temporal, as shame, reproach, scandal, punishments, and the like. By the consideration of these things, I say, does God set a hedge before them.

Providential dispensations[77] are used by the Lord to the same purpose, and these are of two sorts—

Such as are suited to work upon the soul, and to cause it to desist and give over in its lustings and pursuit of sin. Such are afflictions and mercies: "I was wroth, and I smote them" (Isa. 57:17)—"I testified my dislike of their ways by afflictions" (so Hos. 2:9, 11, 12). God chastens men with pains on their bodies; says he in Job, "to turn them from their purpose and to hide sin from them" (Job 33:17-19). And other ways he has to come to them and touch them, as in their names, relations, estates, and desirable things; or else he heaps mercies on them, that they may consider whom they are rebelling against. It may be [that] signal[78] distinguishing mercies are made their portion for many days.

Such as actually hinder the soul from pursuing sin, though it be resolved so to do. The various ways whereby God does this we must afterward consider. These are the ways, I say, whereby the soul is dealt with, after the law of indwelling sin has cast off for a season the influencing power of the law of

[77] provisions, orderings
[78] significant, remarkable, out of the ordinary

grace. But now, when lust rises up to rage or madness, it will also contemn[79] all these, even the rod, and him that has appointed it. It will rush on shame, reproaches, wrath, and whatever may befall it; that is, though they be presented unto it, it will venture upon them all. Rage and madness is fearless. And this it does two ways—

It possesses the mind, that it suffers not the consideration of these things to dwell upon it, but renders the thoughts of them slight and evanid[80]; or if the mind do force itself to a contemplation of them, yet it interposes between it and the affections, that they shall not be influenced by it in any proportion to what is required. The soul in such a condition will be able to take such things into contemplation, and not at all to be moved by them; and where they do prevail for a season, yet they are insensibly wrought off from the heart again.

By secret stubborn resolves to venture all upon the way wherein it is. And this is the second branch of this evidence of the power of sin, taken from the opposition that it makes to the law of grace, as it were by the way of force, strength, and violence. The consideration of its deceit does now follow.

[Chapter 8]

The second part of the evidence of the power of sin, from its manner of operation, is taken from *its deceitfulness.* It adds, in its working, deceit unto power. The efficacy of that must needs be great, and is carefully to be watched against by all such as value their souls, where power and deceit are combined, especially advantaged and assisted by all the ways and means before insisted on.

Before we come to show wherein the nature of this deceitfulness of sin does consist, and how it prevails thereby, some testimonies shall be briefly given in unto the thing itself, and some light into the general nature of it.

That sin, indwelling sin, is deceitful, we have the express testimony of the Holy Ghost: "Take heed that you be not hardened by the deceitfulness of sin" (Heb. 3:13). Deceitful it is; take heed of it, watch against it, or it will produce its utmost effect in hardening of the heart against God. It is on the account of sin that the heart is said to be "deceitful above all things" (Jer. 17:9). Take a man in other things, and, as Job speaks, though he "would be wise and crafty, he is like the wild ass's colt" (Job 11:12)—a poor, vain, empty

[79] have contempt for, scorn, disdain
[80] evanescent, liable to vanish

nothing; but consider his heart on the account of this law of sin—it is crafty and deceitful above all things. "They are wise to do evil," says the prophet, "but to do good they have no knowledge" (Jer. 4:22). To the same purpose speaks the apostle, "The old man is corrupt according to the deceitful lusts" (Eph. 4:22). Every lust, which is a branch of this law of sin, is deceitful; and where there is poison in every stream, the fountain must needs be corrupt. No particular lust has any deceit in it, but what is communicated unto it from this fountain of all actual lust, this law of sin. And the coming of the "man of sin" is said to be in and with the "deceivableness of unrighteousness" (2 Thess. 2:10). Unrighteousness is a thing generally decried and evil spoken of among men, so that it is not easy to conceive how any man should prevail himself of a reputation thereby. But there is a deceivableness in it, whereby the minds of men are turned aside from a due consideration of it; as we shall manifest afterward. And thus the account which the apostle gives concerning those who are under the power of sin is that they are "deceived" (Titus 3:3). And the life of evil men is nothing but "deceiving, and being deceived" (2 Tim. 3:13). So that we have sufficient testimony given unto this qualification of the enemy with whom we have to deal. He is deceitful; which consideration of all things puts the mind of man to a loss in dealing with an adversary. He knows he can have no security against one that is deceitful, but in standing upon his own guard and defense all his days.

Further to manifest the strength and advantage that sin has by its deceit, we may observe that the Scripture places it for the most part as the head and spring of every sin, even as though there were no sin followed after but where deceit went before (so 1 Tim. 2:13-14). The reason the apostle gives why Adam, though he was first formed, was not first in the transgression is because he was not first deceived. The woman, though made last, yet being first deceived, was first in the sin. Even that first sin began in deceit, and until the mind was deceived the soul was safe. Eve, therefore, did truly express the matter, though she did it not to a good end. "The serpent beguiled me," says she, "and I did eat" (Gen. 3:13). She thought to extenuate[81] her own crime by charging the serpent; and this was a new fruit of the sin she had cast herself into. But the matter of fact was true—she was beguiled before she ate; deceit went before the transgression. And the apostle shows that sin and Satan still take the same course (2 Cor. 11:3). "There is," says he, "the same way of working toward actual sin as was of old: beguiling, deceiving goes before; and sin, that is, the actual accomplishment of it, follows after." Hence, all the

[81] make less serious

great works that the devil does in the world, to stir men up to an opposition unto the Lord Jesus Christ and his kingdom, he does them by deceit: "The devil, who deceives the whole world" (Rev. 12:9). It were utterly impossible men should be prevailed on to abide in his service, acting his designs to their eternal and sometimes their temporal ruin, were they not exceedingly deceived (see also Rev. 20:10.)

Hence are those manifold cautions that are given us to take heed that we be not deceived, if we would take heed that we do not sin (see Eph. 5:6; 1 Cor. 6:9; 15:33; Gal. 6:7; Luke 21:8). From all which testimonies we may learn the influence that deceit has into sin, and consequently the advantage that the law of sin has to put forth its power by its deceitfulness. Where it prevails to deceive, it fails not to bring forth its fruit.

The ground of this efficacy of sin by deceit is taken from the faculty of the soul affected with it. Deceit properly affects the mind; it is the mind that is deceived. When sin attempts any other way of entrance into the soul, as by the affections, the mind, retaining its right and sovereignty, is able to give check and control unto it. But where the mind is tainted, the prevalency must be great; for the mind or understanding is the leading faculty of the soul, and what that fixes on, the will and affections rush after, being capable of no consideration but what that presents unto them. Hence it is, that though the entanglement of the affections unto sin be oftentimes most troublesome, yet the deceit of the mind is always most dangerous, and that because of the place that it possesses in the soul as unto all its operations. Its office is to guide, direct, choose, and lead; and "if the light that is in us be darkness, how great is that darkness!" [Matt. 6:23].

And this will further appear if we consider *the nature of deceit in general*. It consists in presenting unto the soul, or mind, things otherwise than they are, either in their nature, causes, effects, or present respect unto the soul. This is the general nature of deceit, and it prevails many ways. It hides what ought to be seen and considered, conceals circumstances and consequences, presents what is not, or things as they are not, as we shall afterward manifest in particular. It was showed before that Satan "beguiled" and "deceived" our first parents; that term the Holy Ghost gives unto his temptation and seduction. And how he did deceive them the Scripture relates (Gen. 3:4-5). He did it by representing things otherwise than they were. The fruit was desirable; that was apparent unto the eye. Hence Satan takes advantage secretly to insinuate that it was merely an abridgment of their happiness that God aimed at in forbidding them to eat of it. That it was for the trial of their obedience, that certain though not immediate ruin would ensue upon the eating of it, he hides from them; only he proposes the present advantage of knowledge, and so presents the whole case quite otherwise unto them than indeed it was. This is the nature of deceit; it is a representation of a matter under disguise, hiding that which is undesirable, proposing that which indeed is not in it, that the mind may make a false judgment of it: so Jacob deceived Isaac by his brother's raiment[82] and the skins on his hands and neck [Gen. 27:15-16].

Again, deceit has advantage by that way of management which is inseparable from it. It is always carried on by degrees, by little and little, that the whole of the design and aim in hand be not at once discovered. So dealt Satan in that great deceit before mentioned; he proceeds in it by steps and degrees. First, he takes off an objection, and tells them they shall not die; then proposes the good of knowledge to them, and their being like to God thereby. To hide and conceal ends, to proceed by steps and degrees, to make use of what is obtained, and thence to press on to further effects, is the true nature of deceit. Stephen tells us that the king of Egypt "dealt subtly," or deceitfully, "with their kindred" (Acts 7:19). How he did it we may see in Exodus 1. He did not at first fall to killing and slaying of them, but says, "Come, let us deal wisely," beginning to oppress them (v. 10). This brings forth their bondage (v. 11). Having got this ground to make them slaves, he proceeds to destroy their children (v. 16). He fell not on them all at once, but by degrees. And this may suffice to show in general that sin is deceitful, and the advantages that it has thereby.

For the way, and manner, and progress of sin in working by deceit, we have it fully expressed, "Every man is tempted when he is drawn away of his own lust, and enticed. Then when lust has conceived, it brings forth sin: and sin, when it is finished, brings forth death" (James 1:14-15). This place, declaring the whole of what we aim at in this matter, must be particularly insisted on. In the foregoing verse the apostle manifests that men are willing to drive the old trade, which our first parents at the entrance of sin set up with, namely, of excusing themselves in their sins and casting the occasion and blame of them on others. It is not, say they, from themselves, their own nature and inclinations, their own designings, that they have committed such and such evils, but merely from their temptations; and if they know not where to fix the evil of those temptations, they will lay them on God himself, rather than go without an excuse or extenuation of their guilt. This evil in the hearts of men the apostle rebukes: "Let no man say when he is tempted, I am tempted of God: for God cannot be tempted with evil, neither does he tempt

[82] garments, clothing

any man" (James 1:13). And to show the justness of this reproof, in the words mentioned he discovers the true causes of the rise and whole progress of sin, manifesting that the whole guilt of it lies upon the sinner, and that the whole punishment of it, if not graciously prevented, will be his lot also.

We have, therefore, as was said, in these words the whole progress of lust or indwelling sin, by the way of subtlety, fraud, and deceit, expressed and limited by the Holy Ghost. And from hence we shall manifest the particular ways and means whereby it puts forth its power and efficacy in the hearts of men by deceitfulness and subtlety; and we may observe in the words—

First, *the utmost end aimed at in all the actings of sin, or the tendency of it in its own nature, and that is death:* "Sin, when it is finished, brings forth death," the everlasting death of the sinner; pretend what it will, this is the end it aims at and tends unto. Hiding of ends and designs is the principal property of deceit. This sin does to the uttermost; other things innumerable it pleads, but not once declares that it aims at the death, the everlasting death of the soul. And a fixed apprehension of this end of every sin is a blessed means to prevent its prevalency in its way of deceit or beguiling.

Secondly, *the general way of its acting toward that end is by temptation:* "Every man is tempted of his own lust." I purpose not to speak in general of the nature of temptations, it belongs not unto our present purpose; and, besides, I have done it elsewhere.[83] It may suffice at present to observe that the life of temptation lies in deceit; so that, in the business of sin, to be effectually tempted, and to be beguiled or deceived, are the same. Thus it was in the first temptation. It is everywhere called the serpent's beguiling or deceiving, as was manifested before: "The serpent beguiled Eve," that is, prevailed by his temptations upon her. So that every man is tempted—that is, every man is beguiled or deceived—by his own lust, or indwelling sin, which we have often declared to be the same.

The degrees whereby sin proceeds in this work of tempting or deceiving are five; for we showed before that this belongs unto the nature of deceit, that it works by degrees, making its advantage by one step to gain another. The first of these consists in *drawing off or drawing away:* "Every man is tempted when he is drawn away of his own lust." The second is in *enticing:* "And is enticed." The third [is] in *the conception of sin:* "When lust has conceived." When the heart is enticed, then lust conceives in it. The fourth is *the bringing forth of sin in its actual accomplishment:* "When lust has conceived it brings forth sin." In all which there is a secret allusion to an adulterous

[83] See Owen's *Of Temptation: The Nature and Power of It,* reprinted in this volume.

deviation from conjugal duties, and conceiving or bringing forth children of whoredom and fornication. The fifth is *the finishing of sin,* the completing of it, the filling up of the measure of it, whereby the end originally designed by lust is brought about: "Sin, when it is finished, brings forth death." As lust conceiving naturally and necessarily brings forth sin, so sin finished infallibly procures[84] eternal death.

The first of these relates to the *mind;* that is drawn off or drawn away by the deceit of sin. The second unto the *affections;* they are enticed or entangled. The third to the *will,* wherein sin is conceived; the consent of the will being the formal conception of actual sin. The fourth to the *conversation* wherein sin is brought forth; it exerts itself in the lives and courses of men. The fifth respects an *obdurate*[85] *course in sinning* that finishes, consummates, and shuts up the whole work of sin, whereon ensues death or eternal ruin. I shall principally consider the three first, wherein the main strength of the deceit of sin does lie; and that because in believers whose state and condition is principally proposed to consideration, God is pleased, for the most part, graciously to prevent the fourth instance, or the bringing forth of actual sins in their conversations; and the last always and wholly, or their being obdurate in a course of sin to the finishing of it. What ways God in his grace and faithfulness makes use of to stifle the conceptions of sin in the womb, and to hinder its actual production in the lives of men, must afterward be spoken unto.

The first three instances, then, we shall insist upon fully, as those wherein the principal concern of believers in this matter does lie. The first thing which sin is said to do, working in a way of deceit, is to draw away or to draw off; whence a man is said to be drawn off, or "drawn away" and diverted—namely, from attending unto that course of obedience and holiness which, in opposition unto sin and the law thereof, he is bound with diligence to attend unto. Now, it is the mind that this effect of the deceit of sin is wrought upon. The mind or understanding, as we have showed, is the guiding, conducting faculty of the soul. It goes before in discerning, judging, and determining, to make the way of moral actions fair and smooth to the will and affections. It is to the soul what Moses told his father-in-law that he might be to the people in the wilderness, as "eyes to guide them" and keep them from wandering in that desolate place [Num. 10:31]. It is the eye of the soul, without whose guidance the will and affections would perpetually

[84] gains, obtains
[85] hardened, unyielding, obstinate

wander in the wilderness of this world, according as any object, with an appearing present good, did offer or present itself unto them.

The first thing, therefore, that sin aims at in its deceitful working is *to draw off and divert the mind from the discharge of its duty.*

There are two things which belong unto the duty of the mind in that special office which it has in and about the obedience which God requires: (1) To keep itself and the whole soul in such a frame and posture as may render it ready unto all duties of obedience, and watchful against all enticements unto the conception of sin; (2) In particular, carefully to attend unto all particular actions, that they be performed as God requires, for matter, manner, time and season, agreeably unto his will; as also for the obviating[86] [of] all particular tenders of sin in things forbidden. In these two things consists the whole duty of the mind of a believer; and from both of them does indwelling sin endeavor to divert it and draw it off.

The first of these is *the duty of the mind in reference unto the general frame and course of the whole soul;* and hereof two things may be considered. That it is founded in a due, constant consideration—(1) of *ourselves,* of sin and its vileness; (2) of *God,* of his grace and goodness: and both these does sin labor to draw it off from.

[The second of these is] *In attending to those duties which are suited to obviate*[87] *the working of the law of sin in a special manner.*

It endeavors to draw it off from a due consideration, apprehension, and sensibleness of its own vileness, and the danger wherewith it is attended. This, in the first place, we shall instance. A due, constant consideration of sin, in its nature, in all its aggravating circumstances, in its end and tendency, especially as represented in the blood and cross of Christ, ought always to abide with us: "Know therefore and see that it is an evil thing and a bitter [thing], that you have forsaken the LORD your God" (Jer. 2:19). Every sin is a forsaking of the Lord our God. If the heart know not, if it consider not, that it is an evil thing and a bitter [thing]—evil in itself, bitter in its effects, fruit, and event—it will never be secured against it. Besides, that frame of heart which is most accepted with God in any sinner is the humble, contrite, self-abasing frame: "Thus says the high and lofty One that inhabits eternity, whose name is Holy; I dwell in the high and holy place, with him also that is of a contrite and humble spirit, to revive the spirit of the humble, and to revive the spirit of the contrite ones" (Isa. 57:15; see also Luke 18:13-14). This becomes a

[86] rendering unnecessary
[87] anticipate, prevent

sinner; no garment sits so decently about him. "Be clothed with humility," says the apostle (1 Pet. 5:5). It is that which becomes us, and it is the only safe frame. He that walks humbly walks safely. This is the design of Peter's advice: "Pass the time of your sojourning here in fear" (1 Pet. 1:17). After that he himself had miscarried by another frame of mind, he gives this advice to all believers. It is not a bondage, servile fear,[88] disquieting and perplexing the soul, but such a fear as may keep men constantly calling upon the Father, with reference unto the final judgment, that they may be preserved from sin, whereof they were in so great danger, which he advises them unto: "If you call on the Father, who without respect of persons judges according to every man's work, pass the time of your sojourning here in fear." This is the humble frame of soul. And how is this obtained? How is this preserved? No otherwise but by a constant, deep apprehension of the evil, vileness, and danger of sin. So was it wrought, so was it kept up, in the approved publican. "God be merciful," says he, "to me a sinner" [Luke 18:13]. Sense of sin kept him humble, and humility made way for his access unto a testimony of the pardon of sin. And this is the great preservative through grace from sin, as we have an example in the instance of Joseph (Gen. 39:9). Upon the urgency of his great temptation, he recoils immediately into this frame of spirit. "How," says he, "can I do this thing, and sin against God?" A constant, steady sense of the evil of sin gives him such preservation, that he ventures liberty and life in opposition to it. To fear sin is to fear the Lord; so the holy man tells us that they are the same: "The fear of the Lord, that is wisdom; and to depart from evil, that is understanding" (Job 28:28). This, therefore, in the first place, in general, does the law of sin put forth its deceit about—namely, to draw the mind from this frame, which is the strongest fort of the soul's defense and security. It labors to divert the mind from a due apprehension of the vileness, abomination, and danger of sin. It secretly and insensibly insinuates lessening, excusing, extenuating thoughts of it; or it draws it off from pondering upon it, from being conversant about it in its thoughts so much as it ought, and formerly has been. And if, after the heart of a man has, through the word, Spirit, and grace of Christ, been made tender, soft, deeply sensible of sin, it becomes on any account, or by any means whatsoever, to have less, fewer, slighter, or less affecting thoughts of it or about it, the mind of that man is drawn away by the deceitfulness of sin.

There are two ways, among others, whereby the law of sin endeavors deceitfully to draw off the mind from this duty and frame ensuing thereon—

---

[88] a fear that enslaves

It does it by a horrible abuse of gospel grace. There is in the gospel a remedy provided against the whole evil of sin, the filth, the guilt of it, with all its dangerous consequents. It is the doctrine of the deliverance of the souls of men from sin and death—a discovery of the gracious will of God toward sinners by Jesus Christ. What, now, is the genuine tendency of this doctrine, of this discovery of grace; and what ought we to use it and improve it unto? This the apostle declares, "The grace of God that brings salvation has appeared to all men, teaching us that, denying ungodliness and worldly lusts, we should live soberly, righteously, and godly, in this present world" (Titus 2:11-12). This it teaches; this we ought to learn of it and by it. Hence universal holiness is called a "conversation that becomes[89] the gospel" (Phil. 1:27). It becomes it, as that which is answerable unto its end, aim, and design—as that which it requires, and which it ought to be improved unto. And accordingly it does produce this effect where the word of it is received and preserved in a saving light (Rom. 12:2; Eph. 4:20-24). But herein does the deceit of sin interpose itself: It separates between the doctrine of grace and the use and end of it. It stays upon its notions, and intercepts its influences in its proper application. From the doctrine of the assured pardon of sin, it insinuates a regardlessness of sin. God in Christ makes the proposition, and Satan and sin make the conclusion. For that the deceitfulness of sin is apt to plead unto a regardlessness of it, from the grace of God whereby it is pardoned, the apostle declares in his reproof and detestation of such an insinuation: "What shall we say then? Shall we continue in sin, that grace may abound? God forbid" (Rom. 6:1). "Men's deceitful hearts," says he, "are apt to make that conclusion; but far be it from us that we should give any entertainment unto it." But yet that some have evidently improved that deceit unto their own eternal ruin, Jude declares: "Ungodly men, turning the grace of God into lasciviousness"[90] (v. 4). And we have had dreadful instances of it in the days of temptation wherein we have lived.

Indeed, in opposition unto this deceit lies much of the wisdom of faith and power of gospel grace. When the mind is fully possessed with, and cast habitually and firmly into, the mold of the notion and doctrine of gospel truth about the full and free forgiveness of all sins in the blood of Christ, then to be able to keep the heart always in a deep, humbling sense of sin, abhorrency of it, and self-abasement for it, is a great effect of gospel wisdom and grace. This is the trial and touchstone of gospel light: If it keeps the heart

---

[89] that is suitable or appropriate to
[90] wantonness, inclination to lust

sensible of sin, humble, lowly, and broken on that account—if it teaches us to water a free pardon with tears, to detest forgiven sin, to watch diligently for the ruin of that which we are yet assured shall never ruin us—it is divine, from above, of the Spirit of grace. If it secretly and insensibly makes men loose and slight in their thoughts about sin, it is adulterate, selfish, false. If it will be all, answer all ends, it is nothing. Hence it comes to pass that sometimes we see men walking in a bondage-frame of spirit all their days, low in their light, mean in their apprehensions of grace; so that it is hard to discern whether covenant in their principles they belong unto—whether they are under the law or under grace; yet walk with a more conscientious tenderness of sinning than many who are advanced into higher degrees of light and knowledge than they—not that the saving light of the gospel is not the only principle of saving holiness and obedience; but that, through the deceitfulness of sin, it is variously abused to countenance[91] the soul in manifold neglect of duties, and to draw off the mind from a due consideration of the nature, desert,[92] and danger of sin. And this is done several ways:

The soul, having frequent need of relief by gospel grace against a sense of the guilt of sin and accusation of the law, comes at length to make it a common and ordinary thing, and such as may be slightly performed. Having found a good medicine for its wounds, and such as it has had experience of its efficacy, it comes to apply it slightly, and rather skins over than cures its sores. A little less earnestness, a little less diligence, serves every time, until the soul, it may be, begins to secure itself of pardon in course; and this tends directly to draw off the mind from its constant and universal watchfulness against sin. He whose light has made his way of access plain for the obtaining of pardon, if he be not very watchful, he is far more apt to become overly formal and careless in his work than he who, by reason of mists and darkness, beats about to find his way aright to the throne of grace; as a man that has often traveled a road passes on without regard or inquiry, but he who is a stranger unto it, observing all turnings and inquiring of all passengers, secures his journey beyond the other.

The deceitfulness of sin takes advantage from the doctrine of grace by many ways and means to extend the bounds of the soul's liberty beyond what God has assigned unto it. Some have never thought themselves free from a legal, bondage frame until they have been brought into the confines of sensuality, and some into the depths of it. How often will sin plead, "This

[91] approve, condone
[92] that which is deserved (such as punishment)

strictness, this exactness, this solicitude is no ways needful; relief is provided in the gospel against such things! Would you live as though there were no need of the gospel? As though pardon of sin were to no purpose?" But concerning these pleas of sin from gospel grace, we shall have occasion to speak more hereafter in particular.

In times of temptation, this deceitfulness of sin will argue expressly for sin from gospel grace; at least, it will plead for these two things:

That there is not need of such a tenacious, severe contending against it, as the principle of the new creature is fixed on. If it cannot divert the soul or mind wholly from attending unto temptations to oppose them, yet it will endeavor to draw them off as to the manner of their attendance. They need not use that diligence which at first the soul apprehends to be necessary.

It will be tendering relief as to the event of sin—that it shall not turn to the ruin or destruction of the soul, because it is, it will, or may be pardoned by the grace of the gospel. And this is true; this is the great and only relief of the soul against sin, the guilt whereof it has contracted already—the blessed and only remedy for a guilty soul. But when it is pleaded and remembered by the deceitfulness of sin in compliance with temptation unto sin, then it is poison; poison is mixed in every drop of this balsam,[93] to the danger, if not death, of the soul. And this is the first way whereby the deceitfulness of sin draws off the mind from a due attendance unto that sense of its vileness which alone is able to keep it in that humble, self-abased frame that is acceptable with God. It makes the mind careless, as though its work were needless, because of the abounding of grace; which is a soldier's neglect of his station, trusting to a reserve, provided, indeed, only in case of keeping his own proper place.

Sin takes advantage to work by its deceit, in this matter of drawing off the mind from a due sense of it, from the state and condition of men in the world. I shall give only one instance of its procedure in this kind. Men, in their younger days, have naturally their affections more quick, vigorous, and active, more sensibly working in them, than afterward. They do, as to their sensible working and operation, naturally decay, and many things befall men in their lives that take off the edge and keenness of them. But as men lose in their affections, if they are not besotted[94] in sensuality or by the corruptions that are in the world through lust, they grow and improve in their understandings, resolutions, and judgments. Hence it is, that if what had place formerly in their affections do not take place in their minds and judgments, they utterly

[93] fragrant ointment used as balm or medication
[94] foolish, especially as it relates to drunkenness

lose them, they have no more place in their souls. Thus men have no regard for, yea, they utterly despise those things which their affections were set upon with delight and greediness in their childhood. But if they are things that by any means come to be fixed in their minds and judgments, they continue a high esteem for them, and do cleave as close unto them as they did when their affections were more vigorous; only, as it were, they have changed their seat in the soul. It is thus in things spiritual. The first and chief seat of the sensibleness of sin is in the affections. As these in natural youth are great and large, so are they spiritually in spiritual youth: "I remember the kindness of your youth, the love of your espousals"[95] (Jer. 2:2). Besides, such persons are newly come off from their convictions, wherein they have been cut to the heart and so made tender. Whatever touches upon a wound is thoroughly felt; so does the guilt of sin before the wound given by conviction be thoroughly cured. But now, when affections begin to decay naturally, they begin to decay also as to their sensible actings and motions in things spiritual. Although they improve in grace, yet they may decay in sense. At least, spiritual sense is not radically in them, but only by way of communication. Now, in these decays, if the soul takes not care to fix a deep sense of sin on the mind and judgment, thereby perpetually to affect the heart and affections, it will decay. And here the deceit of the law of sin interposes itself. It suffers a sense of sin to decay in the affections, and diverts the mind from entertaining a due, constant, fixed consideration of it. We may consider this a little in persons that never make a progress in the ways of God beyond conviction. How sensible of sin will they be for a season. How will they then mourn and weep under a sense of the guilt of it! How will they cordially and heartily resolve against it! Affections are vigorous, and, as it were, bear rule in their souls. But they are like a herb that will flourish for a day or two with watering although it have no root: for, a while after, we see that these men, the more experience they have had of sin, the less they are afraid of it, as the wise man intimates (Eccles. 8:11); and at length they come to be the greatest contemners of sin in the world. No sinner like him that has sinned away his convictions of sin. What is the reason of this? Sense of sin was in their convictions, fixed on their affections. As it decayed in them, they took no care to have it deeply and graciously fixed on their minds. This the deceitfulness of sin deprived them of, and so ruined their souls. In some measure it is so with believers. If, as the sensibleness of the affections decay—if, as they grow heavy and obtuse, great wisdom and grace be not used to fix a due sense of sin upon the mind and judgment, which may provoke, excite, enliven, and stir

[95] betrothals

up the affections every day—great decays will ensue. At first sorrow, trouble, grief, [and] fear affected the mind, and would give it no rest. If afterward the mind does not affect the heart with sorrow and grief, the whole will be cast out, and the soul be in danger of being hardened. And these are some of the ways whereby the deceit of sin diverts the mind from the first part of its safe preserving frame, or draws it off from its constant watchfulness against sin and all the effects of it.

The second part of this general duty of the mind is *to keep the soul unto a constant, holy consideration of God and his grace.* This evidently lies at the spring-head of gospel obedience. The way whereby sin draws off the mind from this part of its duty is open and known sufficiently, though not sufficiently watched against. Now, this the Scripture everywhere declares to be the filling of the minds of men with earthly things. This it places in direct opposition unto that heavenly frame of the mind which is the spring of gospel obedience: "Set your affection on things above, not on things on the earth"—or set your minds (Col. 3:2). As if he had said, "On both together you cannot be set or fixed, so as principally and chiefly to mind them both." And the affections to the one and the other, proceeding from these different principles of minding the one and the other, are opposed, as directly inconsistent: "Love not the world, neither the things that are in the world. If any man love the world, the love of the Father is not in him" (1 John 2:15). And actings in a course suitable unto these affections are proposed also as contrary: "You cannot serve God and mammon" [Matt. 6:24]. These are two masters whom no man can serve at the same time to the satisfaction of both. Every inordinate minding, then, of earthly things is opposed unto that frame wherein our minds ought to be fixed on God and his grace in a course of gospel obedience.

Several ways there are whereby the deceitfulness of sin draws off the mind in this particular; but the chief of them is by pressing these things on the mind under the notion of things lawful, and, it may be, necessary. So all those who excuse themselves in the parable from coming in to the marriage-feast of the gospel, did it on account of their being engaged in their lawful callings—one about his farm, another his oxen—the means whereby he ploughed in this world [Luke 14:16-24]. By this plea were the minds of men drawn off from that frame of heavenliness which is required to our walking with God; and the rules of not loving the world, or using it as if we used it not, are hereby neglected. What wisdom, what watchfulness, what serious frequent trial and examination of ourselves is required, to keep our hearts and minds in a heavenly frame, in the use and pursuit of earthly things, is not my present business to declare. This is evident, that the engine whereby the deceit of sin draws off and turns aside the mind in this matter is the pretense of the lawfulness of things about which it would have it exercise itself; against which very few are armed with sufficient diligence, wisdom, and skill. And this is the first and most general attempt that indwelling sin makes upon the soul by deceit—*it draws away the mind from a diligent attention unto its course in a due sense of the evil of sin, and a due and constant consideration of God and his grace.*

[Chapter 9]

How sin by its deceit endeavors to draw off the mind from attending unto that holy frame in walking with God wherein the soul ought to be preserved, has been declared; proceed we now to show *how it does the same work in reference unto those special duties by which the designs, workings, and prevalency of it may in a special manner be obviated and prevented.*

Sin, indeed, maintains an enmity against all duties of obedience, or rather with God in them. "When I would do good," says the apostle, "evil is present with me" [Rom. 7:21]—"Whenever I would do good, or whatsoever good I would do (that is, spiritually good, good in reference unto God), it is present with me to hinder me from it, to oppose me in it." And, on the other side, all duties of obedience do lie directly against the actings of the law of sin; for as the flesh in all its actings lusts against the Spirit, so the Spirit in all its actings lusts against the flesh. And therefore every duty performed in the strength and grace of the Spirit is contrary to the law of sin: "If you through the Spirit do mortify the deeds of the flesh" (Rom. 8:13). Actings of the Spirit of grace in duties does this work. These two are contrary. But yet there are some duties which, in their own nature and by God's appointment, have a peculiar influence into the weakening and subduing the whole law of sin in its very principles and chief strengths; and these the mind of a believer ought principally in his whole course to attend unto; and these does sin in its deceit endeavor principally to draw off the mind from. As in diseases of the body, some remedies, they say, have a specific quality against distempers; so, in this disease of the soul, there are some duties that have a special virtue against this sinful distemper. I shall not insist on many of them, but instance only in two, which seem to me to be of this nature—namely, that by God's designation *they have a special tendency toward the ruin of the law of sin.* And then we shall show *the ways, methods, and means which the law of sin uses to divert the mind from a due attendance unto them.* Now, these duties are—

first, *prayer,* especially private prayer; and, secondly, *meditation.* I put them together because they much agree in their general nature and end, differing only in the manner of their performance; for by meditation I intend meditating upon what respect and suitableness there is between the word and our own hearts, to this end, that they may be brought to a more exact conformity. It is our pondering on the truth as it is in Jesus, to find out the image and representation of it in our own hearts; and so it has the same intent with prayer, which is to bring our souls into a frame in all things answering the mind and will of God. They are as the blood and spirits in the veins that have the same life, motion, and use. But yet, because persons are generally at a great loss in this duty of meditation, having declared it to be of so great efficacy for the controlling of the actings of the law of sin, I shall in our passage give briefly two or three rules for the directing of believers to a right performance of this great duty, and they are these:

Meditate of God with God; that is, when we would undertake thoughts and meditations of God, his excellencies, his properties, his glory, his majesty, his love, his goodness, let it be done in a way of speaking unto God, in a deep humiliation and abasement of our souls before him. This will fix the mind, and draw it forth from one thing to another, to give glory unto God in a due manner, and affect the soul until it be brought into that holy admiration of God and delight in him which is acceptable unto him. My meaning is that it be done in a way of prayer and praise—speaking unto God.

Meditate on the word in the word; that is, in the reading of it, consider the sense in the particular passages we insist upon, looking to God for help, guidance, and direction, in the discovery of his mind and will therein, and then labor to have our hearts affected with it.

What we come short of in evenness and constancy in our thoughts in these things, let it be made up in frequency. Some are discouraged because their minds do not regularly supply them with thoughts to carry on their meditations, through the weakness or imperfection of their inventions. Let this be supplied by frequent returns of the mind unto the subject proposed to be meditated upon, whereby new senses will still be supplied unto it. But this by the way.

These duties, I say, among others (for we have only chosen them for an instance, not excluding some others from the same place, office, and usefulness with them), do make a special opposition to the very being and life of indwelling sin, or rather faith in them does so. They are perpetually designing its utter ruin. I shall, therefore, upon this instance, in the pursuit of our present purpose, do these two things: (1) show the *suitableness and useful-*

ness of this duty, or these duties (as I shall handle them jointly), unto the ruining of sin; (2) show the *means* whereby the deceitfulness of sin endeavors to draw off the mind from a due attendance unto them.

For the first, observe:

That it is the proper work of the soul, in this duty, *to consider all the secret workings and actings of sin,* what advantages it has got, what temptations it is in conjunction with, what harm it has already done, and what it is yet further ready to do. Hence David gives that title unto one of his prayers: "A prayer of the afflicted, when he is overwhelmed, and pours out his complaint before the LORD" (Psalm 102). I speak of that prayer which is attended with a due consideration of all the wants, straits,[96] and emergencies of the soul. Without this, prayer is not prayer; that is, whatever show or appearance of that duty it has, it is no way useful, either to the glory of God or the good of the souls of men. A cloud it is without water, driven by the wind of the breath of men. Nor was there ever any more present and effectual poison for souls found out than the binding of them unto a constant form and usage of I know not what words in their prayers and supplications, which themselves do not understand. Bind men so in their trades or in their businesses in this world, and they will quickly find the effect of it. By this means are they disenabled from any due consideration of what at present is good for them or evil unto them; without which, to what use can prayer serve, but to mock God and delude men's own souls? But in this kind of prayer which we insist on, the Spirit of God falls in to give us his assistance, and that in this very matter of finding out and discovering the most secret actings and workings of the law of sin: "We know not what we should pray for as we ought, but he helps our infirmities" (Rom. 8:26); he discovers[97] our wants unto us, and wherein chiefly we stand in need of help and relief. And we find it by daily experience, that in prayer believers are led into such discoveries and convictions of the secret deceitful work of sin in their hearts, as no considerations could ever have led them into. So David, in Psalm 51, designing the confession of his actual sin, having his wound in his prayer searched by the skillful hand of the Spirit of God, he had a discovery made unto him of the root of all his miscarriages, in his original corruption (v. 5). The Spirit in this duty is as the candle of the Lord unto the soul, enabling it to search all the inward parts of the belly. It gives a holy, spiritual light into the mind, enabling it to search the deep and dark recesses of the heart, to find out the subtle and

[96] difficulties, distresses
[97] reveals, demonstrates

deceitful machinations,[98] figments, and imaginations of the law of sin therein. Whatever notion there be of it, whatever power and prevalency in it, it is laid hand on, apprehended, brought into the presence of God, judged, condemned, bewailed. And what can possibly be more effectual for its ruin and destruction? For, together with its discovery, application is made unto all that relief which in Jesus Christ is provided against it, all ways and means whereby it may be ruined. Hence, it is the duty of the mind to "watch unto prayer" (1 Pet. 4:7), to attend diligently unto the estate of our souls, and to deal fervently and effectually with God about it. The like also may be said of meditation, wisely managed unto its proper end.

In this duty there is wrought upon the heart *a deep, full sense of the vileness of sin,* with a constant renewed detestation of it; which, if anything, undoubtedly tends to its ruin. This is one design of prayer, one end of the soul in it—namely, to draw forth sin, to set it in order, to present it unto itself in its vileness, abomination, and aggravating circumstances, that it may be loathed, abhorred, and cast away as a filthy thing (as Isa. 30:22). He that pleads with God for sin's remission, pleads also with his own heart for its detestation (Hos. 14:3). Herein, also, sin is judged in the name of God; for the soul in its confession subscribes unto God's detestation of it and the sentence of his law against it. There is, indeed, a course of these duties which convinced persons do give up themselves unto as a mere covert[99] to their lusts; they cannot sin quietly unless they perform duty constantly. But that prayer we speak of is a thing of another nature, a thing that will allow no composition with sin, much less will serve the ends of the deceit of it, as the other, formal prayer, does. It will not be bribed into a secret compliance with any of the enemies of God or the soul—no, not for a moment. And hence it is that oftentimes in this duty the heart is raised to the most sincere, effectual sense of sin and detestation of it that the soul ever obtains in its whole course of obedience. And this evidently tends also to the weakening and ruin of the law of sin.

This is the way appointed and blessed of God to obtain strength and power against sin: "Does any man lack? Let him ask of God" (James 1:5). Prayer is the way of obtaining from God by Christ a supply of all our wants, assistance against all opposition, especially that which is made against us by sin. This, I suppose, need not be insisted on; it is, in the notion and practice, clear to every

[98] plottings, schemings, cunning designs
[99] shelter

believer. It is that wherein we call, and upon which the Lord Jesus comes in to our succor[100] with suitable "help in time of need" (Heb. 4:16).

Faith in prayer countermines[101] *all the workings of the deceit of sin;* and that because the soul does therein constantly engage itself unto God to oppose all sin whatsoever: "I have sworn, and I will perform it, that I will keep your righteous judgments" (Ps. 119:106). This is the language of every gracious soul in its addresses unto God: the inmost parts thereof engage themselves to God, to cleave to him in all things and to oppose sin in all things. He that cannot do this cannot pray. To pray with any other frame is to flatter God with our lips, which he abhors. And this exceedingly helps a believer in pursuing sin unto its ruin; for—

If there be any secret lust that lies lurking in the heart, he will find it either rising up against this engagement, or using its artifices[102] *to secure itself from it.* And hereby it is discovered, and the conviction of the heart concerning its evil furthered and strengthened. Sin makes the most certain discovery of itself; and never more evidently than when it is most severely pursued. Lusts in men are compared to hurtful and noisome beasts; or men themselves are so because of their lusts (Isa. 11:4-6). Now, such beasts use themselves to their dens and coverts, and never discover themselves, at least so much in their proper nature and rage, as when they are most earnestly pursued. And so it is with sin and corruption in the heart.

If any sin be prevalent in the soul, it will weaken it and take it off from the universality of this engagement unto God; it will breed a tergiversation[103] unto it, a slightness in it. Now, when this is observed, it will exceedingly awaken a gracious soul, and stir it up to look about it. As spontaneous lassitude,[104] or a causeless weariness and indisposition of the body, is looked on as the sign of an approaching fever or some dangerous distemper, which stirs up men to use a timely and vigorous prevention, that they be not seized upon by it, so is it in this case. When the soul of a believer finds in itself an indisposition to make fervent, sincere engagements of universal holiness unto God, it knows that there is some prevalent distemper in it, finds the place of it, and sets itself against it.

While the soul can thus constantly engage itself unto God, it is certain that sin can rise unto no ruinous prevalency. Yea, it is a conquest over sin,

---

[100] assistance, relief
[101] counterplots
[102] trickeries
[103] equivocation, falsification by vague or ambiguous language
[104] listlessness, lethargy

a most considerable conquest, when the soul does fully and clearly, without any secret reserve, come off with alacrity[105] and resolution in such an engagement (as Ps. 18:23). And it may upon such a success triumph in the grace of God, and have good hope, through faith, that it shall have a final conquest, and what it so resolves shall be done; that it has decreed a thing, and it shall be established. And this tends to the disappointment, yea, to the ruin of the law of sin.

If the heart be not deceived by cursed hypocrisy, this engagement unto God will greatly influence it unto a peculiar diligence and watchfulness against all sin. There is no greater evidence of hypocrisy than to have the heart like the whorish woman to say, "'I have paid my vows,' now I may take myself unto my sin" (Prov. 7:14); or to be negligent about sin, as being satisfied that it has prayed against it. It is otherwise in a gracious soul. Sense and conscience of engagements against sin made to God do make it universally watchful against all its motions and operations. On these and sundry other accounts does faith in this duty exert itself peculiarly to the weakening of the power and stopping of the progress of the law of sin. If, then, the mind be diligent in its watch and charge to preserve the soul from the efficacy of sin, it will carefully attend unto this duty and the due performance of it, which is of such singular advantage unto its end and purpose. Here, therefore—

Sin puts forth its deceit in its own defense. It labors to divert and draw off the mind from attending unto this and the like duties. And there are, among others, three engines, three ways and means, whereby it attempts the accomplishment of its design:

It makes advantage of its weariness unto the flesh. There is an aversation, as has been declared, in the law of sin unto all immediate communion with God. Now this duty is such. There is nothing [that] accompanies it whereby the carnal part of the soul may be gratified or satisfied, as there may be somewhat of that nature in most public duties, in most that a man can do beyond pure acts of faith and love. No relief or advantage, then, coming in by it but what is purely spiritual, it becomes wearisome, burdensome to flesh and blood. It is like traveling alone without companion or diversion, which makes the way seem long, but brings the passenger with most speed to his journey's end. So our Savior declares, when, expecting his disciples, according to their duty and present distress, should have been engaged in this work, he found them fast asleep: "The spirit," says he, "indeed is willing, but the flesh is weak" (Matt. 26:41); and out of that weakness grow their indisposition

[105] eagerness, liveliness, speed

unto and weariness of their duty. So God complains of his people: "You have been weary of me" (Isa. 43:22). And it may come at length unto that height which is mentioned, "You have said, Behold, what a weariness is it! And you have snuffed at it, says the LORD of hosts" (Mal. 1:13). The Jews suppose that it was the language of men when they brought their offerings or sacrifices on their shoulders, which they pretended wearied them, and they panted and blew as men ready to faint under them, when they brought only the torn, and the lame, and the sick. But so is this duty oftentimes to the flesh. And this the deceitfulness of sin makes use of to draw the heart by insensible[106] degrees from a constant attendance unto it. It puts in for the relief of the weak and weary flesh. There is a compliance between spiritual flesh and natural flesh in this matter—they help one another; and an aversation unto this duty is the effect of their compliance. So it was in the spouse (Song 5:2, 8). She was asleep, drowsing in her spiritual condition, and pleads her natural unfitness to rouse herself from that state. If the mind be not diligently watchful to prevent insinuations from hence—if it dwell not constantly on those considerations which evidence an attendance unto this duty to be indispensable—if it stir not up the principle of grace in the heart to retain its rule and sovereignty, and not to be dallied with by foolish pretenses—it will be drawn off; which is the effect aimed at.

The deceitfulness of sin makes use of corrupt reasonings, taken from the pressing and urging occasions of life. "Should we," says it in the heart, "attend strictly unto all duties in this kind, we should neglect our principal occasions, and be useless unto ourselves and others in the world." And on this general account, particular businesses dispossess particular duties from their due place and time. Men have not leisure to glorify God and save their own souls. It is certain that God gives us time enough for all that he requires of us in any kind in this world. No duties need to jostle one another, I mean constantly. Special occasions must be determined according unto special circumstances. But if in anything we take more upon us than we have time well to perform it in, without robbing God of that which is due to him and our own souls, this God calls not unto, this he blesses us not in. It is more tolerable that our duties of holiness and regard to God should entrench upon the duties of our callings and employments in this world than on the contrary; and yet neither does God require this at our hands, in an ordinary manner or course. How little, then, will he bear with that which evidently is so much worse upon all accounts whatsoever! But yet, through the deceitfulness of

[106] imperceptible

sin, thus are the souls of men beguiled. By several degrees they are at length driven from their duty.

It deals with the mind, to draw it off from its attendance unto this duty, by a tender of a compensation to be made in and by other duties; as Saul thought to compensate his disobedience by sacrifice [1 Sam. 13:8-9]. "May not the same duty performed in public or in the family suffice?" And if the soul be so foolish as not to answer, "Those things ought to be done, and this not to be left undone" [Matt. 23:23], it may be ensnared and deceived. For, besides a command unto it, namely, that we should personally "watch unto prayer," there are, as has been declared, sundry advantages in this duty so performed against the deceit and efficacy of sin, which in the more public attendance unto it, it has not. These [duties] sin strives to deprive the soul of by this commutation,[107] which by its corrupt reasonings it tenders unto it.

I may add here that which has place in all the workings of sin by deceit—namely, *its feeding the soul with promises and purposes of a more diligent attendance unto this duty when occasions will permit.* By this means it brings the soul to say unto its convictions of duty, as Felix did to Paul, "Go your way for this time; when I have a convenient season, I will call for you" [Acts 24:25]. And by this means oftentimes the present season and time, which alone is ours, is lost irrecoverably. These are some of the ways and means whereby the deceit of sin endeavors to draw off the mind from its due attendance unto this duty, which is so peculiarly suited to prevent its progress and prevalency, and which aims so directly and immediately at its ruin. I might instance also in other duties of the like tendency; but this may suffice to discover the nature of this part of the deceit of sin. And this is the first way whereby it makes way for the further entangling of the affections and the conception of sin. When sin has wrought this effect on anyone, he is said to be "drawn away," to be diverted from what in his mind he ought constantly to attend unto in his walking before the Lord. And this will instruct us to see and discern where lies the beginning of our declensions[108] and failings in the ways of God, and that either as to our general course or as to our attendance unto special duties. And this is of great importance and concern unto us. When the beginnings and occasions of a sickness or distemper of body are known, it is a great advantage to direct in and unto the cure of it. God, to recall Zion to himself, shows her where was the "beginning of her sin" (Mic. 1:13). Now, this is that which for the most part is the beginning of sin unto

[107] substitution, exchange

[108] moral decline

us, even the drawing off the mind from a due attendance in all things unto the discharge of its duty. The principal care and charge of the soul lies on the mind; and if that fail of its duty, the whole is betrayed, either as unto its general frame or as unto particular miscarriages. The failing of the mind is like the failing of the watchman in Ezekiel [33:6]; the whole is lost by his neglect. This, therefore, in that self-scrutiny and search which we are called unto, we are most diligently to inquire after. God does not look at what duties we perform, as to their number and tale, or as to their nature merely, but whether we do them with that intension of mind and spirit which he requires. Many men perform duties in a road or course, and do not, as it were, so much as think of them; their minds are filled with other things, only duty takes up so much of their time. This is but an endeavor to mock God and deceive their own souls. Would you, therefore, take the true measure of yourselves, consider how it is with you as to the duty of your minds which we have inquired after. Consider whether, by any of the deceits mentioned, you have not been diverted and drawn away; and if there be any decays upon you in any kind, you will find that there has been the beginning of them. By one way or other your minds have been made heedless, regardless, slothful, uncertain, being beguiled and drawn off from their duty. Consider the charge (Prov. 4:23, 25-27). May not such a soul say, "If I had attended more diligently; if I had considered more wisely the vile nature of sin; if [I] had not suffered my mind to be possessed with vain hopes and foolish imaginations, by a cursed abuse of gospel grace; if I had not permitted it to be filled with the things of the world, and to become negligent in attending unto special duties—I had not at this day been thus sick, weak, thriftless, wounded, decayed, defiled. My careless, my deceived mind, has been the beginning of sin and transgression unto my soul." And this discovery will direct the soul unto a suitable way for its healing and recovery; which will never be effected by a multiplying of particular duties, but by a restoring of the mind (Ps. 23:3).

And this, also, does hence appear to be the great means of preserving our souls, both as unto their general frame and particular duties, according to the mind and will of God—namely, to endeavor after a sound and steadfast mind. It is a signal grace to have "the spirit of power, and of love, and of a sound mind" (2 Tim. 1:7)—a stable, solid, resolved mind in the things of God, not easily moved, diverted, changed, not drawn aside; a mind not apt to hearken after corrupt reasonings, vain insinuations, or pretenses to draw it off from its duty. This is that which the apostle exhorts believers unto: "Therefore, my beloved brethren, be steadfast, unmovable, always abounding in the work of the Lord" (1 Cor. 15:58). The steadfastness of our minds abiding in their duty is the cause of all our unmovableness and fruitfulness in obedience; and so Peter tells us that those who are by any means led away or enticed "fall from their own steadfastness" (2 Pet. 3:17). And the great blame that is laid upon backsliders is that they are not steadfast: "Their heart was not steadfast" (Ps. 78:37). For if the soul be safe, unless the mind be drawn off from its duty, the soundness and steadfastness of the mind is its great preservative. And there are three parts of this steadfastness of the mind: (1) full purpose of cleaving to God in all things; (2) a daily renovation and quickening of the heart unto a discharge of this purpose; (3) resolutions against all dalliances or parleys about negligences in that discharge—which are not here to be spoken unto.

[Chapter 10]

We have not as yet brought unto an issue the first way of the working of the deceit of sin—namely, in *its drawing away of the mind from the discharge of its duty,* which we insist upon the longer upon a double account:

First, *because of its importance and concern.* If the mind be drawn off—if it be tainted, weakened, turned aside from a due and strict attendance unto its charge and office—the whole soul, will, and affections are certainly entangled and drawn into sin; as has been in part declared, and will afterward further appear. This we ought therefore to give diligent heed unto, which is the design of the apostle's exhortation: "Therefore we ought to give the more earnest heed to the things which we have heard, lest at any time we should let them slip" (Heb. 2:1). It is a failure of our minds, by the deceitfulness of sin, in losing the life, power, sense, and impression of the word, which he cautions us against. And there is no way to prevent it but by giving of most "earnest heed unto the things which we have heard," which expresses the whole duty of our minds in attending unto obedience.

Secondly, *because the actings and workings of the mind being spiritual [and thus affected by sin], are such as the conscience unless clearly enlightened and duly excited and stirred up [against the mind's sin], [the mind] is not affected with [them], so as to take due notice of them.* Conscience is not apt to exercise reflex acts upon the mind's failures, as principally respecting the acts of the whole soul. When the affections are entangled with sin (of which afterward), or the will begins to conceive it by its express consent, conscience is apt to make an uproar in the soul, and to give it no rest or quiet until the soul be reclaimed, or itself be one way or other bribed or debauched; but these neglects of the mind being spiritual, without very diligent attendance they are seldom taken notice of. Our minds are often in the Scriptures called our spirits—as, "Whom I serve with my spirit" (Rom. 1:9)—and are distinguished from the soul, which principally intends the affections in that distribution, "Sanctify you wholly, your whole spirit and soul" (1 Thess. 5:23)—that is, your mind and affections. It is true, where the [word] "spirit" is used to express spiritual gifts, it is, as unto those gifts, opposed to our "understanding" (1 Cor. 14:15), which is there taken for the first act of the mind in a rational perception of things; but as that word is applied unto any faculty of our souls, it is the mind that it expresses. This, then, being our spirit, the actings of it are secret and hidden, and not to be discovered without spiritual wisdom and diligence. Let us not suppose, then, that we dwell too long on this consideration, which is of so great importance to us, and yet so hidden, and which we are apt to be very insensible of; and yet our carefulness in this matter is one of the best evidences that we have of our sincerity. Let us not, then, be like a man that is sensible, and complains of a cut finger, but not of a decay of spirits tending unto death. There remains therefore, as unto this head of our discourse, the consideration of the charge of the mind in reference unto particular duties and sins; and in the consideration of it we shall do these two things: (1) show what is required in the mind of a believer in reference unto particular duties; (2) declare the way of the working of the deceit of sin, to draw it off from its attendance thereunto. The like also shall be done with respect unto particular sins, and their avoidance.

For the right performance of any duty, it is not enough that the thing itself required be performed, but that it be universally squared and fitted unto the rule of it. Herein lies the great duty of the mind—namely, to attend unto the rule of duties and to take care that all the concerns of them be ordered thereby. Our progress in obedience is our edification or building. Now, it is but a very little furtherance unto a building that a man bring wood and stones, and heap them up together without order; they must be hewed and squared, and fitted by line and rule, if we intend to build. Nor is it unto any advantage unto our edification in faith and obedience that we multiply duties, if we heap them upon one another, if we order and dispose them not according to rule; and therefore does God expressly reject a multitude of duties, when not universally suited unto the rule: "To what purpose is the multitude of your sacrifices?" (Isa. 1:11), and, "They are a trouble unto me; I am weary to bear them" (v. 14). And therefore all acceptable obedience is called a proceeding according unto "rule" (Gal. 6:16); it is a canonical or regular obedience. As letters in the alphabet heaped together signify nothing, unless they are disposed into their proper order, no more do our duties without this disposal.

That they be so is the great duty of the mind, and which with all diligence it is to attend unto: "Walk circumspectly" (Eph. 5:15), exactly, accurately, that is, diligently, in all things; take heed to the rule of what you do. We walk in duties, but we walk circumspectly in this attention of the mind.

There are *some special things which the rule directs unto that the mind is to attend in every duty.* As—

That, as to the matter of it, it be full and complete. Under the law no beast was allowed to be a sacrifice that had any member wanting,[109] any defect of parts. Such were rejected, as well as those that were lame or blind. Duties must be complete as to the parts, the matter of them. There may be such a part of the price kept back as may make the tendering of all the residue unacceptable. Saul sparing Agag and the fattest of the cattle [1 Sam. 15:9] rendered the destroying of all the rest useless. Thus, when men will give alms, or perform other services, but not unto the proportion that the rule requires, and which the mind by diligent attention unto it might discover, the whole duty is vitiated.[110]

As to the principle of it—namely, that it be done in faith, and therein by an actual derivation of strength from Christ, without whom we can do nothing (John 15:5). It is not enough that the person be a believer, though that be necessary unto every good work (Eph. 2:10), but also that faith be peculiarly acted in every duty that we do; for our whole obedience is the "obedience of faith" (Rom. 1:5)—that is, which the doctrine of faith requires, and which the grace of faith bears or brings forth. So Christ is expressly said to be "our life" (Col. 3:4), our spiritual life; that is, the spring, author, and cause of it. Now, as in life natural, no vital act can be performed but by the actual operation of the principle of life itself; so, in life spiritual, no spiritually vital act—that is, no duty acceptable to God—can be performed but by the actual working of Christ, who is our life. And this is no other way derived unto us but by faith; whence says the apostle, "Christ lives in me: and the life which I now live in the flesh I live by the faith of the Son of God" (Gal. 2:20). Not only was Christ his life, a living principle unto him, but he led a life—that is, discharged vital actions in all duties of holiness and obedience—by the faith of the Son of God, or in him, deriving supplies of grace and strength from him thereby. This, therefore, ought a believer diligently to attend unto—namely, that everything he does to God be done in the strength of

[109] i.e., missing or lacking
[110] invalidated, rendered incomplete, impaired

Christ; which wherein it consists ought diligently to be inquired into by all who intend to walk with God.

In this respect unto rule, the manner of the performance of every duty is to be regarded. Now, there are two things in the manner of the performance of any duty which a believer, who is trusted with spiritual light, ought to attend unto—

First, *that it be done in the way and by the means that God has prescribed with respect unto the outward manner of its performance.* And this is especially to be regarded in duties of the worship of God, the matter and outward manner whereof do both equally fall under his command. If this be not regarded, the whole duty is vitiated. I speak not of them who suffer themselves to be deluded by the deceitfulness of sin, utterly to disregard the rule of the word in such things, and to worship God according to their own imaginations; but of them principally who, although they in general profess to do nothing but what God requires, and as he requires it, yet do not diligently attend to the rule, to make the authority of God to be the sole cause and reason both of what they do and of the manner of the performance of it. And this is the reason that God so often calls on his people to consider diligently and wisely, that they may do all according as he had commanded.

Second, *the affections of the heart and mind in duties belong to the performance of them in the inward manner.* The prescriptions and commands of God for attendance hereunto are innumerable, and the want hereof renders every duty an abomination unto him. A sacrifice without a heart, without salt, without fire—of what value is it? No more are duties without spiritual affections. And herein is the mind to keep the charge of God—to see that the heart which he requires be tendered to him. And we find also that God requires special affections to accompany special duties: "He that gives, with cheerfulness"—which, if they are not attended unto, the whole is lost (cf. Rom. 12:8; 1 Cor. 9:7).

The mind is to attend unto the ends of duties, and therein principally the glory of God in Christ. Several other ends will sin and self impose upon our duties: especially two it will press hard upon us with—first, *satisfaction of our convictions and consciences;* secondly, *the praise of men;* for self-righteousness and ostentation are the main ends of men that are fallen off from God in all moral duties whatsoever. In their sins they endeavor for to satisfy their lusts; in their duties, their conviction and pride. These the mind of a believer is diligently to watch against, and to keep up in all a single eye to the glory of God, as that which answers the great and general rule of all our obedience: "Whatsoever you do, do all to the glory of God" [1 Cor. 10:31]. These and the like things, I say, which are commonly spoken unto, is the mind of a believer obliged to attend diligently and constantly unto, with respect unto all the particular duties of our walking before God. Here, then, lies no small part of the deceit of sin—namely, to draw the mind off from this watch, to bring an inadvertency upon it, that it shall not in these things keep the watch and charge of the Lord. And if it can do so, and thereby strip our duties of all their excellencies which lie in these concerns of them that the mind is to attend unto, it will not much trouble itself nor us about the duties themselves. And this it attempts several ways:

First, *by persuading the mind to content itself with generals, and to take it off from attending unto things in particular instances.* For example, it would persuade the soul to rest satisfied in a general aim of doing things to the glory of God, without considering how every particular duty may have that tendency. Thus Saul thought that he had fulfilled his own duty, and done the will of God, and sought his glory in his war against Amalek, when, for want of attendance to every particular duty in that service, he had dishonored God and ruined himself and his posterity (1 Samuel 15). And men may persuade themselves that they have a general design for the glory of God, when they have no active principle in particular duties tending at all that way. But if, instead of fixing the mind by faith on the peculiar advancing the glory of God in a duty, the soul contents itself with a general notion of doing so, the mind is already diverted and drawn off from its charge by the deceitfulness of sin. If a man be traveling in a journey, it is not only required of him that he bend his course that way, and so go on; but if he attend not unto every turning, and other occurrences in his way, he may wander and never come to his journey's end. And if we suppose that in general we aim at the glory of God, as we all profess to do, yet if we attend not unto it distinctly upon every duty that occurs in our way, we shall never attain the end aimed at. And he who satisfies himself with this general purpose, without acting it in every special duty, will not long retain that purpose either. It does the same work upon the mind, in reference unto the principle of our duties, as it does unto the end. Their principle is that they be done in faith, in the strength of Christ; but if men content themselves that they are believers, that they have faith, and do not labor in every particular duty to act faith to lead their spiritual lives, in all the acts of them, by the faith of the Son of God, the mind is drawn off from its duty. It is particular actions wherein we express and exercise our faith and obedience; and what we are in them, that we are, and no more.

Secondly, *it draws off the mind from the duties before mentioned by insinuating a secret contentment into it from the duty itself performed, as to the matter of it.* This is a fair discharge of a natural conscience. If the duty be performed, though as to the manner of its performance it come short almost in all things of the rule, conscience and conviction will be satisfied; as Saul, upon his expedition against Amalek, cries to Samuel, "Come in, you blessed of the Lord; I have performed the commandment of the Lord" [1 Sam. 15:13]. He satisfied himself, though he had not attended as he ought to the whole will of God in that matter. And thus was it with them, "Wherefore have we fasted, say they, and you regard it not?" (Isa. 58:3). They had pleased themselves in the performance of their duties, and expected that God also should be pleased with them. But he shows them at large wherein they had failed, and that so far as to render what they had done an abomination; and the like charge he expresses against them (Isa. 48:1-2). This, the deceitfulness of sin, endeavors to draw the mind unto, namely, to take up in the performance of the duty itself. "Pray you ought, and you have prayed; give alms you ought, and you have given alms; quiet, then, yourself in what you have done, and go on to do the like." If it prevail herein the mind is discharged from further attendance and watching unto duty, which leaves the soul on the borders of many evils; for—

Thirdly, *hence customariness in all duties will quickly ensue, which is the height of sin's drawing off the mind from duty:* for men's minds may be drawn from all duties, in the midst of the most abundant performance of them; for in and under them the mind may be subject unto an habitual diversion from its charge and watch unto the rule. What is done with such a frame is not done to God (Amos 5:25). None of their sacrifices were to God, although they professed that they were all so. But they attended not unto his worship in faith and unto his glory, and he despised all their duties (see also Hos. 10:1). And this is the great reason why professors thrive so little under the performance of a multitude of duties. They attend not unto them in a due manner, their minds being drawn off from their circumspect watch; and so they have little or no communion with God in them, which is the end whereunto they are designed, and by which alone they become useful and profitable unto themselves. And in this manner are many duties of worship and obedience performed by a woeful generation of hypocrites, formalists, and profane persons, without either life or light in themselves, or acceptation with God, their minds being wholly estranged from a due attendance unto what they do by the power and deceitfulness of sin.

As it is in respect of duties, so also it is in respect of sins. There are sundry things in and about every sin that the mind of a believer, by virtue of its office and duty, is obliged to attend diligently unto, for the preservation of the soul from it. Things they are which God has appointed and sanctified to give effectual rebukes and checks to the whole working of the law of sin, and such as, in the law of grace, under which we are, are exceedingly suited and fitted unto that purpose. And these the deceit of sin endeavors by all means to draw off the mind from a due consideration of and attendance unto. Some few of them we shall a little reflect upon:

The first and most general is *the sovereignty of God, the great lawgiver, by whom it is forbidden.* This Joseph fixed on in his great temptation: "How can I do this great wickedness, and sin against God?" (Gen. 39:9). There was in it a great evil, a great ingratitude against man, which he pleads also and insists upon (vv. 8-9); but that which fixed his heart and resolution against it was the formality of it, that it was sin against God, by whom it was severely forbidden. So the apostle informs us that in our dealing in anything that is against the law, our respect is still to be unto the Lawgiver and his sovereignty: "If you judge the law, you are not a doer of the law, but a judge. There is one lawgiver, who is able to save and to destroy" (James 4:11-12). Consider this always: there is one lawgiver, holy, righteous, armed with sovereign power and authority; he is able to save and destroy. Hence sin is called a rebellion, a casting off his yoke, a despising of him, and that in his sovereignty as the great lawgiver; and this ought the mind always practically to attend unto, in all the lustings, actings, and suggestions of the law of sin, especially when advantaged by any suitable or vigorous temptation: "It is God that has forbidden this thing; the great lawgiver, under whose absolute sovereignty I am, in dependence on whom I live, and by whom I am to be disposed of, as to my present and eternal condition." This Eve fixed on at the beginning of her temptation, "God has said, 'You shall not eat of this tree'" (Gen. 3:3); but she kept not her ground, she abode not by that consideration, but suffered her mind to be diverted from it by the subtlety of Satan, which was the entrance of her transgression: and so it is unto us all in our deviations from obedience.

The deceit of sin, of every sin, the punishment appointed unto it in the law, is another thing that the mind ought actually to attend unto, in reference unto every particular evil. And the diversions from this, that the minds of men have been doctrinally and practically attended with, have been an inlet into all manner of abominations. Job professes another frame in himself, "Destruction from God was a terror to me, and by reason of his highness I could not endure" (Job 31:23). Many evils he had mentioned in the foregoing verses, and pleads his innocence from them, although they were such as, upon the account of his greatness and power, he could have committed easily without fear of danger from men. Here he gives the reason that prevailed with him so carefully to abstain from them, "Destruction from God was a terror to me, and by reason of his highness I could not endure." "I considered," says he, "that God had appointed 'death and destruction' for the punishment of sin, and that such was his greatness, highness, and power that he could inflict it unto the uttermost, in such a way as no creature is able to abide or to avoid." So the apostle directs believers always to consider what a "fearful thing it is to fall into the hands of the living God" (Heb. 10:31), and that because he has said, "Vengeance is mine, I will recompense" (v. 30). He is a sin-avenging God that will by no means acquit the guilty; as in the declaration of his gracious name, infinitely full of encouragements to poor sinners in Christ, he adds that in the close, that "he will by no means clear the guilty" (Ex. 34:7)—that he may keep upon the minds of them whom he pardons a due sense of the punishment that is due from his vindictive justice unto every sin. And so the apostle would have us mind that even "our God is a consuming fire" (Heb. 12:29); that is, that we should consider his holiness and vindictive justice, appointing unto sin a meet[111] recompense of reward. And men's breaking through this consideration he reckons as the height of the aggravation of their sins: "They knew that it is the judgment of God, that they which commit such things were worthy of death, yet continued to do them" (Rom. 1:32).

What hope is there for such persons? There is, indeed, relief against this consideration for humbled believing souls in the blood of Christ; but this relief is not to take off the mind from it as it is appointed of God to be a restraint from sin. And both these considerations, even the sovereignty of God and the punishment of sin, are put together by our Savior: "Fear not them which kill the body, but are not able to kill the soul; but rather fear him which is able to destroy both soul and body in hell" (Matt. 10:28).

The consideration of all the love and kindness of God, against whom every sin is committed, is another thing that the mind ought diligently to attend unto; and this is a prevailing consideration, if rightly and graciously managed in the soul. This Moses presses on the people: "Do you thus requite[112] the LORD, O foolish people and unwise? Is not he your Father that bought you? Has he not made you, and established you?" (Deut. 32:6)—"Is this a requital for eternal love, and all the fruits of it? For the love and care of a Father, of a Redeemer, that we have been made partakers of?" And it is

[111] fitting, appropriate
[112] repay

the same consideration which the apostle manages to this purpose, "Having therefore these promises, dearly beloved, let us cleanse ourselves from all filthiness of the flesh and spirit, perfecting holiness in the fear of God" (2 Cor. 7:1). The receiving of the promises ought to be effectual, as to stir us up unto all holiness, so to work and effect an abstinence from all sin. And what promises are these?—namely, that "God will be a Father unto us, and receive us" (2 Cor. 6:17-18); which comprises the whole of all the love of God toward us here and to eternity. If there be any spiritual ingenuity in the soul while the mind is attentive to this consideration, there can be no prevailing attempt made upon it by the power of sin. Now, there are two parts of this consideration—

That which is general in it, that which is common unto all believers. This is managed unto this purpose:

> Behold, what manner of love the Father has bestowed upon us, that we should be called the sons of God: therefore the world knows us not, because it knew him not. Beloved, now are we the sons of God, and it does not yet appear what we shall be: but we know that, when he shall appear, we shall be like him; for we shall see him as he is. And every man that has this hope in him purifies himself, even as he is pure (1 John 3:1-3).

"Consider," says he, "the love of God, and the privileges that we enjoy by it: 'Behold, what manner of love the Father has bestowed upon us, that we should be called the sons of God.' Adoption is a special fruit of it, and how great a privilege is this! Such love it is, and such are the fruits of it, that the world knows nothing of the blessed condition which we obtain and enjoy thereby: 'The world knows us not.' Nay, it is such love, and so unspeakably blessed and glorious are the effects of it, that we ourselves are not able to comprehend them." What use, then, ought we to make of this contemplation of the excellent, unspeakable love of God? Why, says he, "Everyone that has this hope purifies himself." Every man who has been made partaker of this love, and thereupon a hope of the full enjoyment of the fruits of it, of being made like to God in glory, "purifies himself"—that is, in an abstinence from all and every sin, as in the following words is at large declared.

It is to be considered as to such peculiar mercies and fruits of love as every one's soul has been made partaker of. There is no believer but, besides the love and mercy which he has in common with all his brethren, has also in the lot of his inheritance some enclosures, some special mercies, wherein he has a single propriety, he has some joy which no stranger intermeddles with (Prov.

14:10)—particular applications of covenant love and mercy to his soul. Now, these are all provisions laid in by God, that they may be borne in mind against an hour of temptation—that the consideration of them may preserve the soul from the attempts of sin. Their neglect is a high aggravation of our provocations. In 1 Kings 11:9 it is charged as the great evil of Solomon that he had sinned against special mercies, special intimations of love; he sinned after God had "appeared unto him twice." God required that he should have borne in mind that special favor, and have made it an argument against sin; but he neglected it, and is burdened with this sore rebuke. And, indeed, all special mercies, all special tokens and pledges of love, are utterly lost and misspent upon us, if they are not improved unto this end. This, then, is another thing that it is the duty of the mind greatly to attend unto, and to oppose effectually unto every attempt that is made on the soul by the law of sin.

The considerations that arise from *the blood and mediation of Christ* are of the same importance.

Shall I speak of *the inhabitation of the Spirit*—the greatest privilege that we are made partakers of in this world?

It is from the deceit of sin that the mind is *spiritually slothful, whereby it becomes negligent unto this duty.* Now, this sloth consists in four things:

Inadvertency.[113] It does not set itself to consider and attend unto its special concerns. The apostle, persuading the Hebrews with all earnestness to attend diligently, to consider carefully, that they may not be hardened by the deceitfulness of sin, gives this reason of their danger, that they were "dull of hearing" (Heb. 5:11); that is, that they were slothful and did not attend unto the things of their duty. A secret regardlessness is apt to creep upon the soul, and it does not set itself to a diligent marking how things go with it, and what is continually incumbent on it.

An unwillingness to be stirred up unto its duty. "A slothful man hides his hand in his bosom, and will not so much as bring it to his mouth again" (Prov. 19:24). There is an unwillingness in sloth to take any notice of warnings, calls, excitations, or stirrings up by the word, Spirit, judgments—anything that God makes use of to call the mind unto a due consideration of the condition of the soul. And this is a perfect evidence that the mind is made slothful by the deceit of sin, when special calls and warnings, whether in a suitable word or a pressing judgment, cannot prevail with it to pull its hand out of its bosom; that is, to set about the special duties that it is called unto.

Weak and ineffectual attempts to recover itself unto its duty. "As the door

[113] negligence

turns upon its hinges, so does the slothful man upon his bed" (Prov. 26:14). In the turning of a door upon its hinges, there is some motion but no progress. It removes up and down, but is still in the place and posture that it was. So is it with the spiritually slothful man on his bed, or in his security. He makes some motions or faint endeavors toward a discharge of his duty, but goes not on. There where he was one day, there he is the next; yea, there where he was one year, he is the next. His endeavors are faint, cold, and evanid; he gets no ground by them, but is always beginning and never finishing his work.

Heartlessness upon the apprehensions of difficulties and discouragements. "The slothful man says, 'There is a lion without, I shall be slain in the streets'" (Prov. 22:13). Every difficulty deters him from duty. He thinks it impossible for him to attain to that accuracy, exactness, and perfection which he is in this matter to press after, and therefore contents himself in his old coldness, negligence, rather than to run the hazard of a universal circumspection. Now, if the deceit of sin has once drawn away the mind into this frame, it lays it open to every temptation and incursion of sin. The spouse in the Song of Solomon seems to have been overtaken with this distemper (Song 5:2-3); and this puts her on various excuses why she cannot attend unto the call of Christ, and apply herself unto her duty in walking with him.

It draws away the mind from its watch and duty in reference unto sin by surprises. It falls in conjunction with some urging temptation, and surprises the mind into thoughts quite of another nature than those which it ought to insist upon in its own defense. So it seems to have been with Peter: his carnal fear closing with the temptation wherein Satan sought to winnow[114] him [Luke 22:31-32], filled his mind with so many thoughts about his own imminent danger that he could not take into consideration the love and warning of Christ, nor the evil whereunto his temptation led him, nor anything that he ought to have insisted on for his preservation. And, therefore, upon a review of his folly in neglecting those thoughts of God and the love of Christ which, through the assistance of the Holy Ghost, might have kept him from his scandalous fall, he wept bitterly. And this is the common way of the working of the deceit of sin as unto particular evils:

It lays hold on the mind suddenly with thoughtfulness about the present sin, possesses it, takes it up; so that either it recovers not itself at all to the considerations mentioned, or if any thoughts of them be suggested, the mind is so prepossessed and filled that they take no impression on the soul or make no abode in it. Thus, doubtless, was David surprised in the entrance of his

---

[114] separate as chaff from wheat

great sin. Sin and temptation did so possess and fill his mind with the present object of his lust, that he utterly forgot, as it were, those considerations which he had formerly made use of when he so diligently kept himself from his iniquity. Here, therefore, lies the great wisdom of the soul, in rejecting the very first motions of sin, because by parleys with them the mind may be drawn off from attending unto its preservatives, and so the whole rush into evil.

It draws away the mind by frequency and long continuance of its solicitations, making as it were at last a conquest of it. And this happens not without an open neglect of the soul, in want of stirring up itself to give an effectual rebuke, in the strength and by the grace of Christ, unto sin; which would have prevented its prevalency. But of this more shall be spoken afterwards. And this is the first way whereby the law of sin acts its deceit against the soul:

It draws off the mind from attendance unto its charge and office, both in respect of duty and sin. And so far as this is done, the person is said to be "drawn away" or drawn off. He is "tempted"; every man is tempted, when he is thus drawn away by his own lust, or the deceit of sin dwelling in him. And the whole effect of this working of the deceitfulness of sin may be reduced unto these three heads: (1) the remission of a universally watchful frame of spirit unto every duty, and against all, even the most hidden and secret, actings of sin; (2) the omission of peculiar attending unto such duties as have a special respect unto the weakening and ruin of the whole law of sin, and the obviating of its deceitfulness; (3) spiritual sloth, as to a diligent regard unto all the special concerns of duties and sins.

When these three things, with their branches mentioned, less or more, are brought about, in or upon the soul, or so far as they are so, so far a man is drawn off by his own lust or the deceit of sin. There is no need of adding here any directions for the prevention of this evil; they have sufficiently been laid down in our passage through the consideration both of the duty of the mind and of the deceit of sin.

[Chapter 11]

The second thing in the words of the apostle ascribed unto the deceitful working of sin is its *enticing*. A man is "drawn away and enticed." And this seems particularly to respect the affections, as drawing away does the mind. The mind is drawn away from duty, and the affections are enticed unto sin. From the prevalency hereof a man is said to be "enticed," or entangled as with a bait: so the word imports;[115] for there is an allusion in it unto the bait wherewith a fish is taken on the hook which holds him to his destruction. And concerning this effect of the deceit of sin, we shall briefly show two things: (1) What it is to be enticed, or to be entangled with the bait of sin, to have the affections tainted with an inclination thereunto; and when they are so; (2) What course sin takes, and what way it proceeds in, thus to entice, ensnare, or entangle the soul.

For the first: The affections are certainly entangled *when they stir up frequent imaginations about the proposed object which this deceit of sin leads and entices toward.* When sin prevails, and the affections are gone fully after it, it fills the imagination with it, possessing it with images, likenesses, appearances of it continually. Such persons "devise iniquity, and work evil upon their beds"—which they also "practice" when they are able, when "it is in the power of their hand" (Mic. 2:1). As, in particular, Peter tells us that "they have eyes full of an adulteress, and they cannot cease from sin" (2 Pet. 2:14)—that is, their imaginations are possessed with a continual representation of the object of their lusts. And it is so in part where the affections are in part entangled with sin, and begin to turn aside unto it. John tells us that the things that are "in the world" are "the lust of the flesh, the lust of the eyes, and the pride of life" (1 John 2:16). The lust of the eyes is that which by them is conveyed unto the soul. Now, it is not the bodily sense of seeing, but the fixing of the imagination from that sense on such things, that is intended. And this is called the "eyes," because thereby things are constantly represented unto the mind and soul, as outward objects are unto the inward sense by the eyes. And oftentimes the outward sight of the eyes is the occasion of these imaginations. So Achan declares how sin prevailed with him (Josh. 7:21). First, he saw the wedge of gold and Babylonish garment, and then he coveted them. He rolled them, the pleasures, the profit of them, in his imagination, and then fixed his heart upon the obtaining of them. Now, the heart may have a settled, fixed detestation of sin; but yet if a man find that the imagination of the mind is frequently solicited by it and exercised about it, such a one may know that his affections are secretly enticed and entangled.

This entanglement is heightened *when the imagination can prevail with the mind to lodge vain thoughts in it, with secret delight and complacency.* This is termed by casuists,[116] "*Cogitatio morosa cum delectatione*"—an abiding thought with delight; which toward forbidden objects is in all cases

[115] signifies
[116] those who rigidly apply ethical rules

actually sinful. And yet this may be when the consent of the will unto sin is not obtained—when the soul would not for the world do the thing, which yet thoughts begin to lodge in the mind about. This "lodging of vain thoughts" in the heart the prophet complains of as a thing greatly sinful and to be abhorred (Jer. 4:14). All these thoughts are messengers that carry sin to and fro between the imagination and the affections, and still increase it, inflaming the imagination, and more and more entangling the affections. Achan thinks upon the golden wedge [Josh. 7:21], this makes him like it and love it; by loving of it his thoughts are infected, and return to the imagination of its worth and goodly show; and so by little and little the soul is inflamed unto sin. And here if the will parts with its sovereignty, sin is actually conceived.

Inclinations or readiness to attend unto extenuations of sin, or the reliefs that are tendered against sin when committed, manifest the affections to be entangled with it. We have showed, and shall yet further evidence, that it is a great part of the deceit of sin to tender lessening and extenuating thoughts of sin unto the mind. "Is it not a little one?" or, "There is mercy provided," or, "It shall be in due time relinquished and given over"—is its language in a deceived heart. Now, when there is a readiness in the soul to hearken and give entertainment unto such secret insinuations, arising from this deceit, in reference unto any sin or unapprovable course, it is an evidence that the affections are enticed. When the soul is willing, as it were, to be tempted, to be courted by sin, to hearken to its dalliances and solicitations, it has lost its conjugal affections unto Christ and is entangled. This is "looking on the wine when it is red, when it gives its color in the cup, when it moves itself aright" (Prov. 23:31)—a pleasing contemplation on the invitations of sin, whose end the wise man gives us (v. 32). When the deceit of sin has prevailed thus far on any person, then he is enticed or entangled. The will is not yet come to the actual conception of this or that sin by its consent, but the whole soul is in a near inclination thereunto. And many other instances I could give as tokens and evidences of this entanglement: these may suffice to manifest what we intend thereby.

Our next inquiry is: *How, or by what means, [does] the deceit of sin proceed thus to entice and entangle the affections?* And two or three of its baits are manifest herein:

It makes use of its former prevalency upon the mind in drawing it off from its watch and circumspection. Says the wise man, "Surely in vain is the net spread in the sight of any bird" (Prov. 1:17); or "before the eyes of every thing that has a wing," as in the original. If it has eyes open to discern the snare, and a wing to carry it away, it will not be caught. And in vain should the deceit of sin spread its snares and nets for the entanglement of the soul, while the eyes of the mind are intent upon what it does, and so stir up the wings of its will and affections to carry it away and avoid it. But if the eyes be put out or diverted, the wings are of very little use for escape; and, therefore, this is one of the ways which is used by them who take birds or fowls in their nets. They have false lights or shows of things to divert the sight of their prey; and when that is done, they take the season to cast their nets upon them. So does the deceit of sin; it first draws off and diverts the mind by false reasonings and pretenses, as has been showed, and then casts its net upon the affections for their entanglement.

Taking advantage of such seasons, *it proposes sin as desirable, as exceeding satisfactory to the corrupt part of our affections.* It gilds over the object by a thousand pretenses, which it presents unto corrupt lustings. This is the laying of a bait which the apostle in this verse evidently alludes unto. A bait is somewhat desirable and suitable, that is, proposed to the hungry creature for its satisfaction; and it is by all artifices rendered desirable and suitable. Thus is sin presented by the help of the imagination unto the soul; that is, sinful and inordinate objects, which the affections cleave unto, are so presented. The apostle tells us that there are "pleasures of sin" (Heb. 11:25), which, unless they are despised, as they were by Moses, there is no escaping of sin itself. Hence they that live in sin are said to "live in pleasure" (James 5:5). Now, this pleasure of sin consists in its suitableness to give satisfaction to the flesh, to lust, to corrupt affections. Hence is that caution, "Make not provision for the flesh, to fulfill the lusts thereof" (Rom. 13:14), that is, "Do not suffer your minds, thoughts, or affections to fix upon sinful objects, suited to give satisfaction to the lusts of the flesh, to nourish and cherish them thereby." To which purpose he speaks again, "Fulfill not the lust of the flesh" (Gal. 5:16)—"Bring not in the pleasures of sin, to give them satisfaction." When men are under the power of sin, they are said to "fulfill the desires of the flesh and of the mind" (Eph. 2:3). Thus, therefore, the deceit of sin endeavors to entangle the affections by proposing unto them, through the assistance of the imagination, that suitableness which is in it to the satisfaction of its corrupt lusts, now set at some liberty by the inadvertency of the mind. It presents its "wine sparkling in the cup" [Prov. 23:21], the beauty of the adulteress, the riches of the world, unto sensual and covetous persons; and somewhat in the like kind, in some degrees, to believers themselves. When, therefore, I say, sin would entangle the soul, it prevails with the imagination to solicit the heart, by representing this false-painted beauty or pretended satisfactoriness of sin;

and then if Satan, with any peculiar temptation, fall in to its assistance, it oftentimes inflames all the affections and puts the whole soul into disorder.

It hides the danger that attends sin; it covers it as the hook is covered with the bait, or the net spread over with meat for the fowl to be taken. It is not, indeed, possible that sin should utterly deprive the soul of the knowledge of the danger of it. It cannot dispossess it of its notion or persuasion that "the wages of sin is death" [Rom. 6:23], and that it is the "judgment of God that they that commit sin are worthy of death" [Rom. 1:32]. But this it will do—it will so take up and possess the mind and affections with the baits and desirableness of sin, that it shall divert them from an actual and practical contemplation of the danger of it. What Satan did in and by his first temptation, that sin does ever since. At first Eve guards herself with calling to mind the danger of sin: "If we eat or touch it we shall die" (Gen. 3:3). But so soon as Satan had filled her mind with the beauty and usefulness of the fruit to make one wise, how quickly did she lay aside her practical prevalent consideration of the danger of eating it, the curse due unto it; or else relieves herself with a vain hope and pretense that it should not be, because the serpent told her so! So was David beguiled in his great transgression by the deceit of sin. His lust being pleased and satisfied, the consideration of the guilt and danger of his transgression was taken away; and therefore he is said to have "despised the Lord" (2 Sam. 12:9), in that he considered not the evil that was in his heart, and the danger that attended it in the threatening or commination[117] of the law. Now sin, when it presses upon the soul to this purpose, will use a thousand wiles to hide from it the terror of the Lord, the end of transgressions, and especially of that peculiar folly which it solicits the mind unto. Hopes of pardon shall be used to hide it; and future repentance shall hide it; and present importunity of lust shall hide it; occasions and opportunities shall hide it; surprises shall hide it; extenuation of sin shall hide it; balancing of duties against it shall hide it; fixing the imagination on present objects shall hide it; desperate resolutions to venture the uttermost for the enjoyment of lust in its pleasures and profits shall hide it. A thousand wiles it has, which cannot be recounted.

Having prevailed thus far, gilding over the pleasures of sin, hiding its end and demerit, *it proceeds to raise perverse reasonings in the mind, to fix it upon the sin proposed, that it may be conceived and brought forth, the affections being already prevailed upon;* of which we shall speak under the next head of its progress. Here we may stay a little, as formerly, to give some

[117] formal denunciation

few directions for the obviating of this woeful work of the deceitfulness of sin. Would we not be enticed or entangled? Would we not be disposed to the conception of sin? Would we be turned out of the road and way which goes down to death?—let us take heed of our affections; which are of so great concern in the whole course of our obedience, that they are commonly in the Scripture called by the name of the "heart," as the principal thing which God requires in our walking before him. And this is not slightly to be attended unto. Says the wise man, "Keep your heart with all diligence" (Prov. 4:23) or, as in the original, "above" or "before all keepings"—"Before every watch, keep your heart. You have many keepings that you watch unto: you watch to keep your lives, to keep your estates, to keep your reputations, to keep up your families; but," says he, "above all these keepings, prefer that, attend to that of the heart, of your affections, that they be not entangled with sin." There is no safety without it. Save all other things and lose the heart, and all is lost—lost unto all eternity. You will say, then, "What shall we do, or how shall we observe this duty?"

Keep your affections as to their object.

In general. This advice the apostle gives in this very case (Colossians 3). His advice in the beginning of that chapter is to direct us unto the mortification of sin, which he expressly engages in: "Mortify therefore your members which are upon the earth" (v. 5)—"Prevent the working and deceit of sin which wars in your members." To prepare us, to enable us hereunto, he gives us that great direction: "Set your affection on things above, not on things on the earth" (v. 2). Fix your affections upon heavenly things; this will enable you to mortify sin; fill them with the things that are above, let them be exercised with them, and so enjoy the chief place in them. They are above, blessed and suitable objects, meet for and answering unto our affections—God himself, in his beauty and glory; the Lord Jesus Christ, who is "altogether lovely," the "chief of ten thousand" [Song 5:16, 10]; grace and glory; the mysteries revealed in the gospel; the blessedness promised thereby. Were our affections filled, taken up, and possessed with these things, as it is our duty that they should be—it is our happiness when they are—what access could sin, with its painted pleasures, with its sugared poisons, with its envenomed[118] baits, have unto our souls? How should we loathe all its proposals, and say unto them, "Get you hence as an abominable thing!" For what are the vain, transitory pleasures of sin in comparison to the exceeding recompense of reward

[118] poisonous

which is proposed unto us? (Which [is the] argument the apostle presses in 2 Corinthians 4:17-18.)

As to the object of your affections, in a special manner, let it be the cross of Christ, which has exceeding efficacy toward the disappointment of the whole work of indwelling sin: "God forbid that I should glory, save in the cross of our Lord Jesus Christ, whereby the world is crucified unto me, and I unto the world" (Gal. 6:14). The cross of Christ he gloried and rejoiced in; this his heart was set upon; and these were the effects of it—it crucified the world unto him, made it a dead and undesirable thing. The baits and pleasures of sin are taken all of them out of the world, and the things that are in the world—namely, "the lust of the flesh, the lust of the eyes, and the pride of life." These are the things that are in the world; from these does sin take all its baits, whereby it entices and entangles our souls. If the heart be filled with the cross of Christ, it casts death and undesirableness upon them all; it leaves no seeming beauty, no appearing pleasure or comeliness,[119] in them. Again, says he, "It crucifies me to the world; makes my heart, my affections, my desires, dead unto any of these things." It roots up corrupt lusts and affections, leaves no principle to go forth and make provision for the flesh, to fulfill the lusts thereof. Labor, therefore, to fill your hearts with the cross of Christ. Consider the sorrows he underwent, the curse he bore, the blood he shed, the cries he put forth, the love that was in all this to your souls, and the mystery of the grace of God therein. Meditate on the vileness, the demerit, and punishment of sin as represented in the cross, the blood, the death of Christ. Is Christ crucified for sin, and shall not our hearts be crucified with him unto sin? Shall we give entertainment unto that, or hearken unto its dalliances, which wounded, which pierced, which slew our dear Lord Jesus? God forbid! Fill your affections with the cross of Christ, that there may be no room for sin. The world once put him out of the house into a stable, when he came to save us; let him now turn the world out of doors, when he is come to sanctify us.

Look to the vigor of the affections toward heavenly things; if they are not constantly attended, excited, directed, and warned, they are apt to decay, and sin lies in wait to take every advantage against them. Many complaints we have in the Scripture of those who lost their first love, in suffering their affections to decay. And this should make us jealous over our own hearts, lest we also should be overtaken with the like backsliding frame. Wherefore be jealous over them; often strictly examine them and call them to account; supply unto them due considerations for their exciting and stirring up unto duty.

---

[119] attractiveness

[Chapter 12]

The third success of the deceit of sin in its progressive work is *the conception of actual sin.* When it has drawn the mind off from its duty and entangled the affections, it proceeds to conceive sin in order to the bringing of it forth: "Then when lust has conceived, it brings forth sin" [James 1:15]. Now, the conception of sin, in order unto its perpetration, can be nothing but the consent of the will; for as without the consent of the will sin cannot be committed, so where the will has consented unto it, there is nothing in the soul to hinder its actual accomplishment. God does, indeed, by various ways and means, frustrate the bringing forth of these adulterate conceptions, causing them to melt away in the womb, or one way or other prove abortive, so that not the least part of that sin is committed which is willed or conceived; yet there is nothing in the soul itself that remains to give check unto it when once the will has given its consent. Oftentimes, when a cloud is full of rain and ready to fall, a wind comes and drives it away; and when the will is ready to bring forth its sin, God diverts it by one wind or other: but yet the cloud was as full of rain as if it had fallen, and the soul as full of sin as if it had been committed.

This conceiving of lust or sin, then, is its prevalency in obtaining the consent of the will unto its solicitations. And hereby the soul is deflowered of its chastity toward God in Christ, as the apostle intimates (2 Cor. 11:2-3). To clear up this matter we must observe—

That *the will is the principle, the next seat and cause, of obedience and disobedience.* Moral actions are unto us or in us so far good or evil as they partake of the consent of the will. He spoke truth of old who said, "*Omne peccatum est adeo voluntarium, ut non sit peccatum nisi sit voluntarium*"—"Every sin is so voluntary, that if it be not voluntary it is not sin."[120] It is most true of actual sins. The formality of their iniquity arises from the acts of the will in them and concerning them—I mean, as to the persons that commit them; otherwise in itself the formal reason of sin is its aberration from the law of God.

There is a twofold consent of the will unto sin—

That which is *full, absolute, complete, and upon deliberation*—a prevailing consent; the convictions of the mind being conquered, and no principle of grace in the will to weaken it. With this consent the soul goes into

[120] Cf. St. Augustine's *The Free Choice of the Will,* 3.17.49, in *The Fathers of the Church* (Washington, D.C.: Catholic University of America Press, 1968), 59:210.

sin as a ship before the wind with all its sails displayed, without any check or stop. It rushes into sin like the horse into the battle; men thereby, as the apostle speaks, "giving themselves over to sin with greediness" (Eph. 4:19). Thus Ahab's will was in the murdering of Naboth [1 Kings 21]. He did it upon deliberation, by contrivance, with a full consent; the doing of it gave him such satisfaction as that it cured his malady or the distemper of his mind. This is that consent of the will which is acted in the finishing and completing of sin in unregenerate persons, and is not required to the single bringing forth of sin, whereof we speak.

There is *a consent of the will which is attended with a secret renitency and volition of the contrary.* Thus Peter's will was in the denying of his Master. His will was in it, or he had not[121] done it. It was a voluntary action, that which he chose to do at that season. Sin had not been brought forth if it had not been thus conceived. But yet, at this very time, there was resident in his will a contrary principle of love to Christ, yea, and faith in him, which utterly failed not. The efficacy of it was intercepted, and its operations suspended actually, through the violent urging of the temptation that he was under; but yet it was in his will and weakened his consent unto sin. Though it consented, it was not done with self-pleasing, which such full acts of the will do produce.

Although there may be a predominant consent in the will, which may suffice for the conception of particular sins, *yet there cannot be an absolute, total, full consent of the will of a believer unto any sin;* for—

There is in his will a principle fixed on good, on all good: "He would do good" (Rom. 7:21). The principle of grace in the will inclines him to all good. And this, in general, is prevalent against the principle of sin, so that the will is denominated from thence. Grace has the rule and dominion, and not sin, in the will of every believer. Now, that consent unto sin in the will which is contrary to the inclination and generally prevailing principle in the same will, is not, cannot be, total, absolute, and complete.

There is not only a general, ruling, prevailing principle in the will against sin, but *there is also a secret reluctancy in it against its own act in consenting unto sin.* It is true, the soul is not sensible sometimes of this reluctancy, because the present consent carries away the prevailing act of the will, and takes away the sense of the lusting of the Spirit, or reluctancy of the principle of grace in the will. But the general rule holds in all things at all times: "The Spirit lusts against the flesh" (Gal. 5:17). It does so actually, though not

[121] would not have

always to the same degree, nor with the same success; and the prevalency of the contrary principle in this or that particular act does not disprove it. It is so on the other side. There is no acting of grace in the will but sin lusts against it; although that lusting be not made sensible in the soul, because of the prevalency of the contrary acting of grace, yet it is enough to keep those actings from perfection in their kind. So is it in this renitency of grace against the acting of sin in the soul; though it be not sensible in its operations, yet it is enough to keep that act from being full and complete. And much of spiritual wisdom lies in discerning aright between the spiritual renitency of the principle of grace in the will against sin, and the rebukes that are given the soul by conscience upon conviction for sin.

Observe that reiterated, repeated acts of the consent of the will unto sin may beget a disposition and inclinableness in it unto the like acts, that may bring the will unto a proneness and readiness to consent unto sin upon easy solicitations; which is a condition of soul dangerous, and greatly to be watched against.

This consent of the will, which we have thus described, may be considered [in] two ways: (1) as it is exercised about the circumstances, causes, means, and inducements unto sin; (2) as it respects this or that actual sin.

In the first sense there is a virtual consent of the will unto sin in every inadvertency unto the prevention of it, in every neglect of duty that makes way for it, in every hearkening unto any temptation leading toward it; in a word, in all the diversions of the mind from its duty, and entanglements of the affections by sin, before mentioned: for where there is no act of the will, formally or virtually, there is no sin. But this is not that which we now speak of; but, in particular, the consent of the will unto this or that actual sin, so far as that either sin is committed, or is prevented by other ways and means not of our present consideration. And herein consists the conceiving of sin.

These things being supposed, that which in the next place we are to consider is, the way that the deceit of sin proceeds in to procure the consent of the will, and so to conceive actual sin in the soul. To this purpose observe—

That *the will is a rational appetite*—rational as guided by the mind, and an appetite as excited by the affections, and so in its operation or actings has respect to both, is influenced by both.

It chooses nothing, consents to nothing, but "sub ratione boni"—as it has an appearance of good, some present good. It cannot consent to anything under the notion or apprehension of its being evil in any kind. Good is its natural and necessary object, and therefore whatsoever is proposed unto it for its consent must be proposed under an appearance of being either good in itself, or good at present unto the soul, or good so circumstantiate[122] as it is; so that—

We may see hence the reason why the conception of sin is here placed as a consequent of the mind's being drawn away and the affections being entangled. Both these have an influence into the consent of the will, and the conception of this or that actual sin thereby. Our way, therefore, here is made somewhat plain. We have seen at large how the mind is drawn away by the deceit of sin, and how the affections are entangled—that which remains is but the proper effect of these things; for the discovery whereof we must instance in some of the special deceits, corrupt and fallacious reasonings before mentioned, and then show their prevalency on the will to a consent unto sin.

The will is imposed upon by that corrupt reasoning, that grace is exalted in a pardon, and that mercy is provided for sinners. This first, as has been showed, deceives the mind, and that opens the way to the will's consent by removing a sight of evil, which the will has an aversation unto. And this, in carnal hearts, prevails so far as to make them think that their liberty consists in being "servants of corruption" (2 Pet. 2:19). And the poison of it does oftentimes taint and vitiate[123] the minds of believers themselves; whence we are so cautioned against it in the Scripture. To what, therefore, has been spoken before, unto the use and abuse of the doctrine of the grace of the gospel, we shall add some few other considerations, and fix upon one place of Scripture that will give light unto it. There is a twofold mystery of grace—of *walking with God,* and of *coming unto God;* and the great design of sin is to change the doctrine and mystery of grace in reference unto these things, and that by applying those considerations unto the one which are proper unto the other, whereby each part is hindered, and the influence of the doctrine of grace into them for their furtherance defeated. See 1 John 2:1-2: "These things I write unto you, that you sin not. And if any man sin, we have an advocate with the Father, Jesus Christ the righteous: and he is the propitiation for our sins." Here is the whole design and use of the gospel briefly expressed. "These things," says he, "I write unto you." What things were these? Those mentioned in 1 John 1:2: "The life was manifested, and we have seen it, and bear witness, and show unto you that eternal life, which was with the Father, and was manifested unto us"—that is, the things concerning the person and mediation of Christ; and that pardon, forgiveness, and expiation from sin is to be attained by the blood of Christ (v. 7). But to what end and purpose does

[122] verified by circumstances
[123] invalidate, render incomplete, impair

he write these things to them? What do they teach, what do they tend unto? A universal abstinence from sin: "I write unto you," says he, "that you sin not." This is the proper, only, genuine end of the doctrine of the gospel. But to abstain from all sin is not our condition in this world: "If we say that we have no sin, we deceive ourselves, and the truth is not in us" (v. 8). What, then, shall be done in this case? In supposition of sin, that we have sinned, is there no relief provided for our souls and consciences in the gospel? Yes; says he, "If any man sin, we have an advocate with the Father, Jesus Christ the righteous: and he is the propitiation for our sins." There is full relief in the propitiation and intercession of Christ for us. This is the order and method of the doctrine of the gospel, and of the application of it to our own souls—first, to keep us from sin; and then to relieve us against sin. But here enters the deceit of sin, and puts this "new wine into old bottles," whereby the bottles are broken, and the wine perishes, as to our benefit by it. It changes this method and order of the application of gospel truths. It takes up the last first, and that excludes the use of the first utterly. "If any man sin, there is pardon provided," is all the gospel that sin would willingly suffer to abide on the minds of men. When we would come to God by believing, it would be pressing the former part, of being free from sin, when the gospel proposes the latter principally, or the pardon of sin, for our encouragement. When we are come to God, and should walk with him, it will have only the latter proposed, that there is pardon of sin, when the gospel principally proposes the former, of keeping ourselves from sin, the grace of God bringing salvation having appeared unto us to that end and purpose. Now, the mind being entangled with this deceit, drawn off from its watch by it, diverted from the true ends of the gospel, does several ways impose upon the will to obtain its consent—

By a sudden surprise in case of temptation. Temptation is the representation of a thing as a present good, a particular good, which is a real evil, a general evil. Now, when a temptation, armed with opportunity and provocation, befalls the soul, the principle of grace in the will rises up with a rejection and detestation of it. But on a sudden, the mind being deceived by sin, breaks in upon the will with a corrupt, fallacious reasoning from gospel grace and mercy, which first staggers, then abates the will's opposition, and then causes it to cast the scale by its consent on the side of temptation, presenting evil as a present good, and sin in the sight of God is conceived, though it be never committed. Thus is the seed of God sacrificed to Moloch, and the weapons of Christ abused to the service of the devil.

It does it insensibly. It insinuates the poison of this corrupt reasoning by little and little, until it has greatly prevailed. And as the whole effect of the doctrine of the gospel in holiness and obedience consists in the soul's being cast into the frame and mold of it (Rom. 6:17); so the whole of the apostasy from the gospel is principally the casting of the soul into the mold of this false reasoning, that sin may be indulged unto upon the account of grace and pardon. Hereby is the soul gratified in sloth and negligence, and taken off from its care as to particular duties and avoidance of particular sins. It works the soul insensibly off from the mystery of the law of grace—to look for salvation as if we had never performed any duty, being, after we have done all, unprofitable servants, with a resting on sovereign mercy through the blood of Christ, and to attend unto duties with all diligence as if we looked for no mercy; that is, with no less care, though with more liberty and freedom. This, the deceitfulness of sin, endeavors by all means to work the soul from [these things], and thereby debauches the will when its consent is required unto particular sins.

The deceived mind imposes on the will to obtain its consent unto sin by proposing unto it the advantages that may accrue and arise thereby; which is one medium whereby itself also is drawn away. It renders that which is absolutely evil a present appearing good. So was it with Eve (Genesis 3). Laying aside all considerations of the law, covenant, and threats of God, she all at once reflects upon the advantages, pleasures, and benefits which she should obtain by her sin, and reckons them up to solicit the consent of her will. "It is," says she, "good for food, pleasant to the eyes, and to be desired to make one wise" [v. 6]. What should she do, then, but eat it? Her will consented, and she did so accordingly. Pleas for obedience are laid out of the way, and only the pleasures of sin are taken under consideration. So says Ahab: "Naboth's vineyard is near my house, and I may make it a garden of herbs; therefore I must have it" (1 Kings 21). These considerations a deceived mind imposed on his will, until it made him obstinate in the pursuit of his covetousness through perjury and murder, to the utter ruin of himself and his family. Thus is the guilt and tendency of sin hid under the covert of advantages and pleasures, and so is conceived or resolved on in the soul. As the mind being withdrawn, so the affections being enticed and entangled do greatly further the conception of sin in the soul by the consent of the will; and they do it two ways—

By some hasty impulse and surprise, being themselves stirred up, incited, and drawn forth by some violent provocation or suitable temptation, they put the whole soul, as it were, into a combustion, and draw the will into a consent unto what they are provoked unto and entangled with. So was the case of David in the matter of Nabal. A violent provocation from the extreme unworthy carriage of that foolish churl[124] stirs him up to wrath and revenge (1 Sam. 25:13). He resolves upon it to destroy a whole family, the innocent with the guilty (vv. 33-34). Self-revenge and murder were for the season conceived, resolved, consented unto, until God graciously took him off. His entangled, provoked affections surprised his will to consent unto the conception of many bloody sins. The case was the same with Asa in his anger, when he smote the prophet [2 Chron. 16:7-10]; and with Peter in his fear, when he denied his Master [Luke 22:56-60]. Let that soul which would take heed of conceiving sin take heed of entangled affections; for sin may be suddenly conceived, the prevalent consent of the will may be suddenly obtained; which gives the soul a fixed guilt, though the sin itself be never actually brought forth.

Enticed affections procure the consent of the will by frequent solicitations, whereby they get ground insensibly upon it, and enthrone themselves. Take an instance in the sons of Jacob (Gen. 37:4). They hate their brother because their father loved him. Their affections being enticed, many new occasions fall out to entangle them further, as his dreams and the like. This lay rankling[125] in their hearts, and never ceased soliciting their wills until they resolved upon his death. The unlawfulness, the unnaturalness of the action, the grief of their aged father, the guilt of their own souls, are all laid aside. That hatred and envy that they had conceived against him ceased not until they had got the consent of their wills to his ruin. This gradual progress of the prevalency of corrupt affections to solicit the soul unto sin the wise man excellently describes (Prov. 23:31-35). And this is the common way of sin's procedure in the destruction of souls which seem to have made some good engagements in the ways of God: when it has entangled them with one temptation, and brought the will to some liking of it, that presently becomes another temptation, either to the neglect of some duty or to the refusal of more light; and commonly that whereby men fall off utterly from God is not that wherewith they are first entangled. And this may briefly suffice for the third progressive act of the deceit of sin. It obtains the will's consent unto its conception; and by this means are multitudes of sins conceived in the heart which very little less defile the soul, or cause it to contract very little less guilt, than if they were actually committed. Unto what has been spoken concerning the deceitfulness of indwelling sin in general, which greatly evidences its power and efficacy, I shall add, as a close of this discourse, one or two

[124] coarse, ill-natured man
[125] festering, irritating

particular ways of its deceitful actings; consisting in advantages that it makes use of, and means of relieving itself against that disquisition[126] which is made after it by the word and Spirit for its ruin. One head only of each sort we shall here name:

It makes great advantage of the darkness of the mind, to work out its design and intentions. The shades of a mind totally dark—that is, devoid utterly of saving grace—are the proper working-place of sin. Hence the effects of it are called the "works of darkness" (Eph. 5:11; Rom. 13:12), as springing from thence. Sin works and brings forth by the help of it. The working of lust under the covert of a dark mind is, as it were, the upper region of hell; for it lies at the next door to it for filth, horror, and confusion. Now, there is a partial darkness abiding still in believers; they "know but in part" (1 Cor. 13:12). Though there be in them all a principle of saving light—the day-star is risen in their hearts—yet all the shades of darkness are not utterly expelled out of them in this life. And there are two parts, as it were, or principal effects of the remaining darkness that is in believers: (1) *ignorance,* or a nescience[127] of the will of God, either "*juris*" or "*facti*" of the rule and law in general, or of the reference of the particular fact that lies before the mind unto the law; (2) *error and mistakes positively;* taking that for truth which is falsehood, and that for light which is darkness. Now, of both of these does the law of sin make great advantage for the exerting of its power in the soul.

Is there a remaining ignorance of anything of the will of God? Sin will be sure to make use of it and improve it to the uttermost. Though Abimelech were not a believer, yet he was a person that had a moral integrity with him in his ways and actions; he declares himself to have had so in a solemn appeal to God, the searcher of all hearts, even in that wherein he miscarried (Gen. 20:5). But being ignorant that fornication was a sin, or so great a sin as that it became not a morally honest man to defile himself with it, lust hurries him into that intention of evil in reference unto Sarah, as we have it there related. God complains that his people "perished for lack of knowledge" (Hos. 4:6). Being ignorant of the mind and will of God, they rushed into evil at every command of the law of sin. Be it as to any duty to be performed, or as to any sin to be committed, if there be in it darkness or ignorance of the mind about them, sin will not lose its advantage. Many a man, being ignorant of the duty incumbent on him for the instruction of his family, casting the whole weight of it upon the public teaching, is, by the deceitfulness of sin, brought into a

---

[126] formal inquiry, investigation
[127] lack of knowledge

habitual sloth and negligence of duty. So much ignorance of the will of God and duty, so much advantage is given to the law of sin. And hence we may see what is that true knowledge which with God is acceptable. How exactly does many a poor soul, who is low as to notional[128] knowledge, yet walk with God! It seems they know so much, as sin has not on that account much advantage against them; when others, high in their notions, give advantage to their lusts, even by their ignorance, though they know it not.

Error is a worse part or effect of the mind's darkness, and gives great advantage to the law of sin. There is, indeed, ignorance in every error, but there is not error in all ignorance; and so they may be distinguished. I shall need to exemplify this but with one consideration, and that is of men who, being zealous for some error, do seek to suppress and persecute the truth. Indwelling sin desires no greater advantage. How will it every day, every hour, pour forth wrath, revilings, hard speeches; breathe revenge, murder, desolation, under the name perhaps of zeal! On this account we may see poor creatures pleasing themselves every day, as if they vaunted in their excellency, when they are foaming out their own shame. Under their real darkness and pretended zeal, sin sits securely, and fills pulpits, houses, prayers, streets, with as bitter fruits of envy, malice, wrath, hatred, evil surmises, false speakings, as full as they can hold. The common issue with such poor creatures is [that] the holy, blessed, meek Spirit of God withdraws from them and leaves them visibly and openly to that evil, froward, wrathful, worldly spirit, which the law of sin has cherished and heightened in them. Sin dwells not anywhere more secure than in such a frame. Thus, I say, it lays hold in particular of advantages to practice upon with its deceitfulness, and therein also to exert its power in the soul; whereof this single instance of its improving the darkness of the mind unto its own ends is a sufficient evidence.

It uses means of relieving itself against the pursuit that is made after it in the heart by the word and Spirit of grace. One also of its wiles, in the way of instance, I shall name in this kind, and that is the alleviation of its own guilt. It pleads for itself, that it is not so bad, so filthy, so fatal as is pretended; and this course of extenuation it proceeds in two ways—

Absolutely. Many secret pleas it will have that the evil which it tends unto is not so pernicious as conscience is persuaded that it is; it may be ventured on without ruin. These considerations it will strongly urge when it is at work in a way of surprise, when the soul has no leisure or liberty to weigh its suggestions in the balance of the sanctuary; and not seldom is the will imposed

[128] theoretical, conceptual

on hereby, and advantages gotten to shift itself from under the sword of the Spirit—"It is not such but that it may be let alone, or suffered to die of itself, which probably within a while it will do; no need of that violence which in mortification is to be offered; it is time enough to deal with a matter of no greater importance hereafter"—with other pleas like those before mentioned.

Comparatively; and this is a large field for its deceit and subtlety to lurk in—"Though it is an evil indeed to be relinquished, and the soul is to be made watchful against it, yet it is not of that magnitude and degree as we may see in the lives of others, even saints of God, much less such as some saints of old have fallen into." By these and the like pretenses, I say, it seeks to evade and keep its abode in the soul when pursued to destruction. And how little a portion of its deceitfulness is it that we have declared!

[Chapter 13]

Before we proceed to the remaining evidences of the power and efficacy of the law of sin, we shall take occasion from what has been delivered to divert unto one consideration that offers itself from that Scripture which was made the bottom and foundation of our discourse of the general deceitfulness of sin, namely, James 1:14. The apostle tells us that "lust conceiving brings forth sin," seeming to intimate that look what sin is conceived, that also is brought forth. Now, placing the conception of sin, as we have done, in the consent of the will unto it, and reckoning, as we ought, the bringing forth of sin to consist of its actual commission, we know that these do not necessarily follow one another. There is a world of sin conceived in the womb of the wills and hearts of men that is never brought forth. Our present business, then, shall be to inquire whence that comes to pass. I answer, then—

That this is not so is no thanks unto sin nor the law of it. What it conceives, it would bring forth; and that it does not is for the most part but a small abatement[129] of its guilt. A determinate[130] will of actual sinning is actual sin. There is nothing wanting on sin's part that every conceived sin is not actually accomplished. The obstacle and prevention lies on another hand.

There are two things that are necessary in the creature that has conceived sin, for the bringing of it forth: (1) power; and (2) continuance in the will of sinning until it be perpetrated and committed.

[129] reduction, diminution
[130] resolved, settled

Where these two are, actual sin will unavoidably ensue. It is evident, therefore, that that which hinders conceived sin from being brought forth must affect either the power or the will of the sinner. This must be from God. And he has two ways of doing it: (1) by his *providence,* whereby he obstructs the power of sinning; and (2) by his *grace,* whereby he diverts or changes the will of sinning.

I do not mention these ways of God's dispensations thus distinctly, as though the one of them were always without the other; for there is much of grace in providential administrations, and much of the wisdom of providence seen in the dispensations of grace. But I place them in this distinction because they appear most eminent therein—*providence,* in outward acts respecting the power of the creature; *grace,* common or special, in internal efficacy respecting his will. And we shall begin with the first—

When sin is conceived, the Lord obstructs its production by his providence, in taking away or cutting short that power which is absolutely necessary for its bringing forth or accomplishment; as—

Life is the foundation of all power, the principle of operation; when that ceases, all power ceases with it. Even God himself, to evince the everlasting stability of his own power, gives himself the title of "the living God." Now, he frequently obviates the power of executing sin actually by cutting short and taking away the lives of them that have conceived it. Thus he dealt with the army of Sennacherib, when, according as he had purposed, so he threatened that "the LORD should not deliver Jerusalem out of his hand" (2 Kings 18:35). God threatens to cut short his power, that he should not execute his intendment[131] (19:28); which he performs accordingly, by taking away the lives of his soldiers (v. 35), without whom it was impossible that his conceived sin should be brought forth. This providential dispensation in the obstruction of conceived sin, Moses excellently sets forth in the case of Pharaoh: "The enemy said, I will pursue, I will overtake, I will divide the spoil; my lust shall be satisfied upon them; I will draw my sword, my hand shall destroy them. You blow with your wind, the sea covered them: they sank as lead in the mighty waters" (Ex. 15:9-10). Sin's conception is fully expressed, and as full a prevention is annexed unto it. In like manner he dealt with the companies of fifties and their captains, who came to apprehend Elijah (2 Kings 1:9-12). Fire came down from heaven and consumed them, when they were ready to have taken him. And sundry other instances of the like nature might be recorded. That which is of universal concern we have

[131] intention

in that great providential alteration which put a period to the lives of men. Men living hundreds of years had a long season to bring forth the sins they had conceived; thereupon the earth was filled with violence, injustice, and rapine,[132] and "all flesh corrupted his way" (Gen. 6:12-13). To prevent the like inundation of sin, God shortens the course of the pilgrimage of men in the earth, and reduces their lives to a much shorter measure.

Besides this general law, God daily thus cuts off persons who had conceived much mischief and violence in their hearts, and prevents the execution of it: "Blood-thirsty and deceitful men do not live out half their days" [Ps. 55:23]. They have yet much work to do, might they have but space given them to execute the bloody and sinful purposes of their minds. The psalmist tells us, "In the day that the breath of man goes forth, his thoughts perish" (Ps. 146:4): he had many contrivances about sin, but now they are all cut off. So also Ecclesiastes 8:12-13: "Though a sinner do evil a hundred times, and his days be prolonged, yet surely I know that it shall be well with them that fear God, which fear before him: but it shall not be well with the wicked, neither shall he prolong his days, which are as a shadow; because he fears not before God." Howsoever long a wicked man lives, yet he dies judicially, and shall not abide to do the evil he had conceived. But now, seeing we have granted that even believers themselves may conceive sin through the power and the deceitfulness of it, it may be inquired whether God ever thus obviates its production and accomplishment in them, by cutting off and taking away their lives, so as that they shall not be able to perform it. I answer—

That *God does not judicially cut off and take away the life of any of his for this end and purpose*, that he may thereby prevent the execution or bringing forth of any particular sin that he had conceived, and which, without that taking away, he would have perpetrated; for—

This is directly contrary to the very declared end of the patience of God toward them (2 Pet. 3:9). This is the very end of the longsuffering of God toward believers, that before they depart hence they may come to the sense, acknowledgment, and repentance of every known sin. This is the constant and unchangeable rule of God's patience in the covenant of grace; which is so far from being in them an encouragement unto sin, that it is a motive to universal watchfulness against it—of the same nature with all gospel grace, and of mercy in the blood of Christ. Now, this dispensation whereof we speak would lie in a direct contradiction unto it.

This also flows from the former, that whereas conceived sin contains the

[132] pillage, robbery, plunder

whole nature of it, as our Savior at large declares (Matthew 5), and to be cut off under the guilt of it, to prevent its further progress, argues a continuance in the purpose of it without repentance, it cannot be but *they must perish forever who are so judicially cut off*. But God deals not so with his; he casts not off the people whom he did foreknow. And thence David prays for the patience of God before mentioned, that it might not be so with him: "O spare me, that I may recover strength, before I go hence, and be no more" (Ps. 39:13). But yet—

There are some cases wherein God may and does take away the lives of his own, to prevent the guilt that otherwise they would be involved in; as—

In the coming of some great temptation and trial upon the world. God knowing that such and such of his would not be able to withstand it and hold out against it, but would dishonor him and defile themselves, he may, and doubtless often does, take them out of the world, to take them out of the way of it: "The righteous is taken away from the evil to come" (Isa. 57:1)—not only the evil of punishment and judgment, but the evil of temptations and trials, which oftentimes proves much the worse of the two. Thus a captain in war will call off a soldier from his watch and guard, when he knows that he is not able, through some infirmity, to bear the stress and force of the enemy that is coming upon him.

In case of their engagement into any way not acceptable to him, through ignorance or not knowing of his mind and will. This seems to have been the case of Josiah [2 Chron. 34:26-28]. And, doubtless, the Lord does oftentimes thus proceed with his. When any of his own are engaged in ways that please him not, through the darkness and ignorance of their minds, that they may not proceed to further evil or mischief, he calls them off from their station and employment and takes them to himself, where they shall err and mistake no more. But, in ordinary cases, God has other ways of diverting his own from sin than by killing of them, as we shall see afterward.

God providentially hinders the bringing forth of conceived sin, by taking away and cutting short the power of them that had conceived it, so that, though their lives continue, they shall not have that power without which it is impossible for them to execute what they had intended, or to bring forth what they had conceived. Hereof also we have sundry instances. This was the case with the builders of Babel (Genesis 11). Whatever it was in particular that they aimed at, it was in the pursuit of a design of apostasy from God. One thing requisite to the accomplishing of what they aimed at was the oneness of their language; so God says, "They have all one language; and this they begin to do: and now nothing will be restrained from them, that they have imagined to do" (v. 6). In an ordinary way they will accomplish their wicked design. What course does God now take to obviate their conceived sin? Does he bring a flood upon them to destroy them, as in the old world some time before? Does he send his angel to cut them off, like the army of Sennacherib afterward [2 Kings 19:35]? Does he by any means take away their lives? No; their lives are continued, but he "confounds their language," so that they cannot go on with their work (v. 7)—takes away that wherein their power consisted. In like manner did he proceed with the Sodomites (Gen. 19:11). They were engaged in, and set upon the pursuit of, their filthy lusts. God smites them with blindness, so that they could not find the door, where they thought to have used violence for the compassing of their ends. Their lives were continued, and their will of sinning [was continued]; but their power is cut short and abridged. His dealing with Jeroboam was of the same nature (1 Kings 13:4). He stretched out his hand to lay hold of the prophet, and it withered and became useless. And this is an eminent way of the effectual acting of God's providence in the world, for the stopping of that inundation of sin which would overflow all the earth were every womb of it opened. He cuts men short of their moral power, whereby they should effect it. Many a wretch that has conceived mischief against the church of God has by this means been divested of his power, whereby he thought to accomplish it. Some have their bodies smitten with diseases, that they can no more serve their lusts, nor accompany them in the perpetrating of folly; some are deprived of the instruments whereby they would work. There has been, for many days, sin enough conceived to root out the generation of the righteous from the face of the earth, had men strength and ability to their will, did not God cut off and shorten their power and the days of their prevalency. "They search out iniquities; they accomplish a diligent search: both the inward thought of every one of them, and the heart, is deep" (Ps. 64:6). All things are in a readiness; the design is well laid, their counsels are deep and secret; what now shall hinder them from doing whatever they have imagined to do? "But God shall shoot at them with an arrow; suddenly shall they be wounded. So they shall make their own tongue to fall upon themselves" (vv. 7-8). God meets with them, brings them down, that they shall not be able to accomplish their design. And this way of God's preventing sin seems to be, at least ordinarily, peculiar to[133] the men of the world; God deals thus with them every day, and leaves them to pine away[134] in their sins. They

[133] particular to, characteristic of
[134] wither or waste away

go all their days big with the iniquity they have conceived, and are greatly burdened that they cannot be delivered of it.

The prophet tells us that "they practice iniquity that they had conceived, because it is in the power of their hand" (Mic. 2:1). If they have power for it, they will accomplish it: "To their power they shed blood" (Ezek. 22:6). This is the measure of their sinning, even their power. They do, many of them, no more evil, they commit no more sin, than they can. Their whole restraint lies in being cut short in power, in one kind or another. Their bodies will not serve them for their contrived uncleannesses, nor their hands for their revenge and rapine, nor their instruments for persecution; but they go burdened with conceived sin, and are disquieted and tortured by it all their days. And hence they become in themselves, as well as unto others, "a troubled sea that cannot rest" (Isa. 57:20).

It may be, also, in some cases, under some violent temptations, or in mistakes, God may thus obviate the accomplishment of conceived sin in his own. And there seems to be an instance of it in his dealing with Jehoshaphat, who had designed, against the mind of God, to join in affinity with Ahab, and to send his ships with him to Tarshish; but God breaks his ships by a wind, that he could not accomplish what he had designed [2 Chron. 20:37]. But in God's dealing with his in this way, there is a difference from the same dispensation toward others; for—

It is so only in cases of extraordinary temptation. When, through the violence of temptation and craft of Satan, they are hurried from under the conduct of the law of grace, God one way or other takes away their power, or may do so, that they shall not be able to execute what they had designed. But this is an ordinary way of dealing with wicked men. This hook of God is upon them in the whole course of their lives; and they struggle with it, being "as a wild bull in a net" (Isa. 51:20). God's net is upon them, and they are filled with fury that they cannot do all the wickedness that they would.

God does it not to leave them to wrestle with sin, and to attempt other ways of its accomplishment, upon the failure of that which they were engaged in; but *by their disappointment awakens them to think of their condition and what they are doing, and so consumes sin in the womb by the ways that shall afterward be insisted on.* Some men's deprivation of power for the committing of conceived, contrived sin has been sanctified to the changing of their hearts from all dalliances with that or other sins.

God providentially hinders the bringing forth of conceived sin by opposing an external hindering power unto sinners. He leaves them their lives, and leaves them power to do what they intend; only he raises up an opposite power to coerce, forbid, and restrain them. An instance hereof we have in 1 Samuel 14:45. Saul had sworn that Jonathan should be put to death, and, as far as appears, went on resolutely to have slain him. God stirs up the spirit of the people; they oppose themselves to the wrath and fury of Saul, and Jonathan is delivered. So also when King Uzziah would have in his own person offered incense, contrary to the law, eighty men of the priests resisted him, and drove him out of the temple (2 Chron. 26:16-20). And to this head are to be referred all the assistances which God stirs up for deliverance of his people against the fury of persecutors. He raises up saviors or deliverers on Mount Zion "to judge the mount of Edom" [Obad. 21]. So the dragon, and those acting under him, spirited by him, were in a furious endeavor for the destruction of the church (Rev. 12:16); God stirs up the earth to her assistance, even men of the world not engaged with others in the design of Satan; and by their opposition hinders them from the execution of their designed rage. Of this nature seems to be that dealing of God with his own people (Hos. 2:6-7). They were in the pursuit of their iniquities, following after their lovers; God leaves them for a while to act in the folly of their spirits; but he sets a hedge and a wall before them, that they shall not be able to fulfill their designs and lusts.

God obviates the accomplishment of conceived sin by removing or taking away the objects on whom, or about whom, the sin conceived was to be committed. Acts 12:1-11 yields us a signal instance of this issue of providence. When the day was coming wherein Herod thought to have slain Peter, who was shut up in prison, God sends and takes him away from their rage and lying in wait. So also was our Savior himself taken away from the murderous rage of the Jews before his hour was come (John 8:59; 10:39). Both primitive and latter times are full of stories to this purpose. Prison doors have been opened, and poor creatures appointed to die have been frequently rescued from the jaws of death. In the world itself, among the men thereof, adulterers and adulteresses, the sin of the one is often hindered and stifled by the taking away of the other. So wings were given to the woman to carry her into the wilderness, and to disappoint the world in the execution of their rage (Rev. 12:14).

God does this by some eminent diversions of the thoughts of men who had conceived sin. The brethren of Joseph cast him into a pit, with an intent to famish him there (Gen. 37:24). While they were, as it seems, pleasing themselves with what they had done, God orders a company of merchants to come by, and diverts their thoughts with that new object from the killing to the selling of their brother (vv. 25-27); and how far therein they were subservient to the infinitely wise counsel of God we know. Thus, also, when Saul was in the pursuit of David, and was even ready to prevail against him to his destruction, God stirs up the Philistines to invade the land, which both diverted his thoughts and drew the course of his actings another way (1 Sam. 23:27). And these are some of the ways whereby God is pleased to hinder the bringing forth of conceived sin, by opposing himself and his providence to the power of the sinning creature. And we may a little, in our passage, take a brief view of the great advantages to faith and the church of God which may be found in this matter; as—

This may give us a little insight into the ever-to-be-adored providence of God, by these and the like ways in great variety obstructing the breaking forth of sin in the world. It is he who makes those dams, and shuts up those floodgates of corrupted nature, that it shall not break forth in a deluge of filthy abominations, to overwhelm the creation with confusion and disorder. As it was of old, so it is at this day: "Every thought and imagination of the heart of man is evil, and that continually" [Gen 6:5]. That all the earth is not in all places filled with violence, as it was of old, is merely from the mighty hand of God working effectually for the obstructing of sin. From hence alone it is that the highways, streets, and fields are not all filled with violence, blood, rapine, uncleanness, and every villainy that the heart of man can conceive. Oh, the infinite beauty of divine wisdom and providence in the government of the world! for the conservation of it asks daily no less power and wisdom than the first making of it did require.

If we will look to our own concerns, they will in a special manner enforce us to adore the wisdom and efficacy of the providence of God in stopping the progress of conceived sin. That we are at peace in our houses, at rest in our beds, that we have any quiet in our enjoyments, is from hence alone. Whose person would not be defiled or destroyed—whose habitation would not be ruined—whose blood almost would not be shed—if wicked men had power to perpetrate all their conceived sin? It may be the ruin of some of us has been conceived a thousand times. We are beholding to this providence of obstructing sin for our lives, our families, our estates, our liberties, for whatsoever is or may be dear unto us; for may we not say sometimes, with the psalmist, "My soul is among lions: and I lie even among them that are set on fire, even the sons of men, whose teeth are spears and arrows, and their tongue a sharp sword" (Ps. 57:4)? And how is the deliverance of men contrived from such persons? "God breaks their teeth in their mouths, even the great teeth of the young lions" (Ps. 58:6). He keeps this fire from burning, or quenches it when it is ready to break out into a flame. He breaks their spears and arrows, so that sometimes we are not so much as wounded by them. Some he cuts off and destroys; some he cuts short in their power; some he deprives of the instruments whereby alone they can work; some he prevents of their desired opportunities, or diverts by other objects for their lusts, and oftentimes causes them to spend them among themselves, one upon another. We may say, therefore, with the psalmist, "O Lord, how manifold are your works! In wisdom you have made them all: the earth is full of your riches" (Ps. 104:24); and with the prophet, "Who is wise, and he shall understand these things? prudent, and he shall know them? *all* the ways of the Lord are right, and the just shall walk in them: but the transgressors shall fall therein" (Hos. 14:9).

If these and the like are the ways whereby God obviates the bringing forth of conceived sin in wicked men, we may learn hence how miserable their condition is, and in what perpetual torment, for the most part, they spend their days. They "are like a troubled sea," says the Lord, "that cannot rest" [Isa. 57:20]. As they endeavor that others may have no peace, so it is certain that themselves have not any; the principle of sin is not impaired nor weakened in them, the will of sinning is not taken away. They have a womb of sin that is able to conceive monsters every moment. Yea, for the most part, they are forging and framing folly all the day long. One lust or other they are contriving how to satisfy. They are either devouring by malice and revenge, or vitiating by uncleanness, or trampling on by ambition, or swallowing down by covetousness all that stand before them. Many of their follies and mischiefs they bring to the very birth, and are in pain to be delivered; but God every day fills them with disappointment, and shuts up the womb of sin. Some are filled with hatred of God's people all their days, and never once have an opportunity to exercise it. So David describes them: "They return at evening: they make a noise like a dog, and go round about the city" (Ps. 59:6). They go up and down and "belch out with their mouth: swords are in their lips" (v. 7), and yet are not able to accomplish their designs. What tortures do such poor creatures live in! Envy, malice, wrath, revenge devour their hearts by not getting vent. And when God has exercised the other acts of his wise providence in cutting short their power, or opposing a greater power to them, when nothing else will do, he cuts them off in their sins, and to the grave they go, full of purposes of iniquity. Others are no less hurried and diverted by the power of other lusts which they are not able to satisfy. This is the sore travail they are exercised with all their days: if they accomplish their designs they are more wicked and hellish than before; and if they do not, they are filled with vexation[135] and

[135] annoyance

discontentment. This is the portion of them who know not the Lord nor the power of his grace. Envy not their condition. Notwithstanding their outward, glittering show, their hearts are full of anxiety, trouble, and sorrow.

Do we see sometimes the floodgates of men's lusts and rage set open against the church and [the] interest of it, and does prevalency attend them, and power is for a season on their side? Let not the saints of God despond. He has unspeakably various and effectual ways for the stifling of their conceptions, to give them dry breasts and a miscarrying womb. He can stop their fury when he pleases. "Surely," says the psalmist," the wrath of man shall praise you: the remainder of wrath shall you restrain" (Ps. 76:10). When so much of their wrath is let out as shall exalt his praise, he can, when he pleases, set up a power greater than the combined strength of all sinning creatures, and restrain the remainder of the wrath that they had conceived. "He shall cut off the spirit of princes: he is terrible to the kings of the earth" (v. 12). Some he will cut off and destroy, some he will terrify and affright, and prevent the rage of all. He can knock them on the head, or break out their teeth, or chain up their wrath; and who can oppose him?

Those who have received benefit by any of the ways mentioned may know to whom they owe their preservation, and not look on it as a common thing. When you have conceived sin, has God weakened your power for sin, or denied you opportunity, or taken away the object of your lusts, or diverted your thoughts by new providences? Know assuredly that you have received mercy thereby. Though God deal not these providences always in a subserviency to the covenant of grace, yet there is always mercy in them, always a call in them to consider the author of them. Had not God thus dealt with you, it may be this day you had been a terror to yourselves, a shame to your relations, and under the punishment due to some notorious sins which you had conceived. Besides, there is commonly an additional guilt in sin brought forth, above what is in the mere conception of it. It may be others would have been ruined by it here, or drawn into a partnership in sin by it, and so have been eternally ruined by it, all which are prevented by these providences; and eternity will witness that there is a singularity of mercy in them. Do not look, then, on any such things as common accidents; the hand of God is in them all, and that [is] a merciful hand if not despised. If it be, yet God does good to others by it: the world is the better; and you are not so wicked as you would be.

We may also see hence the great use of magistracy[136] *in the world, that great appointment of God.* Among other things, it is peculiarly subservient

[136] human government

to this holy providence, in obstructing the bringing forth of conceived sin—namely, by the terror of him that bears the sword. God fixes that on the hearts of evil men, which he expresses: "If you do that which is evil, be afraid; for he bears not the sword in vain: for he is the minister of God, a revenger to execute wrath on them that do evil" (Rom. 13:4). God fixes this on the hearts of men, and by the dread and terror of it closes the womb of sin, that it shall not bring forth. When there was no king in Israel, none to put to rebuke, and none of whom evil men were afraid, there was woeful work and havoc among the children of men made in the world, as we may see in the last chapters of the book of Judges. The greatest mercies and blessings that in this world we are made partakers of, next to them of the gospel and covenant of grace, come to us through this channel and conduit. And, indeed, this whereof we have been speaking is the proper work of magistracy—namely, to be subservient to the providence of God in obstructing the bringing forth of conceived sin. These, then, are some of the ways whereby God providentially prevents the bringing forth of sin, by opposing obstacles to the power of the sinner. And [yet] by them sin is not consumed, but shut up in the womb. Men are not burdened for it, but with it; not laden in their hearts and consciences with its guilt, but perplexed with its power, which they are not able to exert and satisfy.

The way that yet remains for consideration whereby God obviates the production of conceived sin is his working on the will of the sinner, so making sin to consume away in the womb. There are two ways in general whereby God thus prevents the bringing forth of conceived sin by working on the will of the sinner; and they are: (1) by *restraining* grace; and (2) by *renewing* grace. He does it sometimes the one way, sometimes the other. The first of these is common to regenerate and unregenerate persons, the latter peculiar to believers; and God does it variously as to particulars by them both. We shall begin with the first of them.

God does this, in the way of restraining grace, by some arrow of particular conviction, fixed in the heart and conscience of the sinner, in reference unto the particular sin which he had conceived. This staggers and changes the mind as to the particular intended, causes the hands to hang down and the weapons of lust to fall out of them. Hereby conceived sin proves abortive. How God does this work—by what immediate touches, strokes, blows, rebukes of his Spirit—by what reasonings, arguments, and commotions of men's own consciences—is not for us thoroughly to find out. It is done, as was said, in unspeakable variety, and the works of God are past finding out [Rom. 11:33]. But as to what light may be given unto it from Scripture instances, after we have manifested the general way of God's procedure, it shall be insisted on. Thus, then, God dealt in the case of Esau and Jacob. Esau had long conceived his brother's death; he comforted himself with the thoughts of it, and resolutions about it (Gen. 27:41), as is the manner of profligate sinners. Upon his first opportunity he comes forth to execute his intended rage, and Jacob concludes that he would "smite the mother with the children" (Gen. 32:11). An opportunity is presented unto this wicked and profane person to bring forth that sin that had lain in his heart now twenty years; he has full power in his hand to perform his purpose. In the midst of this posture of things, God comes in upon his heart with some secret and effectual working of his Spirit and power, changes him from his purpose, causes his conceived sin to melt away, that he falls upon the neck of him with embraces whom he thought to have slain. Of the same nature, though the way of it was peculiar, was his dealing with Laban the Syrian, in reference to the same Jacob (Gen. 31:24). By a dream, a vision in the night, God hinders him from so much as speaking roughly to him. It was with him as in Micah 2:1—he had devised evil on his bed; and when he thought to have practiced it in the morning, God interposed in a dream, and hides sin from him, as he speaks (Job 33:15-17). To the same purpose is that of the psalmist concerning the people of God: "He made them to be pitied of all those that carried them captives" (Ps. 106:46). Men usually deal in rigor with those whom they have taken captive in war. It was the way of old to rule captives with force and cruelty. Here God turns and changes their hearts, not in general unto himself, but to this particular of respect to his people. And this way in general does God every day prevent the bringing forth of a world of sin. He sharpens arrows of conviction upon the spirits of men as to the particular that they are engaged in. Their hearts are not changed as to sin, but their minds are altered as to this or that sin. They break, it may be, the vessel they had fashioned, and go to work upon some other. Now, that we may a little see into the ways whereby God does accomplish this work, we must premise the ensuing considerations—

That the general medium wherein the matter of restraining grace does consist, whereby God thus prevents the bringing forth of sin, does lie in certain arguments and reasonings presented to the mind of the sinner, whereby he is induced to desert his purpose, to change and alter his mind, as to the sin he had conceived. Reasons against it are presented unto him, which prevail upon him to relinquish his design and give over his purpose. This is the general way of the working of restraining grace—it is by arguments and reasonings rising up against the perpetration of conceived sin.

That no arguments or reasonings, as such, materially considered, are sufficient to stop or hinder any purpose of sinning, or to cause conceived sin to prove abortive, if the sinner have power and opportunity to bring it forth. They are not in themselves, and on their own account, restraining grace; for if they were, the administration and communication of grace, as grace, were left unto every man who is able to give advice against sin. Nothing is nor can be called grace, though common, and such as may perish, but with respect unto its peculiar relation to God. God, by the power of his Spirit, making arguments and reasons effectual and prevailing, turns that to be grace (I mean of this kind) which in itself and in its own nature was bare reason. And that efficacy of the Spirit which the Lord puts forth in these persuasions and motives is that which we call restraining grace. These things being premised, we shall now consider some of the arguments which we find that he has made use of to this end and purpose—

God stops many men in their ways, upon the conception of sin, *by an argument taken from the difficulty, if not impossibility, of doing that [which] they aim at.* They have a mind unto it, but God sets a hedge and a wall before them, that they shall judge it to be so hard and difficult to accomplish what they intend, that it is better for them to let it alone and give over. Thus Herod would have put John Baptist to death upon the first provocation, but he feared the multitude, because they accounted him as a prophet (Matt. 14:5). He had conceived his murder, and was free for the execution of it. God raised this consideration in his heart, "If I kill him, the people will tumultuate; he has a great party among them, and sedition will arise that may cost me my life or kingdom." He feared the multitude, and durst[137] not execute the wickedness he had conceived, because of the difficulty he foresaw he should be entangled with. And God made the argument effectual for the season; for otherwise we know that men will venture the utmost hazards for the satisfaction of their lusts, as he also did afterward. The Pharisees were in the very same state and condition. They would fain have decried the ministry of John, but durst not for fear of the people (Matt. 21:26); and by the same argument were they deterred from killing our Savior, who had highly provoked them by a parable setting out their deserved and approaching destruction (Matt. 21:46). They durst not do it for fear of a tumult among the people, seeing they looked on him as a prophet. Thus God overawes[138] the hearts of innumerable persons in the world every day, and causes them to desist from attempting to bring forth the sins which they had conceived. Difficulties they shall be sure to meet

[137] dared

[138] restrain or subdue by awe

with; yea, it is likely, if they should attempt it, it would prove impossible for them to accomplish. We owe much of our quiet in this world unto the efficacy given to this consideration in the hearts of men by the Holy Ghost; adulteries, rapines, murders are obviated and stifled by it. Men would engage into them daily, but that they judge it impossible for them to fulfill what they aim at.

God does it *by an argument taken "ab incommodo"*—from the inconveniences, evils, and troubles that will befall men in the pursuit of sin. If they follow it, this or that inconvenience will ensue—this trouble, this evil, temporal or eternal. And this argument, as managed by the Spirit of God, is the great engine in his hand whereby he casts up banks and gives bounds to the lusts of men, that they break not out to the confusion of all that order and beauty which yet remains in the works of his hands. Paul gives us the general import of this argument: "For when the Gentiles, which have not the law, do by nature the things contained in the law, these, having not the law, are a law unto themselves: which show the work of the law written in their hearts, their conscience also bearing witness, and their thoughts the mean while accusing or else excusing one another" (Rom. 2:14-15). If any men in the world may be thought to be given up to pursue and fulfill all the sins that their lusts can conceive, it is those that have not the law, to whom the written law of God does not denounce the evil that attends it. "But though they have it not," says the apostle, "they show forth the work of it; they do many things which it requires, and forbear or abstain from many things that it forbids, and so show forth its work and efficacy." But whence is it that they so do? Why, their thoughts accuse or excuse them. It is from the consideration and arguings that they have within themselves about sin and its consequents, which prevail upon them to abstain from many things that their hearts would carry them out unto; for conscience is a man's prejudging of himself with respect unto the future judgment of God. Thus Felix was staggered in his pursuit of sin when he trembled at Paul's preaching of righteousness and judgment to come (Acts 24:25). So Job tells us that the consideration of punishment from God has a strong influence on the minds of men to keep them from sin (Job 31:1-3). How the Lord makes use of that consideration, even toward his own, when they have broken the cords of his love and cast off the rule of his grace for a season, I have before declared.

God does this same work *by making effectual an argument "ab inutili"*—from the unprofitableness of the thing that men are engaged in. By this were the brethren of Joseph stayed[139] from slaying him: Genesis 37:26-27, "What

---

[139] stopped

profit is it," say they, "if we slay our brother, and conceal his blood?"—"We shall get nothing by it; it will bring in no advantage or satisfaction unto us." And the heads of this way of God's obstructing conceived sin, or the springs of these kinds of arguments, are so many and various that it is impossible to insist particularly upon them. There is nothing present or to come, nothing belonging to this life or another, nothing desirable or undesirable, nothing good or evil, but, at one time or another, an argument may be taken from it for the obstructing of sin.

God accomplishes this work *by arguments taken "ab honesto"*—from what is good and honest, what is comely, praiseworthy, and acceptable unto himself. This is the great road wherein he walks with the saints under their temptations, or in their conceptions of sin. He recovers effectually upon their minds a consideration of all those springs and motives to obedience which are discovered and proposed in the gospel, some at one time, some at another. He minds them of[140] *his own love, mercy, and kindness*—his eternal love, with the fruits of it, whereof themselves have been made partakers; he minds them of *the blood of his Son,* his cross, sufferings, tremendous undertaking in the work of mediation, and the concern of his heart, love, honor, name, in their obedience; minds them of *the love of the Spirit,* with all his consolations, which they have been made partakers of, and privileges wherewith by him they have been entrusted; minds them of *the gospel,* the glory and beauty of it, as it is revealed unto their souls; minds them of the excellency and comeliness of *obedience*—of their performance of that duty they owe to God—of that peace, quietness, and serenity of mind that they have enjoyed therein.

On the other side, he minds them of being a provocation by sin unto the eyes of his glory, saying in their hearts, "Do not that abominable thing which my soul hates"; minds them of their wounding the Lord Jesus Christ, and putting him to shame—of their grieving the Holy Spirit, whereby they are sealed to the day of redemption—of their defiling his dwelling-place; minds them of the reproach, dishonor, scandal, which they bring on the gospel and the profession thereof; minds them of the terrors, darkness, wounds, want of peace, that they may bring upon their own souls. From these and the like considerations does God put a stop to the law of sin in the heart, that it shall not go on to bring forth the evil which it has conceived.

I could give instances in argument of all these several kinds recorded in the Scripture, but it would be too long a work for us, who are now engaged in a design of another nature; but one or two examples may be mentioned.

[140] brings to their mind

Joseph resists his first temptation on one of these accounts: "How can I do this great wickedness, and sin against God?" (Gen. 39:9). The evil of sinning against God, his God, that consideration alone detains him from the least inclination to his temptation. "It is sin against God, to whom I owe all obedience, the God of my life and of all my mercies. I will not do it." The argument wherewith Abigail prevailed on David to withhold him from self-revenge and murder (1 Sam. 25:31), was of the same nature; and he acknowledges that it was from the Lord (v. 32). I shall add no more; for all the Scripture motives which we have to duty, made effectual by grace, are instances of this way of God's procedure.

Sometimes, I confess, God secretly works the hearts of men by his own finger, without the use and means of such arguments as those insisted on, to stop the progress of sin. So he tells Abimelech: "I have withheld you from sinning against me" (Gen. 20:6). Now, this could not be done by any of the arguments which we have insisted on, because Abimelech knew not that the thing he intended was sin; and therefore he pleads that in the "integrity of his heart and innocency of his hands" he did it (v. 5). God turned about his will and thoughts, that he should not accomplish his intention; but by what ways or means is not revealed. Nor is it evident what course he took in the change of Esau's heart, when he came out against his brother to destroy him (Gen. 33:4). Whether he stirred up in him a fresh spring of natural affection, or caused him to consider what grief by this means he should bring to his aged father, who loved him so tenderly; or whether, being now grown great and wealthy, he more and more despised the matter of difference between him and his brother, and so utterly slighted it, is not known. It may be God did it by an immediate, powerful act of his Spirit upon his heart, without any actual intervening of these or any of the like considerations. Now, though the things mentioned are in themselves at other times feeble and weak, yet when they are managed by the Spirit of God to such an end and purpose, they certainly become effectual, and are the matter of his preventing grace.

God prevents the bringing forth of conceived sin by real spiritual saving grace, and that either in the first conversion of sinners or in the following supplies of it—

This is one part of the mystery of his grace and love. He meets men sometimes, in their highest resolutions for sin, with the highest efficacy of his grace. Hereby he manifests the power of his own grace and gives the soul a further experience of the law of sin, when it takes such a farewell of it as to be changed in the midst of its resolutions to serve the lusts thereof. By this he melts down the lusts of men, causes them to wither at the root, that they shall no more strive to bring forth what they have conceived, but be filled with shame and sorrow at their conception. An example and instance of this proceeding of God, for the use and instruction of all generations, we have in Paul. His heart was full of wickedness, blasphemy, and persecution; his conception of them was come unto rage and madness, and a full purpose of exercising them all to the utmost: so the story relates it (Acts 9); so himself declares the state to have been with him (Acts 26:9-12; 1 Tim. 1:13). In the midst of all this violent pursuit of sin, a voice from heaven shuts up the womb and dries the breasts of it, and he cries, "Lord, what will you have me to do?" (Acts 9:6). The same person seems to intimate that this is the way of God's procedure with others, even to meet them with his converting grace in the height of their sin and folly (1 Tim. 1:16): for he himself, he says, was a pattern of God's dealing with others; as he dealt with him, so also would he do with some such-like sinners: "For this cause I obtained mercy, that in me first Jesus Christ might show forth all longsuffering, for a pattern to them which should hereafter believe on him to life everlasting." And we have not a few examples of it in our own days. Sundry persons [who have been] on set purpose going to this or that place to deride and scoff at the dispensation of the word have been met with in the very place wherein they designed to serve their lusts and Satan, and have been cast down at the foot of God. This way of God's dealing with sinners is at large set forth (Job 33:15-18). Dionysius the Areopagite is another instance of this work of God's grace and love. Paul is dragged either by him or before him, to plead for his life, as "a setter forth of strange gods," which at Athens was death by the law. In the midst of this frame of spirit God meets with him by converting grace, sin withers in the womb, and he cleaves to Paul and his doctrine (Acts 17:18-34). The like dispensation toward Israel we have (Hos. 11:7-10). But there is no need to insist on more instances of this observation. God is pleased to leave no generation unconvinced of this truth, if they do but attend to their own experiences and the examples of this work of his mercy among them. Every day, one or other is taken in the fullness of the purpose of his heart to go on in sin, in this or that sin, and is stopped in his course by the power of converting grace.

God does it by the same grace in the renewed communications of it; that is, by special assisting grace. This is the common way of his dealing with believers in this case. That they also, through the deceitfulness of sin, may be carried on to the conceiving of this or that sin, was before declared. God puts a stop to their progress, or rather to the prevalency of the law of sin in them, and that by giving in unto them special assistances needful for their preservation and deliverance. As David says of himself, "His feet were almost gone, his steps had well-nigh slipped" (Ps. 73:2)—he was at the very brink of unbelieving, despairing thoughts and conclusions about God's providence in the government of the world, from whence he was recovered, as he afterwards declares—so is it with many a believer; he is oftentimes at the very brink, at the very door of some folly or iniquity, when God puts in by the efficacy of actually assisting grace, and recovers them to an obediential frame of heart again. And this is a peculiar work of Christ, wherein he manifests and exerts his faithfulness toward his own: "He is able to succor them that are tempted" (Heb. 2:18). It is not an absolute power, but a power clothed with mercy that is intended—such a power as is put forth from a sense of the suffering of poor believers under their temptations. And how does he exercise this merciful ability toward us? He gives forth, and we find in him, "grace to help in time of need" (Heb. 4:16)—seasonable help and assistance for our deliverance, when we are ready to be overpowered by sin and temptation. When lust has conceived and is ready to bring forth—when the soul lies at the brink of some iniquity—he gives in seasonable help, relief, deliverance, and safety. Here lies a great part of the care and faithfulness of Christ toward his poor saints. He will not suffer them to be worried with the power of sin, nor to be carried out unto ways that shall dishonor the gospel, or fill them with shame and reproach, and so render them useless in the world; but he steps in with the saving relief and assistance of his grace, stops the course of sin, and makes them in himself more than conquerors. And this assistance lies under the promise, "There has no temptation taken you but such as is common to man: but God is faithful, who will not suffer you to be tempted above that you are able; but will with the temptation also make a way to escape, that you may be able to bear it" (1 Cor. 10:13). Temptation shall try us—it is for our good; many holy ends does the Lord compass and bring about by it. But when we are tried to the utmost of our ability, so that one assault more would overbear us, a way of escape is provided. And as this may be done several ways, as I have elsewhere declared, so this we are now upon is one of the most eminent—namely, by supplies of grace to enable the soul to bear up, resist, and conquer. And when once God begins to deal in this way of love with a soul, he will not cease to add one supply after another, until the whole work of his grace and faithfulness be accomplished; an example hereof we have (Isa. 57:17-18). Poor sinners there are so far captivated to the power of their lusts that the first and second dealings of God with them are not effectual for their delivery, but he will not give them over; he is in the pursuit of a design of love toward them, and so ceases not until they are recovered. These are the general heads of the second way whereby God hinders the bringing forth of conceived sin—namely, by working on the will of the sinner. He does it either by common convictions or special grace, so that of their own accord they shall let go the purpose and will of sinning that they are risen up unto. And this is no mean way of his providing for his own glory and the honor of his gospel in the world, whose professors would stain the whole beauty of it were they left to themselves to bring forth all the evil that is conceived in their hearts.

Besides these general ways, there is one yet more special, that at once works both upon the power and will of the sinner, and this is *the way of afflictions,* concerning which one word shall close this discourse. Afflictions, I say, work by both these ways in reference unto conceived sin. They work providentially on the power of the creature. When a man has conceived a sin, and is in full purpose of the pursuit of it, God oftentimes sends a sickness and abates his strength, or a loss cuts him short in his plenty, and so takes him off from the pursuit of his lusts, though it may be his heart is not weaned from them. His power is weakened, and he cannot do the evil he would. In this sense it belongs to the first way of God's obviating the production of sin. Great afflictions work sometimes not from their own nature, immediately and directly, but from the gracious purpose and intention of him that sends them. He insinuates into the dispensation of them that of grace and power, of love and kindness, which shall effectually take off the heart and mind from sin: "Before I was afflicted I went astray, but now have I kept your word" (Ps. 119:67). And in this way, because of the predominancy of renewing and assisting grace, they belong unto the latter means, of preventing sin. And these are some of the ways whereby it pleases God to put a stop to the progress of sin, both in believers and unbelievers, which at present we shall instance in; and if we would endeavor further to search out his ways unto perfection, yet we must still conclude that it is but a little portion which we know of him.

PART 3:

The Effect and Strength of Indwelling Sin

[Chapter 14]

We are now to proceed unto other evidences of that sad truth which we are in the demonstration of. But the main of our work being passed through, I shall be more brief in the management of the arguments that do remain.

The Effect of Sin in the Lives of Believers

That, then, which in the next place may be fixed upon is the demonstration which this law of sin has in all ages given of its power and efficacy, by the woeful fruits that it has brought forth, even in believers themselves. Now, these are of two sorts: (1) the great actual eruptions of sin in their lives; (2) their habitual declensions from the frames, state, and condition of obedience and communion with God, which they had obtained—both which, by the rule of James before unfolded, are to be laid to the account of this law of sin, and belong unto the fourth head of its progress, and are both of them convincing evidences of its power and efficacy.

Consider the fearful eruptions of actual sin that have been in the lives of believers, and we shall find our position evidenced. Should I go through at large with this consideration, I must recount all the sad and scandalous failings of the saints that are left on record in the holy Scripture; but the particulars of them are known to all, so that I shall not need to mention them, nor the many aggravations that in their circumstances they are attended with. Only some few things tending to the rendering of our present consideration of them useful may be remarked; as—

They are most of them in the lives of men that were not of the lowest form or ordinary sort of believers, but of men that had a peculiar eminency in them on the account of their walking with God in their generation. Such were Noah, Lot, David, Hezekiah, and others. They were not men of an ordinary size, but higher than their brethren, by the shoulders and upwards, in profession, yea, in real holiness. And surely that must needs be of a mighty efficacy that could hurry such giants in the ways of God into such abominable sins as they fell into. An ordinary engine could never have turned them out of the course of their obedience. It was a poison that no athletic constitution of spiritual health, no antidote, could withstand.

And these very men fell not into their great sins at the beginning of their profession, when they had had but little experience of the goodness of God, of the sweetness and pleasantness of obedience, of the power and craft of sin, of its impulsions, solicitations, and surprises; *but after a long course of walking with God, and acquaintance with all these things, together with innumerable motives unto watchfulness.* Noah, according to the lives of men in those days of the world, had walked uprightly with God some hundreds of years before he was so surprised as he was (Genesis 9). Righteous Lot seems to have been toward the end of his days ere he defiled himself with the abominations recorded [Gen. 19:32-35]. David, in a short life, had as much experience of grace and sin, and as much close, spiritual communion with God, as ever had any of the sons of men, before he was cast to the ground by this law of sin [2 Samuel 11]. So was it with Hezekiah in his degree, which was none of the meanest [2 Chron. 32:25]. Now, to set upon such persons, so well acquainted with its power and deceit, so armed and provided against it, that had been conquerors over it for so many years, and to prevail against them, it argues a power and efficacy too mighty for everything but the Spirit of the Almighty to withstand. Who can look to have a greater stock of inherent grace than those men had; to have more experience of God and the excellency of his ways, the sweetness of his love and of communion with him, than they had? Who has either better furniture to oppose sin with, or more obligation so to do, than they? And yet we see how fearfully they were prevailed against.

As if God had permitted their falls on set purpose, that we might learn to be wary of this powerful enemy, *they all of them fell out when they had newly received great and stupendous mercies from the hand of God, that ought to have been strong obligations unto diligence and watchfulness in close obedience.* Noah was but newly come forth of that world of waters, wherein he saw the ungodly world perishing for their sins, and himself preserved by that astonishable miracle which all ages must admire. While the world's desolation was an hourly remembrancer[1] unto him of his strange preservation by the immediate care and hand of God, he falls into drunkenness [Gen. 9:21]. Lot had newly seen that which every one that thinks on cannot but tremble; he saw, as one speaks, "hell coming out of heaven" upon unclean sinners—the greatest evidence, except the cross of Christ, that God ever gave in his providence of the judgment to come. He saw himself and children delivered by the special care and miraculous hand of God; and yet, while these strange mercies were fresh upon him, he fell into drunkenness and incest [Gen. 19:32-35]. David was delivered out of all his troubles, and had the necks of his enemies given him round about, and he makes use of his peace from a world of trials and troubles to contrive mur-

[1] reminder

der and adultery [2 Samuel 11]. Immediately it was after Hezekiah's great and miraculous deliverance that he falls into his carnal pride and boasting [2 Chron. 32:25]. I say, their falls in such seasons seem to be permitted on set purpose to instruct us all in the truth that we have in hand; so that no persons, in no seasons, with whatsoever furniture of grace, can promise themselves security from its prevalency any other ways than by keeping close constantly to him who has supplies to give out that are above its reach and efficacy. Methinks this should make us look about us. Are we better than Noah, who had that testimony from God, that he was "a perfect man in his generations," and "walked with God" [Gen. 6:9]? Are we better than Lot, whose "righteous soul was vexed with the evil deeds of ungodly men," and is therefore commended by the Holy Ghost [2 Pet. 2:7-8]? Are we more holy, wise, and watchful than David, who obtained this testimony, that he was "a man after God's own heart" [1 Sam. 13:14]? Or better than Hezekiah, who appealed to God himself that he had served him uprightly with a perfect heart [2 Kings 20:3]? And yet what prevalency this law of sin wrought in and over them we see. And there is no end of the like examples. They are all set up as buoys to discover unto us the sands, the shelves, the rocks, whereupon they made their shipwreck, to their hazard, danger, loss, yea, and would have done to their ruin, had not God been pleased in his faithfulness graciously to prevent it. And this is the first part of this evidence of the power of sin from its effects.

It manifests its power in the habitual declensions from zeal and holiness, from the frames, state, and condition of obedience and communion with God whereunto they had attained, which are found in many believers. Promises of growth and improvement are many and precious, the means excellent and effectual, the benefits great and unspeakable; yet it often falls out, that instead hereof decays and declensions are found upon professors, yea, in and upon many of the saints of God. Now, whereas this must needs principally and chiefly be from the strength and efficacy of indwelling sin, and is therefore a great evidence thereof, I shall first evince the observation itself to be true—namely, that some of the saints themselves do oftentimes so decline from that growth and improvement in faith, grace, and holiness which might justly be expected from them—and then show that the cause of this evil lies in that that we are treating of. And that it is the cause of total apostasy in unsound professors shall be after declared. But this is a greater work which we have in hand. The prevailing upon true believers unto a sinful declension and gradual apostasy requires a putting forth of more strength and efficacy than the prevailing upon unsound professors unto total apostasy, as the wind which will blow down a dead tree that has no root to the ground will scarcely shake or bow a living, well-rooted tree. But this it will do. There is mention made in the Scripture of "the first ways of David," and they are commended above his latter (2 Chron. 17:3). The last ways even of David were tainted with the power of indwelling sin. Though we have mention only of the actual eruption of sin, yet that uncleanness and pride which was working in him in his numbering of the people [1 Chron. 21:1] were certainly rooted in a declension from his first frame. Those rushes did not grow without mire. David would not have done so in his younger days, when he followed God in the wilderness of temptations and trials, full of faith, love, humility, brokenness of heart, zeal, tender affection unto all the ordinances of God; all which were eminent in him. But his strength is impaired by the efficacy and deceitfulness of sin, his locks cut, and he becomes a prey to vile lusts and temptations. We have a notable instance in most of the churches that our Savior awakens to the consideration of their condition in the Revelation. We may single out one of them. Many good things were there in the church of Ephesus, for which it is greatly commended (Rev. 2:2-3); but yet it is charged with a decay, a declension, a gradual falling off and apostasy: "You have left your first love. Remember therefore from whence you have fallen, and repent, and do the first works" (vv. 4-5). There was a decay, both inward, in the frame of heart, as to faith and love, and outward, as to obedience and works, in comparison of what they had formerly, by the testimony of Christ himself. The same also might be showed concerning the rest of those churches, only one or two of them excepted. Five of them are charged with decays and declensions. Hence there is mention in the Scripture of the "kindness of youth," of the "love of espousals," with great commendation (Jer. 2:2-3); of our "first faith" (1 Tim. 5:12); of "the beginning of our confidence" (Heb. 3:14). And cautions are given that we "lose not the things that we have wrought" (2 John 8). But what need we look back or search for instances to confirm the truth of this observation? A habitual declension from first engagements unto God, from first attainments of communion with God, from first strictness in duties of obedience, is ordinary and common among professors. Might we to this purpose take a general view of the professors in these nations—among whom the lot of the best of us will be found, in part or in whole, in somewhat or in all, to fall—we might be plentifully convinced of the truth of this observation—

Is their zeal for God as warm, living, vigorous, effectual, solicitous, as it was in their first giving themselves unto God? Or rather, is there not a common, slight, selfish frame of spirit in the room[2] *of it come upon most professors?* Iniquity has abounded, and their love has waxed[3] cold. Was it not of old a burden to their spirits to hear the name, and ways, and worship of God blasphemed and profaned? Could they not have said, with the psalmist, "Rivers of waters run down our eyes, because men keep not your law" (Ps. 119:136)? Were not their souls solicitous about the interest of Christ in the world, like Eli's about the ark [1 Sam. 4:13]? Did they not contend earnestly for the faith once delivered to the saints [Jude 3] and every parcel of it, especially wherein the grace of God and the glory of the gospel was specially concerned? Did they not labor to judge and condemn the world by a holy and separate conversation? And do now the generality of professors abide in this frame? Have they grown, and made improvement in it? Or is there not a coldness and indifference grown upon the spirits of many in this thing? Yea, do not many despise all these things, and look upon their own former zeal as folly? May we not see many, who have formerly been of esteem in ways of profession, become daily a scorn and reproach through their miscarriages, and that justly, to the men of the world? Is it not with them as it was of old with the daughters of Zion (Isa. 3:24), when God judged them for their sins and wantonness?[4] Has not the world and self utterly ruined their profession? And are they not regardless of the things wherein they have formerly declared a singular concern? Yea, are not some come, partly on one pretense, partly on another, to an open enmity unto, and hatred of, the ways of God? They please them no more, but are evil in their eyes. But not to mention such open apostates any further, whose hypocrisy the Lord Jesus Christ will shortly judge, how is it with the best? Are not almost all men grown cold and slack as to these things? Are they not less concerned in them than formerly? Are they not grown weary, selfish in their religion, and so things be indifferent well at home, scarce care how they go abroad in the world? At least, do they not prefer their ease, credit, safety, secular advantages before these things?—a frame that Christ abhors, and declares that those in whom it prevails are none of his. Some, indeed, seem to retain a good zeal for truth; but wherein they make the fairest appearance, therein will they be found to be most abominable. They cry out against errors—not for truth, but for party's and interest's sake. Let a man be on their party and promote their interest, be he never so corrupt

[2] i.e., place
[3] grows, becomes
[4] lack of discipline

in his judgment, he is embraced, and, it may be, admired. This is not zeal for God, but for a man's self. It is not, "The zeal of your house has eaten me up" [Ps. 69:9], but, "Master, forbid them, because they follow not with us" [Mark 9:38]. Better it were, doubtless, for men never to pretend unto any zeal at all than to substitute such wrathful selfishness in the room of it.

Is men's delight in the ordinances and worship of God the same as in former days? Do they find the same sweetness and relish in them as they have done of old? How precious has the word been to them formerly! What joy and delight have they had in attendance thereon! How would they have run and gone to have been made partakers of it, where it was dispensed in its power and purity, in the evidence and demonstration of the Spirit! Did they not call the Sabbath their delight [Isa. 58:13], and was not the approach of it a real joy unto their souls? Did they not long after the converse and communion[5] of saints, and could they not undergo manifold perils for the attainment of it? And does this frame still abide upon them? Are there not decays and declensions to be found among them? May it not be said, "Gray hairs are here and there upon them, and they perceive it not" [Hos. 7:9]? Yea, are not men ready to say with them of old, "What a weariness is it!" (Mal. 1:13). It is even a burden and a weariness to be tied up to the observation of all these ordinances. What need we be at all so strict in the observation of the Sabbath? What need we hear so often? What need this distinction in hearing? Insensibly a great disrespect, yea, even a contempt of the pleasant and excellent ways of Christ and his gospel is fallen upon many professors.

May not the same conviction be further carried on by an inquiry into the universal course of obedience and the performance of duties that men have been engaged in? Is there the same conscientious tenderness of sinning abiding in many as was in days of old, the same exact performance of private duties, the same love to the brethren, the same readiness for the cross, the same humility of mind and spirit, the same self-denial? The steam of men's lusts, wherewith the air is tainted, will not suffer us so to say. We need, then, go no further than this wretched generation wherein we live, to evince the truth of the observation laid down as the foundation of the instance insisted on. The Lord give repentance before it be too late! Now, all these declensions, all these decays, that are found in some professors, they all proceed from this root and cause—they are all the product of indwelling sin, and all evince the exceeding power and efficacy of it: for the proof whereof I shall not

[5] This word is mistakenly printed as "corn-mullion" in the Goold edition.

need to go further than the general rule which out of James we have already considered—namely, that lust or indwelling sin is the cause of all actual sin and all habitual declensions in believers. This is that which the apostle intends in that place to teach and declare. I shall, therefore, handle these two things, and show: (1) that this does evince a great efficacy and power in sin; (2) declare the ways and means whereby it brings forth or brings about this cursed effect—all in design of our general end, in calling upon and cautioning believers to avoid it, to oppose it.

It appears to be a work of great power and efficacy from the provision that is made against it, which it prevails over. There is in the covenant of grace plentiful provision made, not only for the preventing of declensions and decays in believers, but also for their continual carrying on toward perfection; as—

The word itself and all the ordinances of the gospel are appointed and given unto us for this end (Eph. 4:11-15). That which is the end of giving gospel officers to the church is the end also of giving all the ordinances to be administered by them; for they are given "for the work of the ministry"—that is, for the administration of the ordinances of the gospel. Now, what is or what are these ends? They are all for the preventing of decays and declensions in the saints, all for the carrying them on to perfection (so it is said, v. 12). In general, it is for the "perfecting of the saints," carrying on the work of grace in them, and the work of holiness and obedience by them; or for the edifying of the body of Christ, their building up in an increase of faith and love, even of every true member of the mystical body. But how far are they appointed thus to carry them on, thus to build them up? Has it bounds fixed to its work? Does it carry them so far, and then leave them? "No," says the apostle (v. 13). The dispensation of the word of the gospel, and the ordinances thereof, is designed for our help, assistance, and furtherance, until the whole work of faith and obedience is consummate. It is appointed to perfect and complete that faith, knowledge, and growth in grace and holiness, which is allotted unto us in this world. But what and if oppositions and temptations do lie in the way, Satan and his instruments working with great subtlety and deceit? Why, these ordinances are designed for our safeguarding and deliverance from all their attempts and assaults (v. 14), that so being preserved in the use of them, or "speaking the truth in love, we may grow up unto him in all things who is the head, even Christ Jesus" [v. 15]. This is, in general, the use of all gospel ordinances, the chief and main end for which they were given and appointed of God—namely, to preserve believers from all decays of faith and obedience, and to carry them on still toward perfection. These are means which God, the good husbandman,[6] makes use of to cause the vine to thrive and bring forth fruit. And I could also manifest the same to be the special end of them distinctly. Briefly, the word is milk and strong meat, for the nourishing and strengthening of all sorts and all degrees of believers. It has both seed and water in it, and manuring[7] with it, to make them fruitful. The ordinance of the supper is appointed on purpose for the strengthening of our faith, in the remembrance of the death of the Lord, and the exercise of love one toward another. The communion of saints is for the edifying each other in faith, love, and obedience.

There is that which adds weight to this consideration. *God suffers us not to be unmindful of this assistance he has afforded us, but is continually calling upon us to make use of the means appointed for the attaining of the end proposed.* He shows them unto us, as the angel showed the water-spring to Hagar [Gen. 16:7]. Commands, exhortations, promises, threatenings, are multiplied to this purpose (see them summed up in Heb. 2:1). He is continually saying to us, "Why will you die? Why will you wither and decay? Come to the pastures provided for you, and your souls shall live." If we see a lamb run from the fold into the wilderness, we wonder not if it be torn and rent[8] of wild beasts. If we see a sheep leaving its green pastures and watercourses to abide in dry barren heaths, we count it no marvel, nor inquire further, if we see him lean and ready to perish; but if we find lambs wounded in the fold, we wonder at the boldness and rage of the beasts of prey that durst set upon them there. If we see sheep pining in full pastures, we judge them to be diseased and unsound. It is indeed no marvel that poor creatures who forsake their own mercies, and run away from the pasture and fold of Christ in his ordinances, are rent and torn with diverse lusts, and do pine away with hunger and famine; but to see men living under and enjoying all the means of spiritual thriving, yet to decay, not to be fat and flourishing, but rather daily to pine and wither, this argues some secret powerful distemper, whose poisonous and noxious[9] qualities hinder the virtue and efficacy of the means they enjoy. This is indwelling sin. So wonderfully powerful, so effectually poisonous it is, that it can bring leanness on the souls of men in the midst of all precious means of growth and flourishing. It may well make us tremble, to see men living under and in the use of the means of the gospel, preaching, praying, administration of sacraments, and yet grow colder every day than

[6] farmer
[7] fertilizer
[8] ripped, torn
[9] injurious, harmful, unwholesome

others in zeal for God, more selfish and worldly, even habitually to decline as to the degrees of holiness which they had attained unto.

Together with the dispensation of the outward means of spiritual growth or improvement, there are also supplies of grace continually afforded the saints from their head, Christ. He is the head of all the saints; and he is a living head, and so a living head as that he tells us that "because he lives we shall live also" (John 14:19). He communicates spiritual life to all that are his. In him is the fountain of our life; which is therefore said to be "hid with him in God" (Col. 3:3). And this life he gives unto his saints by quickening of them by his Spirit (Rom. 8:11); and he continues it unto them by the supplies of living grace which he communicates unto them. From these two, his quickening of us, and continually giving out supplies of life unto us, he is said to live in us: "I live; yet not I, but Christ lives in me" (Gal. 2:20)—"The spiritual life which I have is not mine own; not from myself was it educed,[10] not by myself is it maintained, but it is merely and solely the work of Christ: so that it is not I that live, but he lives in me, the whole of my life being from him alone." Neither does this living head communicate only a bare life unto believers, that they should merely live and no more, a poor, weak, dying life, as it were; but he gives out sufficiently to afford them a strong, vigorous, thriving, flourishing life (John 10:10). He comes not only that his sheep "may have life," but that "they may have it more abundantly," that is, in a plentiful manner, so as that they may flourish, be fat and fruitful. Thus is it with the whole body of Christ, and every member thereof, whereby it "grows up into him in all things, which is the head, even Christ: from whom the whole body fitly joined together and compacted by that which every joint supplies, according to the effectual working in the measure of every part, makes increase of the body unto the edifying of itself in love" (Eph. 4:15-16). The end of all communications of grace and supplies of life from this living and blessed head is the increase of the whole body and every member of it, and the edifying of itself in love. His *treasures of grace* are unsearchable; his *stores* inexhaustible; his *life,* the fountain of ours, full and eternal; his *heart* bounteous and large; his *hand* open and liberal: so that there is no doubt but that he communicates supplies of grace for their increase in holiness abundantly unto all his saints. Whence, then, is it that they do not all flourish and thrive accordingly? As you may see it oftentimes in a natural body, so is it here. Though the seat and rise of the blood and spirits in head and heart be excellently good and sound, yet there may be a withering member in the body; this somewhat intercepts the

[10] derived, drawn out

influences of life unto it, so that though the heart and head do perform their office, in giving of supplies no less to that than they do to any other member, yet all the effect produced is merely to keep it from utter perishing—it grows weak and decays every day. The withering and decaying of any member in Christ's mystical body is not for the want of his communication of grace for an abundant life, but from the powerful interception that is made of the efficacy of it, by the interposition and opposition of indwelling sin. Hence it is that where lust grows strong, a great deal of grace will but keep the soul alive, and not give it any eminency in fruitfulness at all. Oftentimes Christ gives very much grace where not many of its effects do appear. It spends its strength and power in withstanding the continual assaults of violent corruptions and lusts, so that it cannot put forth its proper virtue toward further fruitfulness. As a virtuous medicine—that is fit both to check vicious and noxious humors,[11] and to comfort, refresh, and strengthen nature, if the evil humor be strong and greatly prevailing—spends its whole strength and virtue in the subduing and correcting of it, contributing much less to the relief of nature than otherwise it would do, if it met not with such opposition; so is it with the eye-salve and the healing grace which we have abundantly from the wings of the Sun of Righteousness. It is forced oftentimes to put forth its virtue to oppose and contend against, and in any measure subdue, prevailing lusts and corruptions. That the soul receives not that strengthening unto duties and fruitfulness which otherwise it might receive by it is from hence. How sound, healthy, and flourishing, how fruitful and exemplary in holiness, might many a soul be by and with that grace which is continually communicated to it from Christ, which now, by reason of the power of indwelling sin, is not only dead, but weak, withering, and useless! And this, if anything, is a notable evidence of the efficacy of indwelling sin, that it is able to give such a stop and check to the mighty and effectual power of grace, so that notwithstanding the blessed and continual supplies that we receive from our Head, yet many believers do decline and decay, and that habitually, as to what they had attained unto, their last ways not answering their first. This makes the vineyard in the "very fruitful hill" to bring forth so many wild grapes; this makes so many trees barren in fertile fields [Isa. 5:1].

Besides the continual supplies of grace that constantly, according to the tenure of the covenant, are communicated unto believers, which keeps them that they thirst no more as to a total indigence, *there is, moreover, a readiness in the Lord Christ to yield peculiar succor to the souls of his, according as*

[11] bodily fluids, thought to be the physical root of the passions

their occasions shall require. The apostle tells us that he is "a merciful High Priest" and "able" (that is, ready, prepared, and willing) "to succor them that are tempted" (Heb. 2:18); and we are on that account invited to "come with boldness to the throne of grace, that we may obtain mercy, and find grace to help in time of need" [Heb. 4:16]—that is, grace sufficient, seasonable, suitable unto any special trial or temptation that we may be exercised with. Our merciful High Priest is ready to give out this special seasonable grace over and above those constant communications of supplies of the Spirit which we mentioned before. Besides the never-failing springs of ordinary covenant grace, he has also peculiar refreshing showers for times of drought; and this is exceedingly to the advantage of the saints for their preservation and growth in grace; and there may very many more of the like nature be added. But now, I say, notwithstanding all these, and the residue of the like importance, such is the power and efficacy of indwelling sin, so great its deceitfulness and restlessness, so many its wiles and temptations, it often falls out that many of them for whose growth and improvement all this provision is made do yet, as was showed, go back and decline, even as to their course of walking with God. Samson's strength fully evidenced itself when he broke seven new withes and seven new cords, wherewith he was bound, as burning tow[12] and as thread [Judg. 16:8-9, 12]. The noxious humor in the body, which is so stubborn as that [which] no use of the most sovereign remedies can prevail against it, ought to be regarded. Such is this indwelling sin if not watched over. It breaks all the cords made to bind it; it blunts the instruments appointed to root it up; it resists all healing medicines, though never so sovereign, and is therefore assuredly of exceeding efficacy. Besides, believers have innumerable obligations upon them, from the love, the command of God, to grow in grace, to press forward toward perfection, as they have abundant means provided for them so to do. Their doing so is a matter of the greatest advantage, profit, sweetness, contentment unto them in the world. It is the burden, the trouble of their souls, that they do not so do, that they are not more holy, more zealous, useful, fruitful; they desire it above life itself. They know it is their duty to watch against this enemy, to fight against it, to pray against it; and so they do. They more desire his destruction than the enjoyment of all this world and all that it can afford. And yet, notwithstanding all this, such is the subtlety, and fraud, and violence, and fury, and urgency, and importunity of this adversary, that it frequently prevails to bring them into the woeful condition mentioned. Hence it is with believers sometimes as it is with men in some places at sea.

[12] coarse flax

They have a good and fair gale of wind, it may be, all night long; they ply their tackling,[13] attend diligently their business, and, it may be, take great contentment to consider how they proceed in their voyage. In the morning, or after a season, coming to measure what way they have made and what progress they have had, they find that they are much backward of what they were, instead of getting one step forward. Falling into a swift tide or current against them, it has frustrated all their labors, and rendered the wind in their sails almost useless; somewhat thereby they have borne up against the stream, but have made no progress. So is it with believers. They have a good gale of supplies of the Spirit from above; they attend duties diligently, pray constantly, hear attentively, and omit nothing that may carry them on their voyage toward eternity; but after a while, coming seriously to consider, by the examination of their hearts and ways, what progress they have made, they find that all their assistance and duties have not been able to bear them up against some strong tide or current of indwelling sin. It has kept them, indeed, [so] that they have not been driven and split on rocks and shelves—it has preserved them from gross, scandalous sins: but yet they have lost in their spiritual frame, or gone backwards, and are entangled under many woeful decays; which is a notable evidence of the life of sin, about which we are treating. Now, because the end of our discovering this power of sin is that we may be careful to obviate and prevent it in its operation; and, because of all the effects that it produces, there is none more dangerous or pernicious than that we have last insisted on—namely, that it prevails upon many professors unto a habitual declension from their former ways and attainments, notwithstanding all the sweetness and excellency which their souls have found in them—I shall, as was said, in the next place, consider by what ways and means, and through what assistance, it usually prevails in this kind, that we may the better be instructed to watch against it.

[Chapter 15]

The ways and means whereby indwelling sin prevails on believers unto habitual declensions and decays as to degrees of grace and holiness is that now which comes under consideration; and they are many—

Upon the first conversion and calling of sinners unto God and Christ, they have usually many fresh springs breaking forth in their souls and refresh-

[13] a ship's rigging; tackle

ing showers coming upon them, which bear them up to a high rate of faith, love, holiness, fruitfulness, and obedience; as upon a land-flood, when many lesser streams run into a river, it swells over its bounds, and rolls on with a more than ordinary fullness. Now, if these springs be not kept open, if they prevail not for the continuance of these showers, they must needs decay and go backwards. We shall name one or two of them:

They have a fresh, vigorous sense of pardoning mercy. According as this is in the soul, so will its love and delight in God, so will its obedience be; as, I say, is the sense of gospel pardon, so will be the life of gospel love. "I say unto you," says our Savior of the poor woman, "her sins, which were many, are forgiven; for she loved much: but to whom little is forgiven, the same loves little" (Luke 7:47). Her great love was an evidence of great forgiveness, and her great sense of it: for our Savior is not rendering a reason of her forgiveness, as though it were for her love; but of her love, that it was because of her forgiveness. Having in the foregoing parable (from v. 40 and onwards) convinced the Pharisee with whom he had to do that he to whom most was forgiven would love most (as v. 43), he thence gives an account of the great love of the woman, springing from the sense she had of the great forgiveness which she had so freely received. Thus sinners at their first conversion are very sensible of great forgiveness; "Of whom I am chief" [1 Tim. 1:15] lies next [to] their heart. This greatly subdues their hearts and spirits unto all in God, and quickens them unto all obedience, even that such poor cursed sinners as they were should so freely be delivered and pardoned. The love of God and of Christ in their forgiveness highly conquers and constrains them to make it their business to live unto God.

The fresh taste they have had of spiritual things keeps up such a savor and relish of them in their souls, as that worldly contentments, whereby men are drawn off from close walking with God, are rendered sapless and undesirable unto them. Having tasted of the wine of the gospel, they desire no other, for they say, "This is best." So was it with the apostles, upon that option offered them as to a departure from Christ, upon the apostasy of many false professors: "Will you also go away?" (John 6:67). They answer by Peter, "Lord, to whom shall we go? you have the words of eternal life" (v. 68). They had such a fresh savor and relish of the doctrine of the gospel and the grace of Christ upon their souls, that they can entertain no thoughts of declining from it. As a man that has been long kept in a dungeon, if brought forth on a sudden into the light of the sun, finds so much pleasure and contentment in it, in the beauties of the old creation, that he thinks he can never be weary of it, nor shall [he] ever be contented on any account to be under darkness again; so is it with souls when first translated into the marvelous light of Christ, to behold the beauties of the new creation. They see a new glory in him that has quite sullied the desirableness of all earthly diversions. And they see a new guilt and filth in sin, that gives them an utter abhorrency of its old delights and pleasures; and so of other things. Now, while these and the like springs are kept open in the souls of converted sinners, they constrain them to a vigorous, active holiness. They can never do enough for God; so that oftentimes their zeal as saints suffers them not to escape without some blots on their prudence as men, as might be instanced in many of the martyrs of old. This, then, is the first, at least one way whereby indwelling sin prepares men for decays and declensions in grace and obedience—*it endeavors to stop or taint these springs.* And there are several ways whereby it brings this to pass—

It works by sloth and negligence. It prevails in the soul to a neglect of stirring up continual thoughts of or about the things that so powerfully influence it unto strict and fruitful obedience. If care be not taken, if diligence and watchfulness be not used, and all means that are appointed of God to keep a quick and living sense of them upon the soul, they will dry up and decay; and, consequently, that obedience that should spring from them will do so also. Isaac dug wells, but the Philistines stopped them, and his flocks had no benefit by them [Gen. 26:18]. Let the heart never so little disuse itself to gracious, soul-affecting thoughts of the love of God, the cross of Christ, the greatness and excellency of gospel mercy, the beauties of holiness—they will quickly be as much estranged to a man as he can be to them. He that shuts his eyes for a season in the sun, when he opens them again can see nothing at all. And so much as a man loses of faith toward these things, so much will they lose of power toward him. They can do little or nothing upon him because of his unbelief, which formerly were so exceedingly effectual toward him. So was it with the spouse in the Song of Solomon (5:2); Christ calls unto her (v. 1) with a marvelous loving and gracious invitation unto communion with himself. She who had formerly been ravished at the first hearing of that joyful sound, being now under the power of sloth and carnal ease, returns a sorry excusing answer to his call, which ended in her own signal loss and sorrow. Indwelling sin, I say, prevailing by spiritual sloth upon the souls of men unto an inadvertency of the motions of God's Spirit in their former apprehensions of divine love, and a negligence of stirring up continual thoughts of faith about it, a decay grows insensibly upon the whole soul. Thus God often complains that his people had "forgotten him," that is, grew unmindful of his love and grace—which was the beginning of their apostasy.

By unframing the soul, so that it shall have formal, weary, powerless thoughts of those things which should prevail with it unto diligence in thankful obedience. The apostle cautions us that in dealing with God we should use reverence and godly fear, because of his purity, holiness, and majesty (Heb. 12:28-29). And this is that which the Lord himself spoke in the destruction of Nadab and Abihu, "I will be sanctified in them that come nigh me" (Lev. 10:3). He will be dealt with in an awful, holy, reverent manner. So are we to deal with all the things of God wherein or whereby we have communion with him. The soul is to have a great reverence of God in them. When men begin to take them into slight or common thoughts, not using and improving them unto the utmost for the ends whereunto they are appointed, they lose all their beauty, and glory, and power toward them. When we have anything to do wherein faith or love toward God is to be exercised, we must do it with all our hearts, with all our minds, strength, and souls; not slightly and perfunctorily,[14] which God abhors. He does not only require that we bear his love and grace in remembrance, but that, as much as in us lies, we do it according to the worth and excellency of them. It was the sin of Hezekiah that he "rendered not again according to the benefits done to him" (2 Chron. 32:25). So, while we consider gospel truths, the uttermost endeavor of the soul ought to be that we may be "changed into the same image" or likeness (2 Cor. 3:18); that is, that they may have their full power and effect upon us. Otherwise, James tells us what our "beholding the glory of the Lord in a glass," there mentioned by the apostle—that is, reading or hearing the mind of God in Christ revealed in the gospel—comes unto:[15] "It is but like unto a man beholding his natural face in a glass: for he beholds himself, and goes away, and straightway forgets what manner of man he was" (James 1:23-24). It makes no impression upon him, begets no idea or image of his likeness in his imagination, because he does it only slightly, and with a transient look. So is it with men that will indeed think of gospel truths but in a slight manner, without endeavoring, with all their hearts, minds, and strength, to have them engrafted upon their souls, and all the effects of them produced in them. Now, this is the way of sinners in their first engagements unto God. They never think of pardoning mercy, but they labor to affect their whole souls with it, and do stir up themselves unto suitable affections and returns of constant obedience. They think not of the excellency of Christ and spiritual things, now newly discovered unto them in a saving light, but they press

[14] routinely, indifferently
[15] results in

with all their might after a further, a fuller enjoyment of them. This keeps them humble and holy, this makes them thankful and fruitful. But now, if the utmost diligence and carefulness be not used to improve and grow in this wisdom, to keep up this frame, indwelling sin, working by the vanity of the minds of men, will insensibly bring them to content themselves with slight and rare thoughts of these things, without a diligent, sedulous[16] endeavor to give them their due improvement upon the soul. As men decay herein, so will they assuredly decay and decline in the power of holiness and close walking with God. The springs being stopped or tainted, the streams will not run so swiftly, at least not so sweetly, as formerly. Some, by this means, under an uninterrupted profession, insensibly wither almost into nothing. They talk of religion and spiritual things as much as ever they did in their lives, and perform duties with as much constancy as ever they did; but yet they have poor, lean, starving souls, as to any real and effectual communion with God. By the power and subtlety of indwelling sin they have grown formal, and learned to deal about spiritual things in an overly manner; whereby they have lost all their life, vigor, savor, and efficacy toward them. Be always serious in spiritual things if ever you intend to be bettered by them.

Indwelling sin oftentimes prevails to the stopping of these springs of gospel obedience, by false and foolish opinions corrupting the simplicity of the gospel. False opinions are the work of the flesh. From the vanity and darkness of the minds of men, with a mixture more or less of corrupt affections, do they mostly proceed. The apostle was jealous over his Corinthians in this matter. He was afraid lest their minds "should by any means be corrupted from the simplicity that is in Christ" (2 Cor. 11:2-3); which he knew would be attended by a decay and declension in faith, love, and obedience. And thus matters in this case often fall out. We have seen some who, after they have received a sweet taste of the love of God in Christ, of the excellency of pardoning mercy, and have walked humbly with God for many years in the faith and apprehension of the truth, have, by the corruption of their minds from the simplicity that is in Christ, by false and foolish opinions, despised all their own experiences, and rejected all the efficacy of truth, as to the furtherance of their obedience. Hence John cautions the elect lady and her children to take heed they were not seduced, lest they should "lose the things that they had wrought" (2 John 8)—lest they should themselves cast away all their former obedience as lost, and a thing of no value. We have innumerable instances hereof in the days wherein we live. How many are there who, not

---

[16] constant, persistent

many years since, put an unspeakable value on the pardon of sin in the blood of Christ—who delighted in gospel discoveries of spiritual things, and walked in obedience to God on the account of them—who, being beguiled and turned aside from the truth as it is in Jesus, do despise these springs of their own former obedience! And as this is done grossly and openly in some, so there are more secret and more plausible insinuations of corrupt opinions tainting the springs and fountains of gospel obedience, and, through the vanity of men's minds, which is a principal part of indwelling sin, getting ground upon them. Such are all those that tend to the extenuation of special grace in its freedom and efficacy, and the advancement of the wills or the endeavors of men in their spiritual power and ability. They are works of the flesh; and howsoever some may pretend a usefulness in them to the promotion of holiness, they will be found to taint the springs of true evangelical obedience, insensibly to turn the heart from God, and to bring the whole soul into a spiritual decay. And this is one way whereby indwelling sin produces this pernicious effect of drawing men off from the power, purity, and fruitfulness attending their first conversion and engagements unto God, bringing them into habitual declension, at least as unto degrees, of their holiness and grace. There is not anything we ought to be more watchful against, if we intend effectually to deal with this powerful and subtle enemy. It is no small part of the wisdom of faith, to observe whether gospel truths continue to have the same savor unto and efficacy upon the soul as formerly they have had; and whether an endeavor be maintained to improve them continually as at the first. A commandment that is always practiced is always new, as John speaks of that of love. And he that really improves gospel truths, though he hears them a thousand times, they will be always new and fresh unto him, because they put him on newness of practice; when to another, that grows common under them, they are burdensome and common unto him, and he even loathes the manna that he is so accustomed unto.

Indwelling sin does this by taking men off from their watch against the returns of Satan. When our Lord Christ comes first to take possession of any soul for himself, he binds that strong man and spoils his goods; he deprives him of all his power, dominion, and interest. Satan being thus dispossessed and frustrated in his hopes and expectations, leaves the soul, as finding it newly mortified to his baits. So he left our Savior upon his first fruitless attempts. But it is said he left him only "for a season" (Luke 4:13). He intended to return again, as he should see his advantage. So is it with believers also. Being cast out from his interest in them, he leaves them for a season, at least comparatively he does so. Freed from his assaults and perplexing temptations, they proceed vigorously in the course of their obedience, and so flourish in the ways of God. But this holds not; Satan returns again, and if the soul stands not continually upon his guard against him, he will quickly get such advantages as shall put a notable interruption upon his fruitfulness and obedience. Hence some, after they have spent some time, it may be some years, in cheerful, exemplary walking with God, have, upon Satan's return, consumed all their latter days in wrestling with perplexing temptations wherewith he has entangled them. Others have plainly fallen under the power of his assaults. It is like a man who, having for a while lived usefully among his neighbors, done good and communicated according to his ability, distributing to the poor, and helping all around about him, at length, falling into the hands of vexatious, wrangling, oppressive men is forced to spend his whole time and revenue in defending himself against them at law, and so becomes useless in the place where he lives. So is it with many a believer: after he has walked in a fruitful course of obedience, to the glory of God and edification of the church of Christ, being afresh set upon, by the return of Satan in one way or other, he has enough to do all the remainder of his life to keep himself alive; in the meantime, as to many graces, woefully decaying and going backward. Now, this also, though Satan has a hand in it, is from indwelling sin; I mean, the success is so which Satan does obtain in his undertaking. This encourages him, makes way for his return, and gives entrance to his temptations. You know how it is with them out of whom he is cast only by gospel conviction; after he has wandered and waited a while, he says he will return to his house from whence he was ejected. And what is the issue? Carnal lusts have prevailed over the man's convictions, and made his soul fit to entertain returning devils. It is so as to the measure of prevalency that Satan obtains against believers, upon advantages administered unto him, by sin's disposing the soul unto an obnoxiousness to his temptations. Now, the way and means whereby indwelling sin does give advantage to Satan for his return are all those which dispose them toward a declension, which shall afterward be mentioned. Satan is a diligent, watchful, and crafty adversary; he will neglect no opportunity, no advantage that is offered unto him. Wherein, then, soever our spiritual strength is impaired by sin, or which way soever our lusts press, Satan falls in with that weakness and presses toward that ruin; so that all the actings of the law of sin are subservient to this end of Satan. I shall therefore only at present mention one or two that seem principally to invite Satan to attempt a return—

It entangles the soul in the things of the world, all which are so many purveyors for Satan. When Pharaoh had let the people go, he heard after a while that they were entangled in the wilderness, and supposes that he shall therefore now overtake them and destroy them. This stirs him up to pursue after them. Satan finding those whom he has been cast out from entangled in the things of the world, by which he is sure to find an easy access unto them, is encouraged to attempt upon them afresh, as the spider to come down upon the strongest fly that is entangled in his web; for he comes by his temptations only to impel them unto that whereunto by their own lusts they are inclined, by adding poison to their lusts, and painting to the objects of them. And oftentimes by this advantage he gets so in upon the souls of men, that they are never well free of him more while they live. And as men's diversions increase from the world, so do their entanglements from Satan. When they have more to do in the world than they can well manage, they shall have more to do from Satan than they can well withstand. When men are made spiritually faint, by dealing in and with the world, Satan sets on them, as Amalek did on the faint and weak of the people that came out of Egypt [Ex. 17:8-16].

It produces this effect by making the soul negligent, and taking it off from its watch. We have before showed at large that it is one main part of the effectual deceitfulness of indwelling sin to make the soul inadvertent, to turn it off from the diligent, watchful attendance unto its duty which is required. Now, there is not anything in reference whereunto diligence and watchfulness are more strictly enjoined than the returning assaults of Satan: "Be sober, be vigilant" (1 Pet. 5:8). And why so? "Because of your adversary the devil." Unless you are exceeding watchful, at one time or other he will surprise you; and all the injunctions of our blessed Savior to watch are still with reference unto him and his temptations. Now, when the soul is made careless and inadvertent, forgetting what an enemy it has to deal with, or is lifted up with the successes it has newly obtained against him, then is Satan's time to attempt a re-entrance of his old habitation; which if he cannot obtain, yet he makes their lives uncomfortable to themselves and unfruitful to others, in weakening their root and withering their fruit through his poisonous temptations. He comes down upon our duties of obedience as the fowls upon Abraham's sacrifice; so that if we watch not, as he did, to drive them away (for by resistance he is overcome and put to flight), he will devour them (Gen. 15:11).

Indwelling sin takes advantage to put forth its efficacy and deceit to withdraw men from their primitive zeal and holiness, from their first faith, love, and works, by the evil examples of professors among whom they live. When men first engage into the ways of God, they have a reverent esteem of those whom they believe to have been made partakers of that mercy before themselves; these they love and honor, as it is their duty. But after a while they find many of them walking in many things unevenly, crookedly, and not unlike the men of the world. Here sin is not wanting to its advantage. Insensibly it prevails with men to a compliance with them. "This way, this course of walking, does well enough with others; why may it not do so with us also?" Such is the inward thought of many that works effectually in them. And so, through the craft of sin the generation of professors corrupt one another. As a stream arising from a clear spring or a fountain, while it runs in its own peculiar channel and keeps its water unmixed, preserves its purity and cleanness, but when it falls in its course with other streams that are turbid and foul, though running the same way with it, it becomes muddy and discolored also; so is it in this case. Believers come forth from the spring of the new birth with some purity and cleanness; this for a while they keep in the course of their private walking with God: but now, when they come sometimes to fall into society with others, whose profession flows and runs the same way with theirs, even toward heaven, but yet are muddied and sullied with sin and the world, they are often corrupted with them and by them, and so decline from their first purity, faith, and holiness. Now, lest this may have been the case of any who shall read this discourse, I shall add some few cautions that are necessary to preserve men from this infection—

In the body of professors there is a great number of hypocrites. Though we cannot say of this or that man that he is so, yet that some there are is most certain. Our Savior has told us that it will be so to the end of the world. All that have oil in their lamps have it not in their vessels [Matt. 25:3]. Let men take heed how they give themselves up unto a conformity to the professors they meet with, lest, instead of saints and the best of men, they sometimes propose for their example hypocrites, which are the worst; and when they think they are like unto them who bear the image of God, they conform themselves unto those who bear the image of Satan.

You know not what may be the present temptation of those whose ways you observe. It may be they are under some peculiar desertion from God, and so are withering for a season, until he send them some refreshing showers from above. It may be they are entangled with some special corruptions, which is their burden, that you know not of; and for any voluntarily to fall into such a frame as others are cast into by the power of their temptations, or to think that will suffice in them which they see to suffice in others whose distempers they know not, is folly and presumption. He that knows such or such a person to be a living man and of a healthy constitution, if he sees him go crawling up and down about his affairs, feeble and weak, sometimes falling, sometimes standing, and making small progress in anything, will he think it sufficient for himself to do so also? Will he not inquire whether the person he sees has not lately fallen into some distemper or sickness that has weakened him and brought him into that condition? Assuredly he will so do. Take heed, Christians; many of the professors with whom you do converse are sick and wounded—the wounds of some of them do stink and are corrupt because of their folly. If you have any spiritual health, do not think their weak and uneven walking will be accepted at your hands; much less think it will be well for you to become sick and to be wounded also.

Remember that of many of the best Christians, the worst only is known and seen. Many who keep up precious communion with God do yet oftentimes, by their natural tempers of freedom or passion, not carry so glorious appearances as others who perhaps come short of them in grace and the power of godliness. In respect of their outward conversation it may seem they are scarcely saved, when in respect of their faith and love they may be eminent. They may, as the King's daughter, be all glorious within, though their clothes be not always of wrought gold. Take heed, then, that you be not infected with their worst, when you are not able, it may be, to imitate them in their best. But to return.

Sin does this work by cherishing some secret particular lust in the heart. This, the soul contends against faintly. It contends against it upon the account of sincerity; it cannot but do so: but it does not make thorough work, vigorously to mortify it by the strength and power of grace. Now, where it is thus with a soul, a habitual declension as to holiness will assuredly ensue. David shows us how, in his first days, he kept his heart close unto God: "I was upright before him, and I kept myself from mine iniquity" (Ps. 18:23). His great care was lest any one lust should prevail in him or upon him that might be called his iniquity in a peculiar manner. The same course steered Paul also (1 Cor. 9:27). He was in danger to be lifted up by his spiritual revelations and enjoyments. This makes him "keep his body in subjection," that no carnal reasonings or vain imagination might take place in him. But where indwelling sin has provoked, irritated, and given strength unto a special lust, it proves assuredly a principal means of a general declension; for as an infirmity and weakness in any one vital part will make the whole body consumptive,[17] so will the weakness in any one grace, which a perplexing lust brings with it, make the soul. It every way weakens spiritual strength. It weakens *confidence* in God in faith and prayer. The *knees* will be feeble, and the *hands* will hang down in dealing with God, where a galling and unmortified lust lies in the

[17] afflicted with consumption, a progressive wasting away of the body

heart. It will take such hold upon the *soul* that it shall not be "able to look up" (Ps. 40:12). It darkens the *mind* by innumerable foolish imaginations, which it stirs up to make provision for itself. It galls the *conscience* with those spots and stains which in and by its actings it brings upon the soul. It contends in the *will* for rule and dominion. An active, stirring corruption would have the commanding power in the soul, and it is ever and anon[18] ready to take the throne. It disturbs the thoughts, and sometimes will even frighten the soul from dealing with it by meditation, lest, corrupt affections being entangled by it, grace loses ground instead of prevailing. It breaks out oftentimes into scandalous sins, as it did in David and Hezekiah, and loads the sinner with sorrow and discouragement. By these and the like means it becomes to the soul like a moth in a garment, to eat up and devour the strongest threads of it, so that though the whole hang loose together, it is easily torn to pieces. Though the soul with whom it is thus do for a season keep up a fair profession, yet his strength is secretly devoured, and every temptation tears and rends his conscience at pleasure. It becomes with such men as it is with some who have for many years been of a sound, strong, athletic constitution. Some secret, hectical distemper seizes on them. For a season they take no notice of it, or, if they do, they think they shall do well enough with it, and easily shake it off when they have a little leisure to attend to it; but for the present, they think, as Samson with his locks cut, they will do as at other times. Sometimes, it may be, they complain that they are not well, they know not what ails them, and it may be rise violently in an opposition to their distemper; but after a while struggling in vain, the vigor of their spirits and strength failing them, they are forced to yield to the power of a consumption. And now all they can do is little enough to keep them alive. It is so with men brought into spiritual decay by any secret perplexing corruption. It may be they have had a vigorous principle of obedience and holiness. Indwelling sin watching its opportunities, by some temptation or other has kindled and inflamed some particular lust in them—for a while, it may be, they take little notice of it. Sometimes they complain, but think they will do as in former times, until, being insensibly weakened in their spiritual strength, they have work enough to do in keeping alive what remains and is ready to die (Hos. 5:13). I shall not add anything here as to the prevention and obviating this advantage of indwelling sin, having elsewhere treated of it peculiarly and apart.

It works by negligence of private communion with God in prayer and meditation. I have showed before how indwelling sin puts forth its deceit-

---

[18] again, i.e., reoccurring

fulness in diverting the soul from watchfulness in and unto these duties. Here, if it prevails, it will not fail to produce a habitual declension in the whole course of obedience. All neglect of private duties is principled by a weariness of God, as he complains, "You have not called upon me, you have been weary of me" (Isa. 43:22). Neglect of invocation proceeds from weariness; and where there is weariness, there will be withdrawing from that whereof we are weary. Now, God alone being the fountain and spring of spiritual life, if there be a weariness of him and withdrawing from him, it is impossible but that there will a decay in the life ensue. Indeed, what men are in these duties (I mean as to faith and love in them), that they are, and no more. Here lies the root of their obedience; and if this fails, all fruit will quickly fail. You may sometimes see a tree flourishing with leaves and fruit, goodly and pleasant. After a while the leaves begin to decay, the fruit to wither, the whole to droop. Search, and you shall find [that] the root, whereby it should draw in moisture and fatness[19] from the earth to supply the body and branches with sap and juice for growth and fruit, has received a wound, is [in] some way perished and does not perform its duty, so that though the branches are flourishing a while with what they had received, their sustenance being intercepted they must decay. So it is here. These duties of private communion with God are the means of receiving supplies of spiritual strength from him—of sap and fatness from Christ, the vine and olive. While they do so, the conversation and course of obedience flourishes and is fruitful—all outward duties are cheerfully and regularly performed; but if there be a wound, a defect, a failing, in that which should first take in the spiritual radical moisture, that should be communicated unto the whole, the rest may for a season maintain their station and appearance, but after a while profession will wither, fruits will decay, and the whole be ready to die. Hence our Savior lets us know: what a man is in secret, in these private duties, that he is in the eyes of God, and no more (Matt. 6:6); and one reason among others is, because they have a more vigorous acting of unmixed grace than any other duties whatsoever. In all or most particular duties, besides the influence that they may have from carnal respects, which are many, and the ways of their insinuation subtle and imperceptible, there is an alloy[20] of gifts, which sometimes even devours the pure gold of grace, which should be the chief and principal in them. In these there is immediate intercourse between God and that which is of himself in the soul. If once

[19] richness, fertility
[20] mixture

sin, by its deceits and treacheries, prevails to take off the soul from diligent attendance unto communion with God and constancy in these duties, it will not fail to effect a declining in the whole of a man's obedience. It has made its entrance, and will assuredly make good its progress.

Growing in notions of truth without answerable practice is another thing that indwelling sin makes use of to bring the souls of believers unto a decay. The apostle tell us that "knowledge puffs up" (1 Cor. 8:1). If it be alone, not improved in practice, it swells men beyond a due proportion; like a man that has a dropsy,[21] we are not to expect that he has strength to his bigness, like trees that are continually running up a head, which keeps them from bearing fruit. When once men have attained to this—that they can entertain and receive evangelical truths in a new and more glorious light or more clear discovery than formerly, or new manifestations of truth which they knew not before, and please themselves in so doing, without diligent endeavors to have the power of those truths and notions upon their hearts, and their souls made conformable unto them—they generally learn so to dispose of all truths formerly known, which were sometimes inlaid in their hearts with more efficacy and power. This has proved, if not the ruin, yet the great impairing of many in these days of light wherein we live. By this means, from humble, close walking, many have withered into an empty, barren, talking profession. All things almost have in a short season become alike unto them—have they been true or false, so they might be debating of them and disputing about them, all is well. This is food for sin; it hatches, increases it, and is increased by it. A notable way it is for the vanity that is in the mind to exert itself without a rebuke from conscience. While men are talking, and writing, and studying about religion, and hearing preaching, it may be with great delight (as those in Ezek. 33:32), [but their] conscience, unless thoroughly awake and circumspect and furnished with spiritual wisdom and care, will be very well pacified, and enter no rebukes or pleas against the way that the soul is in. But yet all this may be nothing but the acting of that natural vanity which lies in the mind, and is a principal part of the sin we treat of. And generally this is so when men content themselves, as was said, with the notions of truth, without laboring after an experience of the power of them in their hearts, and the bringing forth the fruit of them in their lives, on which a decay must needs ensue.

Growth in carnal wisdom is another help to sin in producing this sad effect. "Your wisdom and your knowledge," says the prophet, "it

[21] excessive accumulation of fluid in bodily tissue; edema

has perverted you" (Isa. 47:10). So much as carnal wisdom increases, so much faith decays. The proper work of it is to teach a man to trust to and in himself; of faith, to trust wholly in another. So it labors to destroy the whole work of faith, by causing the soul to return into a deceiving fullness of its own. We have woeful examples of the prevalency of this principle of declension in the days wherein we live. How many a poor, humble, brokenhearted creature, who followed after God in simplicity and integrity of spirit, have we seen, through the observation of the ways and walkings of others, and closing with the temptations to craft and subtlety which opportunities in the world have administered unto them, come to be dipped in a worldly, carnal frame, and utterly to wither in their profession! Many are so sullied[22] hereby that they are not known to be the men they were.

Some great sin lying long in the heart and conscience unrepented of, or not repented of as it ought, and as the matter requires, furthers indwelling sin in this work. The great turn of the life of David, whence his first ways carried the reputation, was in the harboring his great sin in his conscience without suitable repentance. It was otherwise, we know, with Peter, and he had another issue. A great sin will certainly give a great turn to the life of a professor. If it be well cured in the blood of Christ, with that humiliation which the gospel requires, it often proves a means of more watchfulness, fruitfulness, humility, and contentation,[23] than ever before the soul obtained. If it be neglected, it certainly hardens the heart, weakens spiritual strength, enfeebles the soul, discouraging it unto all communion with God, and is a notable principle of a general decay. So David complains, "My wounds stink and are corrupt because of my foolishness" (Ps. 38:5). His present distemper was not so much from his sin as his folly—not so much from the wounds he had received as from his neglect to make a timely application for their cure. It is like a broken bone, which, being well set, leaves the place stronger than before; if otherwise, makes the man a cripple all his days. These things we do but briefly name, and sundry other advantages of the like nature that sin makes use of to produce this effect might also be instanced in; but these may suffice unto our present purpose. Whatever it uses, itself is still the principle; and this is no small demonstration of its efficacy and power.

[22] tainted, marred, defiled
[23] satisfaction, reassurance

[Chapter 16]

The Effect of Sin in the Lives of Unbelievers

It is of the power and efficacy of indwelling sin, as it remains in several degrees in believers, that we are treating. Now, I have elsewhere showed that the nature and all the natural properties of it do still remain in them; though, therefore, we cannot prove directly what is the strength of sin in them, from what its power is in those in whom it is only checked and not at all weakened, yet may we, from an observation thereof, caution believers of the real power of that mortal enemy with whom they have to do.

If the plague does violently rage in one city, destroying multitudes, and there be in another an infection of the same kind, which yet arises not unto that height and fury there, by reason of the correction that it meets with from a better air and remedies used, yet a man may demonstrate unto the inhabitants the force and danger of that infection got in among them by the effects that it has and does produce among others, who have not the benefit of the preventives and preservatives which they enjoy; which will both teach them to value the means of their preservation, and be the more watchful against the power of the infection that is among them. It is so in this case. Believers may be taught what is the power and efficacy of that plague of sin which is in and among them by the effects the same plague produces in and among others, who have not those corrections of its poison and those preservatives from death which the Lord Jesus Christ has furnished them with.

Having then fixed on the demonstration of the power of sin from the effects it does produce, and having given a double instance hereof in believers themselves, I shall now further evidence the same truth or pursue the same evidence of it, by showing somewhat of the power that it acts in them who are unregenerate, and so have not the remedies against it which believers are furnished with. I shall not handle the whole power of sin in unregenerate persons, which is a very large field, and not the business I have in hand; but only, by some few instances of its effects in them, intimate, as I said, unto believers what they have to deal with—

It appears in the violence it offers to the nature of men, compelling them unto sins fully contrary to all the principles of the reasonable nature wherewith they are endued[24] *from God.* Every creature of God has in its creation a law of operation implanted in it, which is the rule of all that proceeds from

[24] endowed

it, of all that it does of its own accord. So the fire ascends upwards, bodies that are weighty and heavy descend, the water flows—each according to the principles of their nature, which give them the law of their operation. That which hinders them in their operation is force and violence; as that which hinders a stone from descending or the fire from going upwards. That which forces them to move contrary to the law of their nature, as a stone to go upwards or the fire to descend, is in its kind the greatest violence, of which the degrees are endless. Now, that which should take a great millstone and fling it upwards into the air, all would acknowledge to be a matter of wonderful force, power, and efficacy.

Man, also, has his law of operation and working concreated with him. And this may be considered two ways—either, first, as it is *common* to him with other creatures; or as *peculiar,* with reference unto that special end for which he was made. Some things are, I say, in this law of nature common to man with other creatures; as to nourish their young, to live quietly with them of the same kind and race with them—to seek and follow after that which is good for them in that state and condition wherein they are created. These are things which all brute living creatures have in the law of their nature, as man also has. But, now, besides these things, man being created in a special manner to give glory to God by rational and moral obedience, and so to obtain a reward in the enjoyment of him, there are many things in the law of his creation that are peculiar to him—as to love God above all, to seek the enjoyment of him as his chief good and last end, to inquire after his mind and will and to yield obedience and the like; all which are part of the law of his nature.

Now, these things are not distinguished so, as though a man might perform the actions of the law of his nature, which are common to him with other creatures, merely from the principles of his nature, as they do; but the law of his dependence upon God, and doing all things in obedience unto him, passes on them all also. He can never be considered as a mere creature, but as a creature made for the glory of God by rational, moral obedience—*rational,* because by him chosen, and performed with reason; and *moral,* because regulated by a law whereunto reason does attend. For instance, it is common to man with other creatures to take care for the nourishing of his children, of the young, helpless ones that receive their being by him. There is implanted in him, in the principles of his nature, concreated with them, a love and care for them; so is it with other living creatures. Now, let other creatures answer this instinct and inclination, and be not hardened against them like the foolish ostrich, into whom God has not implanted this natural wisdom (Job 39:16-17), they fully answer the law of their creation. With man it is not so. It is not enough for him to answer the instinct and secret impulse and inclination of his nature and kind, as in the nourishing of his children; but he must do it also in subjection to God, and obey him therein, and do it unto his glory—the law of moral obedience passing over all his whole being and all his operations. But in these things lie, as it were, the whole of a man, namely, in the things which are implanted in his nature as a creature, common to him with all other living creatures, seconded by the command or will of God, as he is a creature capable of yielding moral obedience and doing all things for his glory. That, then, which shall drive and compel a man to transgress this law of his nature—which is not only as to throw millstones upward, to drive beasts from taking care of their young, to take from cattle of the same kind the herding of themselves in quietness, but, moreover, to cast off, what lies in him, his fundamental dependence on God as a creature made to yield him obedience—must needs be esteemed of great force and efficacy. Now, this is frequently done by indwelling sin in persons unregenerate.

Let us take some few instances—

There is nothing that is more deeply inlaid in the principles of the natures of all living creatures, and so of man himself, than a love unto and a care for the preservation and nourishing of their young. Many brute creatures will die for them; some feed them with their own flesh and blood; all deprive themselves of that food which nature directs them to as their best, to impart it to them, and act in their behalf to the utmost of their power. Now, such is the efficacy, power, and force of indwelling sin in man—an infection that the nature of other creatures knows nothing of—that in many it prevails to stop this fountain, to beat back the stream of natural affections, to root up the principles of the law of nature, and to drive them unto a neglect, a destruction of the fruit of their own loins. Paul tells us of the old Gentiles that they were *astorgoi,* "without natural affection" (Rom. 1:31).That which he aims at is that barbarous[25] custom among the Romans, who oftentimes, to spare the trouble in the education of their children, and to be at liberty to satisfy their lusts, destroyed their own children from the womb; so far did the strength of sin prevail to obliterate the law of nature, and to repel the force and power of it. Examples of this nature are common in all nations; among ourselves, of women murdering their own children, through the deceitful reasoning of sin. And herein sin turns the strong current of nature, darkens all the light of God in the soul, controls all natural principles, influenced with the power of the command and will of God. But yet this evil has, through the efficacy of sin,

[25] uncivilized

received a fearful aggravation. Men have not only slain but cruelly sacrificed their children to satisfy their lusts. The apostle reckons idolatry, and so, consequently, all superstition, among the works of the flesh (Gal. 5:20); that is, the fruit and product of indwelling sin. Now, from hence it is that men have offered that horrid and unspeakable violence to the law of nature mentioned. (So the psalmist tells us in Psalm 106:37-38. The same is again mentioned in Ezekiel 16:20-21, and in sundry other places.) The whole manner of that abomination I have elsewhere declared.[26] For the present it may suffice to intimate that they took their children and burnt them to ashes in a soft fire; the wicked priests that assisted in the sacrifice affording them this relief, that they made a noise and clamor that the vile wretches might not hear the woeful moans and cries of the poor, dying, tormented infants. I suppose in this case we need no further evidence. Naturalists can give no rational account, they can only admire the secret force of that little fish which, they say, will stop a ship in full sail in the midst of the sea; and we must acknowledge that it is beyond our power to give an account of that secret force and unsearchable deceit that is in that inbred traitor, sin, that can not only stop the course of nature, when all the sails of it, that carry it forward, are so filled as they are in that of affections to children, but also drive it backward with such a violence and force as to cause men so to deal with their own children as a good man would not be hired with any reward to deal with his dog. And it may not be to the disadvantage of the best to know and consider that they carry that about them and in them which in others has produced these effects.

The like may be spoken of all other sins against the prime dictates of the law of nature, that mankind is or has been stained and defamed with—murder of parents and children, of wives and husbands, sodomy, incest, and the like enormities; in all which sin prevails in men against the whole law of their being and dependence upon God. What should I reckon up the murders of Cain and Abel, the treason of Judas, with their aggravations; or remind the filth and villainy of Nero, in whom sin seemed to design an instance of what it could debase the nature of man unto? In a word, all the studied, premeditated perjuries; all the designed, bloody revenges; all the filth and uncleanness; all the enmity to God and his ways that is in the world—is fruit growing from this root alone.

It evidences its efficacy in keeping men off from believing under the dispensation of the gospel. This evidence must be a little further cleared—

Under the dispensation of the gospel, there are but few that do believe.

[26] See, for example, chapter 4 of Owen's *A Dissertation on Divine Justice* (*Works,* 10:525-541).

So the preachers of it complain, "Who has believed our report?" (Isa. 53:1), which the apostle interprets of the paucity[27] of believers (John 12:38). Our Savior, Christ himself, tells us that "many are called"—the word is preached unto many—"but few are chosen" [Matt. 22:14]. And so the church complains of its number (Mic. 7:1). Few there be who enter the narrow gate [Matt. 7:14]; daily experience confirms this woeful observation. How many villages, parishes, yea, towns, may we go unto where the gospel, it may be, has been preached many years, and perhaps scarce meet a true believer in them, and one who shows forth the death of Christ in his conversation! In the best places, and most eminent for profession, are not such persons like the berries after the shaking of an olive-tree—two or three in the top of the uppermost boughs, and four or five in the highest branches?

There is proposed to men in the preaching of the gospel, as motives unto believing, everything in conjunction that severally prevails with men to do whatever else they do in their lives. Whatever anyone does with consideration, he does it either because it is reasonable and good for him so to do, or profitable and advantageous, or pleasant, or, lastly, necessary for the avoidance of evil; whatever, I say, men do with consideration, whether it be good or evil, whether it be in the works of this life or in things that lead to another, they do it from one or other of the reasons or motives mentioned. And, God knows, oftentimes they are very poor and mean in their kind that men are prevailed upon by. How often will men, for a very little pleasure, a very little profit, be induced to do that which shall embitter their lives and damn their souls; and what industry will they use to avoid that which they apprehend evil or grievous to them! And any one of these is enough to oil the wheels of men's utmost endeavors, and set men at work to the purpose. But now all these things center in the proposal of the gospel and the command of believing; and every one of them in a kind that the whole world can propose nothing like unto it—

It is the *most reasonable* thing that can be proposed to the understanding of a man, that he who, through his own default, has lost that way of bringing glory to God and saving his own soul (for which ends he was made) that he was first placed in, should accept of and embrace that other blessed, easy, safe, excellent way for the attaining of the ends mentioned, which God, in infinite grace, love, mercy, wisdom, and righteousness, has found out, and does propose unto him. And—

It is the *most profitable* thing that a man can possibly be invited unto,

[27] smallness of number

if there be any profit or benefit, any advantage, in the forgiveness of sins, in the love and favor of God, in a blessed immortality, in eternal glory. And—

It is *most pleasant* also. Surely it is a pleasant thing to be brought out of darkness into light—out of a dungeon unto a throne—from captivity and slavery to Satan and cursed lusts, to the glorious liberty of the children of God, with a thousand heavenly sweetnesses not now to be mentioned. And—

It is *surely necessary,* and that not only from the command of God, who has the supreme authority over us, but also indispensably so, for the avoidance of eternal ruin of body and soul (Mark 16:16). It is constantly proposed under these terms: "Believe, or you perish under the weight of the wrath of the great God, and that forevermore." But now, notwithstanding that all these considerations are preached unto men, and pressed upon them in the name of the great God from day to day, from one year to another, yet, as was before observed, very few there are who set their hearts unto them, so as to embrace that which they lead unto. Tell men ten thousand times that this is wisdom, yea, riches—that all their profit lies in it—that they will assuredly and eternally perish, and that, it may be, within a few hours, if they receive not the gospel; assure them that it is their only interest and concern; let them know that God himself speaks all this unto them—yet all is one, they regard it not, set not their hearts unto it, but, as it were, plainly say, "We will have nothing to do with these things." They will rather perish in their lusts than accept of mercy.

It is indwelling sin that both disenables men unto and hinders them from believing, and that alone. Blindness of mind, stubbornness of the will, sensuality of the affections, all concur to keep poor perishing souls at a distance from Christ. Men are made blind by sin, and cannot see his excellencies; obstinate, and will not lay hold of his righteousness; senseless, and take no notice of their own eternal concerns. Now, certainly that which can prevail with men wise, and sober, and prudent in other things, to neglect and despise the love of God, the blood of Christ, the eternal welfare of their own souls, upon weak and worthless pretenses, must be acknowledged to have an astonishable force and efficacy accompanying it.

Whose heart, who has once heard of the ways of God, can but bleed to see poor souls eternally perishing under a thousand gracious invitations to accept of mercy and pardon in the blood of Christ? And can we but be astonished at the power of that principle from whence it is that they run headlong to their own destruction? And yet all this befalls them from the power and deceit of sin that dwells in them.

It is evident in their total apostasies. Many men not really converted are much wrought upon by the word. The apostle tells us that they do "clean escape from them that live in error" (2 Pet. 2:18). They separate themselves from idolatry and false worship, owning and professing the truth: and they also escape the "pollutions of the world" (v. 20); that is, "the corruption that is in the world through lust," as he expresses it (2 Pet. 1:4)—those filthy, corrupt, and unclean ways which the men of the world, in the pursuit of their lusts, do walk and live in. These they escape from, in the amendment[28] of their lives and ordering of their conversation according to the convictions which they have from the word; for so he tells us that all this is brought about "through the knowledge of the Lord and Savior Jesus Christ"—that is, by the preaching of the gospel. They are so far wrought upon as to forsake all ways of false worship, to profess the truth, to reform their lives, and to walk answerable to the convictions that are upon them. By this means do they gain the reputation of professors: "They have a name to live" (Rev. 3:1), and are made "partakers" of some or all of those privileges of the gospel that are numbered by the apostle (Heb. 6:4-5). It is not my present business to show how far or wherein a man may be effectually wrought upon by the word, and yet not be really wrought over to close with Christ, or what may be the utmost bounds and limits of a common work of grace upon unregenerate men. It is on all hands confessed that it may be carried on so far that it is very difficult to discern between its effects and productions and those of that grace which is special and saving. But now, notwithstanding all this, we see many of these daily fall off from God, utterly and wickedly; some into debauchery and uncleanness, some to worldliness and covetousness, some to be persecutors of the saints—all to the perdition[29] of their own souls. How this comes about the apostle declares in that place mentioned. "They are," says he, "entangled again." To entice and entangle (as I have showed before from James 1:14-15) is the proper work of indwelling sin; it is that alone which entangles the soul, as the apostle speaks (2 Pet. 2:18, 20). They are allured from their whole profession into cursed apostasy through the lusts of the flesh. It prevails upon them, through its deceit and power, to an utter relinquishment of their profession and their whole engagement unto God. And this several ways evinces the greatness of its strength and efficacy—

In that it gives stop or control unto that exceeding greatness of power which is put forth in the word in their conviction and reformation. We see it by experience that men are not easily wrought upon by the word; the most

[28] moral improvement, reformation
[29] ruin, damnation, destruction

of men can live under the dispensation of it all the days of their lives, and continue as senseless and stupid as the seats they sit upon, or the flint in the rock of stone. Mighty difficulties and prejudices must be conquered, great strokes must be given to the conscience, before this can be brought about. It is as the stopping of a river in his course, and turning his streams another way; the hindering of a stone in his falling downwards; or the turning away of the wild ass, when furiously set to pursue his way, as the prophet speaks (Jer. 2:24). To turn men from their corrupt ways, sins, and pleasures; to make them pray, fast, hear, and do many things contrary to the principle of flesh, which is secretly predominant in them, willingly and gladly; to cause them to profess Christ and the gospel, it may be under some trials and reproaches; to give them light to see into sundry mysteries, and gifts for the discharge of sundry duties; to make dead, blind, senseless men to walk, and talk, and do all the outward offices and duties of living and healthy men, with the like attendancies of conviction and reformation, are the effects and products of mighty power and strength. Indeed, the power that the Holy Ghost puts forth by the word, in the staggering and conviction of sinners, in the wakening of their consciences, the enlightening of their minds, the changing of their affections, the awing of their hearts, the reforming of their lives and compelling them to duties, is inexpressible. But now unto all these is there check and control given by indwelling sin. It prevails against this whole work of the Spirit by the word, with all the advantages of providential dispensations, in afflictions and mercies, wherewith it is attended. When sin is once enraged, all these things become but like the withes and cords wherewith Samson was bound before his head was shaven. Cry but to it, "The Philistines are upon you; there is a subtle, a suitable temptation; now show your strength and efficacy"—all these things become like tow that has smelt the fire[30]; conscience is stifled, reputation in the church of God despised, light supplanted, the impressions of the word cast off, convictions digested, heaven and hell are despised: sin makes its way through all, and utterly turns the soul from the good and right ways of God. Sometimes it does this subtly, by imperceptible degrees, taking off all force of former impressions from the Spirit by the word, sullying conscience by degrees, hardening the heart, and making sensual the affections by various workings, that the poor backslider in heart scarce knows what he is doing, until he comes to the very bottom of all impiety, profaneness, and enmity against God. Sometimes, falling in conjunction with some vigorous

[30] coarse flax (tow) that has been charred or, perhaps, has caused the fire to smolder

temptation, it suddenly and at once plunges the soul into a course of alienation from God and the profession of his ways.

It takes them off from those hopes of heaven which, upon their convictions, obedience, and temporary faith or believing, they had attained. There is a general hope of heaven, or at least of the escaping of hell, of an untroublesome immortality, in the most sottish[31] and stupid souls in the world, who, either by tradition or instruction from the word, are persuaded that there is another state of things to come after this life; but it is, in unconvinced, unenlightened persons, a dull, senseless, unaffecting thing, that has no other hold upon them nor power in them but only to keep them free from the trouble and perplexity of contrary thoughts and apprehensions. The matter is otherwise with them who by the word are so wrought upon as we have before declared; their hope of heaven and a blessed immortality is oftentimes accompanied with great joys and exultations, and is a relief unto them under and against the worst of their fears and trials. It is such as they would not part with for all the world; and upon all occasions they retreat in their minds unto it for comfort and relief.

Now, all this by the power of sin are they prevailed with to forego. Let heaven go if it will, a blessed immortality with the enjoyment of God himself, sin must be served, and provision made to fulfill the lusts thereof. If a man, in the things of this world, had such a hope of a large inheritance, of a kingdom, as wherein he is satisfied that it will not fail him, but that in the issue he shall surely enjoy it, and lead a happy and a glorious life in the possession of it many days; if one should go to him and tell him, "It is true, the kingdom you look for is an ample and honorable dominion, full of all good things desirable, and you may attain it; but come, cast away all hopes and expectations of it, and come join with me in the service and slavery of such or such an oppressing tyrant"—you will easily grant he must have some strange bewitching power with him, that should prevail with a man in his wits to follow his advice. Yet thus it is, and much more so, in the case we have in hand. Sin itself cannot deny but that the kingdom of heaven, which the soul is in hope and expectation of, is glorious and excellent, nor does it go about to convince him that his thoughts of it are vain and such as will deceive him, but plainly prevails with him to cast away his hopes, to despise his kingdom that he was in expectation of, and that upon no other motive but that he may serve some worldly, cruel, or filthy and sensual lust. Certainly here lies a secret efficacy whose depths cannot be fathomed.

[31] foolish, especially as it relates to drunkenness

The apostle manifests the power of the entanglements of sin in and upon apostates, in that it turns them off from the way of righteousness after they have known it (2 Pet. 2:21). It will be found at the last day an evil thing and a bitter [thing] that men live all their days in the service of sin, self, and the world, refusing to make any trial of the ways of God, whereunto they are invited. Though they have no experience of their excellency, beauty, pleasantness, safety; yet, having evidence brought unto them from God himself that they are so, the refusal of them will, I say, be bitterness in the latter end. But their condition is yet far worse, who, as the apostle speaks, "having known the way of righteousness," are by the power of indwelling sin "turned aside from the holy commandment." To leave God for the devil, after a man has made some trial of him and his service—heaven for hell, after a man has had some cheering, refreshing thoughts of it—the fellowship of the saints for an ale-house or a brothel-house, after a man has been admitted unto their communion, and tasted of the pleasantness of it; to leave walking in pure, clear, straight paths, to wallow in mire, draughts and filth—this will be for a lamentation: yet this does sin prevail upon apostates unto; and that against all their light, conviction, experiences, professions, engagements, or whatever may be strong upon them to keep them up to the known ways of righteousness.

It evinces its strength in them by prevailing with them unto a total renunciation of God as revealed in Christ, and the power of all gospel truth—in the sin against the Holy Ghost. I do not now precisely determine what is the sin against the Holy Ghost, nor wherein it does consist. There are different apprehensions of it. All agree in this, that by it an end is put to all dealings between God and man in a way of grace. It is a sin unto death. And this does the hardness and blindness of many men's hearts bring them to; they are by them at length set out of the reach of mercy. They choose to have no more to do with God; and God swears that they shall never enter into his rest: so sin brings forth death. A man by it is brought to renounce the end for which he was made, willfully to reject the means of his coming to the enjoyment of God, to provoke him to his face, and so to perish in his rebellion. I have not mentioned these things as though I hoped by them to set out to the full the power of indwelling sin in unregenerate men; only by a few instances I thought to give a glimpse of it. He that would have a fuller view of it had need only to open his eyes, to take a little view of that wickedness which reigns, yea, rages all the world over. Let him consider the prevailing flood of the things mentioned by Paul to be "the fruits of the flesh" (Gal. 5:19-21)—that is, among the sons of men, in all places, nations, cities, towns, parishes; and then let him add thereunto but this one consideration, that the world, which is full of the steam, filth, and blood of these abominations, as to their outward actings of them, is a pleasant garden, a paradise, compared to the heart of man, wherein they are all conceived, and hourly millions of more vile abominations, which, being stifled in the womb by some of the ways before insisted on, they are never able to bring forth to light—let a man, I say, using the law for his light and rule, take this course, and if he have any spiritual discerning, he may quickly attain satisfaction in this matter. And I showed in the entrance of this discourse how this consideration does fully confirm the truth proposed.

[Chapter 17]

The Strength of Indwelling Sin Evidenced by Its Resistance to the Power of the Law

The measure of the strength of any person or defensed city may be well taken from the opposition that they are able to withstand and not be prevailed against. If we hear of a city that has endured a long siege from a potent enemy, and yet is not taken or conquered, whose walls have endured great batteries and are not demolished, though we have never seen the place, yet we conclude it [is] strong, if not impregnable.

And this consideration will also evidence the power and strength of indwelling sin. It is able to hold out, and not only to live, but also to secure its reign and dominion, against very strong opposition that is made to it. I shall instance only in the opposition that is made unto it by the law, which is oftentimes great and terrible, always fruitless; all its assaults are borne by it, and it is not prevailed against. *There are sundry things wherein the law opposes itself to sin, and the power of it;* as—

It discovers it. Sin in the soul is like a secret hectical distemper in the body—its being unknown and unperceived is one great means of its prevalency; or as traitors in a civil state—while they lie hid, they vigorously carry on their design. The greatest part of men in the world know nothing of this sickness, yea, death of their souls. Though they have been taught somewhat of the doctrine of it, yet they know nothing of its power. They know it not so as to deal with it as their mortal enemy, as a man, whatever he be told, cannot be said to know that he has a hectical fever, if he love his life, and set not himself to stop its progress. This, then, the law does—it discovers this enemy; it convinces the soul that there is such a traitor harboring in its bosom: "I had not known sin, but by the law: for I had not known lust, except the law had said, You shall not covet" (Rom. 7:7). "I had not known it," that is, fully, clearly, distinctly. Conscience will somewhat tumultuate about it; but a man cannot know it clearly and distinctly from thence. It gives a man such a sight of it as the blind man had in the gospel upon the first touch of his eyes: "He saw men like trees walking" [Mark 8:24]—obscurely, confusedly. But when the law comes, that gives the soul a distinct sight of this indwelling sin. Again, "I had not known it," that is, the depths of it, the root, the habitual inclination of my nature to sin, which is here called "lust" (as it is in James 1:14). "I had not known it," or not known it to be sin, "but by the law." This, then, the law does—it draws out this traitor from secret lurking places, the intimate recedes of the soul. A man, when the law comes, is no more ignorant of his enemy. If he will now perish by him, it is openly and knowingly; he cannot but say that the law warned him of him, discovered him unto him, yea, and raised a concourse[32] about him in the soul of various affections, as an officer does that discovers a thief or robber, calling out for assistance to apprehend him.

The law not only discovers sin, but discovers it to be a very bad inmate, dangerous, yea, pernicious to the soul: "Was then that which is good"—that is, the law—"made death unto me? God forbid. But sin, that it might appear sin, working death in me by that which is good; that sin by the commandment might become exceeding sinful" (Rom. 7:13). There are many things in this verse wherein we are not at present concerned: that which I only aim at is the manifestation of sin by the law—it appears to be sin; and the manifestation of it in its own colors—it appears to be exceeding sinful. The law gives the soul to know the filth and guilt of this indwelling sin—how great they are, how vile it is, what an abomination, what an enmity to God, how hated of him. The soul shall never more look upon it as a small matter, whatsoever thoughts it had of it before, whereby it is greatly surprised. As a man that finds himself somewhat distempered, sending for a physician of skill, when he comes requires his judgment of his distemper; he, considering his condition, tells him, "Alas! I am sorry for you; the case is far otherwise with you than you imagine: your disease is mortal, and it has proceeded so far, pressing upon your spirits and infecting the whole mass of your blood, that I doubt, unless most effectual remedies be used, you will live but a very few hours"—so it is in this case. A man may have some trouble in his mind and conscience about indwelling sin; he finds all not so well as it should be with him, more from the effects of sin and its continual eruptions than the nature of it, which he hopes to wrestle with. But now, when

[32] running together, flowing together, meeting of things

the law comes, that lets the soul know that its disease is deadly and mortal, that it is exceeding sinful, as being the root and cause of all his alienation from God; and thus also the law proceeds against it.

The law judges the person, or lets the sinner plainly know what he is to expect upon the account of this sin. This is the law's proper work; its discovering property is but preparative to its judging. The law is itself when it is in the throne. Here it minces not the matter with sinners, as we use to do one with another, but tells him plainly, "'You' are the 'man' in whom this exceeding sinful sin does dwell, and you must answer for the guilt of it." And this, methinks, if anything, should rouse up a man to set himself in opposition to it, yea, utterly to destroy it. The law lets him know that upon the account of this sin he is obnoxious to the curse and wrath of the great God against him; yea, pronounces the sentence of everlasting condemnation upon him upon that account. "Abide in this state and perish," is its language. It leaves not the soul without this warning in this world, and will leave it without excuse on that account in the world to come.

The law so follows on its sentence, that it disquiets and affrights the soul, and suffers it not to enjoy the least rest or quietness in harboring its sinful inmate. Whenever the soul has indulged to its commands, made provision for it, immediately the law flies upon it with the wrath and terror of the Lord, makes it quake and tremble. It shall have no rest, but is like a poor beast that has a deadly arrow sticking in its sides, that makes it restless wherever it is and whatsoever it does.

The law stays not here, but also it slays the soul (Rom. 7:9); that is, by its conviction of the nature, power, and desert of this indwelling sin, it deprives him in whom it is of all that life of self-righteousness and hope which formerly he sustained himself with—it leaves him as a poor, dead, helpless, hopeless creature; and all this in the pursuit of that opposition that it makes against this sin. May we not now expect that the power of it will be quelled and its strength broken—that it will die away before these strokes of the law of God? But the truth is, such is its power and strength that it is quite otherwise. Like him whom the poets feign[33] to be born of the earth, when one thought to slay him by casting him on the ground, by every fall he recovered new strength, and was more vigorous than formerly[34]; so is it with all the falls and repulses that are given to indwelling sin by the law: for—

[33] pretend, imagine, as in fictional writing

[34] referring to Antaeus, son of Poseidon and Gaia, who was later killed in mid-air by Hercules, who discovered Antaeus's secret

It is not conquered. A conquest infers two things in respect of the conquered—first, *loss of dominion;* and, secondly, *loss of strength.* Whenever anyone is conquered he is despoiled[35] of both these; he loses both his authority and his power. So the strong man armed, being prevailed against, he is bound, and his goods are spoiled. But now neither of these befalls indwelling sin by the assaults of the law. It loses not one jot of its dominion nor strength by all the blows that are given unto it. The law cannot do this thing (Rom. 8:3); it cannot deprive sin of its power and dominion, for he that "is under the law is also under sin"—that is, whatever power the law gets upon the conscience of a man, so that he fear to sin, lest the sentence and curse of it should befall him, yet sin still reigns and rules in his heart. Therefore says the apostle, "Sin shall not have dominion over you: for you are not under the law, but under grace" (Rom. 6:14); intimating plainly, that though a person be in never so much subjection to the authority of the law, yet that will not exempt and acquit him from the dominion of sin. Yea, the law, by all its work upon the soul, instead of freeing and acquitting it from the reign of sin and bondage unto it, does accidentally[36] greatly increase its misery and bondage, as the sentence of the judge on the bench against a malefactor[37] adds to his misery. The soul is under the dominion of sin, and, it may be, abides in its woeful condition in much security, fearing neither sin nor judgment. The law setting upon him in this condition, by all the ways aforementioned, brings him into great trouble and perplexity, fear and terror, but delivers him not at all. So that it is with the soul as it was with the Israelites when Moses had delivered his message unto Pharaoh; they were so far from getting liberty by it that their bondage was increased, and "they found that they were in a very evil case" (Ex. 5:19). Yea, and we shall see that sin does like Pharaoh; finding its rule disturbed, it grows more outrageously oppressive and doubles the bondage of their souls. This is not, then, the work of the law, to destroy sin, or deprive it of that dominion which it has by nature. Nor does it, by all these strokes of the law, lose anything of its strength; it continues both its authority and its force; it is neither destroyed nor weakened; yea—

It is so far from being conquered that it is only enraged. The whole work of the law does only provoke and enrage sin, and cause it, as it has opportunity, to put out its strength with more power, and vigor, and force than formerly. This the apostle shows at large, Romans 7:9-13. But you will say,

[35] robbed, plundered
[36] non-essentially, incidentally
[37] criminal

"Do we not see it by experience, that many are wrought upon by the preaching of the law to a relinquishment of many sins and amendment of their lives, and to a great contending against the eruptions of those other corruptions which they cannot yet mortify? And it cannot be denied but that great is the power and efficacy of the law when preached and applied to the conscience in a due manner." I answer—

It is acknowledged that *very great and effectual is the power of the law of God.* Great are the effects that are wrought by it, and it shall surely accomplish every end for which of God it is appointed. But yet the subduing of sin is none of its work—it is not designed of God unto that purpose; and therefore it is no dishonor if it cannot do that which is not its proper work (Rom. 8:3).

Whatever effects it have upon some, yet we see that in the most, such is the power and prevalency of sin, that it takes no impression at all upon them. May you not see everywhere men living many years in congregations where the law is powerfully preached, and applied unto the consciences as to all the ends and purposes for which the Lord is pleased to make use of it, and not once be moved by it—that receive no more impression from the stroke of it than blows with a straw would give to an adamant?[38] They are neither convinced by it, nor terrified, nor awed, nor instructed; but continue deaf, ignorant, senseless, secure, as if they had never been told of the guilt of sin or terror of the Lord. Such as these are congregations full of, who proclaim the triumphing power of sin over the dispensation of the law.

When any of the effects mentioned are wrought, it is not from the power of the letter of the law, but from the actual efficacy of the Spirit of God putting forth his virtue and power for that end and purpose; and we deny not but that the Spirit of the Lord is able to restrain and quell the power of lust when he pleases, and some ways whereby he is pleased so to do we have formerly considered. But—

Notwithstanding all that may be observed of the power of the law upon the souls of men, yet it is most evident that lust is not conquered, not subdued, nor mortified by it; for—

Though the course of sin may be repelled for a season by the dispensation of the law, yet the spring and fountain of it is not dried up thereby. Though it withdraws and hides itself for a season, it is, as I have elsewhere showed, but to shift out of a storm, and then to return again. As a traveler, in his way meeting with a violent storm of thunder and rain, immediately

---

[38] a diamond or any very hard substance

turns out of his way to some house or tree for his shelter, but yet this causes him not to give over his journey—so soon as the storm is over he returns to his way and progress again; so it is with men in bondage unto sin. They are in a course of pursuing their lusts; the law meets with them in a storm of thunder and lightning from heaven, terrifies and hinders them in their way. This turns them for a season out of their course; they will run to prayer or amendment of life, for some shelter from the storm of wrath which is feared coming upon their consciences. But is their course stopped? Are their principles altered? Not at all; so soon as the storm is over, [so] that they begin to wear out that sense and the terror that was upon them, they return to their former course in the service of sin again. This was the state with Pharaoh once and again.

In such seasons sin is not conquered, but diverted. When it seems to fall under the power of the law, indeed it is only turned into a new channel; it is not dried up. If you go and set a dam against the streams of a river, so that you suffer no water to pass in the old course and channel, but it breaks out another way, and turns all its streams in a new course, you will not say you have dried up that river, though some that come and look into the old channel may think, perhaps, that the waters are utterly gone. So is it in this case. The streams of sin, it may be, run in open sensuality and profaneness, in drunkenness and viciousness; the preaching of the law sets a dam against these courses—conscience is terrified, and the man dares not walk in the ways wherein he has been formerly engaged. His companions in sin, not finding him in his old ways, begin to laugh at him, as one that is converted and growing precise; professors themselves begin to be persuaded that the work of God is upon his heart, because they see his old streams dried up: but if there have been only a work of the law upon him, there is a dam put to his course, but the spring of sin is not dried up, only the streams of it are turned another way. It may be the man is fallen upon other more secret or more spiritual sins; or if he be beat from them also, the whole strength of lust and sin will take up its residence in self-righteousness, and pour out thereby as filthy streams as in any other way whatsoever. So that notwithstanding the whole work of the law upon the souls of men, indwelling sin will keep alive in them still: which is another evidence of its great power and strength. I shall yet touch upon some other evidences of the same truth that I have under consideration; but I shall be brief in them.

In the next place, then, *the great endeavors of men ignorant of the righteousness of Christ, for the subduing and mortifying of sin, which are all fruitless, do evidence the great strength and power of it.* Men who have no strength against sin may yet be made sensible of the strength of sin. The way whereby, for the most part, they come to that knowledge is by some previous sense that they have of the guilt of sin. This men have by the light of their consciences; they cannot avoid it. This is not a thing in their choice; whether they will or not, they cannot but know sin to be evil, and that such an evil that renders them obnoxious to the judgment of God. This galls the minds and consciences of some so far as that they are kept in awe, and dare not sin as they would. Being awed with a sense of the guilt of sin and the terror of the Lord, men begin to endeavor to abstain from sin, at least from such sins as they have been most terrified about. While they have this design in hand, the strength and power of sin begins to discover itself unto them. They begin to find that there is something in them that is not in their own power; for, notwithstanding their resolutions and purposes, they sin still, and that so, or in such a manner, as that their consciences inform them that they must therefore perish eternally. This puts them on self-endeavors to suppress the eruption of sin, because they cannot be quiet unless so they do, nor have any rest or peace within. Now, being ignorant of that only way whereby sin is to be mortified—that is, by the Spirit of Christ—they fix on many ways in their own strength to suppress it, if not to slay it; as being ignorant of that only way whereby consciences burdened with the guilt of sin may be pacified—that is, by the blood of Christ—they endeavor, by many other ways, to accomplish that end in vain: for no man, by any self-endeavors, can obtain peace with God. Some of the ways whereby they endeavor to suppress the power of sin, which casts them into an unquiet condition, and their insufficiency for that end, we must look into—

They will promise and bind themselves by vows from those sins which they have been most liable unto, and so have been most perplexed with. The psalmist shows this to be one great engine whereby false and hypocritical persons do endeavor to extricate and deliver themselves out of trouble and perplexity. They make promises to God, which he calls flattering him with the mouth (Ps. 78:36). So is it in this case. Being freshly galled with the guilt of any sin, that, by the power of their temptations, they, it may be, have frequently been overtaken in, they vow and promise that, at least for some such space of time as they will limit, they will not commit that sin again; and this course of proceeding is prescribed unto them by some who pretend to direct their consciences in this duty. Conscience of this now makes them watch over themselves as to the outward act of the sin that they are galled with; and so it has one of these two effects—for either they do abstain from it for the time they have prefixed, or they do not. If they do not, as seldom they do, especially if it be a sin that has a peculiar root in their nature and constitution, and is improved by custom into a habit, if any suitable temptation be presented unto them, their sin is increased, and therewith their terror, and they are woefully discouraged in making any opposition to sin; and therefore, for the most part, after one or two vain attempts, or more, it may be, knowing no other way to mortify sin but this of vowing against it, and keeping of that vow in their own strength, they give over all contests, and become wholly the servants of sin, being bounded only by outward considerations, without any serious endeavors for a recovery. Or, secondly, suppose that they have success in their resolutions, and do abstain from actual sins their appointed season, commonly one of these two things ensues—either they think that they have well discharged their duty, and so may a little now, at least for a season, indulge to their corruptions and lusts, and so are entangled again in the same snares of sin as formerly; or else they reckon that their vow and promise has preserved them, and so sacrifice to their own net and drag, setting up a righteousness of their own against the grace of God—which is so far from weakening indwelling sin, that it strengthens it in the root and principle, that it may hereafter reign in the soul in security. Or, at the most, the best success that can be imagined unto this way of dealing with sin is but the restraining of some outward eruptions of it, which tends nothing to the weakening of its power; and therefore such persons, by all their endeavors, are very far from being freed from the inward toiling, burning, disquieting, perplexing power of sin. And this is the state of most men that are kept in bondage under the power of conviction. Hell, death, and the wrath of God, are continually presented unto their consciences; this makes them labor with all their strength against that in sin which most enrages their consciences and most increases their fears—that is, the actual eruption of it: for, for the most part, while they are freed from that they are safe, though, in the meantime, sin lies tumultuating in and defiling of the heart continually. As with running sores, outward repelling medicines may skin them over, and hinder their corruption from coming forth, but the issue of them is that they cause them to fester inwardly, and so prove, though it may be not so noisome and offensive as they were before, yet far more dangerous: so is it with this repelling of the power of corruption by men's vows and promises against it—external eruptions are, it may be, restrained for a season, but the inward root and principle is not weakened in the least. And most commonly this is the issue of this way: that sin, having gotten more strength, and being enraged by its restraint, breaks all its bounds, and captivates the soul unto all filthy abominations; which is the principle, as was before observed, of most of the visible apostasies which we have in the world (2 Pet. 2:19-20). The Holy Ghost compares sinners, because of the odious, fierce, poisonous nature of this indwelling sin, unto lions, bears, and asps (Isa. 11:6-9). Now, this is the excellency of gospel grace, that it changes the nature and inward principles of these otherwise passionate and untamed beasts, making the wolf as the kid, the lion as the lamb, and the bear as the cow. When this is effected, they may safely be trusted in—"a little child may lead them" [Isa. 11:6]. But these self-endeavors do not at all change the nature, but restrain their outward violence. He that takes a lion or a wolf and shuts him up from ravening,[39] while yet his inward violence remains, may well expect that at one time or other they will break their bonds, and fall to their former ways of rapine and violence. However shutting them up does not, as we see, change their natures, but only restrain their rage from doing open spoil. So it is in this case: it is grace alone that changes the heart and takes away that poison and fierceness that is in them by nature; men's self-endeavors do but coerce them as to some outward eruptions. But—

Beyond bare vows and promises, with some watchfulness to observe them in a rational use of ordinary means, men have put, and some do yet put, themselves on extraordinary ways of mortifying sin. This is the foundation of all that has a show of wisdom and religion in the papacy: their hours of prayer, fastings; their immuring[40] and cloistering themselves; their pilgrimages, penances, and self-torturing discipline—spring all from this root. I shall not speak of the innumerable evils that have attended these self-invented ways of mortification, and how they all of them have been turned into means, occasions, and advantages of sinning; nor of the horrible hypocrisy which evidently cleaves unto the most of their observers; nor of that superstition which gives life to them all, being a thing riveted in the natures of some and their constitutions, fixed on others by inveterate[41] prejudices, and the same by others taken up for secular advantages. But I will suppose the best that can be made of it, and it will be found to be a self-invented design of men ignorant of the righteousness of God, to give a check to this power of indwelling sin whereof we speak. And it is almost incredible what fearful self-macerations[42] and horrible sufferings this design has carried men out unto; and, undoubtedly, their blind zeal and superstition will rise in judgment and condemn the horrible sloth and negligence of the most of them to whom the Lord has granted the saving light of the gospel. But what is the end of these things?

[39] seeking prey, devouring
[40] confining within walls
[41] hardened, habitual, deep-rooted
[42] self-inflicted starvation, emaciation

The apostle, in brief, gives us an account (Rom. 9:31-32). They attain not the righteousness aimed at; they come not up unto a conformity to the law: sin is not mortified, no, nor the power of it weakened; but what it loses in sensual, in carnal pleasures, it takes up with great advantage in blindness, darkness, superstition, self-righteousness, and soul-pride, contempt of the gospel and the righteousness of it, and reigns no less than in the most profligate sinners in the world.

The strength, efficacy, and power of this law of sin may be further evidenced from its life and in-being in the soul, notwithstanding the wound that is given unto it in the first conversion of the soul to God; and in the continual opposition that is made unto it by grace. But this is the subject and design of another endeavor.

It may now be expected that we should here add the special uses of all this discovery that has been made of the power, deceit, prevalency, and success of this great adversary of our souls. But as for what concerns that humility, self-abasement, watchfulness, diligence, and application unto the Lord Christ for relief, which will become those who find in themselves, by experience, the power of this law of sin, [these] have been occasionally mentioned and inculcated through the whole preceding discourse; so, for what concerns the actual mortification of it, I shall only recommend unto the reader, for his direction, another small treatise, written long since, unto that purpose, which I suppose he may do well to consider together with this, if he find these things to be his concern.[43] "To the only wise God our Savior, be glory and majesty, dominion and power, both now and ever. Amen" [Rom. 16:27].

---

[43] See Owen's *Of the Mortification of Sin in Believers,* reprinted in this volume.

OUTLINES

AS MUCH AS POSSIBLE, the following outlines are derived from Owen's original system, by which he numbered virtually every point in his discourse. We've attempted to convert this into a comprehensive outline of his arguments so that large swaths of argumentation can be seen at a glance. Our hope is that these outlines will aid you in following his arguments and train of thought. We have also included page numbers embedded into the outline, so that you can easily flip back and forth between the outline and the discourse.

OF THE MORTIFICATION OF SIN IN BELIEVERS

Part 1: The Necessity of Mortification

(Chapter 4)

III. The life, vigor, and comfort of our spiritual life depend much on our mortification of sin (p. 63)
  A. Life, vigor, and comfort are not necessarily connected to mortification (p. 63)
  B. Adoption and justification, not mortification, are the immediate causes of life, vigor, and comfort (p. 64)
  C. However, in the ordinary relationship with God, the vigor and comfort of our spiritual lives depend much on our mortification of sin (p. 64)
    1. Mortification alone keeps sin from depriving us of vigor and comfort (p. 64)
      a) Every unmortified sin will weaken the soul and deprive it of its vigor (p. 64)
        (1) It untunes and unframes the heart itself, by entangling its affections (p. 64)
        (2) It fills the thoughts with contrivances about it (p. 65)
        (3) It breaks out and actually hinders duty (p. 65)
      b) Every unmortified sin will darken the soul and deprive it of its comfort and peace (p. 65)
    2. Mortification prunes all the graces of God and makes room for them in our hearts to grow (p. 65)
    3. As to our peace; as there is nothing that has any evidence of sincerity without it, so I know nothing that has such an evidence of sincerity in it (p. 66)

Part 2: The Nature of Mortification

(Chapter 5)

I. The nature of mortification (p. 69)
  A. What mortification is not (p. 69)
    1. Mortification is not the utter destruction and death of sin (p. 69)
    2. Mortification is not the dissimulation of a sin (p. 70)
    3. Mortification is not the improvement of a quiet, sedate nature (p. 70)
    4. Mortification is not the diversion of sin (p. 71)
    5. Mortification is not just occasional conquests over sin (p. 71)

(Chapter 6)

  B. What mortification is (p. 73)
    1. Mortification consists in a habitual weakening of sin (p. 73)
    2. Mortification consists in constant fighting and contending against sin (p. 76)
    3. Mortification consists in frequent success (p. 77)

(Chapter 7)

II. General directions (p. 78)
  A. There will be no mortification of any sin unless one be a believer (p. 79)

(Chapter 8)

  B. There will be no mortification of any sin without sincerity and diligence in a universality of obedience (p. 86)

(Chapter 9)

III. Particular directions (p. 89)
  A. Consider whether your lust has these dangerous symptoms accompanying it (p. 89)
    1. Inveterateness (p. 90)
    2. Secret pleas of the heart to countenance sin without a gospel attempt to mortify sin (p. 91)
    3. Applying grace and mercy to an unmortified sin (p. 92)
    4. Frequency of success in sin's seduction (p. 92)
    5. Arguing against sin only because of impending punishment (p. 93)
    6. Probable judiciary hardness (p. 94)
    7. When your lust has already withstood particular dealings from God against it (p. 95)

(Chapter 10)

  B. Get a clear and abiding sense upon your mind and conscience of the guilt, danger, and evil of your sin (p. 97)
    1. Consider the guilt of it (p. 97)
      a) Though the power of sin be weakened by inherent grace, yet the guilt of remaining sin is aggravated and heightened by it (p. 98)
      b) God sees a great deal of evil in the working of lust in the hearts of his servants (p. 98)
    2. Consider the danger of it (p. 98)
      a) Of being hardened by deceitfulness (p. 98)
      b) Of some great temporal correction (p. 99)
      c) Of loss of peace and strength (p. 99)
      d) Of eternal destruction (p. 100)
    3. Consider its present evils (p. 101)
      a) It grieves the holy and blessed Spirit (p. 101)
      b) The Lord Jesus Christ is wounded afresh by it (p. 102)
      c) It will take away a man's usefulness in his generation (p. 102)

(Chapter 11)

  C. Load your conscience with the guilt of sin (p. 103)
    1. Begin with generals and descend to particulars (p. 103)
      a) Charge your conscience with that guilt which appears in it from the rectitude and holiness of the law (p. 103)
      b) Bring your lust to the gospel (p. 105)
    2. Descend to particulars (p. 105)
      a) Consider the infinite patience and forbearance of God toward you in particular (p. 105)
      b) Consider the infinitely rich grace of God whereby you have been recovered to communion with him again (p. 106)
      c) Consider all of God's gracious dealings with you (p. 106)
  D. Constantly long and breathe after deliverance from the power of it (p. 106)
  E. Consider whether the distemper is rooted in your nature and increased by your constitution (p. 107)

1. Particular sinful inclinations are an outbreak of original lust in your nature (p. 107)
2. Without extraordinary watchfulness, your nature will prevail against your soul (p. 107)
3. For the mortification of any distemper rooted in the nature of a man, there is one expedient peculiarly suited: bringing the body into subjection (p. 108)
   a) The outward weakening and impairing of the body should not be looked upon as a thing good in itself (p. 108)
   b) The means whereby this is done should not be looked on as things that in themselves can produce true mortification of any sin (p. 108)

F. Consider the occasions and advantages your distemper has taken to exert and put forth itself, and watch against them all (p. 109)

G. Rise mightily against the first actings and conceptions of your distemper (p. 109)

(Chapter 12)

H. Use and exercise yourself to such meditations as may serve to fill you at all times with self-abasement and thoughts of your own vileness (p. 110)
1. Think much of the excellency of the majesty of God and your infinite, inconceivable distance from him (p. 110)
2. Think much of your unacquaintedness with him (p. 111)

(Chapter 13)

I. Do not speak peace to yourself before God speaks it, but hearken to what God says to your soul (p. 118)
1. God reserves the privilege to speak peace to whom, and in what degree, he pleases (p. 119)
2. It is the prerogative of Christ to speak peace to the conscience (p. 119)
   a) Men speak peace to themselves without the detestation of sin and the abhorrence of themselves for it (p. 119)
   b) Men speak false peace to themselves when they rely upon convictions and rational principles to carry them (p. 121)
3. We speak peace to ourselves when we do it slightly (p. 124)
4. If one speaks peace to himself upon any one account of sin, and at the same time has another evil of no less importance lying upon his spirit, without dealing with God, that man cries "Peace" when there is none (p. 125)
5. When men of themselves speak peace to their consciences, it is seldom that God speaks humiliation to their souls (p. 125)

Part 3: The Means of Mortification

(Chapter 14)

IV. Directions for the work itself (p. 131)

A. Set faith at work on Christ for the killing of your sin (p. 131)

B. This whole work is effected, carried on, and accomplished by the power of the Spirit, in all the parts and degrees of it (p. 138)
1. The Spirit alone clearly and fully convinces the heart of the evil and guilt and danger of the corruption, lust, or sin to be mortified (p. 138)
2. The Spirit alone reveals unto us the fullness of Christ for our relief (p. 138)

3. The Spirit alone establishes the heart in expectation of relief from Christ (p. 139)
4. The Spirit alone brings the cross of Christ into our hearts with its sin-killing power (p. 139)
5. The Spirit is the author and finisher of our sanctification (p. 139)
6. In all the soul's addresses to God in this condition, it has support from the Spirit (p. 139)

OF TEMPTATION: THE NATURE AND POWER OF IT

defense, and yet not be wholly able to eject or cast out the poison and leaven that has been injected (p. 161)
1. When Satan has gotten some peculiar advantage against the soul (p. 161)
2. When a man's lusts and corruptions meet with peculiarly provoking objects and occasions, through the condition of life that a man is in, with the circumstances of it (p. 161)

III. How we know when temptation is in its hour (p. 162)
A. How temptation generally attains its hour (p. 162)
1. It causes the mind to converse frequently with evil and produces more thoughts of it (p. 162)
2. When it has prevailed on others, and the soul is not filled with dislike and abhorrency of them and their ways, nor with pity and prayer for their deliverance (p. 162)
3. By complicating itself with many considerations that, perhaps, are not absolutely evil (p. 163)

B. How we may know when any temptation is come to its high noon, and is in its hour (p. 163)
1. By its restless urgency and arguing (p. 163)
2. When it makes a conjunction of affrightments and allurements (p. 163)

IV. Means of preventing temptation prescribed by our Savior (p. 164)
A. Watch (p. 164)
B. Pray (p. 164)

Part 3: The Great Duty of All Believers

(Chapter 3)

I. It is the great duty of all believers to use all diligence in the ways of Christ's appointment, that they fall not into temptation (p. 167)
A. In that compendious instruction given us by our Savior concerning what we ought to pray for, this of not entering into temptation is expressly one head (p. 167)
B. Christ promises this freedom and deliverance as a great reward of most acceptable obedience (p. 168)
C. Consider the general issues of men's entering into temptation (p. 168)
D. Consider ourselves (p. 171)
1. Consider that we are weakness itself (p. 171)
a) In general, all we can look for is from our hearts (p. 171)
(1) Suppose a man is not a believer, but only a professor of the gospel, what can the heart of such a one do? (p. 171)
(2) "He that trusts in his own heart is a fool" (p. 172)
b) The insufficiency of the particular ways and means that such a heart has or can use to safeguard itself in the hour of temptation (p. 172)
(1) Love of honor in the world (p. 172)
(2) Shame, reproach, loss, etc. (p. 173)
(3) They will not wound their own consciences, and disturb their peace, and bring themselves in danger of hell-fire (p. 173)
(a) The peace of such a one may be false peace or security (p. 174)
(b) Suppose the peace cared for, and proposed to safeguard the soul, be true and good, yet when all is laid up in this one bottom, when the

hour of temptation comes, so many reliefs will be tendered against this consideration as will make it useless (p. 174)

(c) The fixing on this particular only is to make good one passage or entrance, while the enemy assaults us round about (p. 174)

(d) The consideration of the vileness of sinning against God (p. 175)

2. Consider the power of temptation to darken the mind (p. 175)
   a) By fixing the imagination and the thoughts upon the object whereunto it tends (p. 175)
   b) By woeful entangling of the affections (p. 176)
   c) Temptation will give oil and fuel to our lusts (p. 176)
3. Consider that temptations are either public or private (p. 177)
   a) Public temptation (p. 177)
      (1) It has an efficacy in respect of God (p. 177)
      (2) The secret insinuation of examples in those that are accounted godly and are professors (p. 178)
      (3) Usually accompanied with strong reasons and pretenses (p. 179)
   b) Private temptation (p. 179)
      (1) Its union and incorporation with lust (p. 179)
      (2) It affects the whole soul (p. 180)
4. Consider Satan's and sin's end in temptation (p. 181)
5. Consider what has been the issue of your former temptations that you have had (p. 181)

II. Objections and answers (p. 181)
   A. First Exchange (p. 182)
      1. Objection: Why should we so fear and labor to avoid temptation when we are to count it all joy (James 1:2)? (p. 182)
      2. Answer (p. 182)
         a) You will not hold by this rule in all things—namely, that a man need not seek to avoid that which, when he cannot but fall into, it is his duty to rejoice therein (p. 182)
         b) Temptations are taken two ways (p. 182)
            (1) Passively (p. 182)
            (2) Actively (p. 182)
   B. Second Exchange (p. 183)
      1. Objection: But was not our Savior Christ himself tempted; and is it evil to be brought into the same state and condition with him? (p. 183)
      2. Answer: Our Savior was tempted; but his temptations are reckoned among the evils that befell him in the days of his flesh (p. 183)
   C. Third Exchange (p. 183)
      1. Objection: If God is faithful not to tempt us beyond what we can bear and he knows how to deliver us out of temptation, why do we need to ask him that we not enter into it? (p. 183)
      2. Answer (p. 184)
         a) He that willfully or negligently enters into temptation has no reason in the world to promise himself any assistance from God, or any deliverance from the temptation whereunto he is entered (p. 184)
         b) Though there be a sufficiency of grace provided for all the elect, that they shall by no temptation fall utterly from God, yet it would make any gracious heart

to tremble, to think what dishonor to God, what scandal to the gospel, what woeful darkness and disquietness they may bring upon their own souls, though they perish not (p. 184)

c) To enter on temptation on this account is to venture on sin "that grace may abound" (p. 184)

Part 4: Particular Cases and General Directions

(Chapter 4)

I. How one knows he has entered into temptation (p. 187)
   A. When a man is drawn into any sin (p. 187)
   B. Temptations have several degrees (p. 187)
   C. When the heart begins secretly to like the matter of the temptation and is content to feed it and increase it by any ways that it may without downright sin (p. 188)
   D. When it comes to pass that a man's lust and any temptation meet with occasions and opportunities for its provocation and stirring up (p. 190)
   E. When a man is weakened, made negligent or formal in duty, when he can omit duties or content himself with a careless, lifeless performance of them, without delight, joy, or satisfaction to his soul (p. 190)

(Chapter 5)

II. General directions to preserve a soul from entering into temptation: watch and pray (p. 192)
   A. A clear, abiding apprehension of the great evil that there is in entering into temptation (p. 192)
   B. It is not a thing in our own power, to keep and preserve ourselves from entering into temptation (p. 194)
      1. The engagement of the grace and compassion of God (p. 195)
      2. The keeping of it in such a frame as, on various accounts, is useful for its preservation (p. 195)
      3. Act in faith on the promise of God for preservation (p. 195)
      4. Weigh these things severally and, first, take prayer into consideration (p. 196)

(Chapter 6)

III. Watch (p. 197)
   A. Watch the seasons wherein men usually do "enter into temptations" (p. 197)
      1. A season of unusual outward prosperity (p. 197)
      2. A time of the slumber of grace, of neglect in communion with God, of formality in duty (p. 198)
      3. A season of great spiritual enjoyments (p. 199)
      4. A season of self-confidence (p. 200)

(Chapter 7)

   B. Watch the heart itself (p. 201)
      1. Labor to know your own heart (p. 201)
      2. Watch against all that is apt to entangle your natural temper or provoke your corruption (p. 203)
      3. Lay in provision in store against the approaching of any temptation (p. 203)

4. In the first approach of any temptation, as we are all tempted, these directions following are also suited to carry on the work of watching, which we are in the pursuit of: (p. 205)
    a) Be always awake, that you may have an early discovery of your temptation (p. 205)
    b) Consider the aim and tendency of the temptation (p. 205)
    c) Meet your temptation in its entrance with thoughts of faith concerning Christ on the cross (p. 206)
    d) If you have been surprised by temptation and entangled unawares, what should you do? (p. 206)
        (1) Beseech God again and again that it may "depart from you" (p. 206)
        (2) Fly to Christ, in a peculiar manner, as he was tempted, and beg of him to give you succor in this "needful time of trouble" (p. 207)
        (3) Look to him who has promised deliverance (p. 207)
        (4) Consider where the temptation has made its entrance, and by what means, and with all speed make up the breach (p. 208)

(Chapter 8)

IV. Another general direction to preserve a soul from entering into temptation: keep the word of Christ's patience (p. 208)
  A. What it means to "keep the word of Christ's patience" (p. 209)
    1. The word of Christ is the word of the gospel (p. 209)
      a) He is patient toward his saints (p. 209)
      b) Toward the elect not yet effectually called (p. 209)
      c) To the perishing world (p. 209)
    2. Things implied in the keeping of this word (p. 210)
      a) Knowledge (p. 210)
        (1) As a word of grace and mercy, to save him (p. 210)
        (2) As a word of holiness and purity, to sanctify him (p. 210)
        (3) As a word of liberty and power, to ennoble him and set him free (p. 210)
          (a) In respect of conscience as to the worship of God (p. 210)
          (b) In respect of ignoble, slavish respects unto the men or things of the world, in the course of our pilgrimage (p. 210)
        (4) As a word of consolation, to support him in every condition (p. 211)
      b) Valuation (p. 211)
      c) Obedience (p. 211)
  B. How "keeping the word of Christ's patience" will be a means of our preservation (p. 212)
    1. It has the promise of preservation (p. 212)
      a) The faithfulness of the Father, who gives it (p. 212)
      b) The grace of the Son, which is the matter of it (p. 212)
      c) The power and efficacy of the Holy Ghost, which puts the promise in execution (p. 213)
    2. This constant, universal keeping of Christ's word of patience will keep the heart and soul in such a frame, as wherein no prevalent temptation can prevail against it (p. 213)
      a) By the mortification of the heart unto the matter of temptations (p. 213)

- b) In this frame the heart is filled with better things and their excellency, so far as to be fortified against the matter of any temptation (p. 214)

3. He that so keeps the word of Christ's patience is always furnished with preserving considerations and preserving principles (p. 215)
    - a) He has preserving considerations (p. 215)
        - (1) The concern of Christ, whom his soul loves, in him and his careful walking (p. 215)
        - (2) The great consideration of the temptations of Christ in his behalf, and the conquest he made in all assaults for his sake and his God, dwell also on his spirit (p. 216)
        - (3) Dismal thoughts of the loss of love, of the smiles of the countenance of Christ, do also frequently exercise such a soul (p. 216)
    - b) He has preserving principles (p. 216)
        - (1) In all things he lives by faith, and is acted by it in all his ways (p. 216)
            - (a) It empties the soul of its own wisdom, understanding, and fullness, that it may act in the wisdom and fullness of Christ (p. 217)
            - (b) Faith engages the heart, will, and power of Jesus Christ for assistance (p. 217)
        - (2) Love to the saints, with care that they suffer not upon our account (p. 217)

C. Examples of professors coming short of keeping the word of Christ (p. 218)
1. Conformity to the world (p. 218)
2. Neglect of duties (p. 218)
3. Strife, variance, and debate among ourselves, woeful judging and despising one another (p. 218)
4. Self-fullness as to principles, and selfishness as to ends (p. 218)

D. Cautions to take in order to be preserved from temptation (p. 219)
1. Take heed of leaning on deceitful assistances (p. 219)
    - a) Your own counsels, understandings, reasonings (p. 219)
    - b) The most vigorous actings, by prayer, fasting, and other such means, against that particular lust, corruption, temptation, wherewith you are exercised and have to do (p. 219)
    - c) The general security of saints' perseverance and preservation from total apostasy (p. 219)
2. Apply yourselves to this great preservation of faithfully keeping the word of Christ's patience, in the midst of all trials and temptations (p. 219)
    - a) Consider wherein the word of Christ's patience is most likely to suffer in the days wherein we live and the seasons that pass over us, and so vigorously set yourselves to keep it in that particular peculiarly (p. 219)
    - b) Consider the works Christ performs in our days and seasons (p. 219)
        - (1) The pouring of contempt upon the great men and great things of the world, with all the enjoyments of it (p. 219)
        - (2) The owning of the lot of his own inheritance in a distinguishing manner, putting a difference between the precious and the vile, and causing his people to dwell alone, as not reckoned with the nations (p. 220)
        - (3) In being nigh to faith and prayer, honoring them above all the strength and counsels of the sons of men (p. 220)
        - (4) In recovering his ordinances and institutions from the carnal

administrations that they were in bondage under by the lusts of men, bringing them forth in the beauty and the power of the Spirit. (p. 220)

c) In this frame urge the Lord Jesus Christ with his blessed promises to give suitable succor at time of need (p. 220)

(Chapter 9)

V. General exhortations related to the duty of watching (p. 220)
  A. If you neglect it, you will certainly enter into temptation and sin (p. 222)
  B. Consider that you are always under the eye of Christ (p. 222)
  C. Consider that if you neglect this duty and so fall into temptation, when you are entangled God may with it bring some heavy affliction or judgment upon you (p. 222)

THE NATURE, POWER, DECEIT, AND PREVALENCY OF INDWELLING SIN

1. Never let us reckon that our work in contending against sin is at an end (p. 255)
2. Its variety, inconsistency, and deceitfulness above all else calls for perpetual watchfulness against it (p. 255)
3. Commit the whole matter with all care and diligence unto God (p. 256)

(Chapter 4)

IV. The natural properties of indwelling sin (p. 257)
- A. Indwelling sin is enmity (p. 257)
- B. Indwelling sin is enmity against God (p. 259)
  - 1. Indwelling sin is universal (p. 260)
    - a) Indwelling sin is universal against all of God (p. 261)
    - b) Indwelling sin is universal against all of the soul (p. 261)
  - 2. Indwelling sin is constant (p. 262)
- C. Indwelling sin is constant (p. 262)

(Chapter 5)

V. The actings and operations of indwelling sin (p. 262)
- A. Aversation (p. 263)
  - 1. In the affections (p. 264)
  - 2. In the mind (p. 265)
  - 3. Directions with respect to our particular duty against this evil (p. 267)
    - a) Constantly keep the soul in a universally holy frame (p. 267)
    - b) Labor to prevent the very beginnings of the workings of this aversation (p. 267)
    - c) Be sure this aversation never prevails to a conquest (p. 268)
    - d) Carry about a constant, humbling sense of this close aversation unto spiritualness that yet lies in our nature (p. 268)
    - e) Labor to possess the mind with the beauty and excellency of spiritual things (p. 269)

(Chapter 6)

- B. Opposition (p. 270)
  - 1. By force (p. 270)
    - a) Sin's general inclination: it lusts (p. 271)
      - (1) In a hidden, close, propensity unto all evil (p. 272)
        - (a) Discovered in its unexpected surprises of the soul into foolish, sinful figments and imaginations (p. 273)
        - (b) Manifested in its readiness and promptness to join and close with every temptation whereby it may possibly be excited (p. 274)
      - (2) In its actual pressing after that which is evil, and actual opposition unto that which is good (p. 275)
    - b) Sin's particular way of contending: it fights or wars (p. 276)
      - (1) In its rebellion against grace, or the law of the mind (p. 277)
        - (a) Opposition unto the general purpose and course of the soul (p. 278)
        - (b) Opposition unto particular duties (p. 279)
      - (2) In its assaulting the soul (p. 279)
        - (a) Its positive actings in stirring up sin (p. 280)

(b) Its importunity and urgency (p. 280)
(c) It entangles the affections and draws them into a combination against the mind (p. 281)

(Chapter 7)

c) Sin's success in this contest: it leads the soul captive to the law of sin (p. 284)
(1) Success in and upon the actings of the law of sin (p. 284)
(a) Much of it is from Satan when the captivating sin has no peculiar footing nor advantage in the nature, constitution, or condition of the sinner (p. 285)
(b) It is from Satan when a lust is prevalent unto captivity, where it brings in no advantage to the flesh (p. 286)
(2) It leads the soul captive not to a particular or actual sin, but to "the law of sin" (p. 286)
(3) This leading captive argues a prevalency against the contrary actings of the will (p. 286)
(a) The power of sin is great (p. 287)
(b) This leading captive intimates manifold particular successes (p. 287)
(c) This leading captive manifests this condition to be miserable and wretched (p. 287)
d) Sin's growth and rage upon success: it comes up to rage and madness (p. 288)
(1) Its nature consists in violent, heady, pertinacious pressing unto evil or sin (p. 288)
(2) Sin does not rise to this height ordinarily, but when it has a double advantage: (p. 289)
(a) That it be provoked, enraged, and heightened by some great temptation (p. 289)
(b) It must be advantaged by some former entertainment and prevalency (p. 289)
(3) What accompanies this rage, its properties, and the effects it produces (p. 290)
(a) There is in it the casting off, for a time at least, of the yoke, rule, and government of the Spirit and law of grace (p. 290)
(b) Madness or rage is accompanied with fearlessness and contempt of danger (p. 291)
(i) When the soul is broken loose from the power of renewing grace, God often deals with it by preventing grace (p. 291)
(ii) These hindrances that God lays in the way of sinners are of two sorts: (p. 292)
(a) Rational considerations (p. 292)
(b) Providential dispensations (p. 292)

(Chapter 8)

2. By deceit (p. 293)
a) The general nature of deceit (p. 295)
(1) It hides (p. 295)
(2) It is carried on by degrees (p. 296)

b) The way, manner, and progress of sin in working by deceit (p. 296)
   (1) Its ultimate aim is death (p. 297)
   (2) Its general way of acting toward that end is by temptation (p. 297)
      (a) Drawing away the mind from its duty (p. 299)
         (i) In general, the duty of the mind is to keep itself and the whole soul in a frame and posture that will render it ready for all duties of obedience (p. 299)
            (a) It endeavors to draw it off from a due consideration, apprehension, and sensibleness of its own vileness and danger (p. 299)
            (b) The duty to keep the soul unto a constant, holy consideration of God and his grace (p. 305)

(Chapter 9)

         (ii) In particular, the duty of the mind is to attend to all actions (e.g., prayer and meditation) that they may be performed as God requires (p. 306)
            (a) Meditate of God with God (p. 307)
            (b) Meditate on the word in the word (p. 307)
            (c) What we lack in evenness and constancy let us make up in frequency (p. 307)
         (iii) The suitableness and usefulness of this duty unto the ruining of sin (p. 307)
            (a) It is the proper work of the soul in this duty to consider all the secret workings and actings of sin (p. 308)
            (b) In this duty there is wrought upon the heart a deep, full sense of the vileness of sin, with a constant renewed detestation of it (p. 309)
            (c) This is the way appointed and blessed of God to obtain strength and power against sin (p. 309)
            (d) Faith in prayer countermines all the workings of the deceit of sin (p. 310)
         (iv) The means whereby the deceitfulness of sin endeavors to draw off the mind from a due attendance unto them (p. 311)
            (a) It makes advantage of its weariness unto the flesh (p. 311)
            (b) It makes use of corrupt reasonings (p. 312)
            (c) It offers a compensation to be made in and by other duties (p. 313)
            (d) It feeds the soul with promises and purposes of a more diligent attendance unto this duty when occasions will permit (p. 313)

(Chapter 10)

         (v) For the right performance of any duty, it is not enough that the thing itself required be performed, but that it be universally squared and fitted unto the rule of it (p. 316)
            (a) There are some special things which the rule directs unto that the mind is to attend in every duty (p. 317)

(i) That it be full and complete (p. 317)
(ii) That it be done in faith (p. 317)
(iii) That it be done in the right manner (p. 318)
(iv) That it attend unto the ends of duties (p. 318)
(b) There are some things about sin which the mind should attend to (p. 320)
(i) The sovereignty of God (p. 321)
(ii) The deceit of sin (p. 321)
(iii) The love and kindness of God (p. 322)
(iv) The inhabitation of the Spirit (p. 324)
(a) It is from the deceit of sin that the mind is spiritually slothful, whereby it becomes negligent unto this duty (p. 324)
(i) Inadvertency (p. 324)
(ii) Unwillingness to be stirred up unto its duty (p. 324)
(iii) Weak and ineffectual attempts to recover itself unto this duty (p. 324)
(iv) Heartlessness upon the apprehensions of difficulties (p. 325)
(b) It draws away the mind from its watch and duty in reference unto sin by surprises (p. 325)
(c) It draws away the mind by frequency and long continuance of its solicitations, making as it were at last a conquest of it (p. 326)

(Chapter 11)

(b) Enticing the affections (p. 326)
(i) What it is to have the affections entangled in sin (p. 327)
(a) When they stir up frequent imaginations about the proposed object which this deceit of sin leads and entices toward (p. 327)
(b) When the imagination can prevail with the mind to lodge vain thoughts in it, with secret delight and complacency (p. 327)
(c) Inclinations or readiness to attend unto extenuations of sin, or the reliefs that are tendered against sin when committed, manifest the affections to be entangled with it (p. 328)
(ii) How sin entangles the affections (p. 328)
(a) It makes use of its former prevalency upon the mind in drawing it off from its watch and circumspection (p. 328)
(b) It proposes sin as desirable and exceeding satisfactory to the corrupt part of our affections (p. 329)
(c) It hides the danger that attends sin (p. 330)
(d) It raises up perverse reasonings in the mind, to fix it upon the sin proposed, that it may be conceived and brought forth (p. 330)
(iii) How to observe this duty (p. 331)
(a) Keep your affections as to their object (p. 331)
(i) In general: fill your affections with heavenly things (p. 331)

(ii) In particular: let the cross of Christ be the object of your affections (p. 332)
(b) Look to the vigor of the affections toward heavenly things (p. 332)

(Chapter 12)

(c) The conception of actual sin in the will (p. 333)
(i) The will is the principle, the next seat and cause, of obedience and disobedience. (p. 333)
(ii) Twofold consent of the will unto sin (p. 333)
(a) That which is full, absolute, complete, and upon deliberation (p. 333)
(b) There is a consent of the will which is attended with a secret renitency and volition of the contrary (p. 334)
(iii) There cannot be an absolute, total, full consent of the will of a believer unto any sin (p. 334)
(a) There is in his will a principle fixed on good (p. 334)
(b) There is also a secret reluctancy in it against its own act in consenting unto sin (p. 334)
(iv) Repeated acts of the consent of the will unto sin may beget a disposition and inclination in it unto the like acts (p. 335)
(v) This consent of the will may be considered two ways: (p. 335)
(a) As it is exercised about the circumstances, causes, means, and inducements unto sin (p. 335)
(b) As it respects this or that actual sin (p. 335)
(i) The will is a rational appetite (p. 335)
(ii) It chooses nothing, consents to nothing, but as it has an appearance of some present good (p. 335)
(iii) The reason why the conception of sin is here placed as a consequent of the mind's being drawn away and the affections being entangled (p. 336)
(a) The will is imposed upon by that corrupt reasoning, that grace is exalted in a pardon, and that mercy is provided for sinners (p. 336)
(b) The deceived mind imposes on the will, to obtain its consent unto sin, by proposing unto it the advantages that may accrue and arise thereby (p. 338)

(Chapter 13)

(d) The bringing forth of sin in its actual accomplishment (p. 342)
(i) When sin is conceived, the Lord obstructs its production by his providence, in taking away or cutting short its power (p. 343)
(a) By taking away life, which is the foundation of all power (p. 343)
(i) God does not judicially cut off and take away the life of any of his (p. 344)

(a) This is directly contrary to the very declared end of the patience of God toward them (p. 344)
(b) They must perish forever who are so judicially cut off (p. 345)
(ii) There are some cases wherein God may and does take away the lives of his own to prevent the guilt that otherwise they would be involved in (p. 345)
(a) In the coming of some great temptation and trial upon the world (p. 345)
(b) In case of their engagement into any way not acceptable to him, through ignorance or not knowing of his mind and will (p. 345)
(b) By taking away and cutting short the power of them that had conceived it (p. 345)
(i) It is so only in cases of extraordinary temptation (p. 347)
(ii) God does it to awaken them to their condition and what they are doing (p. 347)
(c) By opposing an external hindering power unto sinners (p. 347)
(d) By removing or taking away the objects on whom, or about whom, the sin conceived was to be committed (p. 348)
(e) By some eminent diversions of the thoughts of men who had conceived sin (p. 348)
(i) This may give us a little insight into the providence of God (p. 349)
(ii) Our own concerns will in a special manner enforce us to adore the wisdom and efficacy of the providence of God in stopping the progress of conceived sin (p. 349)
(iii) The miserable condition of wicked men (p. 350)
(iv) Do not despair when you see the floodgates of men's lusts and rage set open against the church and the interest of it (p. 351)
(v) Those who have received benefit by any of the ways mentioned may know to whom they owe their preservation, and not look on it as a common thing (p. 351)
(vi) We may also see hence the great use of magistracy in the world, that great appointment of God (p. 351)
(ii) The way whereby God obviates the production of conceived sin is his working on the will of the sinner (p. 352)
(a) By restraining grace (p. 352)
(i) The general medium of restraining grace is in certain arguments and reasonings presented to the mind of the sinner (p. 353)
(ii) No arguments or reasonings as such are sufficient to stop or hinder any purpose of sinning (p. 353)
(iii) Some of the arguments God uses toward this end (p. 354)
(a) By arguments taken from the difficulty, if not impossibility, of doing that they aim at (p. 354)
(b) By arguments taken *ab incommodo* (p. 355)

(c) By arguments *ab inutili* (p. 355)
(d) By arguments taken *ab honesto* (p. 356)
(b) By renewing grace (p. 357)
(i) This is one part of the mystery of his grace and love (p. 357)
(ii) God does it by special assisting grace (p. 358)
(iii) God does it by the way of afflictions (p. 360)

Part 3: The Effect and Strength of Indwelling Sin

(Chapter 14)

I. The effect of sin in the lives of believers (p. 363)
A. The fearful eruptions of actual sin that have been in the lives of believers (p. 363)
1. In Scripture, many of them had a peculiar eminency in them on the account of their walking with God in their generation (p. 363)
2. These men fell not into their great sins after a long course of walking with God (p. 363)
3. They fell when they had newly received great and stupendous mercies from the hand of God (p. 364)
B. It manifests its power in believers' habitual declensions from zeal and holiness (p. 365)
1. Declension from zeal (p. 366)
2. Declension from delight (p. 368)
3. Declension from the universal course of obedience (p. 368)
C. The cause of all actual sin and habitual declensions in believers is indwelling sin (p. 369)
1. It appears to be a work of great power and efficacy from the provision that is made against it, which it prevails over (p. 369)
a) The word itself and all the ordinances of the gospel are appointed and given unto us for this end (p. 369)
b) That which adds weight to this consideration (p. 370)
c) Supplies of grace continually afforded the saints from their head, Christ (p. 371)
d) There is a readiness in the Lord Christ to yield peculiar succor to the souls of his (p. 372)

(Chapter 15)

2. The ways and means whereby indwelling sin prevails on believers unto habitual declensions and decays as to degrees of grace and holiness (p. 374)
a) Their experience during the first conversion and calling of sinners unto God and Christ (p. 374)
(1) They have a fresh, vigorous sense of pardoning mercy (p. 375)
(2) They have a fresh taste of spiritual things (p. 375)
(3) Indwelling sin taints these springs (p. 376)
(a) By sloth and negligence (p. 376)
(b) By unframing the soul (p. 377)
(c) By false and foolish opinions corrupting the simplicity of the gospel (p. 378)
b) Indwelling sin does this by taking men off from their watch against the returns of Satan (p. 379)

(1) It entangles the soul in the things of the world (p. 380)
(2) By making the soul negligent and taking it off from its watch (p. 381)
(3) By the evil examples of professors among whom they live (p. 381)
(4) By cherishing some secret particular lust in the heart (p. 383)
(5) By negligence of private communion with God in prayer and meditation (p. 384)
(6) By growing in notions of truth without answerable practice (p. 386)
(7) By growing in carnal wisdom (p. 386)
(8) By some great unrepented sin lying long in the heart and conscience (p. 387)

(Chapter 16)

II. The effect of sin in the lives of unbelievers (p. 388)
  A. It appears in the violence it offers to the nature of men (p. 388)
    1. Sins against the natural principle of love unto and a care for the preservation and nourishing of their young (p. 390)
    2. All other sins against the prime dictates of the law of nature that mankind is or has been stained and defamed with (p. 391)
  B. It evidences its efficacy in keeping men off from believing under the dispensation of the gospel (p. 391)
    1. Under the dispensation of the gospel, there are but few that do believe (p. 391)
    2. There is proposed to men in the preaching of the gospel, as motives unto believing, everything in conjunction that severally prevails with men to do whatever else they do in their lives (p. 392)
      a) It is most reasonable (p. 392)
      b) It is most profitable (p. 392)
      c) It is most pleasant (p. 393)
      d) It is surely necessary (p. 393)
    3. Indwelling sin both disenables men unto and hinders them from believing the gospel (p. 393)
  C. It is evident in their total apostasies (p. 393)
    1. It gives stop or control unto that exceeding greatness of power which is put forth in the word in their conviction and reformation (p. 394)
    2. It takes them off from those hopes of heaven which, upon their convictions, obedience, and temporary faith or believing, they had attained (p. 396)
    3. It turns them off from the way of righteousness after they have known it (p. 397)
    4. It evinces its strength in them by prevailing with them unto a total renunciation of God as revealed in Christ, and the power of all gospel truth—in the sin against the Holy Ghost (p. 397)

(Chapter 17)

III. The strength of indwelling sin evidenced by its resistance to the power of the law (p. 398)
  A. The law discovers sin (p. 398)
  B. The law discovers sin to be a very bad inmate (p. 399)
  C. The law judges the person (p. 400)
  D. The law disquiets and affrights the soul (p. 400)
  E. The law slays the soul (p. 400)

    1. It is not conquered (p. 401)
    2. It is only enraged (p. 401)
- F. Question*:* It seems that the preaching of the law has an effect on sin (p. 401)
- G. Answers (p. 402)
    1. It is acknowledged that the power of the law of God is very great and effectual (p. 402)
    2. Whatever effects it have upon some, yet we see that in the most, such is the power and prevalency of sin, that it takes no impression at all upon them (p. 402)
    3. When any of the effects mentioned are wrought, it is not from the power of the letter of the law, but from the actual efficacy of the Spirit of God putting forth his virtue and power for that end and purpose (p. 402)
    4. Notwithstanding all that may be observed of the power of the law upon the souls of men, yet it is most evident that lust is not conquered, not subdued, nor mortified by it (p. 402)
        - a) Though the course of sin may be repelled for a season by the dispensation of the law, yet the spring and fountain of it is not dried up thereby (p. 402)
        - b) In such seasons sin is not conquered, but diverted (p. 403)
            - (1) The great endeavors of men ignorant of the righteousness of Christ, for the subduing and mortifying of sin, which are all fruitless, do evidence the great strength and power of it (p. 403)
                - (a) They will promise and bind themselves by vows from those sins which they have been most liable unto, and so have been most perplexed with (p. 404)
                - (b) Beyond bare vows and promises, with some watchfulness to observe them in a rational use of ordinary means, men have put, and some do yet put, themselves on extraordinary ways of mortifying sin (p. 406)
            - (2) The strength, efficacy, and power of this law of sin may be further evidenced from its life and in-being in the soul and in the continual opposition that is made unto it by grace (p. 407)

Glossary

abashment. embarrassment, lack of self-confidence

abatement. reduction, diminution

abstruse. hard to understand

accidental. non-essential, incidental

acted. activated

adamant. a diamond or any very hard substance

adjunct. dependent statement that amplifies meaning

affection. effect

alacrity. eagerness, liveliness, speed

allay. relieve

alloy. mixture

amendment. moral improvement, reformation

anon. (1) again; i.e., reoccurring; (2) presently, soon

appellation. name, designation

apprehension. perception, conception

artifices. trickeries

aslake. slacken, diminish

asp. cobra

attendancy. that which accompanies

aught. anything; i.e., anything worthwhile

avouching. affirming, confessing

aversation. a moral turning away, estrangement, repulsion

balsam. fragrant ointment used as balm or medication

barbarous. uncivilized

bellows. blacksmith's device for blowing air into fire

beseem. suit, become, fit

betimes. in due time

bosses. the projecting parts of a small, handheld shield; i.e., a strong, imposing defense

bottom. found, base (find a basis for); basis, foundation

breach. gap, broken area

buckler. a small, handheld shield

buffett. strike repeatedly

by-respect. private advantage
cankering. festering, corroding, infecting
casuist. one who rigidly applies ethical rules
censorious. critical
churl. coarse, ill-natured man
circumspect. watchful, attentive, cautious
circumstantiate. verified by circumstances
close. consummate, bring to a conclusion
color. embellishment concealing the truth
combustion. consuming as by fire; tumult
comeliness. attractiveness
commination. formal denunciation
commission. authority
commissionate. commissioned, appointed
commutation. substitution, exchange
compassing. attaining, achieving
compellation. address, naming
composition. truce, cessation of hostilities
concomitant. that which accompanies
concreate. create at the same time
concourse. (1) running together, flowing together, meeting; (2) state of being gathered together
consumptive. afflicted with consumption, a progressive wasting away of the body
contemn. have contempt for, scorn, disdain
contentation. satisfaction, reassurance
contexture. context
contrariety. state of being contrary or in opposition to
controverted. made an object of dispute
conversation. way of life
countenance. approve, condone; approval
countermine. counterplot
covert. shelter
cross. contradictory
cruciate. torment, torture
daub. cover, as with plaster
declension. moral decline
dehort. exhort, in an effort to dissuade
defensative. that which defends or protects
deign. condescend

denominate. designate
deportment. behavior
despoil. rob, plunder
desert. that which is deserved (such as punishment)
determinate. resolved, settled
disappointment. undoing of an intended end or use
discover. uncover, reveal, demonstrate
disframe. dismantle, undo
dispensation. provision, ordering
disquisition. formal inquiry, investigation
dissimulation. making unlike; process of becoming unlike
dropsy. excessive accumulation of fluid in bodily tissue; edema
durst. dared
educe. derive, draw out
efficient cause. Aristotle's term for the means or agency by which something comes into being
emulations. jealousies, especially of power and position
endued. endowed
enervate. debilitate, deprive of strength
ensue. follow
envenomed. poisonous
ere. before
espousal. betrothal
evanid. evanescent, liable to vanish
event. result, outcome
evince. prove, provide evidence, make manifest
excision. surgical removal by cutting
execrable. extremely inferior or detestable
expostulate. discuss earnestly
extenuate. make less serious
facile. mild-mannered
facility. aptitude, ease
fain. eagerly, gladly
fallow. plowed but unseeded
fatness. richness, fertility
feign. pretend, imagine, as in fictional writing
filial. pertaining to a son or daughter
flag. decline in vigor or strength
fomes. diseased material

foment. incite, agitate
froward. stubbornly contrary, obstinate
furniture. equipment, weapons
gadding. straggling, roving
gin. trap
good-man. male head of household
haply. by chance
head. (1) ultimate outcome; (2) category, heading; (3) source
hectical. fluctuating but persistent
humor. bodily fluid, thought to be the physical root of the passions
husbandman. farmer
immure. confine within walls
impetuous. (1) vehement; (2) impulsive
import. signify
importunate. persistent, pressing
improvement. (1) exposition, application; (2) enhancement
inadvertency. negligence
incumbent. obligatory
indisposition. disinclination, unwillingness
infirm. feeble
ingenerate. beget, produce
inquest. inquiry, investigation
insensible. (1) apathetic, callous, uncomprehending; (2) imperceptible
insition. engraftment
instant. insistent, constant, faithful
intemperance. lack of moderation; indulgence, especially of intoxicating drink
intendment. intention
intension. intention
interest. share or stake
interposition. interjection, intervention
inveigh. denounce, censure
inveterate. hardened, habitual, deep-rooted
issue. result, outcome
languid. lacking power
lasciviousness. wantonness, inclination to lust
lassitude. listlessness, lethargy
leave. cease
lee. shelter, protection
loathness. unwillingness, reluctance

loose. lack of restraint
machinations. plottings, schemings, cunning designs
magistracy. human government
malefactor. criminal
manuring. fertilizer
mean. lowly, insignificant
meet. fitting, appropriate
metonymy. a figure of speech in which one term is substituted for another term closely associated with it
morose. sullenly melancholy, gloomy
nescience. lack of knowledge
nigh. near
noisome. dangerous, offensive, foul
notional. theoretical, conceptual
noxious. injurious, harmful, unwholesome
obdurate. hardened, unyielding, obstinate
obnoxious. harmfully exposed
obviate. render unnecessary; anticipate, prevent
overawe. restrain or subdue by awe
own. admit, acknowledge, confess to be true
palliate. moderate the seriousness or intensity of
papist. negative label for Roman Catholics, relating to belief in papal supremacy; from the Latin *papa* ("pope")
parley. discuss (especially with an enemy)
party. participant
paucity. smallness of number
peccant. offending, faulty
peculiar. particular, characteristic
peevish. irritable, discontent
perdition. ruin, damnation, destruction
perfunctorily. routinely, indifferently
pernicious. deadly
pertinacious. obstinate, stubborn
perturbation. disturbance, agitation
pervious. permeable, penetrable
physic. remedy, relief, medicine
pine away. wither or waste away
plaster. medicated bandage
popish. negative label for Roman Catholicism, relating to belief in papal supremacy

preventing grace. a special grace that, preceding human willing, protects against further sinning
procure. gain, obtain
prodigality. reckless extravagance, especially with money
professor. one who makes a religious confession; a professing Christian
prosecution. carrying out, execution
quit. (1) conduct; (2) freed or released
raiment. garments, clothing
rankling. festering, irritating
rapine. pillage, robbery, plunder
ravening. seeking prey, devouring
remembrancer. reminder
renitency. resistance, reluctance
rent. ripped, torn
repining. discontentment, grumbling
repose. (1) rest; (2) place, entrust
requite. repay
respite. relief
retention. contention, concern
retirements. privacy, seclusion, leisure
rifled. disordered, ruffled
right. seek to correct or amend
Roman. Roman Catholic
romish. of or relating to the Roman Catholic Church
sedulous. constant, persistent
self-justiciary. one who believes he can attain righteousness by his own action or nature
self-maceration. self-inflicted starvation, emaciation
sensual. perceived by the senses (not necessarily sexual)
shed. diffuse, spread abroad
shut up. summarize, sum up
signal. significant, remarkable, out of the ordinary
sottish. foolish, especially as it relates to drunkenness
stay. stop
strait. short
straits. difficulties, distresses
station. position
succor. assistance, relief
suffer. allow, permit, tolerate

sullied. (1) polluted, soiled; (2) tainted, marred, defiled

sundry. various

supererogation. according to the Roman Catholic doctrine, a superabundance of merit deposited in a spiritual treasury of the Church that can be used by ordinary sinners for the remittance of their sins

swing. liberty, sway

synecdoche. a figure of speech in which the part stands for the whole or the whole stands for the part

tackling. a ship's rigging; tackle

temper. character, disposition

tender. offer

tergiversation. equivocation, falsification by vague or ambiguous language

tittle. a kind of accent in the Hebrew alphabet

trade. course, path, way or manner of life

tow. coarse flax

tumultuate. agitate, disturb, stir up

usurp. seize, take control with power and force

variance. dissent, discord

velleity. inclination, desire

vexation. annoyance

vitiate. invalidate, render incomplete, impair

want. lack

wanton. lacking discipline

wax. grow, become

winnow. separate as chaff from wheat

withe. shackle made of green twigs (see Judg. 16:7, KJV)

without. outside of

wont. wonted. accustom; accustomed

wroth. filled with wrath

wrought. shaped, molded, fashioned

General Index

Scripture Index

1 Corinthians